Chinese Society, second edition
Change, conflict and resistance
*Edited by Elizabeth J. Perry and
Mark Selden*

Ethnicity in Asia
Edited by Colin Mackerras

The Battle for Asia
From decolonization to globalization
Mark T. Berger

**State and Society in 21st Century
China**
*Edited by Peter Hays Gries and
Stanley Rosen*

Japan's Quiet Transformation
Social change and civil society in the
21st century
Jeff Kingston

Confronting the Bush Doctrine
Critical views from the Asia-Pacific
*Edited by Mel Gurtov and
Peter Van Ness*

**China in War and Revolution,
1895–1949**
Peter Zarrow

The Future of US–Korean Relations
The imbalance of power
Edited by John Feffer

Working in China
Ethnographies of labor and workplace
transformations
Edited by Ching Kwan Lee

Korean Society, second edition
Civil society, democracy and the state
Edited by Charles K. Armstrong

Singapore
The state and the culture of excess
Souchou Yao

**Pan-Asianism in Modern
Japanese History**
Colonialism, regionalism and
borders
*Edited by Sven Saaler and
J. Victor Koschmann*

Asia's Great Cities

Each volume aims to capture the heartbeat of the contemporary city from
multiple perspectives emblematic of the authors' own deep familiarity with
the distinctive faces of the city, its history, society, culture, politics and economics, and its evolving position in national, regional and global frame-
works. While most volumes emphasize urban developments since the Second
World War, some pay close attention to the legacy of the *longue durée* in
shaping the contemporary. Thematic and comparative volumes address such
themes as urbanization, economic and financial linkages, architecture and
space, wealth and power, gendered relationships, planning and anarchy, and
ethnographies in national and regional perspective. Titles include:

Bangkok
Place, practice and representation
Marc Askew

Beijing in the Modern World
*David Strand and
Madeline Yue Dong*

Shanghai
Global city
Jeff Wasserstrom

Hong Kong
Global city
Stephen Chiu and Tai-Lok Lui

Representing Calcutta
Modernity, nationalism and the
colonial uncanny
Swati Chattopadhyay

Singapore
Wealth, power and the culture of control
Carl A. Trocki

Asia.com is a series which focuses on the ways in which new information and communication technologies are influencing politics, society and culture in Asia. Titles include:

Japanese Cybercultures
Edited by Mark McLelland and
Nanette Gottlieb

The Internet in Indonesia's
New Democracy
David T. Hill and Krishna Sen

Asia.com
Asia encounters the Internet
Edited by K. C. Ho, Randolph Kluver
and Kenneth C. C. Yang

Chinese Cyberspaces
Technological changes and
political effects
Edited by Jens Damm and
Simona Thomas

Literature and Society is a series that seeks to demonstrate the ways in which Asian Literature is influenced by the politics, society and culture in which it is produced. Titles include:

The Body in Postwar Japanese Fiction
Edited by Douglas N. Slaymaker

Chinese Women Writers and the
Feminist Imagination, 1905–1948
Haiping Yan

Routledge Studies in Asia's Transformations is a forum for innovative new research intended for a high-level specialist readership, and the titles will be available in hardback only. Titles include:

**1. The American Occupation of Japan
and Okinawa***
Literature and memory
Michael Molasky

2. Koreans in Japan*
Critical voices from the margin
Edited by Sonia Ryang

3. Internationalizing the Pacific
The United States, Japan and the
Institute of Pacific Relations in War
and Peace, 1919–1945
Tomoko Akami

4. Imperialism in South East Asia
'A fleeting, passing phase'
Nicholas Tarling

5. Chinese Media, Global Contexts
Edited by Chin-Chuan Lee

6. Remaking Citizenship in Hong Kong
Community, nation and the global city
Edited by Agnes S. Ku and Ngai Pun

7. Japanese Industrial Governance
Protectionism and the licensing state
Yul Sohn

Education and Reform in China

Transformative market reforms in China since the late 1970s have improved living standards dramatically, but have also led to unprecedented economic inequality. During this period, China's educational system was restructured to support economic development, with educational reforms occurring at a startling pace. Today, the educational system has diversified in structure, finance, and content; it has become more market-oriented; and it is serving an increasingly diverse student population. These changes carry significant consequences for China's social mobility and inequality, and future economic prospects.

In *Education and Reform in China*, leading scholars in the fields of education, sociology, demography, and economics investigate the development of educational access and attainment, educational quality, and the economic consequences of being educated in China. *Education and Reform in China* shows that economic advancement is increasingly tied to education in China, even as educational services are increasingly marketized. The volume investigates the varying impact of change for different social, ethnic, economic and geographic groups. Offering interdisciplinary views on the changing role of education in Chinese society, and on China's educational achievements and policy challenges, this book will be an important resource for those interested in education, public policy, and development issues in China.

Emily Hannum is Assistant Professor of Sociology at the University of Pennsylvania, where she is a member of the Graduate Group in Demography, the Graduate Group in Education, and the Center for East Asian Studies.

Albert Park is Associate Professor of Economics and Faculty Associate of the Center for Chinese Studies and International Policy Center at the University of Michigan.

Asia's Transformations
Edited by Mark Selden
Binghamton and Cornell Universities, USA

The books in this series explore the political, social, economic and cultural consequences of Asia's transformations in the twentieth and twenty-first centuries. The series emphasizes the tumultuous interplay of local, national, regional and global forces as Asia bids to become the hub of the world economy. While focusing on the contemporary, it also looks back to analyse the antecedents of Asia's contested rise.

This series comprises several strands:

Asia's Transformations aims to address the needs of students and teachers, and the titles will be published in hardback and paperback. Titles include:

Debating Human Rights
Critical essays from the United States and Asia
Edited by Peter Van Ness

Hong Kong's History
State and society under colonial rule
Edited by Tak-Wing Ngo

Japan's Comfort Women
Sexual slavery and prostitution during World War II and the US occupation
Yuki Tanaka

Opium, Empire and the Global Political Economy
Carl A. Trocki

Chinese Society
Change, conflict and resistance
Edited by Elizabeth J. Perry and Mark Selden

Mao's Children in the New China
Voices from the Red Guard generation
Yarong Jiang and David Ashley

Remaking the Chinese State
Strategies, society and security
Edited by Chien-min Chao and Bruce J. Dickson

Korean Society
Civil society, democracy and the state
Edited by Charles K. Armstrong

The Making of Modern Korea
Adrian Buzo

The Resurgence of East Asia
500, 150 and 50 year perspectives
Edited by Giovanni Arrighi, Takeshi Hamashita and Mark Selden

* Now available in paperback

Critical Asian Scholarship is a series intended to showcase the most important individual contributions to scholarship in Asian Studies. Each of the volumes presents a leading Asian scholar addressing themes that are central to his or her most significant and lasting contribution to Asian studies. The series is committed to the rich variety of research and writing on Asia, and is not restricted to any particular discipline, theoretical approach or geographical expertise.

Education and Reform in China

Edited by Emily Hannum and Albert Park

Routledge
Taylor & Francis Group

LONDON AND NEW YORK

First published 2007 by Routledge
2 Park Square, Milton Park, Abingdon, Oxon OX14 4RN

Simultaneously published in the USA and Canada
by Routledge
270 Madison Ave, New York, NY 10016

Routledge is an imprint of the Taylor & Francis Group, an informa business

Transferred to Digital Printing 2009

© 2007 Editorial selection, © Emily Hannum and Albert Park, © the
contributors

Typeset in Times New Roman by
RefineCatch Limited, Bungay, Suffolk

British Library Cataloguing in Publication Data
A catalogue record for this book is available from the British Library

Library of Congress Cataloging in Publication Data
Education and reform in China / [edited by] Emily Hannum and Albert Park.
p. cm. – (Critical Asian scholarship) Includes bibliographical references.
1. Education – China – 20th century. 2. Education and state – China. 3. China –
History – Cultural Revolution, 1966–1976. I. Hannum, Emily. II. Park,
Albert, 1966–   LA1131.82.E375 2007
370.951'0904 – dc22   2006037470

ISBN10: 0-415-77095-5 (hbk)
ISBN10: 0-415-54705-9 (pbk)
ISBN10: 0-203-96095-5 (ebk)

ISBN13: 978-0-415-77095-8 (hbk)
ISBN13: 978-0-415-54705-5 (pbk)
ISBN13: 978-0-203-96095-0 (ebk)

We dedicate this volume to the memory of Harold W. Stevenson. We were honored by his presence at the China Education and Reform conference, where participants benefited greatly from his insights about the changing nature of China's classrooms. His work on teaching and learning in China and elsewhere continues to inspire.

Contents

Illustrations

Notes on contributors

Yiu Por (Vincent) Chen is an Assistant Professor in the Public Services Graduate Program, DePaul University and a consultant for the Labor Studies Program at the National Bureau of Economic Research. His research investigates labor mobility within and from China, and rural–urban inequality in China. He received his PhD from Columbia University.

Kai-ming Cheng is Chair Professor of Education and Senior Advisor to the Vice-Chancellor, University of Hong Kong. Since 1996, he has also been Visiting Professor at the Harvard Graduate School of Education. He works on education policy, and has recently concentrated on cultural dimensions of education, as well as workplace changes.

Rachel Connelly is a Professor of Economics at Bowdoin College. She received her PhD in Economics in 1985 from the University of Michigan. Her work on human resources in China has concentrated on issues of education and migration.

Alan de Brauw is a Research Fellow at the International Food Policy Research Institute and an Assistant Professor of Economics at Williams College, Williamstown, MA. His research has focused primarily on education and the effects of migration on source households in rural China.

Weili Ding is Assistant Professor, School of Policy Studies and Department of Economics, Queen's University, Kingston, Ontario, Canada. Her research interests include economics of education and the economy of China. She is currently examining residential segregation in urban China. She holds a PhD in Economics from the University of Pittsburgh.

Yanping Fang is Assistant Professor at the Centre for Research in Pedagogies and Practices in the National Institute of Education at Nanyang Technological University, Singapore. Her areas of interest include teacher induction and mathematics curriculum and pedagogy. She holds a PhD from Michigan State University.

Emily Hannum is Assistant Professor of Sociology at the University of

Pennsylvania. Her research focuses on education, child welfare, and social inequality, particularly in China. With Albert Park, she co-directs the Gansu Survey of Children and Families, a study of family, school and community factors that support children's education and healthy development in rural Northwest China. She received her PhD from the University of Michigan.

Steven Lehrer is an Assistant Professor at the School of Policy Studies and Department of Economics, Queen's University, Kingston, Ontario, Canada. He is also a faculty research fellow at the National Bureau of Economic Research. His research interests are in health economics, economics of education, and experimental economics. He received a PhD in Economics from the University of Pittsburgh.

Wen Li is Associate Professor at the Institute of Agricultural Economics, Chinese Academy of Agricultural Sciences, Beijing. Her research is on rural poverty in China.

Zai Liang is Professor of Sociology at the State University of New York at Albany. His major research interests are in internal and international migration, social demography, and Chinese studies. He served as Chair of the Asia and Asian American Section of the American Sociological Association (2005–2006).

Jing Lin is Associate Professor of Education Policy and Leadership at the University of Maryland, College Park. Her work includes *The Red Guards' Path to Violence* (1991), *Education in Post-Mao China* (1993), *The Opening of the Chinese Mind* (1994), and *Social Transformation and Private Education in China* (1999). Lin received her PhD from the University of Michigan.

Margaret Maurer-Fazio is Associate Dean of Faculty and Professor of Economics at Bates College, Lewiston, Maine. Her research focuses on labor market developments in China. She is currently investigating the economic status of China's ethnic minorities and has recently published articles on gender wage differentials and the integration of China's urban labor markets. She holds a PhD from the University of Pittsburgh.

Lynn Paine is an Associate Professor of Teacher Education and an Adjunct Professor of Sociology and Women's Studies at Michigan State University. Her interests are in comparative education and the sociology of education, with a focus on the comparative study of teachers, teaching, and teacher education in China, the United States, and England. She holds a PhD from Stanford University.

Albert Park is Associate Professor of Economics at the University of Michigan, where he is affiliated with the Center for Chinese Studies, the Population Studies Center, and the International Policy Center, Ford

School of Public Policy. His research focuses on economic development in China. He holds a PhD from Stanford University.

Gerard A. Postiglione is Professor of Comparative Sociology of Education and Development at the University of Hong Kong, where he is also Director of the Wah Ching Centre for Research on Education in China. He is co-editor of the journal *Chinese Education and Society*. His recent book is *Education and Social Change in China* (M.E. Sharpe, 2006).

Scott Rozelle is the Helen Farnsworth Senior Fellow and Professor at Stanford University's Freeman Spogli Institute for International Studies. His research focuses almost exclusively on China, and he is Chair of the Board of Academic Advisors of the Center for Chinese Agricultural Policy.

Donald Treiman is Distinguished Professor of Sociology and Director of the California Center for Population Research at the University of California, Los Angeles. His areas of research are social stratification and social demography. Current projects include research on social stratification in China and internal migration in China, as well as cross-national comparative studies of social stratification and mobility. He holds a PhD from the University of Chicago.

Sangui Wang is Professor, School of Agricultural Economics, Renmin University. He was formerly Director, Poverty Research Division, Institute of Agricultural Economics, Chinese Academy of Agricultural Sciences. He is an expert on rural poverty in China, and has collaborated on numerous international research projects with academics and international organizations.

Junsen Zhang is Professor of Economics at the Chinese University of Hong Kong. His research has focused on the economics of family behavior and family-related macro issues, such as ageing, social security, and economic growth, in China and in other countries. He is an editor of the *Journal of Population Economics*, and is Vice President of the Hong Kong Economic Association.

Wei Zhao is Assistant Professor of Sociology in the Department of Sociology and Anthropology at the University of North Carolina at Charlotte. His research focuses on economic and organizational sociology and social stratification. His recent publications are in the areas of social stratification and contractual relationships in China's transitional economy.

Yaohui Zhao is Professor of Economics, China Center for Economic Research, Peking University. She received BA and MA degrees in economics from Peking University and a PhD in economics from the University of Chicago. Her major research area is labor market issues in China.

Zhenzhen Zheng is Professor at the Institute of Population and Labor Economics, Chinese Academy of Social Sciences, Beijing. Her research interests include population and gender issues, such as migration, education, and reproductive health. She received her PhD in demography from Peking University.

Xueguang Zhou is Professor of Sociology at Stanford University. He conducts research on social stratification, interorganizational relationships, and rural governance in China. He also studies the role of reputation in organizing economic activities in the marketplace.

Preface

This book reflects a shared conviction that many challenges facing contemporary society are inherently complex and are best understood from multiple disciplinary and methodological perspectives. Part of this is a function of our training. As PhD students, both of us were International Predissertation Fellows of the Social Science Research Council, a program which provided opportunities for field research and meaningful interaction among faculty and students from different disciplines and area specializations. We are both part of the University of Michigan community of social scientists, which emphasized interdisciplinary social science research long before it became popular elsewhere. As longtime collaborators co-directing a longitudinal study on rural education in Gansu Province in northwest China, we have come to appreciate first-hand the complementarity of our own knowledge and interests.

This book's starting point was a conference with the same title as this volume, which we organized together in 2001 when both of us were at Harvard University, Emily Hannum as Assistant Professor at Harvard's Graduate School of Education and Albert Park as an An Wang Postdoctoral Fellow at the Fairbanks Center for East Asian Research and then Visiting Assistant Professor at the John F. Kennedy School of Government. That conference brought together leading world experts on education in China from the fields of economics, sociology, education, and psychology, and produced an exciting exchange of ideas that gave participants a new appreciation of the value of hearing different perspectives on issues of common concern. About half of the chapters in this volume grew out of papers first presented at that conference, and later updated and revised. The rest were solicited after the conference, in order to ensure that the volume coherently addressed the key issues related to education and reform in China, as we see them.

Emily Hannum and Albert Park

Acknowledgments

For supporting the conference on *Education and Reform in China* at Harvard University in 2001, we acknowledge the Fairbank Center for East Asian Research, the Asia Center, and the China Program of the John. F. Kennedy School at Harvard University, the Spencer Foundation, and the Ford Foundation Beijing Office, and thank Harvard colleagues Merle Goldman, William Kirby, Elizabeth Perry, and Tony Saich, as well as He Jin at the Ford Foundation. We would like to extend our special thanks to Wen Hao Tien at the Fairbank Center for East Asian Research, for her work in organizing the conference.

For outstanding help in editing many of the chapters, we thank N.E. Barr of the Population Studies Center, the University of Michigan, and Tanja Sargent, formerly at the University of Pennsylvania and now at Rutgers University. We are indebted to Mark Selden for his many suggestions on ways to improve the volume. We also thank Wang Feng and an anonymous referee for their helpful comments, and Stephanie Rogers at Routledge for shepherding us through the publication process. We are grateful to Jeff Rubidge for providing a photograph for the cover of this book. Finally, we would like to thank our families for support and patience throughout the process of preparing this book.

1 Introduction

Market reforms and educational opportunity in China

Emily Hannum, Albert Park,
and Kai-Ming Cheng

Introduction

In China, market reforms dating from the late 1970s have brought dramatic if uneven improvements in living standards, along with fundamental changes in class structure and unprecedented economic inequality. The school system, a key vehicle for social mobility in any modern society, has changed radically during the same period. Under China's reform process, the question of how to restructure the educational system to sustain rapid economic development emerged as a significant policy focus. Major changes occurred in educational provision and access, the quality of schooling, and the economic consequences of schooling. By the turn of the century, the educational system had diversified in structure, finance, and content; it had become more marketized; and it was serving an increasingly disparate student body. A combination of economic and educational policy choices ultimately expanded overall access and created new space for local curricular and financial innovations. These choices also exacerbated disparities in school resources across urban–rural, regional, and socio-economic lines. At the same time, market reforms created a labor market that increasingly rewarded the highly educated.

The studies contained in this volume offer a snapshot of China's educational achievements and persisting policy challenges around the turn of the century. Collectively, the sociologists, economists, and educational researchers included here offer diverse, complementary insights on four important issues in reform-era education: (1) the evolution of educational provision; (2) progress and disparities in educational access and attainment; (3) educational quality and qualitative disparities; and (4) the changing economic consequences of being educated. The introduction discusses the significance of each of these issues, and highlights key findings of chapters in this volume. We begin by setting the context, with a brief depiction of the educational system and policy priorities just prior to market reforms.

Education on the eve of market reforms

While many of the educational shifts that have accompanied market reforms in China have global parallels, the starting point was unusual. For over a decade prior to market reforms, China experienced the "Great Proletarian Cultural Revolution," a far-reaching and chaotic social movement that brought a radical agenda to the forefront of politics and educational policy making. In 1966, Mao Zedong proclaimed the start of a new educational era in which political recommendation and class background became the primary means of determining progress through the educational system (Unger 1984).

When schools reopened after the initial chaotic years during which many were closed, the ideological agenda of eliminating class differences, whether urban–rural, worker–peasant, or intellectual–manual, dominated the classroom and the curriculum (Sun and Johnson 1990; Thomas 1986). Labor and political loyalty were valued over academic achievement, and the link between education and occupational achievement was removed (Unger 1984). Urban students were sent to the countryside for re-education (Tsang 2000).

Higher education experienced particularly dramatic disruptions: a discontinuation of the national examination system for admissions; complete stoppage of admissions of undergraduates for six years and of graduate students for 12 years from the start of the Cultural Revolution; initiation of admissions of peasant and working-class students to "attend, manage, and reform universities"; and a 1971 plan to consolidate, close, and reconstruct 106 of 417 institutions of higher education (see Table 1 in Tsang 2000). The Cultural Revolution has been widely viewed as a disaster for higher education in general, and for science and technology training in particular (for example, see Beijing University School of Education and Zhongshan University Institute of Higher Education 2005).

The structure of primary and secondary education was streamlined. Tracking systems were abolished, as were key-point magnet schools, vocational education, and exam-based progressions (Rosen 1984). The educational system was unified so that, in principle, all students studied the same ten-year curriculum in a 5-3-2 structure (Thogersen 1990: 27). Vocational and technical schools were shut down, and, for the first six years, so were secondary teacher training schools (Tsang 2000).

There are few empirical studies of the nature or quality of schools during the Cultural Revolution. However, the curriculum was certainly highly ideological. For example, Julia Kwong's analysis of the contents of primary language textbooks in the early 1970s concluded that "texts devoted their efforts almost exclusively to inculcating in the young the right political attitudes and outlook, even to the extent of almost excluding the pedagogical function of a language text" (1985: 207). Donald Treiman's chapter in this volume sheds some needed light on the quality question. He shows that among otherwise similar people, and, importantly, among people with identical levels of schooling, the cohort of an age to have been in school during the Cultural Revolution ended up with a level of literacy a full year lower than counterparts who would have been in school prior to or after the Cultural Revolution.[1]

While quality may have suffered for those in school, many who would not have previously had access to schooling did gain access during this period. An essential goal of the Cultural Revolution was to undercut differences between the peasantry and the remainder of the population, and, at least temporarily, this appears to have happened. For example, the numbers of teachers and students in rural areas jumped in the 1970s (Hannum 1999). Mean years of schooling attained in a national sample of adults in 1996 suggests that the urban advantage was 3.1 years for cohorts who turned 7 during the Cultural Revolution, compared to 3.7 years for cohorts reaching age 7 in the early years of the People's Republic (Lu and Treiman 2005).[2] Similarly, cross-cohort analyses of census and survey data, as well as published statistics from the Ministry of Education, suggest that the Cultural Revolution era saw a rapid narrowing of gender gaps in primary and secondary education (Hannum and Xie 1994; Hannum 2005; Lu and Treiman 2005).

A few studies have addressed socio-economic disparities in educational attainment during the Cultural Revolution. For data reasons, much of what is available focuses on urban populations. One key study used national 1982 census data on the non-farm population of co-resident fathers and sons (Deng and Treiman 1997). Co-residence in the same households allowed an investigation of the association between the father's socio-economic status and the son's educational attainment across cohorts who would have moved through the school system at different times. Results showed that the advantage of coming from an educated family or an intelligentsia or cadre family was drastically reduced during the Cultural Revolution, but there was a rapid return to normalcy soon thereafter.

A study by Xueguang Zhou and his colleagues modeled entry into different levels of schooling using retrospective life-history reports on the timing of educational experiences of a representative survey of residents of 20 cities in 1993–1994 (Zhou *et al.* 1998). Results showed that coming from an "exploiting class" or middle-class background had no effect on the probability of entering high school or college during the Cultural Revolution, but had significant positive effects in the preceding and subsequent periods. The effects of father's education on entry into these levels of education also varied significantly across historical periods, and were stronger in the models for the post-Cultural Revolution period than during the Cultural Revolution.

A final piece of corroborating evidence comes from a recent study using data from a national—urban and rural—survey conducted in 1996. In this work, Yao Lu and Donald Treiman (2005) found that the effects on years of schooling of parental education and father's occupational status (measured when the child was 14) were smallest for cohorts reaching age 7 during the Cultural Revolution, and greater for preceding and subsequent cohorts.

Expanded access for under-served populations is likely to have been closely linked to policy choices affecting costs to families for educating children during the Cultural Revolution. Opportunity costs to families for education were low, due to the lack of income-generating alternatives under communism, and, in rural areas, the collectivization of agriculture. Moreover, under educational finance arrangements during the Cultural Revolution, it is unlikely that families directly bore many costs of schooling, even in rural areas. Policy documents indicate that much of school finance in China during the Cultural Revolution relied on local community support for *minban*, or people-managed, teachers and schools, which are distinct from *gongban*, or state-managed, teachers and schools. Under this system, many rural primary teachers were forced to work for "work points" instead of a salary, and were re-classified as rural residents (Tsang 2000). The *minban* teachers in general were less qualified than *gongban* teachers and the amount of local support for hiring such teachers undoubtedly varied across communities. Thus, although greater reliance on such teachers increased access to education, significant disparities remained in the quality of education.

Minban education grew rapidly during the Cultural Revolution, first in the countryside and then in urban areas, as educational authorities turned over the direction and financing of state-managed elementary schools to local production teams or brigades, communes, factories, business enterprises, neighborhood revolutionary committees, etc. (Tsang 2000; Wang 2002). During this period, *minban* teachers were paid in grain rations and supplementary cash subsidies by work units based on earned work points, while state teachers received a substantially higher government salary. Dongping Han's (2001) in-depth study of Jimo County in Shandong Province, the single available empirical study of school finance during the Cultural Revolution, showed that virtually every rural child in the county was able to attend primary school at no cost during the latter years of the Cultural Revolution.

In summary, the evidence suggests at least a short-term flattening of rural–urban, gender, and socio-economic disparities in educational access.[3] These trends were a product of both economic and educational policy choices dictated by the political priorities of the era. They are consistent with the overarching educational goal of the Cultural Revolution: to promote a radical socialist agenda of eradicating social differences.

Educational provision under market reforms

With the transition to a more market-oriented economy in the late 1970s and early 1980s, a different agenda came to guide educational policy, as leaders sought to promote market reforms and economic modernization. In March 1978, Deng Xiaoping delivered the opening address at a National Symposium on Science and Technology in Beijing (Beijing University School of Education and Zhongshan University Institute of Higher Education 2005). He reiterated the importance of science and technology for economic modernization, and stated that "the basis for training science and technology talent rests in education" (ibid.: 11; see also Shen 1994).

Policy reforms revolved around perceptions that educational quality was a serious problem at all levels, vocational and technical training were insufficient, and the central administration of education was too rigid (Lewin *et al.* 1994: 19). A complex hierarchy of programs varying in length, quality, curriculum, and financial base supplanted the simple structure of the Cultural Revolution educational system. Educational philosophy in the reform period began to sanction independent thinking (Lee 1996). Classrooms moved away from a focus on egalitarianism and class struggle, instead emphasizing quality, competition, individual talents and the mastery of concepts and skills important in the development of science and technology (Sidel 1982; Broaded 1983; Kwong 1985; Lin 1993: Chapter 1). The exam-based system of progression abolished during the Cultural Revolution was reinstated. Vocational education was reinstated, and the provision of relevant labor market skills was emphasized (Tsang 2000). Higher education, which had been shut down completely for six years at the start of the Cultural Revolution and remained crippled throughout most of the 1970s, was reinvigorated as a means of supplying the high-quality personnel and scientific expertise needed for national development (ibid.).

As part of these reforms, many general secondary schools of inferior quality were shut down or converted to vocational, technical, or agricultural schools, and policy-makers again experimented with alternatives to formal education such as spare-time, paid, correspondence, and television-based schools (Lin 1993: Chapter 2). China's return to household farming in the early 1980s increased the value of farm labor, raising the opportunity cost of schooling.

One of the most critical changes that accompanied market reforms, with important implications for poor, rural communities, was soaring educational costs related, in part, to privatization. After market reforms, families increasingly were expected to pay a substantial share of the costs of schooling their children. Responsibility for paying *minban* teachers fell to rural households after decollectivization in the late 1970s and early 1980s (Wang 2002).[4] Over time, this burden decreased as the government gradually phased out *minban* education in the name of quality upgrading, a process that was to be completed by the year 2000.[5]

More importantly, in the 1980s, the government decided to decentralize the administration and finance of primary, secondary and tertiary education (Tsang 2000), a key educational policy change discussed in greater detail in Chapter 2 by Wen Li, Albert Park, and Sangui Wang. After the reforms, in most regions, provincial, county, township and village governments took responsibility for schools at the tertiary, upper secondary, lower secondary, and primary levels, respectively (Tsang 2000: 13). This reform of educational finance was part of the larger reform of public finance dating from the end of the 1970s (see Park *et al.* 1996). The major objective of financial reform in education was to mobilize new resources for education, and the 1985 reform specified that multiple methods of financing should be sought (Hawkins n.d.; Tsang 2000).

Decentralization has indeed allowed new resources to be mobilized in support of schooling, as wealthier and more entrepreneurial communities became capable of marshaling non-public resources that were previously unavailable to them. For example, Tsang's (2000: 14) research shows that total educational expenditures increased from 34.63 billion *yuan* in 1986 to 90.68 billion *yuan* in 1997 in 1986 constant prices, translating to an average annual growth rate of 9.1 percent over this period.

However, there are vast financial challenges to extending compulsory, quality education to all, especially the rural poor, under such a system (Tsang 2002). In poor rural areas, the ability to mobilize non-governmental resources is slim (Tsang and Ding 2005). Decentralization increased regional disparities in funding for schools, and also increased family educational expenditures required even for compulsory education, especially in poor areas where revenue-starved local governments had no choice but to pass the burden of educational expenditures onto rural households. By the early 2000s, the highest provincial primary educational expenditures per student, in Shanghai, were more than ten times greater than the lowest, with this ratio roughly doubling during the 1990s (Tsang 2002). Case studies in specific regions have found very large differences in educational expenditures within provinces (West 1997; Li, Park, and Wang, this volume). The disequalizing effects of changes in school finance were made worse by rising regional economic inequalities associated with market reforms (Khan and Riskin 2001). By the mid-1990s, the government recognized the problem of rising disparities, and sought to address it by providing earmarked grants to poor and minority regions to support education. Fiscal reforms implemented in 1994 also increased government revenues significantly as well as the share of revenues controlled by the center.

How did all these changes affect inequalities in the quality of public schooling? Chapter 2, by Li, Park, and Wang, studies inequality in educational expenditures per student for rural primary education at the provincial, county, and village levels using national county-level data from 1993 to 2000 and school-level data from Gansu Province for 2000 and 2004. Results show that overall inequality in rural primary school spending among provinces and counties did not change substantially from 1993 to 2000. Inequality associated with differences in rural income per capita was greatest at higher levels of aggregation; rural primary school spending per student was not significantly correlated with income differences within counties, but was significantly associated with income differences between counties, and even more so between provinces. Wage spending was distributed relatively equitably, but was becoming more unequal over time, while operating expenses were much more unequally distributed, but contributing less to inequality over time.

A final dimension of privatization of educational costs in China has been the spectacular revival of private schools, the nature and implications of which are chronicled by Jing Lin in Chapter 3 in this volume.[6] In the Outline of Chinese Education Reform and Development in 1993, the Chinese government officially adopted a new policy that encouraged the development of schools run by social groups and individual citizens (Tsang 2000). Tsang (2000) reports that in 1994, there were an estimated 500 registered non-governmental schools in urban areas, but the number had reached 4000 by the end of 1997. In 1997, non-government schools enrolled 2.55 percent of general secondary enrollment in the Beijing metropolitan area, 3.17 percent in Shanghai, 8.45 percent in Chongqing, and 11.79 percent in Tianjin.[7] Figures are smaller for primary education.

However, a true sense of the scale of private education is difficult to obtain. As Lin observes, these schools are known by a variety of different terms, including *minban* schools or "schools run by social forces." Private schools may encompass a diversity of institutional forms, some with public connections, such that many schools are not easy to categorize as fully private or fully public (see also Tsang 2000). Lin's chapter indicates that these new *minban* schools may be operated by private individuals, private enterprises, private operators with subsidies from the government, public schools with the freedom to secure incomes from non-public sources, and even public institutions (such as universities or government departments) who run schools on the side as an entrepreneurial activity. These schools target elites and the emerging middle class, and, to some degree, the less affluent in both urban and rural areas. Private schools meet the demand for schooling not satisfied by the public school system, and tailor programs to the preferences of parents. However, the often high cost of private schools creates another mechanism for disparities in the quality of education available to different groups of citizens.

These changes have led to the creation of an educational system that is increasingly dependent on resources outside the purview of central government control, including those of families, communities, and the private sector. Such trends are not unique to China. In recent decades, many developed and developing countries have undergone efficiency-oriented education reforms—often involving decentralization and a larger role for private education. Sometimes, these reforms have been part of structural adjustment or related policies called for by international organizations,[8] or as part of a transition strategy for moving from centrally-planned to market-oriented economies. With fiscal decentralization, community financing of schooling often has become increasingly important, tightening the links between the regional level of development and quality of educational services. In East and Southeast Asia, these changes have contributed to rising economic inequality, higher direct costs to individuals for public education, and rising opportunity costs associated with new wage-earning opportunities for children.[9]

The Chinese government has responded to concerns about access problems under the decentralized system with a series of equity-oriented policy proclamations issued throughout the period. Notably, the Law on Compulsory Education of 1986 designated nine years of education, six years of primary and three years of lower secondary, as mandatory for all children, and timetables were set for different regions to achieve full compliance with the law (Ministry of Education 1986). The Education Law of 1995 affirmed the government's commitment to equality of educational opportunity regardless of nationality, race, sex, occupation, property conditions or religious belief (UNESCO 1998). The 1999 Action Plan for Revitalizing Education in the 21st Century confirmed a commitment to implementing compulsory education across the country (Ministry of Education 1999).

Much of the policy attention has centered on how to expand access to underdeveloped rural areas. For example, the recent Western Development campaign, designed to increase public investments in poor Western provinces, emphasized education as an important element (State Council 2000). Numerous educational development projects, funded by both the Chinese government and international agencies, have sought to expand access to schooling in the late 1990s and early 2000s. In 2003, the State Council held the first national working conference since 1949 to formulate plans for the development of rural education, with a focus on protecting access to and improving the quality of compulsory education in rural areas (Postiglione, Chapter 6 in this volume). Among the ideas to emerge from the conference were plans to establish an effective system of sponsorship for poor students receiving compulsory education, such as by exempting poor students from all miscellaneous fees and textbook charges and offering them lodging allowances by the year 2007.

In recent years, questions of access have also emerged for the growing numbers of children of rural unregistered migrants in cities. By some estimates, unregistered rural–urban migrants constitute upwards of 10 percent of the population of some of China's largest cities (Liang 2001), and the children of these migrants are educationally vulnerable. Julia Kwong (2004) has outlined changing policies about migrant children's education. Kwong writes that the 1986 Law on Compulsory Education placed responsibility for educating children with the communities where those children were registered—the sending communities, not the receiving communities. In 1998, the Ministry of Education and the Public Security Bureau issued a document called "The Temporary Plan for the Education of Migrant Children." In this plan, responsibility for providing educational facilities was shifted from the sending to the receiving location. However, as Yiu Por Chen and Zai Liang show in Chapter 7 in this volume, the consequences of this policy have been uneven, with schools in receiving communities often charging fees that are prohibitively costly.

Some under-served communities themselves are responding in innovative ways to gaps in the availability of educational services. For example, Gerard

Postiglione notes in Chapter 6 that in Tibet, the county education bureau has implemented measures to increase attendance by structuring financial incentives to reward student attendance and to make teacher salaries more dependent on attendance, test scores and promotion. A similar phenomenon is emerging in cities, where unregistered schools—referred to by Chen and Liang in this volume as "migrant-sponsored schools"—have emerged, often against great odds, as one of the options available to children of rural migrants living in cities without urban registration. Field-based research in rural China has similarly documented cases of poor communities seeking to start and support their own schools (Ross and Lin 2006). Ironically, the lessening of centralized control over schooling has both contributed to the disparities in public educational finance that create the need for innovation, and offered the flexibility for such innovation to emerge.

Educational attainment and disparity in the reform era

The educational attainment of China's population has increased dramatically in the years since the establishment of the People's Republic in 1949. For example, estimates from a sample of the 2000 census indicate that 88 percent of 80-year-old women report never attending formal schooling, compared to 4 percent of 25–29-year-olds. Similarly, just 2 percent of women in their eighties had a junior high school or higher level of education; among 25–29-year-olds, the figure was 68 percent (Hannum *et al.* 2004: Figure 5). Evidence from a variety of sources indicates that the early years of market transition saw slight contractions in educational access, but that subsequently, the reform period has seen a steady expansion of educational access (Hannum and Liu 2005).

Still, significant disparities in access to basic education in the past continue to affect the life-chances of today's adult population. In this volume, Donald Treiman's chapter shows that adults who are male and who grew up in better-educated, urban families have significantly higher levels of literacy than others. Socio-economic inequalities may actually be intensifying: in other work, Yao Lu and Donald Treiman (2005) have shown that the years-of-schooling advantage attributable to coming from a better educated, higher-status family intensified for cohorts reaching age 7 during the reform period, compared to Cultural Revolution cohorts.[10] Ethnic disparities in education among young adults in the 2000 census are striking: over 11 percent of minorities aged 25 to 34 had not attended formal schooling, compared to just 2 percent of the majority Han population (Hannum *et al.* forthcoming: Table 4).

Were the inequalities apparent in the educational attainment of adult population still affecting children in the reform era? A number of studies through the early 1990s found evidence of significant gaps in educational access by socio-economic status, ethnicity, gender, and geography (Hannum 1999, 2002, 2005; Connelly and Zheng 2003). Evidence from the later 1990s suggests that while enrollment rates rose for both urban and rural residents, and gender differences narrowed, the advantage of urban residents persists, and socio-economic differences in enrollment rates remained striking (Hannum and Liu 2005). Little recent research has sought to quantify changes in ethnic gaps in access to schooling.

In this volume, Rachel Connelly and Zhenzhen Zheng offer a detailed analysis of educational inequalities through the year 2000, using census data (see Chapters 4 and 5). They offer a baseline study of the cohort of Chinese youth born between 1972 and 1980, using census data from 1990. They then offer a statistical update that directly addresses changes between 1990 and 2000. Consistent with early survey results, Connelly and Zheng show that throughout this time period, young people from the most socio-economically disadvantaged families—here defined as rural families with illiterate parents—were still at substantial risk of being unable to access education. In 2000, 11 percent of rural boys and 17 percent of rural girls aged 10–18 whose parents were illiterate had never attended school.

Also consistent with earlier work, in both years, Connelly and Zheng illustrate that place of residence was among the most important factors explaining school enrollment and graduation patterns in China. Despite dramatic increases in rural enrollment rates, urban–rural differences remained substantial in the year 2000: about 12 percentage points for boys, and about 15 percentage points for girls aged 10 to 18.

Moreover, Connelly and Zheng show a growing urban–rural gap beyond the nine years of compulsory education, due to improvements in urban areas outpacing those in rural areas. In urban areas, 72 percent of 18-year-old boys and 76 percent of girls had attended high school, compared to 48 percent of boys and 52 percent of girls in 1990. In rural areas, in 2000, 18 percent of boys and 14 percent of girls had attended high school, compared to 10 percent and 5 percent in 1990.

Geography, other than urban–rural residence, also conditions educational attainment. Connelly and Zheng's multivariate analysis of the 1990 data at the county level shows that counties that were more rural, poorer (in terms of per capita income), and mountainous had fewer 14-year-olds in school. The 1990 census data also show vast regional differences in enrollment rates of 10–18-year-olds by province and rural–urban residence, ranging from a high of 86 percent of boys enrolled in urban Shanghai, to lows of 29 percent of rural girls in Qinghai, and 7 percent of rural girls in Tibet.

Important improvements occurred between 1990 and 2000: rural primary school entrance rates rose in every province, as did primary school completion rates and, with just two exceptions, transitions into middle school. By the year 2000, entry into primary school among rural youth was high, overall: 99 percent for China as a whole. Provinces in the western regions were the only ones with rates under 99 percent, with most in the 95–98 percent range. Notable outliers were Tibet, at 57 percent, and Qinghai, at 86 percent. Thus, by 2000, lack of access to primary school was highly geographically concentrated. Rural rates of transition into middle school were more variable, ranging from 100 percent in Shanghai and 97 percent in Zhejiang, to 64 percent in Yunnan, to 32 percent in Tibet. Thus, for different reasons, at the primary and middle school levels it remains true that the province in which a child lives says a lot about his or her probability of making it through basic education.

Geography is also linked to educational stratification by ethnicity. Minority children disproportionately reside in remote, poor locations that lack the resources to fund high-quality schools, and this reality contributes heavily to the national educational disadvantage observed for minority children (Hannum 2002). In fact, the ethnic gap is primarily a rural problem. For example, Connelly and Zheng show that 3.5 percent of rural minority boys and 6.5 percent of rural minority girls aged 10–18 in the year 2000 had never attended school, compared to 0.34 percent of rural Han boys and 0.61 percent of rural Han girls. Comparable figures for urban children were 0.25 percent for Han boys, 0.12 percent for Han girls, 0.62 percent for minority boys, and 0.17 percent for minority girls. Urban minority children do not face significantly lower chances of school continuation, compared to their Han counterparts. Importantly, Connelly and Zheng's analysis also shows that those minority children who managed to graduate from middle school, whether urban or rural, enjoyed slightly better chances of going on to high school, compared to their Han counterparts.

Overall, Connelly and Zheng's work suggests that access to schooling for minorities is on the rise. Yet, there persists a serious problem of ethnic disparities in access to education; disparities that will translate into lifetime differences in the educational credentials that are increasingly necessary for competitiveness in China's new economy. Collectively, the results from Connelly and Zheng's work suggest that the disadvantaged position of minorities is in large part a problem of impoverished rural children not being able to progress through the early stages of schooling.

Gerard Postiglione's chapter, which uses a case study of rural Tibet, illustrates a number of the mechanisms that serve to disadvantage rural minority children in primary schools. Poor rural schools attended by Tibetans have little of the income-generating potential of urban schools, and for these schools, attracting good teachers is difficult. Further, poverty has a reinforcing effect, as parents in poor rural villages do not necessarily observe examples of education leading to economic improvements and thus are often unwilling to provide financial support for children's schooling. Yet, as important as regional and economic factors are in explaining ethnic differences in education, additional factors are also significant. Postiglione notes that, like many of China's other minorities, Tibetans have cultural traditions that are in many ways dissimilar to Han traditions. One problem is that the content of schooling for minorities may be perceived as being inconsistent, or even oppositional, to minority groups' own traditions.

Anthropological studies among other groups in China similarly suggest that ethnic groups may develop attitudes unfavorable to education if they perceive the school system as incompatible with aspects of their own culture or if they do not observe tangible returns to education among members of their own community (Hansen 1999; Harrell and Ma 1999). For example, Mette Halskov Hansen (1999) argues that educational disparities between the Dai, Naxi, Hani, and Jinuo in Yunnan can be traced to ethnic differences in perceptions of the economic benefits of education and the accord or opposition between cultural heritage and the educational system. Similarly, Stevan Harrell and Lunze Ma (1999) show that expectations of rewards decisively influence educational participation among the Yi ethnic group in Sichuan.

Even when there is not a direct contradiction between minority culture and the content of schooling, what a rural, minority child is learning in school can be vastly different from his or her experiences in everyday life. In such cases, the motivation of students and their families to continue with education can be adversely affected. Postiglione's work suggests that developing educational content that is relevant to the culture of minority children is critical for supporting engagement with the schooling process.

Minorities have been educationally disadvantaged because they are disproportionately likely to reside in poor, rural areas. Girls are not disproportionately represented in these settings, but they have, in the past, been particularly affected when they were in situations of rural poverty. Nationally, gender gaps are narrowing, an unsurprising trend in light of cross-national studies showing a declining disadvantage for girls with better household economic circumstances and economic growth (Hannum 2005; Knodel and Jones 1996). In 1990, Connelly and Zheng showed significant gender differences in enrollment in rural areas, but there were substantial improvements for rural children, particularly girls, by 2000. In 2000, the overall percentage of youth aged 10–18 who were in school ranged from 88.8 percent for urban boys and 89.4 percent for urban girls to 76.6 percent for rural boys and 74.4 percent for rural girls. The figure for rural boys was a 22 percentage point increase from 1990, and the figure for rural girls was a 30 percentage point increase.

These estimates show very small gender differences. However, there was still a disadvantage for rural girls by some measures. In the year 2000, rural girls had the lowest rates of school attendance at every age from 10–18; 88 percent of rural boys, but only 83 percent of rural girls, who finished primary school had gone on to attend middle school.

Moreover, evidence suggests that gender has continued to be a significant modifier of educational opportunities and experiences in some poor rural settings. Research in poor counties in the 1990s found that girls drop out disproportionately starting in middle school (Brown and Park 2002). Connelly and Zheng's 2000 analysis showed that some provinces, including Anhui, Guizhou, Gansu, Jiangxi, and Shandong, continued to show gender gaps of 10 percentage points or more in the transition to middle school for rural populations.

However, even in these areas, girls seem to be making progress. Chapter 9 in this volume, by Emily Hannum and Albert Park, using data from rural Gansu, indicates that socio-economic status is a much more significant determinant of educational outcomes than gender at the primary level, when most children are still enrolled because costs are not prohibitive. Indeed, primary-age rural girls outperform or equal the performance of boys using both achievement and engagement measures, although boys remain somewhat advantaged in terms of educational aspirations. However, other research in rural Gansu suggests that girls' disadvantage has not completely disappeared at the secondary level. As suggested by Connelly and Zheng's findings, by lower secondary school, girls face a significant, if moderate, disadvantage in enrollment (Hannum and Adams 2006). Overall, girls' educational disadvantage is dissipating in China, although there are certain areas where girls' schooling is still at heightened risk.

Just as regional economic inequalities play a role in ethnic and gender disparities, they loom large in the educational problems facing children of another disadvantaged group: rural workers in cities without urban registration, who are typically migrants from much poorer, rural areas. Educational access for the children of temporary migrants is precarious, as Yiu Por Chen and Zai Liang's chapter analyzing recent survey data from Beijing shows (Chapter 7 in this volume). However, the national scale of the problem is difficult to gauge. Chen and Liang review estimates of school-aged temporary migrant children's enrollment rates in different cities, which range widely. However, Chen and Liang make clear that significant numbers of migrant children are not being served by the school system.

Educational quality and qualitative disparities

As educational access has expanded in China, important questions have emerged about quality and qualitative disparities. China's educational policy-makers in the reform period have made quality a top-level priority. What quality means, however, has become broader than achievement on tests. There is a significant movement among policy-makers to promote learner-centered teaching approaches. The so-called "quality education" (*suzhi jiaoyu*) reforms are intended to develop the diverse skills of the whole child, not just promote test-taking skills, and to stimulate critical thinking.[11] The reforms are meant to encourage students to consider multiple answers to the same question and multiple solutions to the same problem.

The quality education initiative is very much in line with current thinking in the global educational research and development communities about the "key competencies" that twenty-first-century education should promote, such as autonomous thinking, active learning, and the ability to adapt and innovate.[12] However, in China, this new orientation may be a remnant of the socialist legacy of manpower planning (*rencai peiyang*). Economic pragmatism and a concern that such skills are essential for workers in the modern economy are at the heart of the motivation for these reforms.

How are key competencies distributed in the population? Treiman's contribution investigates this question in a direct way, with a literacy assessment administered to a nationally representative sample in 1996 (Chapter 8). Treiman shows that this indicator of educational quality is not necessarily synonymous with educational credentials. Net of education, literacy also reflects other work and life experiences, with higher levels of literacy associated with residence in urban versus rural areas and engagement in non-manual versus manual labor.

China's quality education initiative is designed to significantly improve the competencies of students, compared to the traditional practice of didactic teaching. This initiative seeks to address problems of quality by revisiting curriculum content, reexamining subject boundaries, and modifying teaching approaches to involve more intensive student participation. Little is known, yet, about whether the initiative is having the desired effect on students, or even affecting teaching practice, as few empirical studies have investigated teaching practices and their changes under reforms. Jin Xiao's (2005) fieldwork in rural Yunnan Province suggests that the pedagogy in many poor rural schools in this region remains rigidly traditional, and unlikely to facilitate the kinds of adaptive skills thought to be needed for success in the non-farm labor market. On the other hand, Tanja Sargent's (2005) survey research in rural Gansu Province finds striking differences in teacher beliefs about the goals of education in settings where learner-centered teaching reforms have, and have not, been implemented. Regarding practices, her classroom observations and an analysis of student survey responses about classroom interaction suggest that some, but not all, teachers who were working in classrooms that had ostensibly implemented these reforms were adopting practices sanctioned as learner-centered.

One possible barrier to implementing these reforms in the classroom is the persistence of high-stakes tests. From the point of view of Chinese students and their families, performance on high-stakes tests remains the final arbiter of success. For teachers, too, test scores are important. As Chapter 11 by Weili Ding and Steven Lehrer illustrates, China's teacher evaluation and compensation system places emphasis on student test scores as a performance indicator. Lynn Paine and Yanping Fang's fieldwork in Shanghai, discussed in Chapter 10, revealed that teachers felt great pressure to get students to perform well on standardized tests. How the new educational philosophy will coexist with an underlying incentive for both students and teachers to focus on testing remains an important question for research in the coming years, as the meaning of participatory learning and the testing system evolve.

Cultivating teachers who can offer high-quality learning experiences and produce successful test-takers under the new teaching model is a critical challenge. Paine and Fang's Chapter 10 notes that rising demand for education has led children to seek higher educational attainment, which in turn has led to dramatic increases in the number of enrolled students at secondary schools and institutions of higher learning. The system has been challenged to match this growth with a sufficient supply of qualified teachers, to mentor the very high proportion of young teachers in the workforce, and to provide professional development support for implementing new models of teaching and learning.

Critical for understanding the qualitative differences in schools across China are the great disparities in the qualifications of teachers in different schools and communities, as Paine and Fang report. Whether or not they have the appropriate qualifications, many teachers in poor rural areas face late wages and heavy workloads, often while living in poor, remote areas far from urban townships. These difficult living circumstances are likely to diminish teachers' capacity to offer their best effort in the classroom.

The chapters on access and on teachers speak to the fact that poorer children are not only less likely to attend school, but also experience fewer resources in the school system. Chapter 9 by Hannum and Park focuses on Gansu, one of China's poorest provinces, and investigates disparities in the quality of education experienced by rural students. Even in this sample of students—the vast majority of whom could be considered somewhat poor, and all of whom live in rural villages—the findings indicate that the disadvantages of the lowest socio-economic status children are present within the school system, where poorer children have lower levels of achievement, lower aspirations, and less fondness for schooling. These disadvantages can be linked to both poorer home learning environments and to the characteristics of teachers with whom children are paired. This chapter underscores the point that the consequences of poverty for children's schooling are transmitted not only through economic constraints that directly preclude access to schooling, but also in lack of access to myriad other factors that support children's progress *within* the school system.[13]

Finally, it is important to note that parents with money can increasingly buy their way into schools with better climates, more resources, and a more qualified teaching staff. Ding and Lehrer's Chapter 11 reports that in addition to entrance exam scores, monetary payments have begun affecting admissions into high quality public secondary schools in Jiangsu. Lin's Chapter 3 demonstrates that parents with resources can also secure places in better-resourced private schools for students—whether they are academically strong or not. Again, a tension exists between meeting diverse educational needs and maintaining a meritocratic educational system that facilitates economic mobility.

Marketization and the consequences of education

The preceding sections have discussed dramatic educational expansions and persisting socio-economic and geographic disparities in schooling. We have also discussed how policy-makers in the reform period have sought to increase the relevance of schooling to the labor market. To situate these changes in the context of China's broader economic reforms, we next discuss how the links between schooling and work outcomes have changed as China has transformed from a socialist planned economy to a market-oriented system.

It is important to first review some of the main economic policies and trends since market reforms began. In rural areas, periodic markets were re-established in the early 1980s, after many years under socialism in which the allocation of agricultural products was planned. Agricultural decision-making authority was returned to households, who farmed their own plots and were permitted to keep the fruits of their labor after fulfilling grain quotas and paying taxes to the state. Later, as China industrialized rapidly, labor began leaving farms for non-agricultural employment, first in rural township and village enterprises and subsequently in more distant urban centers. This trend has fueled the growth of China's large population of temporary migrant workers.

These trends have important implications for the value of schooling for rural residents. Using recent rural household survey data, Alan de Brauw and Scott Rozelle report in Chapter 12 in this volume that by the year 2000, an additional year of education in rural China increased wages by 6.4 percent among those engaged in wage employment. This rate of return is much greater than estimates for the early reform period, which were uniformly below 4.0 percent (Gregory and Meng 1995; Parish *et al.* 1995; Yang 1997), and almost surely greater than during the socialist period, when work points were distributed in a highly egalitarian manner. Research also finds that the labor market in rural areas increasingly rewards education (de Brauw *et al.* 2002). Studies of rural China have also found that education is becoming the dominant factor that determines whether rural laborers are successful in finding more lucrative off-farm jobs (Zhao 1997; de Brauw *et al.* 2002).[14]

In urban areas, reform occurred less quickly at first, as Chinese leaders sought to protect the interests of urban workers by maintaining the system of state-ownership of enterprises, guaranteed lifetime employment, compressed wage scales, and state-provided health care, housing, and retirement benefits. In the 1980s, firm managers were given more autonomy and more freedom to sell goods on the market and hire workers on a contract basis. However, loss-making enterprises were supported by loans from state-owned banks, and workers had little incentive to leave the security of their state-sector jobs.

Nonetheless, the mobility of workers increased over time, especially as the state gradually abdicated its role of assigning recent graduates to new jobs, and as the non-state sector grew in size. Wei Zhao and Xueguang Zhou find, in Chapter 13, that the returns to education in urban China increased significantly from 1978 to 1993, especially in the non-state sector and among entrepreneurs. While returns were still relatively low in 1993, at less than 4 percent per year of schooling, education did play an important role in providing access to high status jobs and work organizations.

In the 1990s, the market for education in urban areas changed significantly. China witnessed rapid globalization of the economy as trade flourished and millions of new foreign-invested enterprises were established, many seeking to employ China's brightest young workers. By the mid-1990s, the expression "jumping into the ocean" (*xiahai*), or leaving the safety of the state sector for the sea of the private sector, had entered the vernacular. In the late 1990s, China's policy-makers moved ahead with painful economic restructuring of the struggling state-owned enterprise sector, allowing employment within the state sector to become market-determined. The development of a more open labor market increased the premiums placed on the productive skills of workers, even though large regional wage differences remained.

Extending the trend of rising returns found by Zhao and Zhou with a different data source and slightly higher estimates,[15] Junsen Zhang and Yaohui Zhao find in Chapter 14 that the economic returns to a year of education in urban China nearly tripled during the period 1992–2003, rising from 4.0 to 11.4 percent. Interestingly, the gains occurred in nearly every group of workers, whether categorized by gender, public versus private sector, region, or occupation. The returns to college education grew particularly fast. These results for the earlier years are fairly consistent with estimated returns to schooling using the Chinese Household Income Project (CHIP) data for 1988 and 1995 (e.g. Li 2003; Yang 2004; Hauser and Xie 2005).

These findings suggest major and broad-based changes in the functioning of China's labor markets. Estimates of returns to schooling in China in the early reform era were very low by global standards.[16] A recent review of rate-of-return estimates around the world by George Psacharopoulos and Harry Patrinos (2002) found an average rate of return of about 10 percent and a "classic" pattern of falling returns to education by level of economic development and average level of education. China's dramatic increase in the returns to schooling runs counter to that pattern, partly because of China's unique socialist legacy. However, Psacharopoulos and Patrinos also found rising private rates of return to higher education. China's rapid increase in the rates of return to higher education starting from a low base in the early reform period is consistent with this trend.

The role of education has also become important in determining who finds jobs in a new world of high unemployment and uncertainties in the labor market. In the second half of the 1990s, millions of workers were laid off, state-guaranteed employment ended, and employers put an increasing premium on finding and keeping the most productive workers. Beyond its rising importance in income determination, education thus played a key role in distinguishing those workers who were able to keep their jobs from those who were not. Analyzing recent survey data for urban firms and workers, Margaret Maurer-Fazio's Chapter 15 finds that education was protective against lay-offs and that it increased the chances of reemployment. Maurer-Fazio also shows that among reemployed workers, the return to education was even greater than for the continuously employed.

In summary, the economic importance of education has increased substantially in both rural and urban China, affecting both levels of income and the types of jobs and associated occupational statuses that can be attained. This trend creates greater incentives for individuals to invest in education, and at the same time may be a product of the increasing emphasis of policy-makers on increasing the relevance of schooling for work.

Discussion

Collectively, this volume attests to a track record of impressive achievements in education in China. These achievements include successful expansion of basic education and literacy during the socialist period; progress in improving educational attainment levels during the reform period; the creation of a national educational system that rewards merit and provides real opportunity and hope to citizens of all backgrounds; a model system of teacher evaluation and compensation; and aggressive reforms to re-conceptualize and improve educational quality.

Moreover, the work presented here speaks to the rising importance of education as an element of socio-economic inequality in reform-era China. Policy-makers have sought to improve access and quality, and the relevance of schooling for work, and employers competing in the marketplace have been willing to pay higher and higher premiums for workers with more human capital. Simply put, under market reforms, the educational experience has become more accessible, more variable, and more critical for life outcomes than in the past. For these reasons, education increasingly mediates processes of social mobility and change in China. The decisions ahead for educational policy-makers will have repercussions far beyond the school system.

This volume highlights three particular quandaries for Chinese educational policy-makers. First, there are challenges ahead for continued educational expansion. Chapters discuss the scope of and reasons for persisting access disparities by place of residence, socio-economic status, and ethnicity, and make clear that children who still lack access to compulsory schooling are living very different lives than those who do have access. Today, children remaining outside the system are increasingly concentrated in poor and remote rural areas, or occupy a precarious, semi-citizen status in the cities. How to provide a meaningful education for these children—one that not only enrolls them, but also supports their learning and connects them to economic opportunities—is a daunting policy challenge, and a topic worthy of serious research attention.

Second, access disparities tell only part of the story of educational inequality in China. Studies in this volume clearly demonstrate that the school system has become more marketized and more pluralistic. A policy focus on quality, inequities in the availability of financial resources, disparities in the distribution of qualified teachers, and the emerging private sector options chronicled here make clear that educational inequality is no longer just about differences in access. Inequality increasingly concerns what children are experiencing and learning within the system. Yet, we know very little about the scope of these differences. It will be critical in the coming years to devise ways of measuring qualitative differences in school provision. Moreover, a key policy question for the government of China in coming years will be how to balance the important benefits of system diversification and flexibility—mobilization of family and community resources in support of education, and the ability of many families and communities to provide better opportunities and more second chances to their children—against the cost of a system in which educational qualifications increasingly reflect family origins.

Finally, a new challenge is emerging in China, as the educational system must adapt to serve the needs of an increasingly diverse population. Many children in wealthier urban areas now live pampered lives as single children in newly middle-class families. In contrast, large numbers of poor children in rural areas continue to live precariously, without secure access to good nutrition or funding for their education or health care, much less the cultural, social, and economic resources that would place them on par with their urban counterparts. Absolute poverty in China still is nearly entirely a rural phenomenon, so that educating poor rural children will remain the key challenge for increasing educational access for some years to come. At the same time, growing numbers of rural migrant children in cities also face uncertain futures without secure access to an education, and the lack of access to schooling in urban areas may be a barrier to poverty-reducing migration.

China's policy-makers can draw upon the experience of impressive educational gains of recent decades to think through the policy quandaries of the twenty-first century. Yet, they must walk a difficult path, balancing the often-competing goals of expanding access, promoting quality and economic relevance, encouraging innovation in finance and in the classroom, and serving the needs of an ever more diverse student population. Their success will deeply affect the welfare and opportunities of China's future generations.

Acknowledgment

We would like to thank Mark Selden for helpful suggestions on the contents and structure of this chapter.

Notes

1 See Han (2001) for a dissent from common wisdom on education during the Cultural Revolution.
2 Multivariate analyses, which partial out the effects of other background characteristics correlated with rural residence, similarly show that urban Cultural Revolution cohorts were more disadvantaged than urban members of prior cohorts.
3 However, an opposing view based on results from urban Shanghai can be found in Meng and Gregory (2002).

4 Further, the government sought to achieve a qualitative upgrade in the system by eliminating the *minban* teachers altogether by the year 2000 (Wang 2002).
5 However, see chapters Paine and Fang and Postiglione in this volume on the persistence of *minban* teachers.
6 For additional discussion of private schools in China, see Qu (1996).
7 The Tianjin figure refers to both general and vocational secondary school. See Table 7 in Tsang (2000).
8 For example, see Patrinos and Ariasingam (1997).
9 For an overview in East Asia, see Bray (1996).
10 However, Lu and Treiman (2005) show that the gap is actually narrower in the later year than in the earlier year in multivariate results.
11 In 1999, following the Third National Working Conference on Education, the State Council issued "Decisions on Deepening the Educational Reform and Improving Quality-Oriented Education." The full text of the State Council document can be found on the Ministry of Education Web site: http:// www.moe.edu.cn/wenxian/07.htm.
12 See, for example, World Bank (2003) and Rychen and Salganik (2001).
13 For an excellent overview of conditions facing rural students in western China, see Postiglione (2005).
14 See also the studies in West and Zhao (2000).
15 These estimates extend those of Zhao and Zhou, who found rising but still relatively low returns to schooling in urban China up to 1993 (3.5 percent). Zhao and Zhou's estimates of the returns to schooling in 1993 are lower than Zhang and Zhao's. The difference could be due to differences in the variables included, as Zhao and Zhou include party membership and a number of other control variables, while Zhang and Zhao do not.
16 Estimates for urban China from the 1988 Chinese Household Income Project data showed a rate of return of about 3 percent; some earlier estimates for selected urban and rural areas showed no effects or even negative effects (Xie and Hannum 1996).

References

Beijing University School of Education and Zhongshan University Institute of Higher Education (2005) "Retrospect and Analysis of China's Policies with Regard to Students Sent by the State to Other Countries Since 1978," *Chinese Education and Society*, 38(3): 7–62.

Bray, M. (1996) *Counting the Full Cost: Parental and Community Financing of Education in East Asia*, Washington, DC: World Bank.

Broaded, C.M. (1983) "Higher Education Policy Changes and Stratification in China," *The China Quarterly*, 93: 125–141.

Brown, P.H. and Park, A. (2002) "Education and Poverty in Rural China," *Economics of Education Review*, 21(6): 523–541.

Connelly, R. and Zheng, Z. (2003) "Determinants of School Enrollment and Completion of 10 to 18 Year Olds in China," *Economics of Education Review*, 22(4): 379–388.

de Brauw, A., Huang, J., Rozelle, S., Zhang, L., and Zhang, Y. (2002/6) "The Evolution of China's Rural Labor Markets During the Reforms," *Journal of Comparative Economics*, 30(2): 329–353.

Deng, Z. and Treiman, D.J. (1997) "The Impact of the Cultural Revolution on Trends in Educational Attainment in the People's Republic of China," *American Journal of Sociology*, 103(2): 391–428.

Gregory, R. and Meng, X. (1995) "Wage Determination and Occupational Attainment in the Rural Industrial Sector of China," *Journal of Comparative Economics*, 21: 353–374.

Han, D. (2001) "Impact of the Cultural Revolution on Rural Education and Economic Development," *Modern China*, 27(1): 59–90.

Hannum, E. (1999) "Political Change and the Urban–Rural Gap in Basic Education in China, 1949–1990," *Comparative Education Review*, 43(2): 193–211.

Hannum, E. (2002) "Educational Stratification by Ethnicity in China: Enrollment and Attainment in the Early Reform Years," *Demography*, 39(1): 95–117.

Hannum, E. (2005) "Market Transition, Educational Disparities, and Family Strategies in Rural China: New Evidence on Gender Stratification and Development," *Demography*, 42(2): 275–299.

Hannum, E. and Adams, J. (2006) "Gender and Educational Exclusion in Rural China," forthcoming in M. Lewis and M. Lockheed (eds.) *Social Exclusion, Gender and Education: Case Studies from the Developing World*, Washington, DC: Brookings Institute.

Hannum, E., Behrman, J., Wang, M., and Liu, J. (forthcoming) "Education in the Reform Era," in L. Brandt and T. Rawski (eds.) *China's Economic Transition*, Cambridge: Cambridge University Press.

Hannum, E. and Liu, J. (2005) "Adolescent Transitions to Adulthood in China," in J. Behrman, C. Lloyd, N. Stromquist, and B. Cohen (eds.) *Studies on the Transition to Adulthood in Developing Countries*, Washington, DC: National Academy of Science Press.

Hannum, E. and Xie, Y. (1994) "Trends in Educational Gender Inequality in China: 1949–1985," *Research in Social Stratification and Mobility*, 13: 73–98.

Hansen, M.H. (1999) *Lessons in Being Chinese: Minority Education and Ethnic Identity in Southwest China*, Seattle: University of Washington Press.

Harrell, S. and Ma, E. (1999) "Folk Theories of Success: Why Han Aren't Always Best," in G. Postiglione (ed.) *China's National Minority Education: Culture, Schooling and Development*, New York: Falmer Press.

Hauser, S. and Xie, Y. (2005) "Temporal and Regional Variation in Earnings Inequality in Transition between 1988 and 1995," *Social Science Research*, 34: 44–79.

Hawkins, J.N. (n.d.) *Centralization, Decentralization, Recentralization: Educational Reform in China*, Washington, DC: World Bank.

Khan, A.R. and Riskin, C. (2001) *Inequality and Poverty in China in the Age of Globalization*, New York: Oxford University Press.

Knodel, J. and Jones, G. (1996) "Post-Cairo Population Policy: Does Promoting Girls' Schooling Miss the Mark?" *Population and Development Review*, 22: 683–702.

Kwong, J. (1985) "Changing Political Culture and Changing Curriculum: An Analysis of Language Textbooks in the People's Republic of China," *Comparative Education*, 21(2): 197–208.

Kwong, J. (2004) "Educating Migrant Children: Negotiations between the State and Civil Society," *The China Quarterly*, 180: 1073–1088.

Lee, W.O. (1996) "Moral Education Policy: Developments Since 1978: Guest Editor's Introduction," *Chinese Education and Society*, 29 (July–August 1996): 5–12.

Lewin, K., Little, A., Xu, H., and Zheng, J. (1994) *Educational Innovation in China: Tracing the Impact of the 1985 Reforms*, Harlow: Longman.

Li, H.Z. (2003) "Economic Transition and Returns to Education in China," *Economics of Education Review*, 22(3): 317–328.

Liang, Z. (2001) "The Age of Migration in China," *Population and Development Review*, 27: 499–524.

Lin, J. (1993) *Education in Post-Mao China*, Westport, CT: Praeger.

Lu, Y. and Treiman, D.J. (2005) "The Effect of Sibship Size on Educational Attainment in China: Cohort Variations," California Center for Population Research On-Line Working Paper, Series CCPR–052–05: 1–68.

Meng, X. and Gregory, R.G. (2002) "The Impact of Interrupted Education on Subsequent Educational Attainment: A Cost of the Chinese Cultural Revolution," *Economic Development and Cultural Change*, 50(4): 935–959.

Ministry of Education (1986) People's Republic of China Law on Compulsory Education. Beijing: Ministry of Education. (Electronic version posted to http://www.moe.edu.cn/).

Ministry of Education (1999) Action Plan for Revitalizing Education for the 21st Century. (Electronic version posted to http://www.moe.edu.cn/).

Parish, W., Zhe, X.Y., and Li, F. (1995) "Non-farm Work and Marketization of the Chinese Countryside," *The China Quarterly*, 143: 697–730.

Park, A. *et al.* (1996) "Distributional Consequences of Reforming Local Public Finance in China," *The China Quarterly*, 147: 751–778.

Patrinos, H.A. and Ariasingam, D.L. (1997) *Decentralization of Education: Demand-Side Financing*, Washington, DC: World Bank.

Postiglione, G. (2005) "Schooling and Inequality in China," in G. Postiglione (ed.) *Education and Social Change in China*, Armonk, NY: M.E. Sharpe.

Psacharopoulos, G. and Patrinos, H.A. (2002) "Returns to Investment in Education: A Further Update," World Bank Policy Research Working Paper 2881 (September), Washington, DC: World Bank.

Qu, T.H. (1996) "A Brief Description of Current Private School Development in China," *Chinese Education and Society*, 29 (March–April 1996): 31–40.

Rosen, S. (1984) "New Directions in Secondary Education," in R. Hayhoe (ed.) *Contemporary Chinese Education*, Sydney: Croom Helm.

Ross, H. and Lin, J. (2006) "Social Capital Formation through Chinese School Communities," *Research in Sociology of Education 15: Children's Lives and Schooling across Societies*: 43–70.

Rychen, D.S. and Salganik L.H. (eds.) (2001) *Defining and Selecting Key Competencies*, Kirkland, WA: Hogrefe and Huber.

Sargent, T. (2005) "Learner-Centered Reforms and Teacher Beliefs and Practices in Rural Gansu, China," paper presented at the Comparative and International Education Society, Palo Alto, California, March.

Shen, A.P. (1994) "Teacher Education and National Development in China," *Journal of Education*, 176: 57–71.

Sidel, R. (1982) "Early Childhood Education in China: The Impact of Political Change," *Comparative Education Review*, 26(1): 78–87.

State Council (2000) Circular of the State Council on Policies and Measures Pertaining to the Development of the Western Region (October 26, 2000). (Translation posted to The China Economic Information Network, http://ce.cei.gov.cn/).

Sun, H. and Johnson, D. (1990) "From Ti-Yong to Gaige to Democracy and Back Again: Education's Struggle in Communist China," *Contemporary Education*, 61 (Summer): 209–214.

Thogersen, S. (1990) *Secondary Education in China after Mao: Reform and Social Conflict*, Aarhus: Aarhus University Press.

Thomas, R.M. (1986) "Political Rationales, Human Development Theories, and Educational Practice," *Comparative Education Review*, 30 (August): 299–320.

Tsang, M.C. (2000) "Education and National Development in China since 1949: Oscillating Policies and Enduring Dilemmas," Center on Chinese Education, Teachers College, Columbia University, Working Paper D–1, http://www.tc. columbia.edu/centers/coce/publications.htm#(D) (accessed June 1, 2006).

Tsang, M.C. (2002) "Intergovernmental Grants and the Financing of Compulsory Education in China," *Harvard China Review*, 3(2): 15–20. Reference is to electronic edition posted to Center on Chinese Education, Teachers College, Columbia University, http://www.tc.columbia.edu/centers/coce/pdf_files/a1.pdf (accessed June 1, 2006).

Tsang, M.C. and Ding, Y.Q. (2005) "Resource Utilization and Disparities in Compulsory Education in China," *China Review: An Interdisciplinary Journal on Greater China*, 5(1): 1–31.

UNESCO (1998) "World Data on Education: The Country Dossiers (China)," Geneva, Switzerland: UNESCO: IBE Documentation and Information Unit (Internet Databank, http://www.ibe.unesco.org/International/Databanks/Dossiers/ mainfram.htm).

Unger, J. (1984) "Severing the Links between Education and Careers: The Sobering Experience of China's Urban Schools," in J. Oxenham (ed.) *Education versus Qualifications? A Study of Relationships between Education, Selection for Employment, and the Productivity of Labor*, Boston: Allen and Unwin.

Wang, C. (2002) "*Minban* Education: the Planned Elimination of the 'People-Managed' Teachers in Reforming China," *International Journal of Educational Development*, 22(2): 109–129.

West, L. (1997) "Provision of Public Services in Rural PRC," in C. Wong (ed.) *Financing Local Government in the People's Republic of China*, New York: Oxford University Press for the Asian Development Bank.

West, L. and Zhao, Y. (eds.) (2000) *Rural Labor Flows in China*, Berkeley, CA: Berkeley Institute of East Asian Studies.

World Bank (2003) *Lifelong Learning in the Global Knowledge Economy: Challenges for Developing Countries: A World Bank Report*. Washington, DC: The International Bank for Reconstruction and Development.

Xiao, J. (2005) "Rural Classroom Teaching and Non-Farm Jobs in Yunnan," in G. Postiglione (ed.) *Education and Social Change in China*, Armonk, NY: M.E. Sharpe.

Xie, Y. and Hannum, E. (1996) "Regional Variation in Earnings Inequality in Reform-Era Urban China," *American Journal of Sociology*, 101(4): 950–992.

Yang, D. (1997) "Education and Off-Farm Work," *Economic Development and Cultural Change*, 45: 613–632.

Yang, D. (2004) "Determinants of Schooling Returns During Transition: Evidence from Chinese Cities," mimeo.

Zhao, Y. (1997) "Labor Migration and Returns to Rural Education," *American Journal of Agricultural Economics*, 79(4): 1278–1287.

Zhou, X., Moen, P., and Tuma, N.B. (1998) "Educational Stratification in Urban China: 1949–94," *Sociology of Education*, 71(3): 199–222.

Part I

Finance and access under market reforms

2 School equity in rural China

*Wen Li, Albert Park, and
Sangui Wang*

Introduction

Fiscal decentralization has been a key feature of China's economic reforms, leading to the devolution of responsibilities over both revenue collection and public expenditures to lower levels of government—the province, county, township, and village. While a decentralized system improves incentives for local governments to generate revenues and to be responsive to local needs, it can hamper efforts to meet goals of distributional equity. Given overall budget scarcity, it is not surprising that in China decentralization led to greater inequity in the provision of public goods and services across regions. Many poor areas confronted a lack of local government revenues or subsidies from upper levels of government, leading to fiscal crises which prevented local governments from even meeting their salary obligations to government officials and teachers, let alone enabling them to finance high quality public services (Park *et al.* 1996; Wong 1997).

These changes have had a pronounced effect on the equity of public educational expenditures, typically one of the largest budgetary items of local governments (Tsang 1994, 1996; West 1997). Along with decentralization, in order to ensure the adequacy of resources, the government also endorsed greater diversification of the sources of educational finance.[1] However, richer regions generally have more alternative financing options than poorer regions, so diversification may exacerbate rather than ameliorate disparities. By the early 2000s, the highest provincial primary educational expenditures per student, in Shanghai, were more than ten times greater than the lowest, with this ratio roughly doubling during the 1990s (Tsang 2002). Case studies in specific regions have found very large differences in educational expenditures within provinces, and even within counties (West 1997).

Regional differences in educational spending levels translate into differences in the quality of educational services. Quality differences, in turn, may increase disparities in educational attainment, thereby setting the stage for greater income inequality in the future. Zhang and Kanbur (2005) document rising provincial inequality in teacher–student ratios and illiteracy rates during the economic reform period. Connelly and Zheng's chapters in this volume describe significant urban–rural and regional differences in school enrollment rates persisting to the year 2000. Heckman (2005) interprets these large spatial disparities in attainment as evidence of substantial inefficiencies in China's public educational investments.

By the mid-1990s, the government itself had recognized the policy importance of reversing the trend of widening disparities, and began allocating targeted funds to reduce inequities in the public financing of education. Major changes to the fiscal system in 1994 led to increases in both the amount of revenues mobilized and greater control by the center over budgetary allocations, presumably reducing budgetary pressures at all levels and increasing the center's ability to redistribute resources. Concerns over widening disparities and excessive fees led the government to provide greater central financing support for educational costs in poor areas. As early as 1995, the Ministry of Finance and the National Education Commission announced the launch of the Compulsory Education Project in Poor Areas to help mobilize national and local resources to educate the poor. Minority regions also were targeted for special assistance. Also, in the early 2000s, the government announced the reduction and eventual elimination of rural education surcharges.

Although there have been significant changes in local public finance, and educational finance in particular, since the early 1990s, there is a glaring lack of quantitative evidence on the extent of inequality in educational spending and how this has changed over time. This chapter makes several new contributions to the understanding of patterns of school equity in rural China. We focus particular attention on the financing of primary education, the most basic level of education, which involves nearly all children and nearly every local community in the country, most located in rural areas.[2]

First, we examine for the first time inequities at each level of public expenditures, including differences among regions, provinces, counties, and villages. These comparisons are facilitated by published provincial and county-level educational expenditure data, and primary survey data collected by the authors from primary schools in 20 different counties in one of China's poorest provinces, Gansu, in the years 2000 and 2004. This is also the first study, as far as we know, that looks at national county-level data or school-level data over an extended period of time to systematically assess trends in inequality.

Second, the school-level data enable us to look separately at all the sources and uses of funds in rural schools. Of particular importance, we are able to examine village-level financing of education. Official educational statistics do not provide detail down to the individual school level, and other studies based on budgetary data only go down to the township level, the lowest administrative level for which budgetary data is available, or exclude non-governmental sources of financing.

Our analytic approach focuses on calculating inequality measures for all available measures of rural primary school expenditures per student, including specific sources and uses of funds, for each level of analysis (region, province, county, village) and for different years of available data. At the village level, because of limited sample sizes, we focus on mean differences in educational expenditures across relative income groups. When appropriate and data are available, we also report inequality measures for other relevant educational spending or economic variables for purposes of comparison. At each level of analysis, we also investigate the extent to which economic differences measured by rural income per capita lead to differences in educational spending levels.

The rest of the chapter is organized as follows. The next section introduces the data and definitions of education income and expenditure categories. The third section describes changes in the composition of the sources and uses of primary school educational funds, including an inter-regional comparison. The fourth section examines regional and provincial inequality, the fifth section analyzes county-level inequality, and the sixth section analyzes school-level inequality. A final section concludes.

Data and the definitions of sources and uses of funds

For easy reference, in Table 2.1 we list the standard categories of sources and uses of funds according to China's official educational statistics, including the Chinese terms. The sources of funds are divided into five categories: (1) government finance; (2) funds from schools established by social groups

Table 2.1 China's educational funding: source and use categories

Sources	Chinese
1. Government finance	*guojia caizhengxing jiaoyu jingfei*
A. Budgetary	*yusuannei*
B. Extra-budgetary	*yusuanwai*
(i) Special educational fees assessed on rural households	*jiaoyu shuifei fujia*
(ii) Enterprise funds used for enterprise-run schools	*qiye ban xue*
(iii) School-generated revenues	*xuexiao chuangshou*
2. Funds from schools established by social groups or individuals	*shehui tuanti he gongmin geren banxue jingfei*
3. Collective or community contributions	*shehui juanzu he jizi banxue jingfei*
4. School fees and other administrative revenue	*shiye shouru: zhuyao wei xuezafei*
5. Other sources	*qita jiaoyu jingfei*
Uses	
1. Administrative expenditures	*jiaoyu shiyefei zhichu*
A. Wages	*geren bufen*
B. Operating	*gongyong bufen*
2. Infrastructure investment	*jijian feiyong zhichu*

or individuals; (3) collective or community contributions; (4) administrative revenue, mainly from school fees; and (5) other sources. Government finance is divided between budgetary and extra-budgetary sources, with the latter including special educational fees assessed on rural households, enterprise funds used for enterprise-run schools, and school-generated revenues. Expenditures include administrative expenditures and infrastructure investment, with the former divided between wages (and bonuses) and operating expenses.

In this chapter, our analytical focus is on the funding of rural primary education. We draw primarily upon two data sources. One is provincial and county-level data published annually in the *China Educational Finance Yearbook* (*zhongguo jiaoyu jingfei nianjian*). At the provincial level, there is a relatively complete breakdown of sources and uses of rural primary school expenditures. At the county level, four educational finance variables are available in both years: (1) government finance for administrative expenditures on education for all schooling levels; (2) within-budget government administrative expenditures on all schooling levels; (3) within-budget administrative expenditures on rural primary education; and (4) within-budget administrative expenditures on operating expenses of rural primary schools. We examine three years of data, 1993, 1997, and 2000. We also look at the earliest and latest years for which the county data can be linked to data from other sources on county rural income per capita, 1993 and 1999, to study how inequality in spending is related to differences in the level of economic development. The year 1993 is a good base year, because it precedes new fiscal reforms in 1994 that tried to centralize budgetary authority and coincides with the rapid period of growth and economic liberalization that followed Deng's southern tour in 1992.

The second dataset is two waves of primary school data on the sources and uses of funds from a survey we conducted in 20 counties in Gansu Province in 2000 and 2004 as part of the Gansu Survey of Children and Families. The school income and expenditure categories are similar but not identical to the official statistical categories described above. Many primary school principals did not distinguish clearly between within-budget government spending (source 1A in Table 2.1) and funds from extra-budgetary educational fees assessed by local township governments (source 1B(i)), since both types of funds flow to schools from township governments. In our primary school data, these two categories are lumped together in a category labeled "government spending."[3] We also collected data on funds generated by school commercial activities (source 1B(iii)), from collective or social contributions (source 3), student contributions (source 4), and other sources (source 5). The school data do not contain information on some categories (sources 1B(ii) and 2) because the sample does not include any schools that are not village-run or enterprise-run schools.

We also calculate mean rural income per capita in the villages where schools are located based on completed questionnaires from surveys of

20 households in each village conducted as part of the Gansu Survey of Children and Families in both 2000 and 2004.

Changes in the composition of rural primary school financing

Since the distribution of educational resources is related to the specific types of sources and uses of funds, we begin by providing a breakdown of the main sources and uses of primary school funds nationally in 1993, 1997, and 2000 (Table 2.2). The share trends for many items are not unidirectional from 1993 to 2000 but rather show reversals after 1997.

Most significantly, the share of the government budget in total financing decreased from 0.60 in 1993 to 0.56 in 1997, but then increased to 0.67 by 2000 (Table 2.2). At the same time, the share of local taxes and fees showed the opposite pattern, increasing from 0.14 in 1993 to 0.17 in 1997, then falling to 0.12 in 2000. This pattern is consistent with reforms that first encouraged diversification of financing sources to complement public financing, followed by a reversal in response to growing alarm about widening disparities and irresponsible fee-levying which led the government to re-emphasize the primary role of government in financing educational costs. The much smaller shares of revenues from school-generated funds and community funds in 2000 compared with previous years also is consistent with a backlash against diversification of financing sources in the late 1990s, or less need for such financing with more budgetary resources available. However, the share of

Table 2.2 Sources and uses of rural primary school funds, 1993, 1997, and 2000

	1993	*1997*	*2000*
Sources			
Government budget	0.604	0.558	0.665
Local taxes and fees	0.141	0.168	0.124
School-generated	0.028	0.027	0.014
Other budgetary	0.003	0.003	0.000
Community	0.117	0.113	0.035
Student fees	0.090	0.101	0.104
Other	0.016	0.030	0.058
Uses			
Administrative: wages	0.667	0.602	0.731
Administrative: operating	0.215	0.250	0.229
Infrastructure	0.110	0.140	0.040
Budget balance	0.008	0.009	0.000
Uses of budgeted funds			
Administrative: wages	0.935	0.900	0.932
Administrative: operating	0.055	0.078	0.058
Infrastructure	0.011	0.022	0.011

Note: Units are share of total sources, uses, and uses of budgeted funds.

revenue from student fees increased slightly from 1997 to 2000, reaching 10.4 percent of revenues, and the share of revenue from "other sources" nearly doubled from 3 to 6 percent (Table 2.2).

Turning to the expenditure side, not surprisingly, most educational expenditures were spent on teachers' wages. However, the share of wages and bonuses in all uses of funds changed over time, declining from 0.67 in 1993 to 0.60 in 1997, then increasing to 0.73 by 2000 (Table 2.2). Offsetting these changes was an increase and decline of infrastructure spending of similar magnitudes. These changes could reflect a shift in spending priorities from infrastructure investment to raising teachers' salaries, or reflect changes in the sources of school financing if government financing privileges teachers' salaries and infrastructure is financed from non-government revenue.

Regional and provincial inequality in rural primary school financing

We compare education spending levels in different regions of the country, broken down by year and type of expenditure (Table 2.3). Mean per capita spending levels in central and western provinces are presented as a share of mean spending levels in coastal provinces. First, we note that the level of disparities is substantial; in 2000, total expenditures in central and western China were 57.6 and 62.9 percent of that in coastal China. Interestingly, western China spends slightly more than central China, even though it is poorer; this may be partly explained by fewer economies of scale in remote,

Table 2.3 Regional rural primary school expenditures per student (as share of coastal expenditures)

	1993	*1997*	*2000*
Central provinces			
Total	0.600	0.702	0.576
Budgetary	0.614	0.635	0.583
Administrative: wages	0.622	0.616	0.587
Administrative: operating	0.496	0.740	0.535
Infrastructure	0.716	1.171	0.645
Western provinces			
Total	0.639	0.667	0.629
Budgetary	0.824	0.789	0.696
Administrative: wages	0.717	0.655	0.656
Administrative: operating	0.442	0.537	0.514
Infrastructure	0.645	1.089	0.911

Notes: Regional classifications based on those used by the Ministry of Education. Coastal provinces include Beijing, Guangdong, Jiangsu, Jilin, Liaoning, Shandong, Shanghai, Tianjin, Zhejiang; central provinces include Anhui, Fujian, Hainan, Hebei, Heilongjiang, Henan, Hubei, Hunan, Jiangxi, and Shanxi; and western provinces include Chongqing, Gansu, Guangxi, Guizhou, Inner Mongolia, Ningxia, Qinghai, Shaanxi, Sichuan, Tibet, Xinjiang, and Yunnan. Ratios calculated from regional means that weight provincial data by student population.

mountainous areas where class sizes are relatively small. Second, for both central and western regions the overall degree of disparity with the coastal regions decreased from 1993 to 1997, but increased from 1997 to 2000 to slightly surpass the 1993 levels. Given the changes in the composition of fund sources described above, this suggests that increasing regional disparities are associated with increases in the share of financing coming from government budgets. Although the level of regional disparities in budgetary expenditures is less than in total expenditures, the gaps with coastal China are increasing at a faster rate for budgetary expenditures than non-budgetary expenditures. Perhaps richer areas can finance an increasing share of their education costs from budgetary revenues and so do not need to increase alternative financing.

If we examine regional disparities in specific types of spending, we find interesting differences. First, in general, regional disparities are greatest for school operating expenses, followed by wage expenditures, followed by construction expenditures. The greater disparities in operating costs is not surprising given that governments in poor regions often focus their efforts on paying teachers' salaries and ask local communities to finance operating costs. The relatively small disparities in construction expenditures could reflect special programs to fund school construction in poor regions, including by non-governmental organizations, or greater economies of scale of school infrastructure in richer areas where population density is much higher. Table 2.3 also reveals that trends in regional disparities in operating expenditures and infrastructure costs follow the same nonlinear pattern as overall expenditures while regional disparities in personnel expenditures widen continuously over time.

In Table 2.4, we present two commonly used inequality measures, the Gini coefficient and Theil index, to measure provincial inequality for different categories of primary school expenditures for 1993, 1997, and 2000. For both measures, higher values correspond to greater inequality. We are interested in both differences in the levels of inequality across categories and trends in inequality over time. With respect to the former, first we find that inequality in total expenditures is slightly less than inequality in budgetary expenditures, suggesting that extra-budgetary and non-government expenditures are equalizing rather than disequalizing with respect to province-level inequality. This makes sense if relatively poorer provinces compensate for lower spending by raising a larger share of their revenue from non-budgetary sources. Second, we find that among the three mutually exclusive expenditure categories, the order in descending level of inequality is infrastructure, operating expenditures, and wages.

In examining inequality trends, we find different trends for different expenditure categories. Using either inequality measure, inequality in total primary school expenditures per student decreased from 1993 to 1997, but increased from 1997 to 2000 to slightly surpass the initial level of inequality. The results are similar to the trends in regional disparities. Inequality in budgetary expenditures changes very little over time, with the different measures

Table 2.4 Provincial inequality in rural primary school expenditures per capita

		1993		1997		2000	
		estimate	S.E.	estimate	S.E.	estimate	S.E.
Total	Gini	0.190	0.024	0.171	0.027	0.198	0.024
	Theil	0.060	0.014	0.055	0.015	0.069	0.017
Budgetary	Gini	0.219	0.025	0.217	0.025	0.210	0.020
	Theil	0.080	0.019	0.090	0.023	0.084	0.017
Administrative:	Gini	0.184	0.022	0.193	0.022	0.200	0.023
wages	Theil	0.056	0.012	0.066	0.018	0.073	0.019
Administrative:	Gini	0.275	0.053	0.233	0.041	0.232	0.044
operating	Theil	0.139	0.044	0.098	0.029	0.104	0.032
Infrastructure	Gini	0.318	0.045	0.244	0.040	0.273	0.028
	Theil	0.168	0.045	0.105	0.029	0.122	0.023

Notes: Standard errors are estimated by bootstrapping. Inequality measures weight provincial data by student population. Data for Chongqing in 1997 and 1999 are included in Sichuan totals.

showing different trends. Meanwhile, among the three fund use categories, we find that inequality in administrative wages increases over time, inequality in administrative operating expenses decreases over time, and inequality in infrastructure investments decline then rise, with an overall net decline. If government budgets focus on payment of teachers' wages and operating expenses are financed more by non-budgetary and extrabudgetary sources, then the patterns are consistent with rising inequality in budget-financed wage spending, from a lower starting point, and falling inequality in non-budgetary and extra-budgetary financing, from a higher starting point. Overall, there is no evidence of significant changes in provincial inequality in primary school financing.

County inequality in rural primary school financing

In Table 2.5, we present Gini coefficients and Theil indices of inequality over time for the available county-level educational expenditure measures. Recall that these categories differ from those used to examine provincial inequality. The only available rural primary school expenditure variables at the county level are budgetary administrative expenditures per student and budgetary administrative operating expenditures per capita, a subcategory of the former. In addition to reporting results for the set of counties for which we can match data in all three years (1993, 1997, and 2000), we also report results for the larger sample of counties that can be matched in 1997 and 2000. As before, spending on operating expenditures is much more unequal than overall administrative expenditures (including wages). We find that inequality in budgetary administrative expenditures did not change appreciably over time,

Table 2.5 Inequality in county educational expenditures per student, 1993, 1997, and 2000

		1993		1997		2000	
		Coef	S.E.	Coef	S.E.	Coef	S.E.
Administrative (all schools)	Gini	0.330	0.022	0.257	0.033	0.243	0.013
	Theil	0.257	0.047	0.239	0.147	0.108	0.010
	N	1113		1113		1113	
	Gini			0.236	0.019	0.228	0.008
	Theil			0.185	0.089	0.094	0.009
	N			1578		1578	
Administrative budgetary (all schools)	Gini	0.320	0.020	0.230	0.006	0.249	0.009
	Theil	0.244	0.040	0.089	0.006	0.112	0.014
	N	1113		1113		1113	
	Gini			0.221	0.005	0.236	0.008
	Theil			0.082	0.004	0.099	0.011
	N			1578		1578	
Administrative budgetary (rural primary schools)	Gini	0.310	0.008	0.309	0.009	0.309	0.007
	Theil	0.154	0.008	0.164	0.014	0.158	0.009
	N	1113		1113		1113	
	Gini			0.307	0.009	0.304	0.006
	Theil			0.168	0.014	0.153	0.007
	N			1578		1578	
Administrative budgetary: operating (rural primary schools)	Gini	0.492	0.012	0.505	0.011	0.555	0.011
	Theil	0.422	0.023	0.434	0.020	0.541	0.026
	N	898		898		898	
	Gini			0.513	0.011	0.575	0.010
	Theil			0.446	0.020	0.582	0.023
	N			1378		1378	

but that inequality in budgetary operating expenditures increased significantly, with the gini coefficient increasing from 0.492 in 1993 to 0.555 in 2000 and the Theil index increasing from 0.422 to 0.541 over the same period (Table 2.5). The former result is the same as for provincial inequality, but the latter result appears at odds with the earlier finding that provincial inequality in operating expenditures declined over time. However, this latter difference may be entirely due to the fact that the county measure of operating expenditures excludes extra-budgetary and non-government expenditures while the provincial measure does not. Budgetary spending on operating expenses are likely to increase at a slower pace in poorer regions that struggle to meet teachers' wage bills, and richer communities may not perceive a need to raise as much additional funds from alternative sources.

For the purposes of comparison, Table 2.5 also reports changes in inequality measures for all administrative expenditures on education (not just rural primary schools) as well as for the budgetary component of administrative expenditures. Overall, both declined substantially from 1993 to 2000, with only budgetary administrative expenditures showing an increase in inequality in any sub-period (from 1997 to 2000). These results suggest that county-level budget expenditures on primary schools have become relatively more unequal than similar expenditures on higher levels of education. Also, changes in extra-budgetary and non-government expenditures seem to have been equalizing from 1997 to 2000.

Next, we link the county educational expenditure data to other county data on total government revenues and expenditures per capita and rural income per capita in order to examine the relationship between inequality in educational expenditures and inequality in basic economic conditions. The earliest and latest years for which we can successfully match the county data are 1993 and 1999. In all cases, we maintain an identical sample of counties in the two years to ensure that the comparisons are meaningful. In Table 2.6, we first report the Gini coefficient and Theil index for the three county educational expenditure variables, just as in Table 2.5. In addition, we report inequality measures for county total budgetary expenditures per capita, total budgetary revenues per capita, and rural income per capita.[4] All indices are calculated using appropriate population weights. In addition, using a subset of counties in provinces for which we have data on at least 20 counties per province, we calculate the share of the Theil index accounted for by between-province inequality, with remaining variation attributable to within-province inequality.

Similar to the results reported in Table 2.5, we find little change in inequality in administrative budget expenditures per student on rural primary

Table 2.6 Inequality in county educational expenditures per student and economic indicators, 1993 and 1999

	1993			1999		
	Gini	Theil	Theil bw/prov. share (%)	Gini	Theil	Theil bw/prov. share (%)
Administrative budgetary	0.304	0.150	52	0.305	0.160	52
(rural primary schools)	(0.0064)	(0.0062)		(0.0082)	(0.0097)	
Administrative budgetary	0.325	0.245	38	0.278	0.139	62
(all schools)	(0.0181)	(0.0361)		(0.0091)	(0.0100)	
Administrative (all	0.334	0.255	40	0.247	0.111	55
schools)	(0.0181)	(0.0365)		(0.00924)	(0.0105)	
Total govt. budgetary	0.299	0.168	34	0.277	0.154	29
expenditure per capita	(0.0088)	(0.0132)		(0.0123)	(0.0172)	
Total govt. budgetary	0.406	0.312	25	0.341	0.218	18
revenues per capita	(0.0119)	(0.0252)		(0.0149)	(0.0262)	
Rural income per capita	0.246	0.103	55	0.223	0.0806	63
	(0.0073)	(0.0073)		(0.0051)	(0.0037)	

Note: The sample of 1,343 counties with complete data for both years. Numbers in parentheses are bootstrapped standard errors. Theil decompositions based on results for counties in provinces with data points for at least 20 counties.

schools, but a clear reduction in inequality in administrative budget expenditures per student for all schools. One reason for falling inequality may be that inequality in economic conditions of the sample counties also fell, which is verified by the trends reported in Table 2.5. Also, for total educational spending, the share of inequality due to between-province differences increased sharply from 40 percent to 55 percent, even though there is much less change, and in some cases even change in the opposite direction, for total budget expenditures, total budget revenues, and rural income per capita. Given declines in overall inequality, this suggests that the allocation of budgetary dollars to education within provinces became more equalizing over time than between provinces. Finally, rural budgetary expenditure inequality is about equally divided into within-province and between-province components in both years, and this inequality is larger than for total administrative educational expenditures in 1999 but less in 1993. This implies that the falling inequality in total educational expenditures is due to changes in allocations of secondary and higher education and in urban education.

We next examine how administrative budgetary expenditures per student in rural primary schools are related to differences in community wealth (e.g. poverty) versus other factors. To examine this question, we regress the log of the expenditure measure on the log of county rural income per capita. We estimate the relationship across all counties, within provinces (by including provincial dummy variables) and between provinces (by regressing provincial means). Our results presented in Table 2.7 show that the effect of income levels on rural primary school administrative budgetary expenditures was less in 1999 than in 1993 (elasticities of 0.406 and 0.384 in 1993 and 1999). This was true both within provinces and between provinces. Regressivity, however, remains much greater across provinces than within provinces, suggesting that redistribution is more easily realized within provinces.

School-level inequality in rural primary school financing in Gansu Province

In Table 2.8, we summarize the primary school finance data from the Gansu Survey of Children and Families, broken down by equally sized relative income groups (low income, medium income, and high income) for 2000 and

Table 2.7 Elasticity of county rural within-budget administrative expenditures per primary school student with respect to rural income per capita

	All	*Within provinces*	*Between provinces*
1993	0.406***	0.205***	0.522***
1999	0.384***	0.161***	0.409***

Note: *** denotes that the coefficient is statistically significant at the 1 percent significance level. Elasticities are coefficients from log-log regressions.

Table 2.8 Gansu primary school administrative expenditures per student by income group and by sources and uses of funds, 2000 and 2004

	2000				2004			
	Low income	Medium income	High income	All	Low income	Medium income	High income	All
Number of schools	40	40	39	119	36	34	34	104
Admin. income per student	293.50	343.88	473.96	379.96	394.64	407.59	607.78	468.55
Of which:								
Government spending	238.34	287.00	295.49	277.78	325.20	341.39	485.73	382.97
Collective/community	7.18	3.23	14.32	8.41	3.47	0.87	35.14	12.97
Student fees	38.13	41.13	115.01	68.16	63.27	65.34	85.95	71.36
School-generated revenue	7.21	8.20	41.25	20.38	2.70	0.00	0.44	1.08
Other	2.63	4.33	7.88	5.23	0.00	0.00	0.53	0.17
Admin. spending per student	293.50	343.88	473.96	379.96	364.21	382.52	565.45	436.51
Of which:								
Wages	250.79	294.71	302.03	286.26	325.03	342.14	487.08	383.60
Operating expenses	42.71	49.17	171.93	93.70	39.19	46.41	78.37	54.44

Source: Gansu Survey of Children and Families, 2000 and 2004.
Note: Income groups based on village income per capita measured from surveys of 20 households in each village.

2004. Gansu is one of China's poorest provinces, ranking second to last in rural income per capita in 2004. The sample contains the primary schools attended by children in a randomly drawn sample of 100 villages. In 2000, there were large differences in spending levels across primary schools in the province; per student administrative expenditures were 474 *yuan* in the rich income group and only 294 in the low income group. Data for the rich group also differs sharply from the others in the composition of both sources and uses of funds. Richer areas have far greater amounts of non-government revenue, especially from student fees, school-generated revenues, and collective or community contributions. Meanwhile government spending is relatively equal, with schools in the three income groups getting 238, 287, and 295 *yuan* per student. Richer areas also have considerably more funds available for operating expenses (172 *yuan* per student on average, compared to middle income and poor income areas (49 and 43 *yuan* per student). This suggests that non-budgetary finance and local village finance, for which data are not often systematically collected, are disequalizing.

In 2004, real school spending per student increased in all income groups.[5] For the full sample, administrative expenditures per student increased from 380 *yuan* in 2000 to 469 *yuan* in 2004, a 23 percent increase. The increase was highest in percentage terms in the low income group, but much smaller in absolute terms. There are several important changes in the composition of educational financing in 2004 in comparison to 2000.[6] First, government spending increased much faster in the high income group than in other groups, creating significant differences in government support per student that had not existed previously. Second, perhaps relatedly, student fees fell in the high income villages but increased significantly (by more than 50 percent) in the low and medium income villages. Third, school-generated revenues nearly disappeared, likely in response to new concerns about exploiting children's work and providing a safe environment for children following a highly publicized explosion in a workshop of a rural school. Fourth, financing from the collective or local community was disequalizing, with almost no such funds in low and medium income villages. Finally, the data show that spending on wages increased significantly from 2000 to 2004, but spending on operating expenses fell, especially for the high income group.

Next, we estimate the relationship between educational spending and community per capita income levels. Table 2.9 presents elasticities estimated from linear and log-log specifications of primary school spending overall and broken down by sources and uses. An important finding is that none of the expenditure categories have a statistically significant relationship with village income levels when comparing schools within the same county, with the one exception of operating expenditures in 2004. However, the between-county elasticities are uniformly higher than the overall elasticities, in most cases about double, suggesting that much of income-related rural inequality in educational spending in Gansu is associated with between-county differences rather than within county differences.

Table 2.9 Elasticities of Gansu primary school expenditures and revenues per student with respect to village income per capita, 2000 and 2004

Dependent variables	2000			2004		
	All	*Within-county*	*Between-county*	*All*	*Within-county*	*Between-county*
Linear						
Admin. income per student	0.336***	−0.048	0.670***	0.444***	0.038	0.652***
Government spending	0.249****	−0.098	0.549****	0.388****	0.085	0.522***
Collective and community cont.	0.747**	−0.4608	1.794****	3.885****	−0.707	7.296***
Student fees	0.283	0.287	0.280	0.143	−0.037	0.158
School-generated revenue	1.25***	−0.178	2.491***	−1.026	−2.621	−0.305
Other	0.880**	0.776	0.971*	0.968	0.305	0.728
Admin. exp. per student	0.336****	−0.048	0.670***	0.483****	0.152	0.648***
Wages	0.238****	−0.0936	0.525****	0.389****	0.086	0.522***
Operating expenses	0.715****	0.1286	1.224****	1.138****	0.612**	1.522***
Admin. income per student	0.314****	−0.0796	0.601****	0.402**	0.172	0.534***
Logs						
Government spending	0.249****	−0.0206	0.490****	0.489**	0.189	0.598
Admin. exp. per student	0.314****	−0.0796	0.601****	0.448****	0.214	0.562*
Wages	0.2139**	−0.1476	0.481***	0.432*	0.109	0.573
Operating expenses	0.729****	0.2016	1.130***	0.711***	0.409**	0.966***

Notes: *, **, and *** denote that coefficient is statistically significant at the 10, 5, and 1 percent significance levels. For linear specifications, elasticities are calculated at sample means.

The findings for specific types of sources and uses largely verify the patterns seen in the cross-tabulations presented in Table 2.8. In both years, government spending has a much lower elasticity with respect to rural income per capita than overall spending, while other sources of funds have higher elasticities. Similarly, among expenditure categories, wage expenditures are much less associated with income differences (elasticity of 0.213) than are operating expenses (elasticity of 0.715). The magnitudes of the overall elasticities (columns 1 and 4) are nearly all greater in 2004 than in 2000, suggesting that the relationship between spending and local income levels increased over time. This is especially true for funds from collective or community sources, and operating expenditures. Two categories of funding, school-generated revenue and other revenue, are no longer correlated in a statistically significant way with rural income per capita. The between-county effects of income levels, however, do not show any clear change compared to 2000, suggesting that it is the impact of within-county income differences that has increased.

Conclusion

In this chapter, we have analyzed inequality in rural primary school educational expenditures at different administrative levels (region, province, county, and village) at different points in time. Unlike earlier research from the 1980s and early 1990s that finds rising inequality in school spending associated with China's fiscal decentralization, one main finding of our analysis is that overall, there was little change in inequality in rural primary school spending during the period 1993 to 2000, and there is evidence of reductions in educational spending for other schooling levels. The lack of an increase in inequality of rural primary school spending at the provincial or county levels holds, whether one looks at total expenditures or focuses on the government component of expenditures. At the same time, the mean expenditures per student have increased significantly over time in real terms.

This by no means implies that the Chinese government should be complacent about attacking the large disparities that remain, especially across regions and between urban and rural areas. Unequal access to quality education undermines the social objective of providing equal opportunity to all citizens as well as the economic development goal of increasing the level of human capital of the entire labor force.

The second main finding of this chapter is that inequality in educational spending associated with differences in income levels is greater at higher levels of aggregation. Differences in spending of primary schools within the same county are not very great, regardless of village income levels, but differences across counties with different income levels are substantial, and across provinces even greater. We do find that between-province and between-county differences in income had less of an effect on within-budget primary school expenditures from 1993 to 1999, and some suggestive evidence that within-county differences in income may have become more important from 2000 to 2004 in Gansu. Overall, our results suggest that equalization efforts through redistributive transfers are failing the most between higher levels of government, and suggest that efforts to increase redistribution should focus on higher levels of government.

Finally, we find significant differences in the level of inequality of different sources and uses of funds. According to our analysis of the county-level data, inequality in wage spending is much less than inequality in operational expenses, although there is evidence from both the county and school data that inequality in wage spending is increasing while inequality in operational expenses is decreasing (although not the budgetary component of such expenses). Perhaps in accordance with government policy, schools are reducing the importance of extra-budgetary and non-government financing sources over time. According to the Gansu data, in recent years, poor villages spent less real *yuan* per student on operational expenses over time, which is not surprising given the priority given to paying salaries and the lack of non-budgetary revenue sources in such areas. These results suggest that providing greater financing for the operating expenses of schools in poor areas merits attention.

Acknowledgments

Data collection for the Gansu Survey of Children and Families was supported by The Spencer Foundation Small and Major Grants Programs, by NIH Grants 1R01TW005930-01 and 5R01TW005930-02, and by a grant from the World Bank.

Notes

1 Efforts to promote diversification began as early as 1988 and were codified in the Education Law of 1995, Article 53, which stated that the state should institute a system of educational finance in which fiscal allocations constitute the main source, to be supplemented by funds through a variety of avenues in order to gradually increase the input of financial resources directed to education and ensure that state-run educational institutions had stable sources of funding (Wang 2000).
2 Using county data for 1997, Pan (2000) finds that inequality in primary school financing is greater than inequality in secondary school financing.
3 Note that this definition is not the same as source 1 in Table 2.1.
4 County budgetary data are available from *China County Socio-economic Statistics Compendium 2000*. Rural income per capita are National Statistical Bureau data.
5 All 2004 variables are deflated to 2000 real values using the province-specific rural consumer price index.
6 One difference in the school questionnaires used in 2000 and 2004 was that total sources and uses of funds were forced to balance in 2000, but not in 2004.

References

China County Socio-economic Statistics Compendium 2000 (2000) Beijing: China Statistical Press.

China Educational Finance Yearbook (various years) Beijing: China Statistical Press.

Heckman, J. (2005) "China's Human Capital Investments," *China Economic Review*, 16: 50–70.

Pan, T. (2000) "Regional Disparities in China's County-Level Educational Investments and Analysis of Influencing Factors (woguo xianji yiwu jiaoyu touzi de diqu chayi jiqi yingxiang yinsu fenxi)," *Education and Economics (jiayu yu jingji)*, 4: 36–44.

Park, A., Rozelle, S., Wong, C. and Ren, C. (1996) "Distributional Consequences of Reforming Local Public Finance in China," *The China Quarterly*, 147: 751–778.

Tsang, M. (1994) "Costs of Education in China: Issues of Resource Mobilization, Equality, Equity, and Efficiency," *Education Economics*, 2: 287–312.

Tsang, M. (1996) "Financial Reform of Basic Education in China," *Economics of Education Review*, 15: 423–444.

Tsang, M. (2002) "Intergovernmental Grants and the Financing of Compulsory Education in China," *Harvard China Review*, 3(2): 15–20.

Tsang, M. and Ding, Y. (2005) "Resource Utilization and Disparities in Compulsory Education in China," *China Review*, 5: 1–31.

Tsui, K. (1997) "Economic Reform and Attainment in Basic Education in China," *The China Quarterly*, 149: 104–127.

Wang, R. (2000) "Provincial Expenditure Review: Education Financing," unpublished report to the World Bank.

West, L. (1997) "Provision of Public Services in Rural PRC," in C. Wong (ed.) *Financing Local Government in the People's Republic of China*, New York: Oxford University Press for the Asian Development Bank, pp. 213–282.

West, L. and Wong, C. (1995) "Fiscal Decentralization and Growing Regional Disparities in Rural China: Some Evidence in the Provision of Social Services," *Oxford Review of Economic Policy*, 2: 70–84.

Wong, C. (1997) "Rural Public Finance," in C. Wong (ed.) *Financing Local Government in the People's Republic of China*, New York: Oxford University Press for the Asian Development Bank, pp. 167–212.

The World Bank (1999) *Strategic Goals for Chinese Education in the 21st Century*, Washington, DC: The World Bank.

Zhang, X. and Kanbur, R. (2005) "Spatial Inequality in Education and Health Care in China," *China Economic Review*, 16: 189–204.

3 Emergence of private schools in China

Context, characteristics, and implications

Jing Lin

Emergence of private schools in modern China

China has a long history of private education. Beginning almost two and a half millennia ago when the great philosopher Confucius (551–479 BC) founded the first private school and continuing through the mid-twentieth century, private education has played a prominent role in the provision of both higher and basic education in China. For example, in 1947, 79 of the 207 universities in the country were private, as were 56 percent of all primary schools and 84 percent of all secondary schools in Beijing, Tianjin, Nanjing, Shanghai, and Wuhan (Mei 1994).

However, private schools, which comprised 40 percent of all schools in the country by 1949 (Zhang 1995), all but disappeared after the Chinese Communist Party (CCP) came to power. Transforming China into a socialist state-ownership system, the government devoted the first part of the 1950s to eliminating private businesses and institutions throughout the country. By 1956, nearly all private schools had been closed down or converted into public schools. Operating under a centralized system, schools in the country adopted a uniform curriculum developed by the Ministry of Education, and the educational system was re-designed to serve the state-controlled economy, giving schools little autonomy. By 1976, when the Cultural Revolution came to an end, there were literally no private schools left in China.

Private schools began to reappear in China in the early 1980s, when control over education began to relax under the government's reform policies. Initially, private education took the form of evening classes, weekend schools, or correspondence universities, helping unsuccessful students to prepare to retake the National University Entrance Exam, or offering learning opportunities to those who wanted to improve their educational credentials or develop specialized vocational or cultural skills. However, private education began an explosive period of development beginning in 1992, after the late paramount leader Deng Xiaoping reaffirmed the government's staunch commitment to economic reform. By this time, China had undergone 12 years of economic reform and opening, and a wealthy class was re-appearing, leading entrepreneurs to pursue money-making opportunities in education.

Tremendous demand for high quality education and a lack of places in universities combined to bring forth a new stage of development in private education in China.

The first private school to thrust private education into the national spotlight was the Guangya Primary School, founded in August 1992, in the city of Chengdu in Sichuan Province. Dubbed the "first school for aristocrats in China," it attracted international attention because of its expensive tuition and fees, "new teaching methods" borrowed from the West that were supposed to ensure high-quality teaching, and superior learning conditions (including computers, color TVs, and pianos, installed in air-conditioned classrooms). Other features of the school, such as small class sizes, a boarding system, comfortable living conditions, and foreign instructors hired to teach all subjects in English, also aroused much curiosity.

Following the example of Guangya, similar private schools sprang up throughout the country, especially from 1992 to 1995 when the country experienced unprecedented economic development. By 1997, southern Guangdong Province had more than 70 elite private schools and Beijing city had more than 40 (Zhang and Wang 1998). Private schools charging more moderate fees also appeared in large numbers during this time. Even in the under-developed province of Guangxi, an astonishing 400 private schools were reportedly opened in 1993. By the end of 1995, the country's private schools included 20,780 kindergartens, 3,159 primary and secondary schools, 672 vocational schools, 1,209 universities—21 of which had been granted the right to issue degrees recognized by the state—and about 35,000 private short-term training schools and other private schools focused on the cultural and social lives of citizens. Together, these schools enrolled approximately 6.5 million people (Wang 1996).

In the first decade of the twenty-first century, the trend toward private education in China continues unabated. In December 2002, the Minban Education Promotion Law was passed, and in 2003, the country had over 70,000 private schools of all kinds, enrolling 14.16 million students. Among these schools, 55,000 were day care centers, enrolling 4.8 million children; 5,676 were primary schools, enrolling 2.75 million students; 3,651 were junior high schools, enrolling 2.57 million students; 2,679 were senior high schools, enrolling 1.41 million students; and 1,430 were vocational schools, enrolling 815,000 students. Private higher learning institutions of all kinds numbered 1,279, enrolling 1.81 million students. By 2005, 175 private universities had been approved to issue diplomas, enrolling 810,000 students (*China Education News*, December 27, 2005). Several dozen private universities have expanded from small colleges renting makeshift campuses to large operations owning spacious campuses enrolling 10,000–40,000 students each.

In fact, the number of private primary and secondary schools may be much higher than indicated by the official figures. For example, it is likely that county townships and rural villages have set up private schools but do not report them to higher levels of government, and there may be hundreds of vocational and technical schools that operate through franchise arrangements but are not officially counted. Given this potential for large numbers of unofficial schools, either currently in operation or in the process of being set up, exact counts have been difficult to obtain.

From 1995 to 2006, I visited nearly 40 private primary and secondary schools in Beijing, Shenyang, Dalian, Shanghai, Guangzhou, Guilin, and a local county in Guangxi as part of a sponsored research project. I also visited a dozen private universities and have maintained close collaboration with some of them. The types of institutions I visited included elite private schools, ordinary urban/township private schools, rural private schools, and private universities. I also visited more than a dozen elite public schools (or "key" schools) and ordinary public schools. This chapter, which describes the current state of private education in China, draws upon my observations of and interactions with private school/university founders, administrators, teachers, and students during these visits.

Private education touches on important issues of school choice, equality, efficiency, educational reform, and the formation of civil society. In some countries, because children's access to elite private schools has been closely connected to parents' political and economic power, private schools have been criticized for reproducing social class hierarchies (Baird 1977; Cookson and Persell 1985; Griggs 1985; Kane 1992). Private schools thrive on decentralization and promote competition. In developing countries, private education may be a necessary solution to the rising demand for education, particularly at the secondary level. The rapid re-emergence of private schools in China has been accompanied by concerns about the role and impact of private education, including who has access to what kinds of schools, how much autonomy schools should assume, and how private schools fit with the ideal of public education in training socialist citizens.

Definition of private education

Many terms have been used for the non-public schools founded in China during the past two decades. For example, they have been called "private schools," "nongovernmental schools," "schools run by social forces," "people-run schools," and "community schools." The first widely publicized government policy on private schools, Regulation on Schools Run by Social Forces, instituted in July 1997, stipulates its application to all schools run by "businesses and government organizations, social groups and other social organizations and individuals, using non-government educational financial resources, to provide schooling and other forms of education to society." The definition of private education used here encompasses all educational institutions completely or largely privately funded, as well as schools for which considerable decision-making power rests in private hands, although the state may provide resources or exercise some control.[1]

Private schools in China generally have more power than public schools to determine their educational goals, curriculum, teaching approaches, program development, internal management model, school developmental plan, and administrative structure. This makes them similar to private schools in other countries as well as to those existing in China up to the year 1949. Using terms such as "schools run by social forces" may be confusing but this term reflects the wide spectrum of groups who control the direction, funding or the administration of the school. Notably, however, private education institutions in China, functioning under a socialist political system, do not have total freedom from government regulations. Instead, they need to comply with a range of rules and requirements set by the government. For example, primary and secondary schools have to use the textbooks designated by the government, which can be supplemented with additional materials chosen by the school. Some schools are co-founded with public schools or sponsored by local governments. Despite these restrictions, these institutions still meet the defining criteria that "the ultimate feature of private schools is that they possess a high degree of autonomy while education is provided as a public undertaking" (Lin and Du 1996).

Context of private education development

The re-emergence of private schools in China was propelled by rapid economic development and new demands from society. Economic reform policies introduced in the 1980s injected autonomy and incentives into the country's agricultural and industrial systems. Throughout the 1980s, China registered double-digit GDP growth rates. During the 1990s, the rate of growth was extremely high in the first part of the decade, causing the government to put a sudden brake on bank lending, and consequently leading to slower growth rates of less than 10 percent during the last few years of the decade. In the first decade of the twenty-first century, the government set a target rate of 8 percent of GDP per year, which has been exceeded in most years. This rapid economic growth led to significant improvements in real per capita disposable income in rural and urban areas from the start of reforms in 1978 to 2000.

Along with this nationwide increase in incomes, a new stratum of people who "got rich first" quickly emerged (Bi 1994). This group includes those who own their own businesses or are working for highly profitable organizations. They have wide social connections that translate into lucrative contracts or kickbacks. They own cars and apartments or houses, items that may cost an ordinary family many years of savings. The appearance of a new wealthy elite has stirred up discussion about the formation of a new class structure in China.

My own research revealed that a highly elite group of individuals exist who possess political, economic, and/or intellectual capital that gives them a very advantageous financial position. They are government officials, well-educated intellectuals, university graduates with skills sought by foreign corporations, private entrepreneurs, real estate agents, consultants, and movie and other entertainment stars. Meanwhile, I also identified a group of people best described as a "latent middle class." This class includes the millions of state employees who live in housing provided by the government or their employers; salaried workers, journalists, central and local government officials, office clerks, bank clerks, employees of utility companies, and university teachers. These people all had incomes much higher than that reported on their salary slips—through bonuses, fees, kickbacks, and moonlighting. The new elites and the "latent middle class" laid the foundation for the appearance of elite private schools.

In addition to increases in income, another important factor in the demand equation is the Chinese people's long tradition of valuing education. The imperial examination system established during the Sui Dynasty (581–618) connected educational attainment with power, wealth, honor and prestige. Rich and poor people alike invested in their sons' education with the hope that they would pass the examination and bring fame and prosperity to the family. This system, which lasted 1,400 years, has created what John Ogbu (1994) termed "educational optimism" in the minds of the Chinese people. Wanting their sons and daughters to become "dragons" and "phoenixes," Chinese parents are willing to make great investments in their children's education, and make significant sacrifices if needed. This cultural orientation is the foundation for high demand for quality education that the public schools system has not been able to meet.

Along with having the means and the incentive to secure a high quality education for their children, the value of education is further heightened in the country's development of a market economy. The great influx of foreign investment and the appearance of hundreds of thousands of private enterprises ushered in a competitive job system in which educational credentials increasingly determine one's position, income, and social prestige (see chapters by de Brauw and Rozelle and Zhang and Zhao in this volume).

An additional factor increasing the value placed on education is the changing family structure in modern China. The single-child family planning policy instituted since the late 1970s has drastically changed child-rearing practices. In the single-child nuclear family, the child is the center of attention, and many are spoiled by an abundance of material resources. On the other hand, these children, having no siblings, also experience loneliness, isolation and frustration. Parents who are busy with work also long for a school environment in which their child can be kept away from negative social influences (Wu and Wang 1995). Divorced parents also want a supervised environment for their children when they are busy working. Divorce is on the rise in China. In the city of Guangzhou, the divorce rate increased by 185 percent from the early 1980s to 1996 (Xiao 1996). Higher divorce rates and the breakdown of extended family cohabitation have led more families to place children in elite private boarding schools for full-time care. Children of divorced parents comprised about a quarter of the student body in some schools I visited.

While Chinese society and Chinese families have undergone fundamental changes, public schools have been slow to make adjustments. Under the government's centralized control, they continue to be administered by a large bureaucratic system which gives little or no leeway to schools with respect to curriculum or administration. Further, funding shortages have led to dwindling resources in many public schools. Since 1986, the central government has undertaken fiscal decentralization, shifting funding responsibilities to local schools which had to raise their own funds to cover one-third to one half of their operating costs (see Chapter 2 by Li, Park, and Wang). This change caused many schools to rely on charging fees of all kinds to supplement their revenue.

China has the world's largest educational system. Primary education is compulsory and in 1996, 136.2 million students were enrolled in primary schools (an enrollment ratio of 98.8 percent). In addition, 50.5 million students were enrolled in junior secondary schools (an enrollment ratio of 82 percent); 10.1 million more students studied in various types of secondary vocational or technical schools (including 1.92 million students in technical workers' training schools), accounting for 56.8 percent of the total enrollment of students at the senior secondary school level; 3.1 million students were enrolled in adult secondary specialized schools; and 83.4 million students were enrolled in adult technical training schools (*China Facts and Figures* 1997).

In contrast to the high participation at the primary and secondary levels, however, enrollment rates in higher education were vastly lower. Throughout the 1980s and early 1990s, only 4 percent of students could enroll in universities. In 1996, China had 1,032 general universities that enrolled 966,000 new undergraduate students and had 3.0 million undergraduate students nation-wide. In 1996, 945,000 new students enrolled in more than 1,000 institutions of adult higher education, including 80,000 enrolled in TV courses (*China Facts and Figures* 1997). Based on these figures, many high school graduates in China failed to go on to higher education in the mid-1990s, despite significant progress over a decade and a half of reforms. The public school system is thus under tremendous pressure to meet the population's needs for kindergartens, secondary schools, and especially higher education.

The situation in rural areas is even worse than in urban areas. As described in Chapter 5 by Connelly and Zheng, partly due to a lack of ability to pay required fees, in 2000, about 17 percent of rural female primary school graduates and about 12 percent of male primary school graduates failed to go on to junior secondary schools, and among junior high graduates, only about 21 percent of rural girls and about 25 percent of rural boys go on to senior high schools. A great number of schools are poorly equipped, their teachers are underpaid, and their administrators lack the funds to organize educational activities.

In urban cities and townships, quality education is available only to a very small number of students studying in key schools. "Key" secondary schools, which serve only 4 percent of all students, usually boast a 90–99 percent admission rate to universities; in most ordinary schools (except those in major urban cities) the vast majority of students are unable to enter universities. Because most key schools are built in urban areas, only a very small number of rural children have access to them. Lack of access to quality education has prompted many rural and urban parents to seek alternatives to the public education system for their children, which has generated a huge demand for private schools.

Characteristics of private schools

Private schools in China can be categorized by the clientele they serve, how much they cost, and what they offer to students. The distinguishing features of several types of private schools are briefly described below.

Elite private schools

I define elite private schools as those that charge more than 10,000 *yuan* in tuition and fees per year. Despite rapid economic growth, in the late 1990s, the average annual income for Chinese families was 4,000 to 10,000 *yuan*, which means that elite schools are beyond the reach of most Chinese.

In 1994, about 100 elite private schools operated throughout the country, and the number increased rapidly in the following years. For example, in 1997, Guangdong Province alone had more than 70 elite schools that enrolled about 110,000 students, and Beijing and Shenyang each had more than 40 such schools (Zhang and Wang 1998).

Among the elite schools I visited, the founders included former schoolteachers and administrators who were frustrated by the rigidity of the public school curriculum and inefficiency of school administration. Some of them received overseas support in founding their schools, while others drew from their own savings or pooled money together from like-minded people. They tended to advocate teaching students multiple skills, using innovative educational methods, and instilling in students long-forgotten cultural values such as filial piety and frugality.

Many high-profile elite school founders were companies and private entrepreneurs who were attracted by the lucrative profit promised by private schools. A school that charges 20,000 *yuan* in tuition per year and enrolls 1,000 students can take in 20 million *yuan* annually. After subtracting costs, some schools can rake in a hefty 50 percent in profits. Furthermore, state regulations allow school investors to purchase up to 500 mu of land (or 82 acres) usually at highly subsidized rates. Founders also see the opportunity of using the school to run businesses that are shielded from paying state taxes.

During the booming early years of real estate development (1992–1996), many elite private schools were established by real estate companies to attract buyers for their housing development projects. China-trained scholars, returned overseas Chinese, and businessmen from Hong Kong and Taiwan were also involved. One school I visited was founded by two scholars with doctoral degrees in education. Trained in China, they wanted to translate their knowledge into practice and explore new ways of furthering China's educational reforms. Businessmen from Hong Kong and Taiwan were also drawn to the potential for high profits and have collaborated with local residents to set up elite schools.

Key schools have been another player in the establishment of elite private schools. In China's dual-track public school system, key schools have decisive advantages over ordinary schools in obtaining funding from the government as well as in generating revenues on their own. Their reputation for accepting only the best students who are taught by the most qualified teachers has tremendous appeal to parents. Key schools have taken advantage of this strong social demand by setting up "offspring" schools that are affiliated with the key school, using the facilities of the key school and employ teachers of the key school. The income is funneled back to the key school for bonuses and school improvement projects. These schools usually charge over 10,000 *yuan* per year in tuition. One school in Shanghai charges 40,000 *yuan* per year in the name of donations to the school.

Principals of elite schools tend to be experienced educators, and the majority are former administrators of well-known public schools who achieved high professional recognition in their careers. Some are business entrepreneurs who were previously teachers. A few have obtained graduate or doctoral degrees in China or from abroad. While most principals are individuals hired by the school owners, some founders are principals themselves. The hired principals work in teams or independently. In the mid-1990s, their salary ranged from 1,000 to 3,000 *yuan* per month, a relatively high salary by Chinese standards at the time. For the most part, the principals are considered "high-level *dagongzhai*," or "expensive hired hands," who perform intellectual work for the owners. The owners maintain tight control over school affairs, particularly school finance, allowing the hired principals little say in how tuition is collected or disbursed. The principal's chief responsibility is overseeing teaching activities and motivating teachers to fulfill the goals set by the owners. One school I visited had a video monitoring system that allowed the principal to watch the teaching activities in every classroom. The primary task for him, as for other principals, was to ensure students' academic progress and parents' satisfaction, which was the lifeline for the school to attract students.

The teaching force in elite schools is usually formed of retired teachers (especially initially), teachers on unpaid leave from public schools, young teachers who have just graduated from teacher education colleges, teachers who have resigned from their jobs in public schools, or part-time teachers who moonlight for extra income. A higher pay scale is a significant benefit of teaching in elite schools. In the mid-1990s, the teachers' salary range was

600–1,800 *yuan* per month, which was significantly higher than the monthly range of 400–800 *yuan* for teachers in most public schools. Having an apartment, as well as the prospect of moving from a small town to a large city, also attracts a large number of applicants to teaching positions in elite schools.

Elite private schools, like public schools, are expected to comply with requirements set by the Ministry of Education for the national standardized curriculum, and to follow national guidelines on course offerings and learning progress. Educators in all the elite schools I visited reported that their schools go considerably beyond what is required by the state, and that, in particular, English and computer science are core subjects taught to students from an early age. While public schools begin English language instruction in grade four, elite schools start from grade one, or even earlier. One kindergarten I visited started to immerse children in an English-speaking environment at the age of 3.

To offer high-quality instruction in English, which elite schools pitch as the working language of the twenty-first century, some schools hire foreign teachers who are paid much higher salaries than Chinese teachers (usually 2,000–5,000 *yuan* per month, with a free apartment, and funds to travel the country during the summer). These teachers use movies, records, plays, and reading materials to teach, and students are encouraged to listen to and practice spoken English. Great emphasis is placed on mastering the standard pronunciation so that no Chinese accent can be detected.

Extracurricular activities comprise a major part of the curriculum in elite schools. These are intended to help build a sense of community among students, to foster self-confidence, and to stimulate interest in learning. For example, one school I visited urged students to develop "twelve abilities" that included aerobics, fast calculation, dancing and singing, photography, calligraphy, and socializing. Others specialize in traditional music, and all schools have orchestras or bands.

To support this range of educational and extracurricular activities, many elite schools have their own computer lab, library, theater, piano practice room, dancing room, audio-visual lab, multimedia classrooms, etc. They install TV sets in the classroom, and have an arsenal of musical instruments and sports equipment. Some schools have tennis courts and indoor or outdoor swimming pools. They also have professional quality running tracks. One school in the south that I visited had a huge theater for school gatherings. Another school had a huge open ground around the school building with pavilions and bridges above small ponds. In 2003, I visited a newly established school in Shanghai. The school had dozens of huge buildings with spacious classrooms and dormitories, and a canal runs through the campus, giving students the sense of being close to nature. These highly visible aspects of elite private schools have attracted much attention and criticism as well.

Ordinary private schools

Despite the fanfare surrounding elite private schools, a large number of private schools in China are ordinary schools serving the needs of the general public. Ordinary private schools cater to the demands of parents who are salaried workers, officials, and rural peasants. They charge moderate fees and operate under vastly different conditions than elite schools. They can be urban/township schools, rural schools, single-sex vocational schools, vocational technical schools, arts schools, medical schools, or other types of schools. They offer primary, secondary, post-secondary, or vocational/technical/specialized education. In some regions, ordinary private schools have become a main provider of education, side by side with public schools.

Urban or township ordinary private schools are located in cities or county townships. The majority of them offer senior high school education while some also operate a junior high school section. Some urban migrant communities also have set up their own primary schools (see Chapter 7 by Chen and Liang).

Founders are typically business entrepreneurs, private school alumni, or social or political activists who see running schools as a positive way to contribute to society. Founders also include conscientious citizens who have pooled funds to set up private schools for students who are excluded from the education system because of a lack of schools (Lin 1993). Retired teachers and school administrators are often the main force initiating ordinary private schools. In China, the retirement age for public school teachers and administrators is 50–55 for women and 60 for men. At this age, many teachers are still energetic or even at the peak of their careers, and thus seek to enrich their lives and supplement their retirement incomes by teaching in an established private school or by setting up their own schools.

These schools usually begin operations with the rental of a few classrooms and the purchase of some necessary equipment. Catering to the salaried class, they generally keep tuition in the range of 500–1,500 *yuan* per year, although some charge as much as 4,000 per semester depending on the school's location and the provision of room and board. In general, schools base their tuition on the ability of local residents to pay, with schools in larger cities charging higher fees.

Most teachers in these schools are middle-aged former or retired public school teachers who take up teaching mainly to earn extra income. These teachers work part-time and have limited supervisory responsibilities. The schools also hire a few full-time teachers whose main responsibilities are to supervise the students' daily life and provide coaching in the evening as well as discipline and moral guidance. Generally, these schools have great difficulty attracting young and capable teachers, as they cannot afford to provide them such benefits as pensions, medical insurance, or housing. Teacher turnover and the number of aged teachers are significantly higher in ordinary urban or township schools than in elite schools. The curriculum offered by these schools is usually very similar to that of regular public schools. Athletic teams, hobby groups, and other extracurricular activities are organized, but these do not comprise the main part of the school's curriculum. In fact, they are often removed to make more time for academic subject learning. Most schools cannot afford to teach piano or provide music courses, and although some offer computer courses, others have no computers at all. English learning relies on textbooks and a tape-recorder. Some schools have only the minimum accoutrements of teaching: a blackboard, tables and chairs. Class size averages 40–70 students, which means that students receive little individualized attention and are largely independent learners.

Rural private schools are another type of ordinary private school. They have appeared in large numbers in response to the growing rural–urban inequity caused by under-funding of rural public schools. Many rural public schools suffer from low teaching quality and shortage of funds for even the most basic needs in teaching. The schools therefore charge parents numerous fees. Rural households, with little cash, often find it very difficult to pay these fees. Unlike urban cities where families have only one child, rural families typically have several children. The cost of public education is unbearable for many of the poor.

Having a strong desire for their children to receive as much education as possible, rural residents have sought alternatives to local public schools, which have included setting up their own private schools. For example, I visited a county in 1993 that had four private secondary schools but no private primary schools. Yet in 1995 when I returned, the rural residents had established four private primary schools in just one township, with another six scheduled to be opened that same year. In an adjacent county, half of the primary schools were funded by individuals and overseas sources. In one school I visited, the village head, Chen, who had 10 grandchildren and knew the hardships that villagers faced in coming up with money to pay local public school fees, organized villagers to build a low-fee school. Every family in his village contributed 10 *yuan* to the project, and Chen asked an old friend who used to be a principal in another province to return and serve as the principal. Chen himself oversaw all other administrative affairs, including getting the villagers to make their own bricks to build another school building as the school's reputation spread and students from nearby villages began coming.

Another school I visited was built in one day by 400 villagers, just before local government officials came to tear down the school. "Adults and children, young and old, as long as they could carry a brick, all came to help," a villager said, describing their determination to have their own school. The school was funded by a local businessman who himself had experienced the difficulty of paying public school fees for his five children. The school eventually obtained the necessary permissions to operate and had about 200 students when I visited in 1996.

Tuition and fees charged by rural private schools tend to be low and affordable for most rural families. For example, in the mid-1990s, the Guomin Middle School in Nanle County, Henan Province, charged each boarding student 200 *yuan* per term; and the private Kuang Liangzhi Junior High School in Bazhong County, Sichuan Province charged only 70 *yuan* per student (Zhu 1994). The schools I visited generally charged 100–150 *yuan* per semester for primary students and 300–500 *yuan* per semester for secondary students. Schools also take students' financial circumstances into consideration. For example, they allow students short of cash to use rice, wheat, vegetables, or fruits to substitute for tuition. Some schools reduced fees for especially poor students. The proximity of these schools is another advantage. They tend to be within easy walking distance of residents, a convenience which was appreciated by parents, especially those with girls, who were often kept at home because of the long distance to school. In fact, the rural private schools I visited enrolled more girls than boys, a ratio also affected by boys' tendency to leave home for higher income work in cities to the south.

Salaries for teachers in these rural private schools are rather low. Two teachers remarked to me that they make only enough to buy rice, but not enough to buy vegetables and meat. The teachers are mostly high school graduates, who are considered well educated in poorer regions.

Rural private schools adhere to the national curriculum and teach according to the guidelines established by the Ministry of Education. Teaching methods are traditional lecturing and rote learning, but the schools also include vocational training in their curriculum, such as courses on crop cultivation, domestic animal care, sewing, and electronic machine repair. To supplement this curriculum and generate revenue, the schools often maintain workshops and vegetable gardens.

Students generally study very hard, as they know how difficult it is for their parents to raise the money to send them to schools. In a rural school visited by the author, the students' average scores in a countywide mid-term exam surpassed that of a local public school, averaging 89 out of 100 for the two main subjects, Chinese and math, in comparison to an average score of 60 for the adjacent public school.

Rural private schools are usually set up with very limited funds. Although some schools have their own buildings, others rent or hold classes in run-down buildings. Some also have to rent tables and chairs, while others ask students to carry their own tables and chairs to school. Most schools do not have teaching equipment and facilities for scientific experiments, foreign language education, or sports. One school I visited only had two ping-pong tables made of mud brick, and a basketball hoop. Because the schools rely on tuition to survive, and tuition is generally modest, they seldom have any extra money to improve their teaching conditions significantly.

Single-sex schools are another type of ordinary private school, though not all single-sex schools are private. In 1993, China had about 100 public and private single-sex schools nationwide (Yan 1993). Single-sex private schools include comprehensive regular all-girls high schools, all-girls vocational high schools, and post-secondary vocational training colleges for young women. Some are founded by private entrepreneurs, scholars or social organizations, others are set up by local governments. In 1995, 1996, 1999, and 2003, I visited nine single-sex schools (two of which I have visited several times). Of these, two were public schools, three were private general schools, two were vocational schools, and two were colleges operated by women's organizations. In prominent places, they all posted that their goal of education is for girls to become independent, strong, self-confident and self-respecting. These schools claim to defy the cultural tradition of "male superiority and female inferiority" and aim at raising the consciousness of girls and nurturing the personal and intellectual development of girls. They cater their teaching to female students' characteristics, and train students with skills to find job opportunities in China's booming market economy. Hairdressing, cosmetics, waitressing, and secretarial skills were the focus of vocational education, while for the general all-girls schools, academic learning as well as the "cultivation of feminine strength" were emphasized.

Education for girls was mostly carried out in all-girls schools in precommunist China. After 1949, and especially during the Cultural Revolution period, all-girls schools were closed down or merged with all-boy schools to form co-ed schools. In the mid-1980s, an all-girls school reopened in Shanghai. This was a school that was attended by famous women in China and from abroad, and is now a key public school. Private all-girls education appeared mainly after 1992, along with other types of private schools. There are four reasons for its reappearance: (1) parents' desire to provide a safe environment for their daughters; (2) the need for continuing education for young girls who cannot get into a senior regular high school; (3) the great increase in service sector jobs in China's economy; and (4) the low pass rates for girls in the national university entrance exam, which prompted some people to seek teaching methods and environments appropriate to girls' learning style and psychological development.

Single-sex schools for girls have appeared in cities as well as the countryside, and in developed as well as underdeveloped areas of the country. In 1996, the first private all-girls school in Beijing was opened by a famous scholar who wanted to restore the tradition of single-sex education in Beijing. An all-girls school I visited in northeastern China was set up by a businessman engaged in international trade. To attract students, he recruited a retired principal from a public school by offering an annual salary of 50,000 *yuan*, a spacious apartment, and a car for her use. Under the leadership of this principal, the school was very successful. In 1996, the school charged students 8,000 *yuan* per year in tuition and fees and had an enrollment of 400 students. Parents of these students belonged mostly to the latent middle class. Instead of focusing on stereotypical feminine activities, the school taught students to wrestle, to drive, to use computers, and to speak fluent English. They arranged a curriculum that helped girls become more confident about their abilities, more employable in the very competitive job market, and more able to gain access to higher education. In other schools I visited, however, girls are taught to cultivate their "feminine strengths" of elegance, perseverance and softness while achieving academically and developing self-confidence.

Private universities

Since the relaxation of government control over education in the early 1980s, China's public universities have been unable to meet all the new demand for higher education. In 1980, China had a total of 675 universities enrolling around 1.5 million students. Although the number of universities increased throughout the 1980s, as the previously closed universities were re-opened and new ones were constructed, only half a million out of 20 million university applicants were admitted each year. In the early 1990s, admissions increased to about 900,000 students per year, still far below social demand; and in 1996, the country enrolled 5.83 million students in 1,032 regular (four-year) higher learning institutions (see Lin 1999). To put this in perspective internationally, China had 1,175 public universities for 1.2 billion people, as of 1993, whereas in 1985, Japan had 890 universities for its 120 million people (Xu 1993). Lack of university places creates fierce competition. Research has explored the extreme stress of "examination hell" in Japan and South Korea (Ogura 1987; Kwak 1991; Zeng 1996) but the "hell" experienced by Chinese students is even more torturous given the smaller ratio of places to hopeful students (Lin and Chen 1995).

The government has had difficulty expanding public higher education fast enough to keep up with demand. In the 1990s, training a university student cost about 8,000–10,000 *yuan* per year. As we have discussed, the government is hardly able to shoulder this financial burden for millions of additional students.

Furthermore, public universities in the country urgently need to be upgraded. According to Deguang Yang (1993), public universities in China were given little autonomy by the government, which maintained bureaucratic control over nearly all activities in universities, restricting their ability to improve efficiency and management. Up to the year 1993, the state government still maintained the model of planned enrollments and planned job assignments. Under this strict centralized control, universities had very limited decision-making power over curriculum, personnel, property management, equipment, admissions, program changes, or job assignments. Consequently, the majority of universities suffered from inefficiency and a lack of vitality—this in spite of high teacher–student and teacher–staff ratios (1:5.3 and 1:3.0, respectively, in 1993) (Yang 1993).

It is in this context that private universities reappeared, beginning in the early 1980s. Starting off as primarily evening or weekend classes or schools providing remedial education, private higher education made great strides by the mid-1990s, prompting the government to adopt new regulations on their administration (Zhang 1994). The number of private universities increased rapidly after 1992. By 1994, China had more than 800 private universities, compared to 1,075 public universities and 1,256 adult higher learning institutions; and by 1997, China had more than 1,200 private universities, exceeding the number of public universities (see Lin 1999).

Although private universities may offer programs similar to those of public universities, most cannot confer degrees without the approval of the Ministry of Education, and their students must participate in the National Higher Education Examination for Self-Learning Students. It was not until 2005 that, after nearly two decades of effort, 24 private universities won approval to offer undergraduate degrees (Zhao 2005).

In the mid-1990s, I visited four private universities and found a distinctive characteristic of private universities was their independence, which gives them autonomy in administration and decision-making, but also enables them to be flexible in meeting the demands of students and their parents. Tuition and fees are the main source of income for private universities. A survey of 100 private universities in 1994 found that in 82 universities, 90 percent of revenue came from student tuition and fees. Because funding is mostly from private sources, private universities have autonomy in the allocation of funds, whereas in public universities, "money for buying soy sauce cannot be used to buy salt" (Li 1993).

Founders of private universities include retired professors and administrators from public universities, retired government officials, various social organizations, individual citizens, business enterprises, joint-venture economic organizations, learned societies and academic research associations, or alumni associations.

In the 1990s, retired university teachers formed the core of the teaching staff. Male professors in China retire at age 60 and females at age 55. After retirement, many are still quite energetic and look for opportunities to continue work. In the early 1990s, three well-known universities, Peking University, Qinghua University, and Shanghai Jiaotong University, retired nearly 1,300 teachers with job titles ranging from senior lecturers to full professors. These retirees possessed rich teaching experience and were fully covered by their former employers in terms of pensions and medical insurance. They thus formed the core faculty of a private university founded in 1993 which grew to admit 12,000 students in 2004.

In the beginning, most private universities have only a few or no permanent teachers. A survey of 200 private universities found that only 20 percent of teachers are long-term employees; the rest are temporary (Dong 1995). Some universities are able to be selective and pay high salaries to attract experienced professors from famous universities nearby (Chen 1993), but most university teachers are hired on "more work–more pay" contracts under which they are paid for each course taught. More recently, however, full-time and younger faculty have become much more common and in many cases comprise the majority of the workforce. This has occurred along with the expansion of private universities and a gradual improvement of pay and working conditions.

A striking feature of most private universities in the early stages was that they had a streamlined bureaucratic structure and were not burdened by having to provide housing and various benefits to large staffs. This allowed private universities to explore new ways of conducting education and enabled them to create their own market niche (Yang 1993). Their small size allows them to be focused and practice-oriented, and to base their programs on the needs of students, which in turn enables their graduates to be competitive in the job market. In general, private universities eagerly fill the "gaps" left by public universities and are especially concerned with developing courses that will enhance students' employment opportunities in new economic sectors. They place little or no restrictions on students' gender, age, occupation, or even education level. The students they accept differ from those in public institutions in intellectual endowments, educational preparation, occupational and life experiences, tastes and interests, family environment, economic status, and many other aspects. Flexibility in operations and a streamlined internal management system are what underlie the rapid development of private higher learning institutions (Li 1993).

Given that private universities lack social prestige and are often poorly equipped, the majority of high school graduates understandably opt for public universities if their examination results qualify them to do so. They enroll in private universities only after they fail to be admitted to a good public university.

In the beginning stage, most private universities had to rent classrooms. Most lacked appropriate space and equipment for administration and sports activities. Dining facilities and dormitories for students tended to be very run-down. However, an increasing number of private universities, after years of operation and accumulation, have built their own teaching buildings and purchased necessary equipment and facilities. They have expanded along with public universities after the government loosened tuition control and allowed public universities to expand 35 percent every year for several years, starting in 1998. In 2003, 12 private universities became so-called "10,000-person universities," meaning they were able to enroll over 10,000 students.

In sum, despite their problems, private universities have become a major force in higher education in China, and they have made positive contributions to the development of the country's higher education system (China National Institute of Educational Research 1995). They supplement the inadequate provision of public higher education, helping to satisfy the aspirations of individual citizens for knowledge and skill acquisition. They provide diversity in higher education and serve as examples of new directions for educational reform. They cater to the needs of local economic and social development and focus on training a large number of practically-oriented, skilled personnel. They have developed distinctive approaches to creating educational programs (specialties), using faculty, charging tuition fees, administrating and managing internal resources, and collaborating with industrial and commercial enterprises. The pace of private university development has quickened in the twenty-first century, and it remains to be seen whether or not some prestigious private universities will come onto the scene as the quality of education they provide improves.

Equality, choice, and private education in China

What are the implications of private education development in China? Do private schools, and especially elite private schools, serve to perpetuate social class inequality in Chinese society? Should choice be allowed in Chinese education?

Private education touches on fundamental issues in education: equality, choice, and efficiency. With the spread of democratic ideals in the twentieth century, it has become widely accepted that education is not a privilege but an inherent human right, and that all human beings are entitled to receive education, regardless of their social class, gender, race, and ethnicity. Countries throughout the world have made basic education compulsory for their citizens, and enrollment ratios in many developing countries are fast catching up with those in developed countries.

Many people believe that public education serves the role of a social equalizer, providing similar opportunities to all citizens to develop their potential to the fullest. Some proponents of public education argue that it is a key symbol of equality, indispensable for any democratic system. In this view, private schools serve only the rich and powerful, and thus perpetuate social inequality.

However, public schools have also been criticized. First, they have not always been able to provide equal educational opportunity for all children. For example, in the United States, the best public schools are in fact rather exclusive, usually located in wealthy neighborhoods. Public education also has been viewed as giving government too much control over schools and denying autonomy to teachers and parents, the actors who are most directly concerned with education. Furthermore, many unequal practices take place within public schools, such as tracking systems that legitimize discrimination against less powerful minority and working-class students (Oakes 1985; Lin 1993; Zeng *et al.* 1997).

These and other problems in public schools have led some people to strongly support private education. Proponents argue that parents should have the right to choose schools, and that this choice is a fundamental right. Private education places more power in the hands of educators and may foster higher quality curricula. It may also enhance educational opportunities for children who have been unsuccessful in a public school environment. People have different attributes and abilities, and private schools can better cater to the different interests and needs of students striving to develop their potential. Further, society's demands for education are diverse, which means that schools should be evaluated using multiple criteria (Tan 1994).

In China, similar debates have taken place since the re-emergence of private schools under economic reform. The development of private education in China has resulted from a combination of factors: the tremendous need for education, shortages in funding, and problems in public schools and universities. Just as in Western countries, the Chinese government has been hesitant to support private education for fear it would weaken the public schools, and, in China's case, the fear that it might change the nature of the socialist education system. However, the trend seems to be unstoppable, for private schools give Chinese education a much-needed dimension—diversity. Diversity in school development increases educational opportunities for some children. Ordinary private schools, for example, open doors to those excluded by the public school system. They allow rural and urban students, who would otherwise have to drop out, a chance to stay in school. And all-girls schools, searching for ways to help girls that are helpful for them to learn, open windows to new ways of conducting education. Private vocational schools, arts schools, medical colleges, and other types of schools widen employment opportunities for millions of young people who cannot otherwise attend a university. Private universities, despite their many problems, give hope to people that they can obtain higher learning in any number of areas.

Elite private schools, charging high fees and offering excellent learning conditions, have also conducted valuable experiments in educational reform. For example, they promoted many stimulating extracurricular activities to help students develop physical, social, cultural, and creative skills. They pay particular attention to helping students cultivate a sense of community, and encourage students to think and explore for themselves.

Although it is difficult to evaluate the extent to which private schools perpetuate class differences, it is very evident that private education helps address a great need in China, where educational funding is inadequate to fulfill the demand for educational services. Further, competition in educational services leads to greater accountability in the public schooling system and greater motivation for teachers and administrators.

The reappearance of private schools in China has historical significance. Not only does it signify the re-emergence of a long tradition of private education in the country, it gives part of the power of running education back to the citizenry. Private schools have broadened the channels for educational investment and fundamentally changed the concept of education as a solely government-run enterprise. Private schools bring together the state, society, and individual citizens to share the obligation to develop education (including compulsory education) for all. They demonstrate the tremendous potential and enthusiasm for private education in Chinese society.

What are the prospects for private schools in China? While the numbers of private schools have recently grown relatively slowly, internal expansion has led to the continuous growth of private education. Schools I visited in the mid- and late-1990s admitted 300–500 students, but now they have 3,000–6,000 students. Private universities, after major expansions in enrollment, are taking measures to improve the quality of their teaching and the efficiency of their administration. Many elite private schools and ordinary private schools have built their reputations and found their places in the market, but those of low quality have shut down or are being phased out. Overall, government policies to regulate and support private education have trailed behind grassroots initiatives. In fact, reluctance to give private schools and universities full autonomy has been a source of dissatisfaction and complaints. In order for private schools and universities to play a bigger role, supportive policies and financial support from the central and local governments are needed. In all, although private education has gone from the initial stage to the second stage of consolidation and expansion, it may take years of struggle for them to be fully recognized by society and the government. Some private universities, realizing the challenges ahead, have taken as their motto to become a "famous university in one hundred years." We shall see.

Note

1 For example, many private universities are not completely private in nature. Some are affiliated with state-owned colleges and institutes, contracted to be self-sufficient while having to pay an annual fee to the sponsoring organization. Some are *de facto* state institutions which change their name for the sake of generating profit for the organization. Some are spin-off subsidiaries of state organizations.

References

Baird, L.L. (1977) *The Elite Schools: A Profile of Prestigious Independent Schools*, Lexington, MA: D. C. Heath.

Bi, C. (1994) "Exploring the Practice and Theory of Chinese Private Schools," in Z. Zhang (ed.), *Theory and Practice of Private and Nongovernmental Schools*, Beijing: China Workers' Publishing House, pp. 225–41.

China Education News, www.edu.cn (accessed December 27, 2005).

China Facts and Figures, 1997 (1997) Beijing: New Star Publishers, p. 80.

China National Institute of Educational Research (1995) *A Study on NGO-sponsored and Private Higher Education in China*, Beijing: China National Institute of Educational Research.

Cookson, P.W. and Persell, C.H. (1985) *Preparing for Power: America's Elite Boarding Schools*, New York: Basic Books.

Dong, M. (1995) "The Present Situation, Problems and Strategies of China's Private Higher Education," *World of Education Run by Social Forces*, 6: 6–7.

Griggs, C. (1985) *Private Education in Britain*, London: The Falmer Press.

Kane, P.R. (1992) "What Is an Independent School?," in P.R. Kane (ed.), *Independent Schools, Independent Thinkers*, San Francisco: Jossey-Bass Publishers, pp. 1–4.

Kwak, B. (1991) "Examination Hell in Korea Revisited," *Koreana*, 5: 45–55.

Li, W. (1993) "A Waterfront Pavilion Gets the Moonlight First: Enlightenment of

Locally-run Schools on Reform of Adult Education," *Private Higher Education*, 4: 16–17.

Lin, J. (1993) *Education in Post-Mao China*, New York: Praeger.

Lin, J. (1999) *Social Transformation and Private Education in China*, New York: Praeger.

Lin, J. and Chen, Q. (1995) "Academic Pressure and Impact on Students' Growth in China," *McGill Journal of Education*, 30: 149–168.

Lin, R. and Du, Z. (1996) "On Laws Concerning Private Higher Education," *World of Education Run by Social Forces*, 3: 14–15.

Mei, R. (1994) "Private Schools in Contemporary China: Part 2," *Administration of Secondary and Primary Schools*, 5: 20–22.

Oakes, J. (1985) *Keeping Track: How Schools Structure Inequality*, New Haven, CT: Yale University Press.

Ogbu, J. (1994) "Racial Stratification and Education in the United States: Why Inequality Persists," *Teachers College Record*, 96: 265–298.

Ogura, Y. (1987) "Examination Hell: Japanese Education's Most Serious Problem," *The College Board Review*, 144: 8–30.

Qiu, C. (1996) "Money, Right, Law," *Private Education*, 6: 12–13.

Tan, S. (1994) "On the Issue of Educational Equality in Our Country at Present," *Educational Research*, 6: 14–18.

Wang, M. (1996) "Create a New Phase for Schools Run by Social Forces," *World of Education Run by Social Forces*, 4: 4–6.

Wu T. and Wang, F. (1995) "SOS! 'Poor' Students are Enjoying High Consumption," *Administration of Primary and Secondary Schools*, 10: 21–22.

Xiao Y. (1996) "Divorce: A Great Revolution in 1996," *Behavioral Science (Xi'an)*, 2: 4–10.

Xu, J. (1993) "Break a Road for Privately Run Schools," *World of Higher Education Run by Social Forces*, 4: 20–22.

Yan, J. (1993) "Adult Women's Education Today," *Half the Sky*, 3: 13.

Yang, D. (1993) "We Should Actively and Steadily Develop Universities Run by Social Forces," *China Higher Education Research*, 2: 11–14.

Zeng, K. (1996) "Prayer, Luck, and Spiritual Strength: The Desecularization of Entrance Examination Systems in East Asia," *Comparative Education Review*, 40: 264–279.

Zeng, R. *et al.* (1997) *Report on a Study of 50 Schools in Hong Kong*, Hong Kong: Hong Kong Institute of Educational Research.

Zhang, K. and Wang, W. (1998) "Current Condition, Problems and Strategies of Private Secondary and Primary School Development," *Administration of Secondary and Primary Schools*, 1: 20–23.

Zhang, W. (1994) "Current Laws and Regulations on Schools Run by Social Forces in Our Country," in Z. Zhang (ed.), *Theory and Practice of Private and Nongovernmental Schools*, Beijing: China Workers' Publishing House, pp. 330–352.

Zhang, Z. (1995) *Development, Prospects, Difficulties and Strategies for Private Schools in China*, Beijing: Central Institute for Educational Studies.

Zhao Yifeng (2005) "Private Universities Approved to Offer Undergraduate Degree Education Increases by 18 Bringing the Total Number to 24," http://learning. sohu.com/20051119/n240755337.shtml.

Zhu, Y. (1994) "A Sharp Look at Minban Schools," *The Future and Development*, 6: 39–42.

4 Educational access for China's post-Cultural Revolution generation

Enrollment patterns in 1990

Rachel Connelly and Zhenzhen Zheng

Introduction

China's first post-Cultural Revolution generation came through school in a period of rapid social change. Reforms in the economy promoted increases in standards of living, reductions in poverty, and increases in community wealth available to support education. However, the same reforms brought new disparities. Income inequality grew substantially, particularly between the urban and coastal areas, on the one hand, and the rural interior areas, on the other. Within education, academic meritocracy was again being touted as the criterion for academic advancement, but the ability to pay increasingly served as an important element of children's educational progress. Funding was decentralized, increasing the disparity of resources available to education (see Chapters 1 and 2 of this volume and Adams and Hannum 2005). Davis (1989: 581) characterized China's educational structures in the late 1980s as "more fragmented, less egalitarian, and more stratified than (at any point) since the late 1950s." The stratifying trend was also significant beyond the school system, as social disparities in the educational attainment of students passing through education in this period established the foundation for current and future economic inequalities.

It is in this context—the return to meritocracy, increasing income disparity, and rapidly changing economic fortunes—that we examine the school enrollment pattern of Chinese youth. Using the one-percentage sample of the Chinese Census of 1990, we are able to capture the generation born from 1972 to 1980, who are the first young people to live in the post-Cultural Revolution world. They were also the first generation to come of age completely in the era of economic reform. On the other hand, 1990 is very early in the process of economic reform and many areas had not yet experienced increases in real wealth or increased opportunity for migration. There is no expectation that the world of education represented by this statistical portrait in 1990 represents enrollment patterns at the start of the twenty-first century, and, in fact, the next chapter highlights the changes in school enrollment and graduations rates over the ten-year period between the 1990 and 2000 censuses. Instead, this portrait is offered as a

The determinants of enrollment

benchmark from which we can measure the effect of the sweeping changes of the 1990s.

The large sample size of the 1990 census allows a detailed description of enrollment rates across the country at the province, county, and village level. The census also permits investigation of potential covariates such as parental education, number of siblings, and family composition. The census lacks information on grade attainment, but does distinguish between primary school enrollments and middle school enrollments. It also lacks specific information on household income. We have added county-level income measures, which capture some of the income-related differences, but income disparity within a county is largely unaccounted for.

Our analysis of school enrollment is informed by an economic model of individual or family decision-making. One of the main determinants of school enrollment and completion is the opportunity cost of the student's time, which is expected to differ substantially across China depending on the local economy, the proximity to large population centers, and cultural differences. Another important determinant of schooling outcomes is income. Both household income and community-level income are expected to affect educational outcomes. Economic reforms played a role in changing education patterns, as they affected both the opportunity costs and income levels of various groups within the population. For example, opportunity costs may have changed differently for boys and girls. Income growth differed substantially by location and terrain. How opportunity costs of staying in school change with the type of economic development China is experiencing and how changes in communities' fortunes affect educational outcomes are empirical questions that our cross-sectional analysis begins to analyze by contrasting enrollment rates across rural versus urban residence, gender, ethnicity (at least Han versus non-Han), household background characteristics, and geographical regions with different economic fortunes.

The main findings of our analysis, findings that echo previous work on Chinese education, are that place of residence and sex, and the interactions between them, were the most important categories for understanding school enrollment and graduation patterns in China. Rural girls seem to be triply disadvantaged in enrollment and graduation rates: first, because they live in a rural area as compared to an urban area; second, because they are girls, not boys; and third, because China's family planning policy, paired with a tradition of son preference, has made it more likely that a girl has siblings. Children with siblings, especially girls with siblings, are less likely to be enrolled and less likely to complete primary or middle school. Rural boys were also substantially disadvantaged compared to urban boys and girls. A number of other demographic variables also affected educational attainment. Parental education and the number and sex of siblings were all significant determinants of enrollment and graduation rates at both the county and individual level. Contextual variables also mattered, such as the proportion of children 10–18 years old in the village who were in school, the terrain of the county of residency, and per capita income of the county. Ethnicity was found to be related to enrollment and graduation rates, but with a less consistent pattern. At the national level, there are large differences between Han and non-Han enrollment rates, but at the county level, most of these differences are explained by differences in average income and terrain. However, at the individual level, non-Han children were found to be significantly less likely to have initially enrolled in primary school, and less likely to have enrolled in middle school, given that they finished primary school.

The Chinese context

In 1990, Chinese colleges and universities could only accommodate a small percentage of college-age youth. Because of this, the main factors limiting the attainment of higher education in China are on the supply side. However, at the other end of the education spectrum, the first nine years of schooling, the decision to stay in school or not is driven by both demand and supply. On the demand side, we can consider students who leave school "early" as those for whom the opportunity costs plus direct costs of staying in school are greater than the benefits. Both costs and benefits of staying in school are expected to differ substantially across location, as some of the normal equilibrating forces within the labor market are thwarted by the Chinese registration system (*hukou*), which has tied people's official residence to the area of their birth. In addition, income levels are expected to affect demand, both because poor families may be credit-constrained (Brown and Park 2002) and because education has a consumption aspect, which is expected to behave as any normal good.

There are important supply side considerations as well, especially at the middle school level. In 1980, the Chinese Central Government passed the "Resolution on Universalization of Primary Education," which required that primary education be universalized in the 1980s. In 1984, the average "involvement rate" of first year school-aged children reached 95 percent (that is, 95 percent of children of first year school age entered school), according to official government statistics (He 1996). However, in May 1985, a "Resolution on Educational System Reform" was passed, which assigned total responsibility for primary education to the local government. This reform has resulted in increased inequality of funding between rural and urban schools and among rural schools (Hannum 1999; Tsang 2000).

The following year, in April 1986, the 6th National People's Congress passed the Law of Compulsory Education, which officially made nine years of schooling compulsory throughout China while reaffirming that the fiscal responsibility for compulsory education is that of local government (He 1996). The State promises in that same law to help local areas with compulsory education expenses in regions with economic difficulties and in minority areas (Article 12 of the Law of Compulsory Education). The implementation of universal nine-year compulsory schooling (six years of primary school, three years of middle school) was to be carried out in different phases depending on local circumstances. Three types of areas were distinguished on the basis of level of socio-economic development: (1) developed areas; (2) moderately developed areas; and (3) underdeveloped areas. Level of socio-economic development was defined by per capita GDP, per capita net income, and the proportion of rural industry product value in rural GDP (Yang and Han 1990). By 1990, all areas were expected to have primary education available for all students, but the moderately developed areas and the under-developed areas were not expected to have completed the transition to universal compulsory middle school.

In reality, according to official Chinese government statistics, by 1990, only 76 percent of the counties had realized universal primary education, though the population of those counties was 91 percent of the total national popula-tion (He 1996). Even where slots were technically available, many rural stu-dents needed to travel a long way to middle school, forcing them to live away from their families during the week. In addition, many of these schools were poorly funded and inadequately staffed, and conditions for living and learn-ing were poor. Parents may have been reluctant to have their children away from home or living in these conditions, due to the poor quality of education being offered.

Economic reforms in China, and accompanying rapid economic growth, led to increased wealth in both urban and some rural areas, although the rural areas closer to the coast or to large urban area did better than interior areas. This increase in wealth, for the most part, meant that more resources were available for education, increasing the quality and availability of middle school education in rural areas. The increased educational resources, keeping everything else constant, would be predicted to increase the probability that students complete nine grades.

However, the increased income came about through substantial economic reforms, especially decollectivization in favor of the household responsibility system of agriculture. This change shifted the location of much decision-making from state or local authorities to individual households (see Chapter 1 of this volume for more details on the effect of decollectivization). Rural families' incomes became much more closely linked to their own work efforts than in the collective period. While this change was seen as mainly positive, providing the incentives for hard work and increased productivity, there were also some negative consequences. Specifically, the implementation of the household responsibility system meant that families could reap direct benefits from the use of their children's labor. For this reason, rural families faced new incentives to pull their children out of school before graduation.

Increased light manufacturing jobs similarly offered new incentives for pulling some students out of school. This change likely affected rural stu-dents more than urban students, since many of the employers in urban areas seem to have rules against hiring anyone who has not graduated from middle school, while rural enterprises did not have such rules. The consequences of increasing numbers of manufacturing jobs for educational outcomes depend on how strictly prohibitions against hiring middle school dropouts were enforced and the level of migration. If restrictions were strictly enforced and if young people perceive migrating to the cities as an option, then attractive manufacturing jobs in urban areas may serve to reduce the rate of school dropouts, even in rural areas. If the restrictions against hiring middle school dropouts were largely ignored, then light manufacturing jobs may have tempted more students to drop out of middle school.

Previous research on educational attainment in China

The analysis of educational attainment in developing countries is often limited by lack of data. Yet, given the importance of education as a determinant of individual income and, more generally, of well-being, understanding determinants of educational attainment is of great importance both for understanding inequality and for informing policy. Common themes of rural/ urban and gender disparity can be found in most countries. Family size, parental education, and parental income also play important roles in each study.

In the Chinese academic literature, we found ten studies of Chinese education in the ten years between 1989 and 1998. These studies each make use of aggregate data from the State Education Commission, which provides province-level measures of school enrollment by grade and sex. Many of the studies also analyze small-scale surveys. For example, Yang and Han (1991) present results from a random sample of nine provinces and 60 counties collected in April 1989. Their analyses focused on the reasons why primary and middle students repeat grades and why they drop out. Having to repeat a grade is one of the reasons students give for dropping out. They found that grade repetition is more likely to affect middle school dropping out than primary school dropping out. It is unclear whether grade repetition actually causes dropping out or whether it simply tags students at risk of dropping out. Parents and teachers identified economic factors, geographic factors, the temptation of temporary jobs, the overcrowding of schools, lack of resources within the school, and lack of teachers as factors contributing to early school leaving. Most of the other Chinese studies concentrated on the poor Western region of China and on various national minority populations. In some areas of Western China, school entrance rates are 20 points lower than the national average and girls appear to be particularly disadvantaged (Zhou *et al.* 1995).

In the English-language academic literature, there has been a recent flurry of studies on reform-era Chinese education. Knight and Song (1993, 1996) use the 1988 China Income Project Survey data to explore the determinants of educational attainment. Knight and Song (1996) focus specifically on differences in educational attainment by place of residence. They find large differences by location of residence, with urban residence a substantial positive predictor of increased educational attainment in the population of

Chinese 16 years of age and older. Broaded and Liu (1996) concentrate on urban youth's transition from compulsory middle school to voluntary and supply constrained high school. They analyze a sample of 670 students from 15 classrooms in Wuhan in 1992. Their careful study shows the importance of gender as a determinant of both educational aspirations and high school enrollment, even in a large urban area in China.

Hannum (1999, 2005) used aggregate data from the 1990 Chinese Census and tabular State Education Commission data to show rising urban–rural differences in basic educational provision and enrollment in the years leading up to 1990, and a slowdown in the trend of progress toward gender equality in basic education in the earliest reform years. Combining census data with microdata from the rural component of the 1988 Chinese Household Income Project (CHIP) survey and the 1992 National Sample Survey of the Situation of Chinese Children, Hannum (2002, 2003, 2005) showed an interaction between rural poverty and gender inequality in enrollments, and documented the significance of poverty in producing observed ethnic disparities in enrollment.

More recent data are presented in Knight and Song (2000) and Brown and Park (2002). Knight and Song use 1995 CHIP data to explore an intra-household bargaining model. They find that boys have a higher probability of enrollment at all levels and that children whose mother has a higher education level than the father are more likely to be in school, especially boys. Brown and Park use a 1997 dataset of rural residents in six poor counties in six provinces of China to explore issues of the roles of credit constraints, women's empowerment, and school quality on enrollment, test scores, and the probability of repeating a year. They find that children in more wealthy families in their poor counties have higher test scores and are less likely to repeat a grade. Children in families with severe credit constraints are less likely to be enrolled. They also find evidence of gender bias, in which girls who are doing poorly in school are more likely to drop out of primary school, whereas boys usually stay in school through middle school.

Our study of the 1990 Census microdata files provides a complement to these studies. The census provides us with a broad-based data source that is large enough to measure community effects as well as individual effects. We include older children aged 15–18 in the analysis so that middle school attendance and graduation can be studied. Further, school enrollment rates calculated from census data are less likely to be overstated than some of the data collected by the Ministry of Education, since most census respondents would have little incentive to falsify school enrollment answers. The chief drawback of the 1990 Census is the lack of data on household income. To partially address this limitation, we include information on county level income and terrain from the 1990 County Databook of the Statistical Bureau of China.

Patterns in enrollment across provinces, rural/urban residence, and sex

This section provides a description of school enrollment rates across China using the one-percentage sample from the 1990 Chinese Census. Based on our earlier discussion of expected differences, here we consider differences in enrollment rates across locations, rural versus urban residence and the sex of the student. Table 4.1, row 1, shows that the average in-school rates among

Table 4.1 Percentage of 10–18-year-olds in school by province, sex, and location of residence

	Boys		Girls	
	Urban	Rural	Urban	Rural
All China	73.64	54.55	71.96	44.37
Han	73.83	54.99	72.01	45.05
Non-Han	71.16	50.33	71.25	37.80
Provinces				
Beijing	82.70	71.02	85.89	68.18
Tianjin	85.40	64.74	87.87	60.77
Hebei	75.64	56.78	71.49	52.61
Shanxi	69.82	51.88	69.52	48.33
Inner Mongolia	67.05	53.11	71.58	46.10
Liaoning	77.86	59.37	75.04	57.10
Jilin	71.58	54.63	73.30	53.24
Heilongjiang	70.12	54.74	72.80	49.80
Shanghai	86.34	69.34	80.08	72.67
Jiangsu	76.36	63.14	71.77	53.02
Zhejiang	64.78	44.32	57.80	39.31
Anhui	65.99	52.76	62.09	37.00
Fujian	74.05	50.95	67.59	38.76
Jiangxi	72.42	53.88	70.03	35.45
Shangdong	76.04	59.53	75.21	47.34
Henan	72.07	54.47	67.28	44.72
Hubei	77.75	53.94	73.25	44.00
Hunan	71.52	55.42	68.78	43.74
Guangdong	79.57	66.94	76.26	55.53
Guangxi	71.54	59.14	71.50	48.06
Hainan	69.25	66.02	59.48	58.69
Sichuan	69.79	46.50	69.59	36.57
Guizhou	64.34	52.58	55.93	34.61
Yunnan	76.39	50.65	75.35	36.30
Tibet	73.33	14.01	50.00	6.95
Shaanxi	75.69	54.52	74.69	48.93
Gansu	74.48	52.63	74.56	36.91
Qinghai	74.37	40.07	76.68	29.32
Ningxia	74.15	53.23	75.86	39.97
Xinjiang	67.57	49.32	67.42	49.32

youth aged 10–18 in 1990 were 73.6 percent for urban boys, 72.0 percent for urban girls, 54.6 percent for rural boys, and 44.4 percent for rural girls. Rows 2 and 3 show that there is little difference between Han and non-Han rates in urban areas, but in rural areas, non-Han rates are almost five percentage points less for boys and more than seven percentage points less for girls. Table 4.1 also presents the percentage in school by sex, location of residence, and province. Proportions varied considerably across provinces, from highs in the 80 percent range in the urban centers of Shanghai, Beijing and Tianjin to lows in the 30 percent range for rural girls in the interior provinces of Gansu, Yunnan, Guizhou, Sichuan, Jiangxi. Tibet was a real outlier, with extremely low rates of rural enrollments for both boys and girls. Despite differences in level, the ordinal pattern was identical across all provinces. Urban rates were always higher than rural rates, often by 20 percentage points or more; girls usually had lower rates than boys did, with small differentials in the urban areas and larger differentials in rural areas.

Further analysis by age of the children shows that this urban/rural gender pattern was consistent over single year age groups as well. The percentage enrolled by age was very similar between urban boys and girls until age 17, when urban boys begin to overtake urban girls. Comparing rural girls and boys by single year of age, we find that rural girls had lower rates of school enrollment at every age and that the differential between rural boys and girls increased with age, except at the highest ages. Finally, comparing urban boys with rural boys and urban girls with rural girls, the gap between urban and rural enrollment rates increased with age.

Communities can differ in the percentage of children who ever attend school, in the percentage who drop out of school before completion, and in the percentage of children who go on to higher levels of education. In China from 1978–1986 (the approximate years when the cohort being examined would have entered school for the first time), the vast majority of children did start school. Still, differences in the opportunity to attend primary school between rural and urban youth and between boys and girls were clear. Only one half of 1 percent of urban youth, both boys and girls, never attended school. For rural youth, comparable figures were 3 percent for rural boys and 8.5 percent for rural girls. In cross-tabulations of never-enrollment with other household characteristics, educational level of one's parents, the number of younger siblings, county income levels, the terrain of the county of residence, ethnicity, and age were all correlated with attendance for rural youth. For urban youth, attendance was fairly consistent across categories, with the exception of parents' education. For rural girls, having an illiterate parent, having two or more younger siblings, living in a mountainous county and being non-Han all increased the odds substantially of never attending school.

Table 4.2, column 1 shows the inverse percentage—the percentage of all youth aged 10–18 who ever attended school by province and location of residence. These data show particularly high rates of never attending

Table 4.2 Selected education rates by province

		Primary school		Middle school		High school
		Attendance	Graduation	Attendance	Graduation	Attendance
Total	Rural	94.29	87.06	62.47	83.6	18.28
	Urban	99.47	98.73	97.24	97.82	56.59
Beijing	Rural	99.1	97.66	93.41	95.83	33.33
	Urban	99.66	99.68	99.03	99.68	80.39
Tianjin	Rural	98.65	92.17	79	84.29	27.12
	Urban	99.92	96.94	98.51	93.21	75.73
Hebei	Rural	97.82	96.12	69.04	94.08	12.69
	Urban	99.66	98.84	97.19	99.26	56.19
Shanxi	Rural	98.72	96.2	66.85	92.79	13.15
	Urban	99.58	98.76	98.39	98.91	47.25
Inner Mongolia	Rural	95.46	88.36	65.15	81.4	14.72
	Urban	99.17	98.62	96.6	98.13	45.45
Liaoning	Rural	99.18	94.37	72.04	78.88	16.92
	Urban	99.72	99.59	98.84	99.16	54.99
Jilin	Rural	98.06	90.38	64.5	70.87	9.44
	Urban	99.6	99.21	98.41	98.62	46.27
Heilongjiang	Rural	97.68	88.45	63.1	73.92	25.68
	Urban	99.52	98.77	96.3	97.09	46.67
Shanghai	Rural	99.66	95.77	95.18	82.05	23.96
	Urban	99.81	99.77	98.86	100	73.82
Jiangsu	Rural	98.35	93.1	73.01	85.79	19.13
	Urban	99.63	98.93	97.5	97.8	58.2
Zhejiang	Rural	98.16	91.24	71.65	87.5	21.61
	Urban	100	99.11	97.83	97.55	55.56
Anhui	Rural	90.11	80.49	58.48	81.39	12.52
	Urban	99.43	98.03	95.04	97.79	52.54
Fujian	Rural	95	77.12	58.99	70.72	25.78
	Urban	99.38	97.45	97.39	92.04	65.41
Jiangxi	Rural	94.36	75.46	60.26	73.27	24.92
	Urban	99.58	99.12	97.24	97.29	57.91
Shangdong	Rural	96.83	94.79	66.05	93.64	14.43
	Urban	99.82	99.37	99	99.82	60.77
Henan	Rural	96.1	94.73	60.3	90.76	14.07
	Urban	99.61	99.53	97.7	99.02	57.62
Hubei	Rural	97.13	85.07	63.51	78.02	22.54
	Urban	99.38	99.29	98.39	99.45	63.37
Hunan	Rural	97.85	86.71	63.18	77.85	25.79
	Urban	99.77	99.32	97.44	97.51	55.65
Guangdong	Rural	97.95	84.79	64.87	83.21	19.74
	Urban	99.44	98.39	95.9	95.84	64.01
Guangxi	Rural	95.4	82.72	47.37	83.05	15.8
	Urban	99.61	98.97	92.03	97.33	48.86
Hainan	Rural	96.37	81.43	73.33	75.9	26.98
	Urban	97.19	92.23	91.95	94.07	58.56
Sichuan	Rural	95.86	87.13	53.63	76.26	17.39
	Urban	99.46	99.01	97.2	97.26	56.27

Guizhou	Rural	81.7	67.73	55.33	75.89	13.54
	Urban	98.74	96.07	95.32	93.24	46.38
Yunnan	Rural	81.15	69.81	54.9	74.07	27
	Urban	99.81	99.11	96.57	97.83	63.33
Tibet	Rural	18.97	40	20	–	–
	Urban	81.48	57.14	50	–	–
Shaanxi	Rural	92.73	87.55	68.93	83.33	22.57
	Urban	99.74	99.32	98.08	98.82	63.88
Gansu	Rural	77.29	80.09	64.65	85.96	25.74
	Urban	99.3	97.54	97.48	99.65	43.55
Qinghai	Rural	52.72	74.13	66.04	85	35.29
	Urban	98.72	98.78	97.53	100	47.95
Ningxia	Rural	73.97	80.49	72.73	77.14	29.63
	Urban	99.66	98.7	98.68	96.72	64.41
Xinjiang	Rural	95.42	89.83	58.91	91.35	34.91
	Urban	97.77	96.37	95.22	97.17	58.55

school for rural residents of the Southwestern provinces of Guizhou and Yunnan and the Western provinces of Tibet, Gansu, Qinghai, and Ningxia.

Youth who began school but are not currently in school may have completed school or may have dropped out in the middle. In order to differentiate between these two possibilities, we focus on youth at age 14. Based on a system of nine years of compulsory education, most students should still be in school at age 14. In fact, our analysis shows that the majority of those not in school at age 14 had dropped out of school, while only a small percentage of youth had graduated from middle school by this age. Of the urban boys, 87.4 percent of those who ever started school were still in school at age 14, 4 percent had dropped out and 8.6 percent had finished middle school and not gone on to high school. For urban girls, 87.4 percent of those who ever started school were still in school at age 14, 3.6 percent had dropped out and 9 percent had finished middle school and not gone on to high school. Again, the urban pattern was fairly consistent across boys and girls, with just slightly more boys dropping out, but slightly less boys stopping after the ninth grade. Rural youth at age 14 were substantially less likely to be in school. Rural youth also showed substantial differences between the boys and the girls. Of the rural boys, 63.2 percent of those who started school were still in school at age 14, 30 percent had dropped out and 6.8 percent had finished middle school and not gone on to high school. For rural girls, 48.1 percent were still in school at age 14, 45.1 percent had dropped out and 6.8 percent had finished middle school and not gone on to high school. The gender difference in the rate of completing middle school of 4 percent in urban areas and 30–45 percent in rural areas is a stark reminder of the enormous gap that existed in 1990 between urban and rural China.

Our analyses showed that the transition from primary school to middle school was the location of much of the dropping out before completing middle school. Recall that attending middle school in a rural area often involved leaving home and boarding at the township school during the week. For the urban boys aged 14 who entered primary school but did not complete middle school, 42.7 percent finished primary school and did not enter middle school. The comparable percentage for urban girls was 63.7 percent, for rural boys was 59.1 percent and for rural girls was 62.2 percent. Here it is striking to find such a large gap between urban boys and girls. Recall that a very small percentage of urban youth, less than 4 percent, dropped out of school by age 14. Of this small number, girls were more likely to have completed primary school and not entered middle school, while more of the boys tended to drop out in the middle of middle school. In rural areas, the numbers not completing school were much more substantial. Thus, 17.1 percent of all rural boys aged 14 and 25.7 percent of all rural girls completed primary school and did not enter middle school.

Table 4.2 shows the full set of transition percentages by province and rural/urban residence. Each column uses the number of students who have completed the previous transition as the population. So, for example, column 2 reports the percentage of students who finished primary school out of all those who began primary school, and column 3 reports the percentage of students who began middle school out of all those who finished primary school. Rows 1 and 2 give the national averages for rural and urban residences. Across the provinces, we can see substantial differences in these transition rates. For example, comparing rural youth in Guangxi and Guangdong, youth in both provinces had a high rate of initial attendance, 95.40 percent and 97.95 percent respectively, and a very similar rate of graduating from primary school, 82.72 percent versus 84.79 percent. However, these provinces exhibited a substantial difference in attending middle school conditional on primary school completion: 47.37 percent versus 64.87 percent. Students who started middle school in Guangxi were as likely to finish as those students from Guangdong, with completion rates of 83.05 percent for Guangxi and 83.21 percent for Guangdong.

County patterns

The large sample size and broad coverage of the 1990 census data allow us to look beyond province-level differences. When we examined data at the county level, we found very substantial differences between counties even in the same province. No clear pattern of difference between coastal areas and the interior emerged. Instead, northern counties seemed to have higher rates of enrollment than did southern, but striking variation exists within geographic regions. For example, Hebei province, which surrounds Beijing, had a rural male enrollment rate of 56.78 percent and an urban rate for boys of 75.64 percent (see Table 4.1, row 3). Yet, in Hebei, we found county enrollments rates ranging from 30.5 percent to 100 percent for boys.

A multivariate analysis of the county rates presented in Table 4.3 revealed

Table 4.3 Determinants of county proportions of 14-year-olds in school

	Proportion of all 14-year-olds in school	*Difference in prop. of 14-year-old boys and girls in school*
Proportion of 14-year-olds who are in primary school	0.074* (0.029)	0.081* (0.031)
Proportion rural	−31.083** (4.246)	14.555** (4.739)
Proportion non-Han	−2.707 (2.246)	−6.132* (2.421)
Total fertility rate	−7.35** (1.057)	3.476** (1.176)
County per capita income	0.009** (0.002)	−0.003 (0.002)
Hill county	−1.145 (1.470)	−0.964 (1.584)
Mountain county	−5.464** (1.445)	0.623 (1.571)
South coastal	4.011* (1.774)	5.516** (1.917)
Southwest	−2.474 (2.247)	4.722 (2.422)
Mid-coastal	−5.656** (1.485)	6.153** (1.615)
South central	−7.568** (1.780)	7.987** (1.941)
Proportion of 14-year-olds in school		−0.015 (0.040)
Constant	105.092** (4.603)	−13.514* (6.502)
Observations	736	736
R-squared	0.4	0.15

Notes: The total fertility rate was constructed as the average number of children born to the cohort of women who were born between 1935 and 1960. Its role in the regression is a measure of average family size in the cohort of students.

Standard errors in parentheses * significant at 5 percent level; ** significant at 1 percent level.

that while some of the differences in attendance across counties can be explained by differences in average per capita income and in the terrain, the mid-coastal provinces and south central provinces still had significantly lower attendance rates for 14-year-olds. The four regional dummies were chosen to correspond with the map regions that seem to be correlated with differences in school enrollment rates. The proportion of in-school 14-year-olds still in primary school was included as a control for differences in the average age of school entry and because of the relationship found in other studies between grade repetition and dropping out.

As shown in Table 4.3, column 1, the R-squared for this model is 40 percent, which indicates that the included variables have a substantial amount of predictive power in this cross-sectional context. Most of the included variables were significant predictors of the county enrollment rate. Counties that were more rural and counties that were mountainous had lower proportions of 14-year-olds in school. Higher average family size, measured by the constructed total fertility rate for mothers of the cohort of 10–18-year-olds, also lowered the proportion of 14-year-olds who were in school. Higher county level per capita income was correlated with higher enrollment rates at age 14. Having a higher proportion of 14-year-olds in primary school had a small positive effect on the proportion in school, perhaps because students wait until they have completed primary school before dropping out. Finally, having controlled for all these variables, counties in the south central and the mid-coastal areas had significantly lower enrollment rates, while the counties in the south coastal region had higher rates. These regional results may represent cultural differences or may be the result of a differing opportunity costs of staying in school attributable to the large number of light manufacturing jobs in the southern areas and more skilled employment needs in the mid coast area.

Table 4.3, column 2, shows the multivariate analysis of the gender gap in school enrollment rates for 14-year-old boys and girls. A positive coefficient indicates that the characteristic increases the size of the county gender gap, while a negative coefficient indicates that the characteristic reduces the size of the county gender gap. For example, if the county is mainly rural, the gender gap of enrollment at age 14 was greater. Interestingly, terrain and per capita income do not explain the gender gap, though they were important predictors of enrollment rates. The last variable included is the county enrollment rate. This variable is also insignificant, which tells us that the size of the gender gap is uncorrelated with the level of enrollment. South coastal, mid-coastal, and south central regions all had significantly larger gender gaps than the rest of China. Controlling for region, income, and terrain, counties with larger minority populations had significantly smaller gender gaps. Thus, the gender gap is larger in Han-dominated counties in the southern part of China, holding everything else constant. This analysis shows the importance of separating the issue of enrollment level from the issue of gender gap in enrollment. Some areas with very low levels of the enrollment do not exhibit large gender gaps while some areas with relatively high enrollment of boys have substantially lower enrollments for girls.

Differences in household characteristics

Both parental education and family size are expected to affect educational attainment, based on a simple economic cost/benefit analysis. Our analyses of the 1990 census data show a very consistent pattern of parental education on school enrollment status of children: the higher the level of parental education, the larger the proportion of the group who were enrolled in school. The differentials across parental education groups were largest for rural girls: 26.26 percent of rural girls whose parents were both illiterate were in school, compared to 43.05 percent of those with one parent with some primary education and 58.22 percent if one parent attended middle school.

In terms of family size, cross-tabulations also show a very consistent pattern of negative effects of large families on school enrollment, even in urban areas. Each additional sibling lowered the proportion of youth enrolled in school by almost the same proportion, except for rural girls going from no sibling to one sibling. For example, the in-school rate is 74.2 percent for rural boys with no siblings, 71.3 percent for rural boys with one sibling, 58.4 percent for rural boys with two siblings. For rural girls, 60.0 percent of the girls with no siblings are in school compared to 67.3 percent of those with one sibling, and 50.7 percent of those with two siblings. The negative effect of large family size may be due to financial constraints or quantity/quality tradeoffs. The same pattern emerged when we considered the number of younger siblings only and the number of younger brothers only.

Multivariate analyses also showed that the negative effect of having a sibling was significant for rural youth for each educational transition; that is, having a sibling lowered the probability of starting school, lowered the probability of completing primary school having started school, lowered the probability of starting middle school having finished primary school, etc. (Connelly and Zheng 2003). Since girls in China in 1990 were much more likely to have a sibling, through the combination of strong son preference and China's strict family planning policy, girls in rural China were disadvantaged in education both as a result of the difference between the marginal effects on boys and girls of having a sibling and the difference in the probability of having a sibling. This indirect disadvantage increases the direct negative effect of being female that emerges in multivariate analyses of rural enrollment.

Community characteristics

While household characteristics are expected to be important predictors of school enrollment, there is also the expectation that characteristics of the location of residence will affect enrollment. One reason is that the financing of education is mainly local. Thus, local economic fortunes should affect community expenditures on schools, independent of household wealth. In addition, community expectations of the appropriate level of school attainment may also influence enrollment. Since marriage markets are mainly local in rural China, boys and girls with education levels below the community average may find it difficult to find a marriage partner. On the flip side, it maybe difficult to convince a 14-year-old to attend middle school if few of his or her cohort are still in school.

To test these hypotheses, we included the proportion of the village youth aged 10–18 who were currently in school and county levels of per capita income in our multivariate analysis of individual level school enrollment. The Chinese villages were large enough that individual behavior could be considered independent of the village average. We found that living in a village where a higher proportion of youth, aged 10 to 18, attended school had a large and consistent effect on individual enrollment and graduation transitions. Furthermore, for the lower educational categories of primary school attendance, primary school graduation and middle school attendance, village in-school rates had significantly larger effects for girls than boys.

Higher county per capita income was found to be positively correlated with the probability of a rural youth being enrolled in primary school, middle school, and high school but not with the probability of finishing primary school or middle school, given that one is enrolled. These results are consistent with Hannum's findings that village poverty levels affected enrollments for rural youth, net of household socio-economic background. They are also consistent with Brown and Park's findings that school quality (which we are assuming is correlated with county per capita income) affects the duration of primary school enrollment independent of individual and household characteristics.

Conclusion

In this chapter, we have sought to provide a statistical portrait of Chinese school enrollment patterns of youth aged 10 to 18, using data from the 1990 census data of China. While overall levels of school enrollment were high, especially for a country with China's level of per capita income, the data reveal substantial variations between urban and rural residents, and between boys and girls, particularly between boys and girls in the rural areas. Tables 4.1 and 4.2 also show substantial variation across provinces even after separating out rural and urban children. Table 4.2 shows that provinces differed in the pattern of educational transitions, that is, that some provinces seemed to fare better with initial enrollments, while others had particularly high or low rates of transition from primary school to middle school or from middle school to high school. In addition, our research showed that there is substantial geographical variation in enrollment rates of 14-year-olds even within provinces. One cannot point to a single region of China and say that the "problem" was confined to this region. As Table 4.3 shows, terrain and income played important roles in explaining differences in county-level enrollment rates, but regional differences remained. Mid-coastal, south coastal, and south central provinces had a particularly large gender gap in 14-year-old enrollment rates, which may represent cultural factors or differences in the opportunity cost of girls' and boys' time in these regions.

Multivariate analyses done at the individual level, referred to above and reported fully in Connelly and Zheng (2003) reveal a consistent set of correlates with enrollment. Rural versus urban residence and sex were, by far, the most prominent among these. In addition, parental education, the number of siblings, and village in-school rates each had consistent effects on all educational milestones. Having a sibling lowers the probability that a rural youth attends primary school, graduates from primary school, attends middle school, graduates from middle school and attends high school. Parents' educational attainment is correlated with the child's educational status in each analysis. Village level in-school rates also have a powerful effect on the probability that an individual youth attended school or graduated. In addition, in rural areas, girls' educational status at the lower levels was more positively affected than boys' was by higher village rates. This result suggests that there may be positive externalities, especially to girls, in terms of increased enrollment when a community raises its enrollment rates or makes middle school more accessible. Finally, county-level wealth measures were consistently positive in their predictive power for rural areas.

Our findings are consistent with the many other studies done in China that were cited above and also with similar studies done in other developing countries in different parts of the world. For example, in every country where researchers have applied these determinants of educational attainment models, parental schooling is an important determinant of youth enrollment. In addition, in China as elsewhere, larger family sizes reduce the probability of school attendance and graduation. And while other studies do not include village in-school rates as we did, several other studies have found the importance of location of residence as a determinant of enrollment.

For future research, better measures of differences in school availability and school quality are needed in order to differentiate between supply and demand causes of differentials. Brown and Park (2002) offer a good example of the value of these variables, but their data are confined to 472 youths in six counties. A larger, broader-based study with data like that in Brown and Park's is needed.

References

Adams, J. and Hannum, E. (2005) "Children's Social Welfare in China, 1989–1997: Access to Health Insurance and Education," *The China Quarterly*, 181: 100–121.

Broaded, C.M. and Liu, C. (1996) "Family Background, Gender and Educational Attainment in Urban China," *The China Quarterly*, 145: 53–86.

Brown, P. and Park, A. (2002) "Education and Poverty in Rural China," *Economics of Education Review*, 21(6): 523–541.

Connelly, R. and Zheng, Z. (2003) "Determinants of School Enrollment and Completion of 10 to 18 Year Olds in China," *Economics of Education Review*, 22: 379–388.

Davis, D. (1989) "Chinese Social Welfare: Policies and Outcomes," *The China Quarterly*, 119: 577–597.

Hannum, E. (1999) "Political Change and the Urban–Rural Gap in Basic Education in China," *Comparative Education Review*, 43(2): 193–211.

Hannum, E. (2002) "Ethnic Differences in Basic Education in Reform-Era Rural China," *Demography*, 39(1): 95–117.

Hannum, E. (2003) "Poverty and Basic Education in Rural China: Communities, Households, and Girls' and Boys' Enrollment," *Comparative Education Review*, 47(2): 141–159.

Hannum, E. (2005) "Market Transition, Educational Disparities, and Family Strategies in Rural China: New Evidence on Gender Stratification and Development," *Demography*, 2: 275–299.

He, D. (1996) *Dangdai Zhongguo Jiaoyu (Shang)* (*Education in Contemporary China* (Vol. 1)), Beijing: Dangdai Zhongguo Chubanshe (Contemporary China Press).

Knight, J. and Song, L. (1993) "The Determinants of Educational Attainment in China," in K. Griffin and R. Zhao (eds.), *The Distribution of Income in China*, London: Macmillan Press.

Knight, J. and Song, L. (1996) "Educational Attainment and the Rural–Urban Divide in China," *Oxford Bulletin of Economics and Statistics*, 58(1): 83–117.

Knight, J. and Song, L. (2000) "Differences in Educational Access in Rural China," Working Paper, Department of Economics, University of Oxford.

Tsang, M. (2000) "School Choice in People's Republic of China," Teachers College, Columbia University, New York, Occasional Paper 9, November.

Yang, N. and Han, M. (1990) "A Preliminary Cost-Benefit Analysis of Rural Education in Three Categories of Regions and its Implication for the Generalization of Compulsory Education" (Qianxi Sanlei Diqu Nongcun Jiaoyu de Xiaoyi jiqi dui Puji Yiwu Jiaoyu de Yingxiang), in State Education Development Research Center (Zhongguo Jiaoyu Fazhan de Hongguan) (ed.) *The Background, Current Situation and Trend of China's Education Development (Guojia Jiaoyu Fazhan Yanjiu Zhongxin Bian)*, Beijing: Zhuoyue Press.

Yang, N. and Han, M. (1991) "School Enrollment, Dropping Out, and Grade Repetition in Primary and Middle School in China" (Woguo Xiaoxue, Chuzhong Xuesheng Chuoxue he Liuji Wenti Yanjiu), *Education and Research (Jiaoyu Yanjiu)*, 3: 45–57.

Zhou, W., Yu, Q., and Wu, S. (1995) "The Analysis of Girls' Educational Problems in Ling Sha Hui Minority," *Nationalities Education Research* (in Chinese).

5 Enrollment and graduation patterns as China's reforms deepen, 1990–2000

Rachel Connelly and Zhenzhen Zheng

Introduction

This chapter builds on Chapter 4, and offers a statistical portrait of enrollment and graduation patterns in the 2000 Chinese Census. Looking at school enrollment and attainment in 2000 provides us with an important insight into the effect of economic and institutional reforms of the 1990s. As is well known by now, the decade of the 1990s marked an unprecedented period of rapid economic, social, and institutional change throughout China. Overall, per capita GDP grew 8.9 percent annually between 1991 and 2000 in real terms (National Bureau of Statistics 2005: Table 3.3: 53).

However, while all areas within China experienced an increase in income, the most substantial increases were experienced in urban areas. The estimate of the annual increase in per capita income for living expenses for rural areas is 4.3 percent (National Bureau of Statistics 2005). Along with rising income has come growing income inequality. As the old maxim goes, "The rich are getting richer and the poor are getting poorer." Well, perhaps not poorer, in terms of general consumption, however, in the area of education, this maxim is surely true because changes in school financing in China begun in the mid-1980s, discussed in Chapters 1 and 2, have led to increased use of school fees and an ever-growing quality gap between urban and rural schools (ibid.).

Our analysis of the 2000 census data shows that China has made tremendous progress towards its goal of universal education through the ninth grade. School initiation rates are up in every province, as are school completion rates. There is still work to be done in rural areas in terms of middle school completion. However, on every measure, the 1990s have been a decade of substantial progress. One area of concern is that the gap in senior high school attendance has widened over the decade; while there has been increased attendance of senior high school in rural areas, the increase in attendance in urban areas outpaced the increase in rural areas, causing the gap to widen. We provide further details on this finding below.

In addition to the goal of increasing educational attainment in general, central and local governments of China have been working during this decade to close the educational gender gap. There have been a number of both governmental and non-governmental initiatives aimed specifically at keeping rural girls in school. The analysis of the 1990 census data in Chapter 4 showed that a substantial gender gap existed in rural areas, but it also showed that there were large differences in the size of the gap both between provinces and even within the same province. How the gender gap has changed over the ten years between censuses is another focus of this chapter.

The remainder of this chapter is organized as follows. The next section provides a snapshot of school enrollment rates for China as a whole using rural–urban and male–female categories, as residence status and gender were key lines of stratification in 1990. These national rates are compared with our previous findings from the 1990 census to explore the changes that have occurred over the decade. Then, we explore the interrelationship among other relevant demographic characteristics such as parents' education, sex, and location in terms of school enrollment rates using the 2000 data. Next, we move beyond school enrollment rates, to explore educational transitions, such as the percentage entering school, the percentage graduating for primary school, and the percentage entering middle school. The last two empirical sections of the chapter consider provincial and gender differences. Finally, we conclude the chapter with an overall assessment of progress in the 1990s.

Enrollment and attainment rates by location of residence and sex of the child

In 2000, the overall proportion of youth aged 10–18 who are in school in China ranges from 88.8 percent for urban boys, 89.4 percent for urban girls, 76.6 percent for rural boys, and 74.4 percent for rural girls. These are impressive numbers for a developing country, and represent a tremendous increase from 10 years ago. Comparing the rates from 1990 and 2000, we find increases in both urban and rural areas. The increase in rural areas is particularly heartening, with rural boys increasing 22 percentage points since 1990 and rural girls increasing by 30 percentage points. Urban rates increased by 15 percentage points for boys and 17 for girls.

The top rows of Table 5.1 show that the pattern of school enrollment by age for 2000 and the percentage point increases from 1990. Comparing the urban and rural youth in 2000, the gap between urban and rural rates clearly increases as the children age. At ages 10 and 11, the proportion of rural boys and girls who are enrolled in school is close to the urban rates. But by the time a child reaches 13 or 14, the urban/rural gap is evident and is substantial by age 15 and 16. Rural girls have the lowest rates of school attendance at every age from 10 to 18. The differential between rural boys and girls increases as the child ages, except at the very highest ages. The gender gap in rural education is explored more fully in the section on the gender gap below.

Columns 4–8 of Table 5.1 show that progress has been made from 1990 to 2000 across the age distribution. The largest improvements can be seen at ages 14 and 15. These are the ages when most students are in middle school.

Table 5.1 Percentage of youth 10–18 years of age who are currently in school of those who ever enrolled, 2000, and percentage change, 1990 to 2000

	Percentage currently in school, 2000				Difference 2000–1990			
	Rural boys	Rural girls	Urban boys	Urban girls	Rural boys	Rural girls	Urban boys	Urban girls
Total	76.62	74.44	88.80	89.40	20.64	26.95	14.78	17.06
Age								
10	99.21	99	99.52	99.61	1.45	2.94	1.05	1.71
11	98.59	97.97	99.3	99.13	3.94	8.77	4.36	4.15
12	97.1	95.44	98.81	98.87	8.32	15.92	3.98	4.38
13	94.01	90.43	97.55	98.4	14.14	24.21	6.37	4.18
14	84.63	80.04	96.39	95.69	21.87	33.36	9.13	8.56
15	65.74	60.05	90.3	92.26	22.19	29.67	15.33	16.62
16	45.44	40.15	82.83	84.84	18.29	22.61	22.37	23.34
17	28.28	23.65	72.41	74.34	12.83	13.99	28.06	34.17
18	16.47	13.28	48.97	49.53	7.06	7.74	22.99	25.72
Parents' Education								
Illiterate	59.34	58.03	65.38	72.13	16.03	23.12	11.6	21.66
Primary School	68.36	65.45	73.6	74.8	14.02	20.87	10.27	12.14
Middle School +	81.21	79.3	89.92	90.42	14.01	19.89	11.67	14.08
Younger Sibs								
0	79.87	77.64	90.4	91.37	20.75	27.65	13.12	14.34
1	75.03	76.32	82.22	85.31	17.34	25.78	9.72	13.35
2	65.02	66.41	76.29	78.91	12.22	18.84	14.38	14.74
3+	58.24	57.38	73.77	72.11	4.36	12.67	0.1	1.23
Ethnicity								
Han	77.5	75.25	89.05	89.43	21.61	27.95	14.92	17.07
Non-Han	69.14	67.3	85.8	89.07	11.44	17.63	13.23	17.03

There has been a tremendous increase in the proportion of rural youth who attend middle school. In 1990, 62.5 percent of the rural youth who had graduated from primary school went on to middle school. In 2000, the comparable number is 86.1 percent. This is strong evidence that the Compulsory Education Law of 1986, which officially made nine years of schooling compulsory throughout China, has been effective in increasing school attendance beyond primary school.

As we saw in Chapter 4, not every 14-year-old who is enrolled in school is in middle school. However, progress has been made on this front as well. While in 1990, 34 percent of rural boys and 32 percent of rural girls who were still in school were in primary school at age 14, the comparable numbers for 2000 are 16 percent for rural boys and 17 percent for rural girls, showing that rural children are beginning school at an earlier age in 2000, compared to 1990, and perhaps they are also going to school more continually and therefore do not have to repeat grades as often. Still, in 2000, the rural proportions are substantially higher than the urban proportions, signaling that more improvement is possible.

What is the status of those 14- and 15-year-olds who are not in school in 2000? The majority of those not in school at age 14 and 15 in rural areas have dropped out of school, while a small percentage of urban youth have graduated from middle school by this age.

Since the vast majority of students should have completed middle school by age 18, we next consider the percentage of 18-year-olds who have graduated from middle school and the percentage who have initiated senior high school. There has been a substantial increase in middle school completion between 1990 and 2000 in rural China. In 1990, 48 percent of all 18-year-old rural boys had graduated from middle school. In 2000, that number is 77 percent. The rate for rural girls is slightly lower in 2000 with 72 percent of all 18-year-old rural girls having graduated from middle school, but that number represents an even greater improvement from the 33 percent of rural girls in 1990 who had graduated from middle school.

The rate of senior high school attendance has also increased over the decade for both rural and urban youth. In urban areas in 2000, 72 percent of 18-year-old boys had attended high school compared to 48 percent in 1990. The numbers for urban girls are similar, with 76 percent having attended high school in 2000, compared to 52 percent in 1990. Rural rates are still low compared to urban rates; in 2000, 18 percent of rural boys and 14 percent of rural girls had attended high school, compared to 10 percent and 5 percent in 1990.

Beyond location and sex—changes in enrollment and attainment rates by other demographic characteristics

As shown in Chapter 4, parental education, family size, ethnicity, and migrant status were all related to enrollment in 1990. The bottom rows of Table 5.1

summarize the changes between 1990 and 2000 in overall enrollment rates of those youth who ever attended school by selected demographic characteristics. The positive numbers throughout columns 5–8 show that enrollment rates have increased in 2000 compared to 1990 in every category. Rural girls appear have made the most gains in the decade, which seems like good news all around. One trend that is especially encouraging is the enrollment gains made by rural girls with one younger sibling. Rural girls are more likely to have younger siblings than rural boys due to continuing son preference, which is particularly strong for second births. Rural girls aged 10 to 18 with a younger sibling are 26 percentage points more likely to be in school in 2000 than they were in 1990.

Beyond school enrollment rates: changes in the percentage never attending, percentage attending middle school and high school

The percentage of youth enrolled in school as presented thus far is affected by a number of factors: the school initiation rate, that is, the percentage of children who begin school; the speed with which students complete school; and percentage of children who continue on in school after initiation. One would hope that the higher school enrollment rates shown in Table 5.1 translate into higher initiation rates and more children transitioning on to higher levels of education but neither is guaranteed. In addition, if children are starting school earlier, the school enrollment rate of 10–18-year-olds would be reduced, everything else held constant. Above, we presented some evidence that rural students are entering school at an earlier age, which would lower the percentage of 10–18-year-olds currently in school, everything else held constant. In this section, we consider the educational transition rates that, when combined, affect the value of the school enrollment rates already presented.

The percentage of youth in China aged 10–18 in 2000 who have never attended school is quite low, less than one percentage point, except for rural girls for whom the figure is 1.25 percent. These numbers represent substantial increases compared to 1990. The never attended rate for rural girls in particular went down 7.26 points, while for rural boys it went down 2.38 points. Only those children with neither parent ever attending school show substantial rates of never attending, (17 percent for rural girls and 11 percent for rural boys) but the number of children in this category is small.

Beyond the goal of increasing school initiation rates, the 1986 Law of Compulsory Education had as its goal to increase middle school attendance and graduation. Table 5.2 shows the national progress made toward that goal. Columns 1–4 represent youth aged 15–18 who have attended middle school as a percentage of those youth aged 15–18 who graduated from primary school. In our analysis of the 1990 rates, we found that this transition was the location of most of the exiting from the educational endeavor. Again, there is much to feel good about in this table. Some 88 percent of rural boys and 83 percent of rural girls who finish primary school, go on to attend middle

Table 5.2 Percentage of youth 15–18 years of age who have ever attended middle school of those who graduated from primary school, 2000, and percentage change, 1990 to 2000

	Percentage attended middle school, 2000				Difference 2000–1990			
	Rural boys	Rural girls	Urban boys	Urban girls	Rural boys	Rural girls	Urban boys	Urban girls
Total	88.48	83.30	98.67	98.71	19.39	28.73	1.76	1.14
Age								
15	90.27	85.9	98.88	99.18	17.89	28.56	1.8	1.98
16	89.12	83.64	99.01	98.91	19.83	28.33	1.68	0.6
17	87.83	82.26	98.92	98.72	20.24	28.18	1.88	1.35
18	86.13	80.56	97.88	98.03	19.08	29.05	0.82	0.63
Parents' Education								
Illiterate	64.01	58.47	92.68	93.55	6.35	16.61	4.97	1.7
Primary S	81.84	74.31	95.08	94.33	14.59	23.35	0.52	−1.46
Middle S +	93.88	90	99.04	99.13	11.74	20.35	0.7	0.48
Younger Sib								
0	89.4	83.5	99.12	99.27	21.34	28.68	2.1	1.16
1	88.96	85.25	97.18	98.16	19.46	30.47	−0.03	0.5
2	85.63	81.38	96.15	95.52	16.7	27.39	1.3	−1.4
3+	80.11	77.24	96.97	90.91	10.66	22.68	−0.08	−6.47
Ethnicity								
Han	90.37	85.16	98.79	98.85	20.59	30.06	1.76	1.18
Non-Han	72.81	67.73	97.3	97.02	12.9	20.43	2.15	0.95

school. These numbers are 19 percentage points higher for rural boys and 29 percentage points higher for rural girls than they were 10 years before. Rural girls with one sibling are 30 percentage points more likely to attend middle school than they were in 1990. This change signals a reduction of the gender gap, because the gender gap is exacerbated by rural girls being more likely to have siblings than rural boys.

Table 5.3 considers the transition from graduating from middle school to attending high school. These results are included here because the transition from graduating from middle school to attending high school is the location of significant decision-making for urban youth. Columns 7 and 8 show the substantial gains made by urban youth at this transition point. Urban girls aged 17 or 18 who graduate from middle school (recall that almost all urban youth do graduate from middle school) are 25 percentage points more likely to attend high school in 2000 than they were in 1990. The comparable number for urban boys is 24 percentage points. The only groups to show a decline in this transition are non-Han rural boys and girls. This may be attributable to the larger number of children graduating from middle school. In the past,

Table 5.3 Percentage of youth 17–18 years of age who have ever attended high school of those who graduated from middle school, 2000 and percentage change, 1990 to 2000

	Percentage attended high school, 2000				Difference 2000–1990			
	Rural boys	Rural girls	Urban boys	Urban girls	Rural boys	Rural girls	Urban boys	Urban girls
Total	24.54	20.68	79.39	81.84	4.43	5.13	22.58	25.47
Age								
17	26.44	21.44	83.12	83.66	6.8	5.96	22.76	26.33
18	22.81	20	75.59	80.13	2.29	4.38	22.11	24.66
Parents' Education								
Illiterate	14.65	14.18	42.11	41.18	−1.44	1.7	14.78	13.47
Primary S	18.12	15.58	56.9	62.5	−0.65	2.35	16.12	22.97
Middle S+	28.95	24	81.64	83.81	4.14	3.93	16.62	19.22
Younger Sib								
0	25.98	20.41	82.44	85.8	5.2	4.25	25.08	29.16
1	23.95	22.63	69.37	73.91	5.63	6.39	15.09	16.1
2	21.99	19.28	63.53	68.5	1.43	3.21	16.3	17.57
3+	17.29	15.26	28.57	57.69	−3.27	0.43	−30.74	0.91
Ethnicity								
Han	17.1	18.45	73.85	79.49	5.26	5.56	23.25	25.65
Non-Han	25.23	20.87	79.9	82.03	−5.41	−1.47	14.36	23.3

when graduation rates from middle school were much lower, only the top students would continue and thus, those top students were more likely to transition into high school. Now that graduating from middle school is less selective, it is not surprising that a smaller percentage would go on to high school.

Changes in transition rates across provinces

The analysis of the 1990 data presented in Chapter 4 showed substantial educational differences across provinces and even within provinces. The 2000 results are no different in this regard. There are substantial differences across provinces as shown in Table 5.4. Table 5.4 focuses on rural youth only, as that is the location of most of the variation, except for attending high school. Table 5.4, columns 1–5 show rates of rural youth's educational transitions by province in 2000. Each column uses the number of students who have completed the previous transition as the population. Populations are also limited by age to avoid the problem that some younger students may still be in process. So, for example, column 2 reports the percentage of 15–18-year-olds who finished primary school out of all those who began primary school, and

Table 5.4 Selected conditional educational transitions of rural youth by province, 2000, and percentage change, 1990 to 2000

	Percentage 2000					Difference 2000–1990				
	Ever Attend	Grad P.S	Attend M.S	Grad M.S	Attend H.S	Ever Attend	Grad P.S	Attend M.S	Grad M.S	Attend M.S
Total	99.05	98.22	86.09	87.54	22.82	4.76	11.16	23.62	3.94	4.54
Beijing	99.69	100	95.19	95.1	68.04	0.59	2.34	1.78	-0.73	34.71
Tianjin	100	100	91.63	91.46	14.67	1.35	7.83	12.63	7.17	-12.45
Hebei	99.77	99.7	92.81	83.43	12.7	1.95	3.58	23.77	-10.65	0.01
Shanxi	99.67	99.79	86.74	93.96	25.33	0.95	3.59	19.89	1.17	12.18
Inner Mongolia	99.32	98.18	80.3	89	15.36	3.86	9.82	15.15	7.6	0.64
Liaoning	99.78	99.36	86.79	93.62	19.42	0.6	4.99	14.75	14.74	2.5
Jilin	99.6	98.48	79.23	84.5	16.16	1.54	8.1	14.73	13.63	6.72
Heilongjiang	99.19	98.4	82.45	88.86	8	1.51	9.95	19.35	14.94	-17.68
Shanghai	99.74	100	94.31	100	52.46	0.08	4.23	-0.87	17.95	28.5
Jiangsu	99.68	99.23	92.02	94.83	23.73	1.33	6.13	19.01	9.04	4.6
Zhejiang	99.69	99.71	97.12	96.76	37.96	1.53	8.47	25.47	9.26	16.35
Anhui	99.66	99.39	88.88	83.01	12.1	9.55	18.9	30.4	1.62	-0.42
Fujian	99.8	99.38	93.03	91.94	26.12	4.8	22.26	34.04	21.22	0.34
Jiangxi	99.46	98.56	88.12	87.3	20.52	5.1	23.1	27.86	14.03	-4.4
Shandong	99.56	99.3	89.57	87.99	21.85	2.73	4.51	23.52	-5.65	7.42
Henan	99.83	99.37	91.4	90.13	22.56	3.73	4.64	31.1	-0.63	8.49
Hubei	99.68	99.31	85.23	93.19	18.83	2.55	14.24	21.72	15.17	-3.71
Hunan	99.76	99.42	88.55	94.6	30.79	1.91	12.71	25.37	16.75	5
Guangdong	99.77	98.71	89.92	78.87	32.16	1.82	13.92	25.05	-4.34	12.42
Guangxi	99.59	96.59	79.03	82.52	21.67	4.19	13.87	31.66	-0.53	5.87
Hainan	98.62	97	85.57	69.87	17.43	2.25	15.57	12.24	-6.03	-9.55
Chong Qing	99.51	99.24	83.11	91.14	29.17	NA	NA	NA	NA	NA

Sichuan	97.64	98.37	79.99	92.59	16.99	1.78	11.24	26.36	16.33	-0.4
Guizhou	96.3	87.61	68.94	61.52	11.16	14.6	19.88	13.61	-14.37	-2.38
Yunnan	97.27	93.34	64	80.04	22.54	16.12	23.53	9.1	5.97	-4.46
Shaanxi	99.51	98.69	87.63	85.66	36.69	6.78	11.14	18.7	2.33	14.12
Gansu	95.94	97.28	78.28	82.25	29.5	18.65	17.19	13.63	-3.71	3.76
Qinghai	85.59	89.44	65.22	95.83	13.04	32.87	15.31	-0.82	10.83	-22.25
Ningxia	95.09	91.16	78.85	83.52	30.26	21.12	10.67	6.12	6.38	0.63
Xinjiang	98.86	98.13	78.39	85.54	23.74	3.44	8.3	19.48	-5.81	-11.17
Tibet	56.68	80.82	32.2	57.14	25	37.71	40.82	12.2	NA	NA

Note: The sample for each progressive transition only includes those youth who have completed the last transition. In addition, the sample potentially graduated from primary school and attending middle school is limited to youth aged 15–18 and the sample potentially graduated from middle school and attending high school is limited to youth 17 and 18 years of age. Also note that data for Chongqing are not available, since in 1990 Chongqing was part of Sichuan. This also means that the change in Sichuan is not precisely accurate since the rates in 1990 include rural Chongqing and the rates in 2000 exclude rural Chongqing. Since areas around large cities often have higher incomes it is probably the case that the included rural Chongqing residents had higher enrollment rates than those in other parts of Sichuan, implying that the differences in rates for Sichuan between 1990 and 2000 are likely to be underestimates. The rates for higher levels of education in Tibet were not available in 1990 because of the very limited cell sizes.

column 3 reports the percentage of 15–18-year-olds who began middle school out of all those who finished primary school. Across the provinces, we can see substantial differences in these transition rates. For example, comparing rural youth in Yunnan and Sichuan, youth in both provinces had a high rate of initial attendance, 97.27 percent and 97.64 percent respectively, and similar rates of graduating from primary school, 93.34 percent versus 98.37 percent. However, these provinces exhibited a substantial difference in attending middle school conditional on primary school completion: 64 percent versus 79.99 percent. Students who started middle school in Yunnan were also less likely to finish as those students from Sichuan, with completion rates of 80.04 percent for Yunnan and 92.59 percent for Sichuan. Of the students who graduated middle school, a larger percentage go on to high school from Yunnan, 22.54 percent, compared with 16.99 percent from Sichuan. As we discussed above, this may be the result of the Yunnan students being more self-selected, since the previous transition rates were lower.

Table 5.4, columns 6–10 highlight differences in the percentage change in educational transitions across provinces. In a few categories in a few provinces, negative numbers appear, indicating that the rates were lower in 2000 than 1990. All the incidences of negative rates appear in the last two columns, where the issue of changing levels of self-selection are the greatest. Another possible cause for the higher level transitions is that some of the rural youth have already migrated away from these areas. Finally, the negative transitions may also be real, if they reflect increasing opportunity cost of youths' time, as rural youth continue to migrate to urban and southern coastal areas in larger and larger numbers over this ten-year period.

The gender gap across provinces

Table 5.5 presents the difference between rural boys and girls transition rate to middle school by province for 1990 and 2000, as the biggest gender gaps are generally found in rural decisions to attend middle school. Positive numbers mean the rate is higher for boys than girls. Negative numbers mean the rate is higher for girls. In general, the gender gap by province has narrowed substantially over this ten year period. By comparing columns 1 and 2, we see that substantial progress has been made in narrowing the gap in provinces which had the largest gaps in 1990. Some provinces still show substantial (albeit narrowing) gaps in 2000. In Guizhou, boys who finished primary school are 14 percentage points more likely to attend middle school than girls. Other provinces with large gaps at the point of middle school attendance in 2000 are Gansu, Jiangxi, and Shandong.

Conclusion

Evidence provided in this chapter shows that substantial progress has been made in attaining the Chinese national government's goal of universal

Table 5.5 Comparison of rural gender gap by province in attending middle school, 1990 and 2000

	1990 *Difference in rural boys and girls percentage attending middle school*	*2000* *Difference in rural boys and girls percentage attending middle school*
Beijing	5.75	−2.68
Tianjin	−3.69	1.1
Hebei	7.46	1.56
Shanxi	3.86	4.66
Inner Mongolia	9.88	4.39
Liaoning	−0.32	1.19
Jilin	3.58	3.12
Heilongjiang	3.34	1.47
Shanghai	−1.82	2.66
Jiangsu	17.61	7.01
Zhejiang	13.95	2.08
Anhui	23.14	10.1
Fujian	17.02	6.1
Jiangxi	24.95	12.44
Shandong	18.53	8.05
Henan	14.55	4.75
Hubei	19.65	7.14
Hunan	16.6	1.79
Guangdong	25.64	7.3
Guangxi	15.31	3.91
Hainan	0	3.78
Chong Qing	NA	3.32
Sichuan	18.09	4.85
Guizhou	20.72	13.95
Yunnan	14.62	6.44
Shaanxi	0	−2.08
Tibet	8.51	0.82
Gansu	13.89	10.29
Qinghai	−2.39	−4.35
Ningxia	13.63	8.9
Xinjiang	−1.79	5.99

Note: A positive number means the rate is higher for boys than girls. A negative number means the rate is higher for girls.

education for all children through the ninth grade. An increase in enrollment and graduation rates was seen in every province at every age level. While there is still a large rural–urban gap in the probability of finishing ninth grade, that gap has narrowed over the ten-year period from 1990 to 2000. By the time of the 2000 census, the probability of finishing middle school, given that one begins middle school, is 87 percent for rural boys and 88 percent for rural girls. The gap between rural boys' and rural girls' educational attainment has also narrowed substantially over this period.

Of course, there is still room for improvement and there are still areas of concern. Increasing local fees for education cause hardship for poor, cash-strapped farmers in many rural areas and jobs in urban areas continue to pull some rural youth out of middle school. In addition, while rural areas have made great strides in graduating students from middle school, urban areas have increased the number of students attending senior high school or vocational school. This has led to an even larger gap in attending high school between urban and rural dwellers. These are among the challenges Chinese local officials and national leaders need to face in the future as well as the challenge of increased migration to urban areas which makes the rural–urban education gap even more important as many of those rural educated young people will become a potential underclass of urban residents in the next few decades.

Reference

National Bureau of Statistics (2005) *China Statistical Yearbook 2005*, Beijing: China Statistics Press.

6 School access in rural Tibet

Gerard A. Postiglione

Introduction and rationale

China's ethnic minority population of over 110 million has enjoyed dramatic educational gains in the years since the beginning of the reform era, but most minority ethnic groups still have levels of literacy and educational attainment that are below the national average (N.A. 2000). Fourteen years after the Law on Compulsory Education came into force in 1986, only 85 percent of the Chinese population found themselves covered by the nine-year compulsory education provision (N.A. 2003). The remaining portion of the population, especially from the western regions of China, included diverse ethnic cultures, and new market forces presented significant challenges to the stated policy goals of universal access to basic education (see, for example, N.A. 2000c; N.A. 2001b).

This chapter uses a case study of rural Tibet to focus attention on school access issues facing many of the largely rural ethnic minority populations in China. While Tibet is in some respects unique among minority regions in China, it does illustrate significant links between the economy and the culture that cross the boundaries of region, school, and family. The chapter begins with an overview of ethnic minority education in China and a discussion of related policies and problems in different minority regions. Within this context, the chapter reviews selected educational issues in Tibet and then focuses on findings from a field study of one rural county. The chapter looks at family, school, and community influences on educational opportunities and presents results with four organizing themes in mind: (1) social equality; (2) economic development; (3) cultural autonomy; and (4) national unity. Results suggest a number of measures that could further improve school participation rates in Tibet and elsewhere, these measures are discussed in the final section of the chapter.

Minority education in China

Indigenous minorities residing in remote regions of developing countries usually attain literacy and basic education later than the mainstream population

(McDermott 1987; Trueba *et al.* 1989). In fact, the challenge of ethnic minority education in developing countries, especially for girls, has become a matter of international urgency (UNESCO 2000). Modern states are now expected to ensure educational access and equity for all. The cultural dimensions of ethnic minority education, particularly language and religion, increase the complexity of the task at a time when globalization has increased the salience of regional cultures (Berberoglu 1995; Friedman 1997; Smith 1997). This is especially true for China.

The demand by ethnic minorities for schools to elevate the status of their culture within the national framework has become ubiquitous. Yet, the content of schooling reflects the state's view of the nature of ethnic inter-group processes. This view is evident in Fei Xiaotong's influential concept of *duoyuan yiti geju*—plurality and unity within the configuration of the Chinese nation—which delineates a process by which all ethnic group cultures move toward a unified national culture (Fei 1991). China's state schools conserve a particular brand of national culture (*zhonghua minzu wenhua*). In short, they are challenged by the responsibility to conserve ethnic minority cultures within a national context that places a premium on Han Chinese cultural capital (Heberer 1989; Gladney 1991; Dikotter 1992; Mackerras 1994, 1995; Harrell 1996; Liu and Faure 1996). This responsibility includes educating ethnic minorities, adequately and accurately representing their ethnic heritage, linking the content of schooling to their cultural values and beliefs, socializing them into a national identity, ensuring equitable educational and work opportunities, and linking minority education to economic development of minority communities.

The size, distribution, and diversity of China's ethnic minority populations make fulfilling these responsibilities a daunting task. China's minorities are widely distributed across the country, with 33.4 percent residing in the southwest, 27.3 percent occupying five west-central provinces, 20.7 percent living in five northwest provinces, and only 17.4 percent spread around the eastern regions of the country (Xia 2001: 9). China's minorities can be differentiated according to a number of criteria: population size; the nature of group identifications; inter-group cultural and linguistic diversity; the strength of religious traditions; family values, size, structure, and gender ideology; use of a written and/or spoken language; the size, location, and terrain of the region(s) the group occupies; the proportion that inhabits an autonomous province, prefecture, county, or town; proximity to and relationship with other ethnic groups, including the Han; whether any neighboring Han are migrants or indigenous residents; whether the group is urban or rural, agricultural or pastoral, border or inland, or concentrated or dispersed; whether members of the group's ethnic nationality also live across the border in other countries, either as minorities or the principal nationality; whether the group has a significant overseas or refugee community; and finally, whether the group has a separate tradition of foreign relations with peoples of another part of the world (Postiglione 2000).

Given minority groups' cultural, regional, and developmental differences, China has had to take care not to respond to their educational needs as if they were a single entity. Rather, national minority educational policies are supposed to be designed to be implemented flexibly to account for the unique conditions faced in different minority regions. Practice, however, is another matter, as policies may be interpreted by the agenda of the regional leader in power at any particular period of time. The degree of autonomy practiced in educational matters by ethnic minorities is still an issue for research and investigation.

Nevertheless, the government has made development in its western regions a top priority for the new century. Domestic and internationally sponsored development projects are focusing more on minority education, especially nine-year compulsory education. The state has implemented a number of measures to improve educational access and decrease dropout rates for ethnic minorities. For instance, special subsidies for education are provided in minority regions and boarding schools have been built when the distance between home and school affects attendance. Also, native-language teaching, including the provision of textbooks in minority languages, is supported through secondary school for some minorities; in all, 21 languages are being used in the schools attended by ethnic minorities. Beyond the level of compulsory education, minorities are eligible to have points added to their examination scores (*jiafen*), especially for college and university, and exams may be taken in some minority languages. Remedial classes (*yuke ban*) are arranged for minority freshmen in some key point universities. Nationality schools and colleges, including ethnic minority teacher training colleges, are provided and subsidized (Guo and Wei 1995).

Aside from policies specifically designed for ethnic minorities, there are other measures intended to improve school access and quality in poor, rural areas. The State Council in 2003 held the first national working conference since 1949 to formulate plans for the development of education in rural areas. The document that resulted from the meeting, "Decisions of the State Council to Further Strengthen Education in Rural Areas," reaffirmed the importance of education in rural areas to the construction of an affluent society. The document proposed to strengthen efforts to achieve the "two basics" and improve the quality of nine-year compulsory education in 372 counties in western China within five years. It also reaffirmed the role of vocational and adult education to solve problems of agriculture in rural areas. Among the more specific proposals are the implementation of a county-centered management system of compulsory education to improve the mechanism that guarantees education funds, and the establishment of a sound system that provides full sponsorship for the education of poor students and protects the right of school-aged children in rural areas to receive compulsory education. The document further specified that, by 2007, all poor students receiving compulsory education would be exempt from miscellaneous fees and textbook charges and would receive lodging allowances. The "Decisions" also included provisions to speed up the reform of personnel systems in schools, improve teacher quality, implement distance-education programs, strengthen leadership, and mobilize society to support rural education.

Despite the policy–practice gap, certain successes have been achieved. The numbers of ethnic minority students attending all levels of the education system have continually increased, and numbers of several of the 55 officially designated minorities stand above the national average, including the Koreans, Russians, Daurs, Mans, Ewenkis, Elunquns, Tatars, and Xibes (N.A. 1995). Yet, only in primary schools and middle-level teacher training colleges (for training primary school teachers) are ethnic minority teacher and student enrollments proportionate to their size in the national population (see Tables 6.1 and 6.2; see also N.A. 1986: 5, 9, 16, 17; N.A. 1997; N.A. 2000a).

Further, persistent educational problems are not always reflected in official statistics. For example, according to Ministry of Education data, in eight western provinces and regions with large ethnic minority populations, including Inner Mongolia, Xinjiang, Tibet, Qinghai, Ningxia, Guangxi, Guizhou, and Yunnan, 93.62 percent of minority children of primary school age were attending in 1996 (see World Bank 2004). Although 12 years of schooling was virtually universalized in Beijing and Shanghai by the beginning of the twenty-first century, the education system in rural areas struggled to provide six to nine years of basic education. Some rural areas had to endure run-down schools, inadequately prepared teachers, unattractive teaching materials, inefficient school management, inadequate community participation and support, and high dropout and repetition rates. Whereas 16 provinces in eastern China had an enrollment rate of 99.5 percent, those in the northwest and southwest remained below this mark. In Tibet, for example, the percentage of the relevant age group that was enrolled in school for basic education was 81.3 percent in 1998 (Xia *et al.* 1999: 71). However, official figures on enrollment mask high dropout rates. The scope of gender disparities—and even the existence of gender disparities—also differ between advanced coastal areas and poor and remote areas of northwest and southwest China (for example, see Connelly and Zheng's Chapters 4 and 5 in this volume).

China's civilizing project of national schooling in ethnic minority regions is challenged by factors both common to all regions and specific to some ethnic communities. Part of the story is linked directly to the poverty of many minority areas. As market forces begin to take hold, students are pulled away from school, family, and community by new income opportunities, making lack of attendance and discontinuation serious problems. Other factors include the importance of children's contribution to household labor, the inability of parents to pay school fees, the distance from home to school, the irrelevance of curriculum to rural life, the poor conditions of some schools, and a lack of trained teachers, in particular those needed for ethnic minority native-language teaching (Postiglione *et al.* 1995).

Part of the story is also cultural, as minority groups can show resistance to

Table 6.1 Number of minority students (×10,000) and their percentage of the national population at different levels of the education system in 1980, 1985, 1996, 1999, and 2003

	1980	*1985*	*1996*	*1999*	*2003*
Kindergarten	47,426	341,784	883,200	818,500	1,177,500
Percentage	0.41	2.31	3.31	3.52	5.88
Special Schools	521[a]	786[a]	11,100	11,700	25,600
Percentage	1.57	1.87	3.47	3.15	7.01
Primary Schools	7,522,153	9,548,050	12,510,700	12,141,800	11,207,000
Percentage	5.14	7.14	9.19	8.96	9.59
Vocational Schools	14,592	87,445	245,700	241,500	652,300
Percentage	3.21	3.80	5.19	4.52	17.38
Junior Secondary	–	–	–	–	87,400
Percentage	–	–	–	–	12.07
Senior Secondary	–	–	–	–	564,900
Percentage	–	–	–	–	5.31
General Sec. Schools	1,992,954	2,244,707	3,701,900	4,632,900	6,544,600
Percentage	3.61	4.76	6.45	6.84	14.47
Junior Secondary	–	–	–	–	5,263,300
Percentage	–	–	–	–	7.95
Senior Secondary	–	–	–	–	1,281,300
Percentage	–	–	–	–	6.52
Teacher Training Schools	44,669	49,825	90,200	97,100	–
Percentage	9.26	8.92	10.25	10.72	
Technical Schools	39,312	66,491	210,500	279,600	–
Percentage	5.16	6.40	6.29	6.58	
Tertiary Education	42,944	94,095	196,800	247,700	697,600
Percentage	3.75	5.52	6.51	6.06	6.55
Post-graduate	356	1,550	–	–	–
Percentage	1.64	1.77			

Sources: *Achievements of Education in China 1980–85* (1986); *Essential Statistics in Education in China* (1997); *Educational Statistics Yearbook of China* (2000).

Note: [a] Defined as schools for the deaf and blind.

aspects of schooling that encroach upon their ethnic culture and identity formation, and, at the same time, do not yield promised economic rewards (see, for example, Gladney 1999). In fact, the ability of state-sponsored minority education to address the cultural and economic dimensions of school access is crucial to its success, making this an area of growing interest in China (N.A. 2000c; Ha and Teng 2001). Despite this interest, however, little literature in China subscribes to the cultural discontinuity hypothesis—or the idea that poor academic performance among some minority groups is largely due to cultural and linguistic differences between their home environment

Table 6.2 Number of minority teachers (×10,000) and their percentage of the national population at different levels of the education system in 1980, 1985, 1996, 1999, and 2003

	1980	1985	1996	1999	2003
Kindergarten	6,783	14,697	33,200	323,000	26,200
Percentage	1.65	2.67	3.74	3.70	4.28
Special Schools	125[a]	209[a]	1,600	1,600	1,500
Percentage	2.60	2.86	6.08	5.06	5.09
Primary Schools	329,371	397,770	515,500	545,100	570,900
Percentage	5.98	7.39	8.99	9.30	10.01
Vocational Schools	739	5,551	18,200	16,200	30,900
Percentage	3.21	3.93	5.91	5.02	14.70
Junior Secondary	–	–	–	–	3,000
Percentage	–	–	–	–	9.72
Senior Secondary	–	–	–	–	27,900
Percentage	–	–	–	–	4.98
General Sec. Schools	112,331	125,560	233,400	271,400	333,400
Percentage	3.71	4.73	6.74	7.07	13.89
Junior Secondary	–	–	–	–	267,300
Percentage	–	–	–	–	7.71
Senior Secondary	–	–	–	–	66,100
Percentage	–	–	–	–	6.18
Teacher Training Schools	2,570	3,178	6,000	6,100	–
Percentage	6.94	6.9	9.53	9.89	
Technical Schools	3,517	5,985	12,200	12,500	–
Percentage	3.86	4.67	5.98	5.91	
Tertiary Education	7,808	12,775	22,000	23,300	36,300
Percentage	3.16	3.71	5.46	5.46	5.01
Post-graduate	–	–	–	No fig.	–

Sources: *Achievements of Education in China 1980–85* (1986); *Essential Statistics in Education in China* (1997); *Educational Statistics Yearbook of China* (2000).

Note: [a] Defined as schools for the deaf and blind.

and the school environment in which they are expected to learn the values of the dominant majority. Instead, the literature tends to blame poor perform-ance on the "low cultural level" of certain ethnic groups. Although some Western literature criticizes China's education system for its neglect of minor-ity cultures, several Han Chinese scholars have pointed out that this Western view fails to explain why about ten minorities in China do better education-ally than the Han majority. John Ogbu's work in the United States adds nuance to this perspective, noting the distinction between voluntary minor-ities, or those who emigrate out of choice to a new place, and involuntary minorities, or those who are indigenous to a region (e.g. Ogbu 1991). The logic is that voluntary minorities are more disposed to accept the new society and its education system, while indigenous minorities may resist state schooling and develop an oppositional identity in the face of pressure to assimilate on unequal terms. Resistance will be particularly strong if indigenous minorities view the education system as a way to strip them of their own culture and identity without giving them equal opportunity in the wider society. If, on the other hand, indigenous minorities believe they can use education to achieve success, they will often surmount the obstacles posed by cultural divergencies.

Recent literature on ethnic minority education in China lends some credence to this logic. For instance, Mackerras (1999) raised the possibility that the revival of ethnic minority culture may be in part a reaction to the expansion of state schooling, which challenges the value systems of ethnic minorities. Gladney (1999) has pointed out that Han Chinese often view minority culture as backward and minority religious education as lacking value— perceptions that result in a marginalization of minorities. Stites (1999) notes that China's need to produce a viable system of bilingual education has been hampered because ethnic minority languages are "not entirely autonomous systems that can be easily engineered to promote the central government's goals for social, political and economic development." Sautman (1999) believes that efforts to "Sinicize" (*Hanhua*) the origins and identities of minority peoples result in opposition to educational efforts that recognize the special characteristics of minorities, that favor regionally autonomous policies, and that give minorities preferences in admission to higher education. Harrell and Ma's (1999) research on the Yi highlights the damage done by the civilizing mission of an education system that treats ethnic minority culture as backward (*luohou*), and shows the key role of minority teachers in helping the Yi to outperform the Han in school. Hansen's (1999) research takes a similar position by showing in detail how the civilizing project resulted in schools teaching the Tai people in southwest China that they are members of a backward minority group. Upton's (1999) examination of Tibetans in Sichuan province finds that, despite Western criticism, Tibetan language textbooks contain a fair amount of content relevant to Tibetan cultural life, though not as much as Tibetans crave. She writes that "forceful lessons about Tibetan culture can be taught to students through lessons that derive from works that are culturally and historically distinct." Though Harrell and Ma's (1999) research emphasizes the civilizing mission of state-sponsored minority education, they also draw important lessons from Ogbu's folk theory of success, by which they explain why some sectors of the Yi population actually outperform their Han Chinese neighbors.

Thus, the literature reveals differing interpretations of ethnic minority educational access in China and highlights a growing tension among four interrelated themes: social equality, economic development, cultural autonomy, and national unity. The literature emphasizes the sociological link between culture and economic development within the national context, and makes it clear that education and social development policies that ignore this link are doomed to fail. National policies for economic development have led to uneven patterns, especially in minority regions. If ethnic minorities associate school participation with a high likelihood of economic success—success that might improve their status and power within the national mainstream—then the probability of attendance will be higher. However, since ethnic minority regions are usually located in poor regions where economic opportunities are minimal, tendencies to resist schooling, or merely to assign it a low priority, are also possible.

Education can be a key mechanism to build national unity. However, to do so, it must bring sufficient numbers of ethnic minority students into the upper levels of the education system. National policies for ethnic minority education aim to do this through a number of measures, including boarding schools, bilingual education, ethnic minority teacher training, preferential admission policies, and special subsidies. Despite these policies, improving educational access often clashes with the theme of cultural autonomy, and using education to serve economic development has not always led to stronger national integration.

In the remainder of this chapter, we consider how state policies and economic and cultural factors interact to affect educational participation among Tibetans in a rural community of the Tibetan Autonomous Region (TAR). In the pages that follow, I provide an overview of the situation in Tibet, emphasizing the overall educational context, the educational problems, and the educational policies. We then draw on fieldwork in one county to offer a more detailed investigation of household perspectives on rural schools, and of factors affecting rural school attendance and discontinuance.

The Tibetan case

Context

The Tibetan Autonomous Region, at 1.2 million square kilometers, comprises 12.5 percent of the area of China, but it is home to only 0.002 percent of the population (Zhang 1995). In many ways, Tibet is remote from mainstream China. Tibetans possess a distinctive culture dating back more than a thousand years, with a complex religious tradition and writing system (Goldstein 1989, 1997; Smith 1996). Tibet's population lives at extraordinarily high altitudes, predominantly plateau, averaging 3,600 meters above sea level and surrounded by mountains. Tibetans are dispersed across a region that stretches far beyond the TAR; more Tibetans live in the surrounding provinces of Sichuan, Qinghai, Gansu, and Yunnan than in the TAR. All told, they occupy 3.8 million square kilometers of China—an area about half the size of the United States.

Although Beijing assumed responsibility for the management of Tibet in 1951, little changed in the traditional feudal structure of Tibet until the Dalai Lama fled after the uprising in 1959 and there was an in-migration of larger numbers of non-Tibetan officials. The TAR was established in 1965, and land was redistributed and administered by People's Communes (Grunfeld 1996). The Cultural Revolution wrought havoc and destruction, and was followed by an admission of errors after the death of Chairman Mao and the rise of Deng Xiaoping. Communes were abandoned in 1984. Despite the popular image of Tibetans as nomadic herders, the proportions of Tibetans engaged in agriculture and herding have been in dispute. However, only about 10 percent of TAR Tibetans live in urban regions (Iredale *et al.* 2001).

The TAR is more ethnically homogenous than any other provincial-level entity in China, with an estimated 95.5 percent of the 1990 population being ethnic Tibetan (Iredale *et al.* 2001: 138–139; N.A. 2001a). This proportion far exceeds the homogeneity of key nationalities in China's four other autonomous regions: 48 percent Uighur in the Xinjiang Uighur Autonomous Region, 33 percent Hui in the Ningxia Hui Autonomous Region, 35 percent Zhuang in the Guangxi Zhuang Autonomous Region, and 15 percent Mongol in the Mongol Autonomous Region (Economic and Development Department of the State Ethnic Affairs Commission and Department of Integrated Statistics of the State Statistical Bureau 1998: 302). However, the Han Chinese population of Tibet is growing rapidly. TAR Tibetans comprise about half of the population of the capital city of Lhasa, and the proportion of Tibetans in the entire TAR population declined to 92 percent in 2000 (N.A. 2001a).

Education policies

Monastery education dominated before 1951, and still exerts a strong influence. The first modern school in Lhasa was established in 1951. The Seventeen Point agreement signed between the Tibetans and Chinese in 1951 stated that: "the spoken and written language and the school education of the Tibetan nationality shall be developed step by step in accordance with the actual conditions of Tibet" (Sino-Tibetan Agreement 1951). This agreement permitted monasteries to remain the principal educational institutions. Many children of the wealthy elite were sent for cadre training in Beijing and elsewhere. By 1959, shortly after the Dali Lama fled to India, Tibet's educational system was brought closer in line with the rest of China. Nevertheless, monastery education, with its emphasis on recitation of the scriptures, still exerts a strong influence on modern education (Mackerras 1999).

The gradualist approach to minority education was abandoned during the Great Leap period, when the Preparatory Committee for the Establishment of the TAR emphasized the establishment of community schools, many of which were later closed due to their poor quality (N.A. 1999). Expansion occurred quickly after 1965 and leveled off in 1978, when the emphasis shifted from quantity to quality. With the dissolution of the communes in 1984, many parents withdrew their children from school to labor in the household. The open policy after the Cultural Revolution also led many children to attend monasteries instead of the poor and under-staffed state schools (Bass 1998: 215; Geng and Wang 1989).

Throughout the years, Tibet remained several steps behind other parts of China in the development of modern educational institutions. Most notably, there has been a lack of qualified teachers. In Tibet, by 1998, the percentages of teachers with appropriate qualifications were 63 percent in upper secondary, 72 percent in lower secondary, and 59 percent in primary school (Xia *et al.* 1999). To improve the teaching force, an upper limit of 2,000 substitute (*daike*) teachers was set in 2000. At the same time, plans called for training 10,000 teachers between 1995 and 2003. This figure included 550 in higher education, 400 in middle-level specialized schools, 750 in senior secondary, 2,600 in junior secondary, and 5,700 in primary school. In the meantime, 1,377 *minban* teachers were to receive training (Xia *et al.* 1999).

At the First Tibet Work Forum in 1980, many Han cadres were transferred out and those who remained were told to study Tibetan language. Tibetan was to be the first language of education and public life; however, today the Chinese language dominates government and public organizational life. The Second Work Forum in 1984 extended Tibetan medium instruction into secondary school, while also sending Tibetan secondary students to schools in other parts of China, and recruiting teachers from around the country to come to Tibet (Bass 1998: 215).

The Third Education Work Meeting in 1987 emphasized the improvement of teacher training, and of education management in government-sponsored schools (N.A. 1999: 62). The Fourth Education Work Meeting in 1993, along with the Fifth the following year, emphasized local responsibility for education, and the separation of school management levels. The new plan meant that the village would manage lower primary schools, the township would manage upper primary schools, and the county would manage secondary schools. The enrollment target for 2000 was 80 percent, with three years of compulsory education popularized in the remote nomadic areas, six years in the agricultural areas, and nine years in the city (N.A. 1999: 64). The Fifth Education Work Meeting in 1994 supported consolidation and boarding schools to improve quality. It also aimed to strengthen the teaching force and the quality of teaching, eliminate the *minban* schools and convert *minban* teachers to *gongban* teachers (N.A. 1999: 64).

Urban regions benefited more than the rest of the TAR from these improvements, and this is particularly reflected in the dropout rate from primary school. Catriona Bass has pointed out that while the TAR media and government information suggest a severe dropout problem, official statistics report relatively low dropout rates. Bass cites a variety of reasons for high rates of school leaving. These include inadequate provision of school places, low teacher quality, long distances between homes and schools, irrelevant curricula, lack of textbooks, and labor shortages in households (Bass 1998: 78–80). Challenges particular to Tibet include the language of instruction and the strength of religious practice. Few village people can speak Chinese, and religion surrounds most aspects of daily life. Children who are able to progress from the village lower primary school through the township upper primary school have to spend an entire year in the county junior secondary school studying Chinese before they begin their regular study.

It is not surprising that by 1990, less than 20 percent of the TAR Tibetans had a primary education and few had much more. By the end of the century, illiteracy and semi-literacy stood slightly above 50 percent, and enrollment in junior secondary school stood below 25 percent. Urban enrollment is high, but many remote regions have only universalized three-year compulsory education (N.A. 2001a).

By 2000, around the time this research was conducted, the TAR had more than 4,000 schools: 820 primary and secondary schools, 3,033 teaching points (or incomplete primary schools), 110 regular and vocational secondary schools, and 4 institutions of higher education. These schools served about 360,000 TAR students in all forms and levels of education, and were staffed by about 19,000 teachers. The rate of qualified teachers at the primary, middle, and upper secondary schools was 67 percent, 77 percent, and 75 percent, respectively. The official figures for 2000 indicate that 6 percent of the region's population had achieved nine-year compulsory education, largely in the urban areas where most of the Han reside, 70 percent had achieved six-year compulsory education, and 22 percent had achieved or nearly achieved three-year compulsory education (N.A. 2001a).

As a group, TAR Tibetans have one of the lowest education levels in the country. The official enrollment rate for all school-aged children in basic education was 83.4 percent in 1999, surpassing the 80 percent target set for 2000 (N.A. 2001a).

A number of China's educational policies apply specifically to Tibet, the best-known of which are the three-guarantees (*sanbao*) policy, which provided for free tuition, food, and lodging for all children at school, and the inland school policy (*neidi xizang ban*), which sends primary school graduates to secondary schools in 19 provinces, autonomous regions, and municipalities of China. In addition, there are other measures that apply to all ethnic minority regions, including bilingual education, boarding schools in nomadic areas, and ethnic minority teacher training. Despite these policies, however, efforts to improve educational access have often clashed with issues of cultural autonomy. Using education to serve economic development has not always led to stronger national integration. Since most Tibetans live in rural areas, further investigation into the regional context is needed to better understand how family perspectives relate to increased educational access and participation.

Research site

The region of study was the county of Penam (*Bailang*), on the southern banks of the Yarlong River, about 290 kilometers from Lhasa. The county was formally established in August 1959 and encompasses about 2,460 square kilometers. The county seat has a post office, bank, school, hospital, theater, and other services. Tibetans account for 99.82 percent of the population of about 40,000, which is spread over 11 townships, including two herding townships, and 113 villages. The entire area consists of a small amount of cultivated arable land surrounded by grasslands and forested area. The county's altitude ranges from 3,850 to 5,300 meters, with three mountains above 5,700 meters. Its semi-nomadic, semi-rural inhabitants produce barley, spring and winter wheat, potatoes, peas, and rapeseed, and the local economy also depends in some way or another on yaks, oxen, horses, donkeys, mountain goats, sheep, and pigs. Fish are also plentiful and forest resources support traditional family-produced handicrafts and grain oil products. Other locally produced goods include boots, mattresses, perfume, and fertilizer. The township where I spent most of my time hugs a tributary of the Nianchu River. It is located in the middle of a deep 24-km-long ravine.

At the turn of the twenty-first century, Penam's 40,000-plus inhabitants had 68 schools, including one county middle school, one county primary school, 55 teaching points, 344 educational workers, and 285 teachers. The official figures provided by the county education department were that, of Penam's 7,305 students, 450 attended secondary schools and 6,855 were in primary school, attending central primary schools (3,648) or teaching points (3,207). The official gross enrollment rate provided for the county was 90.2 percent, though my fieldwork led me to view this figure as highly inflated.

The township where the fieldwork took place had 11 administrative villages, with 589 households and 4,556 people (2,277 males and 2,279 females). There were seven village-based schools with 567 students, plus one central primary school with 241 students. The *sanbao* policy (covering school, boarding, and meals) was cancelled in 1997, and parents were required to pay a portion of the book fees.

The historical development of education in the township helps explain the state of education at the turn of this century. The first period of this township's school development under the new government control was from 1960 to 1966, when seven *minban* schools were built. During the second phase of development—the communal period from 1967 to 1980—each production team had a school, and the total number increased to 10. By 1979, the official figure provided for enrollment rate was 79 percent, or about 300 students.

The third period was 1981 to 1992, when the rural production responsibility system began, and children were needed in family production. The township population increased by 18.5 percent from 1980 to 1991, and the total enrollment rate dropped to 35.7 percent, or 728 students, which included only 11.4 percent of all school-age girls. Three schools were consolidated during this period (Jiacuo 1995).

School non-enrollment and discontinuation were major challenges during the land reform period of the early 1980s that broke down the commune system established during the Cultural Revolution. There was little incentive to send children to school that were poorly managed with few trained teachers. Beginning in 1985, the county government began to institute new measures that included better salaries for *minban* teachers. By 1989, the township government had set up a system of rules and regulations (*guizhang zhidu*), which included fines for not attending school. However, these were ineffective in decreasing the school dropout rate. As one official put it, "People did as they pleased and there was not even a party organization."

In 1984, the county used 6,969 *yuan* to build the Sukang School—the township central primary school. In 1992, the township built a 100-sqm school in Tingzhuo village; it had two rooms, one of which was an office. In 1992, 260 students attended Sukang Central Primary School. It had 8 teachers in 9 rooms, 32 sets of desks and chairs, 10 blackboards, and 3 recorders, with no ink, pens, paper, or maps. The schools had a little land, so they planted and sold barley.

Of the township's 4,136 residents in 1990, one had a middle-level specialized education, eight had a junior secondary education, and 463 had some primary schooling. Five percent of residents over the age of six were literate. At that time, parents with four children had to send three to school; those with three children had to send two to school. In China, primary school age is usually seven to 12 years, but in rural Tibet, children begin primary school later and some graduate at about 17 years of age. Less than half (45 percent) of all students passed their exams in 1990. Of 50 students, about 16 went on to either the Dujing township or Penam county middle school. Most township residents seem to consider it enough to have only a few years of education, but those who finished school would often become illiterate after several years. In 30 years, 1,500 residents attended township schools, but only 471 received education above primary level, and 68 percent became illiterate again. Ten percent of the graduates became Lamas or Nigu (nuns) after graduation (four of the county's 20 monasteries are in the township). In 1990, the township also provided some adult education, largely for women. It was initially organized in three night schools, but two soon closed for lack of students. Sukang Central Primary School became the sole night school for adult literacy classes. Staffed by *minban* teachers, it was supported by the Township Women's Federation and the Village Committee. Newspaper reading was the primary method used. If someone did not do homework, they were fined five *mao*. This money was used to keep the school open. In 1985, there were penalties for missing school of 15 *yuan* (the first semester of primary one) and 20 *yuan* (for the second semester).

By the late 1990s, the regional government aimed to greatly increase school enrollments, but obstacles remained. The township suffered from a lack of basic infrastructure (power and roads), health and medical resources, and other basic services. The schools were located at a distance from population centers, had insufficient resources, and lacked trained teachers. Although instruction in Tibetan language helped integrate schooling to the indigenous culture, other aspects of daily life, including local agriculture and animal husbandry practices, religious beliefs, and many common cultural traditions, were unrelated to school life. The main challenge for the education system was to increase the villagers' commitment to the schools, in terms of their children's attendance and their contributions in money and time.

Research approach

The research project upon which this chapter is based was a field study begun in December 1998 and carried on through September 2001. The aim was to examine selected factors that contributed to school attendance and discontinuation in rural Tibet, where most of the region's Tibetan population reside. Of particular interest were the perspectives of Tibetan families as they relate to schooling and the TAR's policies to improve access to education. Field methods were used, including unstructured, in-depth interviews, semi-structured survey questionnaires, and observation. Benam (Bailang) county in south central Tibet was selected because it was representative of poor semi-agricultural, semi-nomadic counties, familiar to the research team, and accessible. Discussions were held with education officials, and in-depth interviews were conducted with families, school personnel, and students at the village level. Almost all families from four villages of Mag township, 153 in all, were sampled. There is no intention to generalize these finding to rural villages across Tibet. With little field research on rural education in Tibet to act as a base, this approach was used to gain a better understanding of the role of and perceptions toward schools in rural villages.

The survey instrument was designed based on an initial visit to the county project villages, and based on experience with similar studies in other ethnic minority regions of western China. After being translated into Tibetan, the survey instrument was piloted in Gongga county and revised. The research team was trained and the principal researcher worked in the field with the team on two occasions. Background documents were collected and interviews were conducted, which provided a basis for designing the survey instrument. While in the field, the researcher lived in the village school, from which he was able to visit households and speak with teachers and students.

The initial interviews were open-ended, focusing on the basic household characteristics, perspectives toward the school, school participation, teacher contact, school costs, and educational relevance. The survey questionnaire, which was derived from the interviews, was implemented by the trained research team, who recorded answers to questions and kept notes on household characteristics that could be relevant to the aim of the study. These case studies of households were used as a way to gain an understanding of the factors that act to support or resist schooling.

Because village life revolved around the growing seasons, the initial interviews were generally conducted in winter, mid-summer, or after the harvest. Although herding was a year-round activity, the pace was less urgent than in agriculture. School-aged children contributed significantly to herding because it often required little more than watching over and moving a small number of animals from one place to another. Households would also work together during harvest season, when children played an even more essential role. During the interviews, I was able to move from the village school where I lived to the households and usually spent a morning or an afternoon at each household.

Though the surveys were carried out by trained researchers, they were used to gather only general information on household situation, attitudes, and issues related to the school. Percentages are reported here when they seem meaningful in the context of other investigation. The survey data were gathered from households in four neighboring villages: Sokang, Mongkang, Gokhang, and Goetoe.

Results

Results are presented to illustrate key problems of school access and discontinuance within the context of the measures in effect to alleviate these problem. Discussion centers on household characteristics and perspectives of parents. In visiting the village residents for the initial household interviews, I found that most families lived in a three- to five-room house on two floors, the lower occupied by animals and the upper floor containing a kitchen, bedroom, storeroom, and prayer room. Usually the household compound was draped with prayer flags at each corner of the roof, and surrounded by white walls. Families also had a common sitting area used in good weather that would be open to light and air from the outside. Otherwise the cooking area was used to receive guests.

In terms of financial situation, more than 60 percent of the families viewed themselves in the middle-income range and, with the exception of one family that classified itself as rich, the rest saw themselves as poor. A government initiative for those families that remained poor after the land reform would move them to new areas (*xin kaifa*), and also aimed at settling nomadic families, who were usually poorer than agricultural families. About 65 percent of the villagers had no skills outside of basic farming and animal husbandry. A small number had some skills in carpentry, weaving, masonry, and painting. The demands of the household economy made it necessary for many families to borrow money, and about two-thirds reported some kind of loan. Usually the loans came from relatives or from the monastery, though about 5 percent were given by banks. Despite the *sanbao* policy, which was cancelled and later reinstituted, families with children in school were more likely to borrow money. Of the 153 families, 36 percent had taken loans, ranging in price from 20 to about 4,000 *yuan*, the average being 732 *yuan*.

Life and prosperity were inseparable from owning land and valuable animals, especially animals that contributed to family labor. The amount of land owned by households ranged from 2 to 48 *mu*, with the average being around 10 *mu*. Over 90 percent of the families owned sheep, goats, cows and dzo (male hybrid of a yak and a domesticated cow). A smaller proportion owned an ox or yak. Horses were owned by about one-third of families. Others had donkeys, pigs and a few chickens. About 15 percent of the families had a tractor worth a few thousand *yuan*. About 30 percent had battery-powered tape recorders used for playing music and about 20 percent had a hand- or foot-powered sewing machine. Loans impacted ability to pay school fees, number of animals impacted children's contribution to household labor, and the lack of household machinery, such as tractors and sewing machines, gave less opportunity for school to capitalize on technical education opportunities.

Parents were asked to respond to a series of questions in terms of their oldest school-age child. When the topic of sending children to school arose, most parents mentioned the benefit of being able to read and write Tibetan and do simple calculations. Some respondents said that the process of storing barley for transport and sale could be improved if one possessed basic arithmetic skills. One quarter associated schooling with having a better life and about one-fifth of those with a child in school saw schooling as a path to becoming a local government official. These three reasons for sending children to school—being literate in Tibetan and math; having a better life; and becoming a local official—were sometimes associated with one another in the interviews. Only one in ten associated schooling with learning a manual skill, and very few associated it with getting a moral education or becoming a good citizen, serving the public, or being a good parent—which are traditionally associated with a monastery education. Significantly, only one in ten reported the belief that schooling increases the possibility to earn more income, revealing a significant difference between official and popular perspectives on the subject.

Of the 153 families surveyed in the first county, 103 had children of school age (between 6 and 15). Of these, 26 families reported having only one child, and 12 of these children attended school. Thirty-two families reported having two children, and 38 of these children attended school. Among the 27 families reporting three children, 47 children attended school. Of the 13 families who reported having four children, 29 children attended school. Five families reported having five children, with 12 of these children attending school. I visited several homes with more children, in one case as many as ten children, which means that some families may have under-reported the number of their children during the survey. Of this township's 248 school-age children (127 girls and 121 boys), 138 attended school (61 girls and 77 boys), and 110 did not (66 girls and 44 boys).

The results yield two notable observations. First, the proportion of girls to boys is much higher than in other parts of rural China, where many demographers attribute the low proportion to pre-natal sex selection. Second, only about 56 percent of all of the school-age children in this study attended school, which is a rate below official figures.

Although the compulsory age of schooling begins at age 6 in China, most children in rural Tibet do not begin school until a year or two after this age. In the study sample, attendance rates are below 40 percent for children of ages 6 and 7, and they reach a high of 100 percent of girls and boys at age 8. The rate remains at 100 percent for boys age 9 and 10, but falls thereafter from about 85 percent among boys 11 and 12, to 60 percent for boys age 13 and 14, to 33 percent for boys age 15. Attendance rates for girls in this sample are lower at all ages and the trend is more erratic. Rates dip from 80 to 60 percent and then rise back to 80 percent for girls at ages 9, 10, and 11; then they fall and rise again (from 36 to 19 to 29 percent) for girls age 13, 14, and 15. Clearly, less than half of all children under age 8 or over age 14 attend school. After a peak around age 8, attendance rates generally fall off to about one-third by age 15.

The major reason children miss school is to work at home with farming and livestock. In the 103 families with school-aged children who were asked about household labor affecting school attendance, 42 percent said it sometimes has an effect. Although teachers and officials assumed that household labor responsibilities contributed to school discontinuation, parents did not see this as a problem in school attendance or homework assignments. Most parents (61 percent) said their child spent less than an hour on homework a night, and this may be why parents did not think household chores interfered with school homework assignments. Over two-thirds (69 percent) said they checked on homework most or some of the time, but about 68 percent said they did not understand it some or all of the time, and only one-third (32 percent) said they understood it most of the time. When it came to the content of schooling, the ethnic culture of the region was clearly reflected in parents' responses. Two-thirds of the parents said their children liked studying Tibetan the most, while only 13 percent named mathematics and 18 percent named Chinese as their children's favorite subject. Almost two-thirds (63 percent) of the parents believed that Tibetan was the most useful subject, which was two to three times the proportion who believed it was Chinese.

The county authorities had few options for mandating school attendance, but they had a point system for rewarding school attendance, as a the county education department official explained:

> For each day a student attends school, points are earned. Each point is worth two *mao*. Daily points are dependent on the grade level. A P1 (Primary One) student earns 1 point, P2 earns 1.5 points, P3 earns 2 points, P4 earns 2.5 points, P5 earns 3 points, and P6 earns 4 points. There is a total of 270 days of school per year, not counting 36 Sundays and public holidays and teacher meetings. Moreover, if a student has perfect attendance for the entire year, that student earns 10 *mao* for each day of school attended. This measure was instituted as an interim measure when the attendance rates were extremely low.

> If a child does not come to school, there are three possible effects: (1) If the student is sick, no points are deducted from his or her total. (2) If the student receives permission to miss school, no points are deducted.

If the student misses more than 20 days, points must be deducted of two points per day. (3) If the student skips school or cuts out, not only are points deducted, but also there is a fine of four points.

At the school level, the point system was explained this way by the principal:

When a student attends a day in primary one, they can get 0.15 *yuan*, year two is 0.20 *yuan*. For example, the total this year for two villages was 114.81 *yuan*, which is 2.43 for each person. If the student ever skipped class, the penalty is 0.20 *yuan*, if it goes over four days, the penalty is 30 *yuan*. This came to 503.78 this past year for the two villages. At the annual parents' meeting, the commitment is honored in cash. In this way, through the point system, students can come to school and learn culture, as well as earn money.

At the school level, another minor measure accommodates the demands of the harvest seasons, as a principal of a township primary school explained: "In the busy spring and winter seasons, we use a '*xunhuo*' measure, which means that the school is called off and students are sent home. However, this period cannot go beyond seven days."

The principal also explained that parents had become more cooperative in sending their children to school in recent years, but not for educational reasons:

Up until a few years ago, [support from parents] was not very good. The people's understanding of education was not very deep. There was still the contradiction between family labor needs and schooling. Each year, there were 10 or more children that did not come to school. Now that has passed. Now, many families send their children to school because they are compelled.

As the century ended, school access and non-attendance was receiving a good deal of attention in the TAR. From the regional point of view, education was seen as a development strategy to help improve standards of living. In the national context, education was viewed as an area in which the TAR lagged far behind other regions in China. While many rural Tibetans viewed state schooling as an imposition from above, they also began to see that it might be one path to a better life. Rural Tibetans were aware that going to school could lead to a position in the local county government, especially through attending the boarding schools (*neidi Xizangban*) for Tibetan secondary school students that are located in Chinese cities around the country. Urban Tibetans were more aware of the link between schooling and opportunities in the expanding Han Chinese world of the TAR. For those who had sent a family member to the city to work (*dagong*), it became clear that being literate in Tibetan and mathematics was not enough. Tibetans felt growing frustration with Han Chinese who had the upper hand in urban economic life and who preferred to hire other Han, rather than Tibetans.

Because Tibetan families did not always recognize the relevance of available schooling to community development or the rigors of daily life, the role of Tibetan schoolteachers became very important. Teachers could better understand the link between state schooling, cultural values, improved standards of living, and community development. Moreover, preparing Tibetan children to compete with the increasing number of Han Chinese coming into the TAR cast education in a different light. Young men returning to their villages shared their experiences about urban life and reported that speaking Chinese could increase job opportunities, even if the Han Chinese tended to discriminate against Tibetan workers.

Discussion

Educational access and school discontinuation in rural Tibet can be linked both to John Ogbu's notion of involuntary minorities and the folk theories of success pointed out by Stevan Harrell and Ma Erzi among the rural Yi population in southwestern Sichuan. In short, only if ethnic minorities associate school participation with a high likelihood of economic success, enough to improve their status and power within the national mainstream, will the probability of school attendance be significantly improved. Such an associative discourse would be nested within larger overlapping state ideological themes of social equity, economic development, cultural autonomy, and national integration. These themes constitute an elaborate context for rural Tibetans and the manner in which the themes are heard and interpreted, experienced and decoded, will matter to the reformulation of folk theories of school success and resistance.

The state ideological themes can be based in a number of ways on social practices initiated by measures implemented by county education bureaus to increase attendance by offering financial incentives to students and making teacher salaries more dependent on attendance, test scores, and promotion. However, many rural schools provide only a subsistence learning environment. There is a gap between the quality of teaching at the village, township and county levels, with many villages still relying on *minban* teachers. Children who live in villages closer to the township school are advantaged, and children in households remote from village schools are less likely to attend school. Schools accord opportunities for girls and for boys, but attitudes in school and at home affect attendance rates, which drop off faster for girls than boys as they move up the school grade ladder. Families are aware of equity issues and have been concerned about school costs since the *sanbao* policy was discontinued, and book fees were introduced. Rising costs do not augur well for the development of folk theories of success.

Economic development guides educational policy in China and special subsidies have been made available for ethnic minority regions. Given the poverty of rural Tibet, funding for education takes up 20 percent of the government budget and spending is not transparent. While flexibility to structure financial incentives was capitalized upon by one county, this is more the exception than the rule across counties. Schools in rural areas have little of the income-generating potential of urban schools, and attracting good teachers is difficult, without increased funding. As the graduates of the inland Tibetan secondary schools (*neidi ban*) return and find government positions much harder to come by, some can be found teaching at township level rural schools. It is not yet clear how they compare with the graduates of TAR teacher training colleges, in terms of both teaching methods and ability to strengthen the connection between education and the local community economy.

Although it has taken families quite some time to see the benefits of schooling, they have long been willing to send at least one of their children to school for two to three years. It matters a great that a significant number of families have come to believe that education can lead not only to government positions, but to increased skills for helping the household economy and increasing their income. If the schools offer a better quality education that translates into visible results, rural parents will, in all likelihood, provide more support for schools, and even be willing to pay nominal school fees.

As more Tibetan students from the inland Tibetan schools return and as more Tibetan students within the TAR demonstrate their abilities to excel in language, math and science, the extent to which Tibetan rural culture is transformed into a form of social capital that acts to strengthen school achievement and ethnic identity remains an open question. Regardless, the increased relevance of schooling to the local environment would strengthen support for schooling, increase attendance rates, and possibly facilitate the engagement of rural communities in thinking about how their culture and way of life connects and integrates with the larger national social and economic environment. In this sense, the case of rural Tibet illustrates the issues facing minority education in other parts of China. Like most other minorities, Tibetans have deep religious traditions, and a set of values and beliefs, which have helped them survive in harsh natural environments over many generations. Tibet is treated like other minority areas of China with respect to special education policies and measures, including special subsidies, preferential admission, and bilingual education. There are also special policies that apply only to Tibetans, including the *sanbao* and inland Tibetan secondary schools. This is also due to the fact that Tibet is the only one of the five ethnic minority autonomous provinces-level entities where the major ethnic group constitutes over half of the population. Despite the special educational policies, Tibet still has the lowest literacy and educational attainment levels of any province-level entity in China. This can be rightfully attributed to the remoteness of the region and levels of poverty. Yet, it could also be attributed to the negative incentive for innovation and experimentation in education areas that deal with policies of language and culture.

Acknowledgment

The author acknowledges financial support for research provided by the Hong Kong Research Grants Council.

References

Achievements of Education in China 1980–85 (Zhongguo jiaoyu chengjiu tongji ziliao 1980–1985). (1986) Beijing: People's Education Press.

Bass, C. (1998) *Education in Tibet: Policy and Practice Since 1950*, London: Zed Books.

Berberoglu, B. (ed.) (1995) *The National Question: Nationalism, Ethnic Conflict and Self-Determination in the 20th Century*, Philadelphia, PA: Temple University Press.

Dikotter, F. (1992) *The Discourse on Race in Modern China*, Hong Kong: Hong Kong University Press.

Economic and Development Department of the State Ethnic Affairs Commission, and Department of Integrated Statistics of the State Statistical Bureau (1998) *Zhongguo Minzu Tongji Nianjian 1997*, Beijing: Minzu Chubanshe.

Economic and Development Department of the State Ethnic Affairs Commission, and Department of Integrated Statistics of the State Statistical Bureau (1999) *Zhongguo Minzu Tongji Nianjian 2000*, Beijing: Minzu Chubanshe.

Educational Statistics Yearbook of China 1999 (Zhongguo jiaoyu shiye tongji nianjian 1999) (2000) Beijing: People's Education Press.

Essential Statistics in Education in China (Zhongguo jiaoyu shiye fazhan tongji jiankuang) (1997) Beijing: Department of Planning and Construction, State Education Commission.

Fei, X.T. (1991) *Zhonghua Minzu Yanjiu Xin Tance (New Explorations in China's Ethnic Studies)*, Beijing: Chinese Academy of Social Sciences Publishing House.

Friedman, J. (1997) "Being in the World: Globalization and Localization," in M. Featherstone (ed.) *Global Culture: Nationalism, Globalization and Modernity*, London: Sage Publications.

Geng, J.S. and Wang, X.H. (1989) *Xizang Jiaoyu Yanjiu (Research on Education in Tibet)*, Beijing: Zhongyang Minxu Xueyuan Chubanshe.

Gladney, D.C. (1991) *Muslim Chinese: Ethnic Nationalism in the People's Republic*, Cambridge, MA: The Council of East Asian Studies and Fellows of Harvard University.

Gladney, D.C. (1999) "Making Muslims in China," in G. Postiglione (ed.) *China's National Minority Education: Culture, Schooling and Development*, New York: The Falmer Press.

Goldstein, M.C. (1989) *A History of Modern Tibet, 1913–1951: The Demise of the Lamist State*, Los Angeles: University of California at Los Angeles.

Goldstein, M.C. (1997) *China, Tibet and the Dali Lama*, Berkeley, CA: The University of California Press.

Grunfeld, T. (1996) *The Making of Modern Tibet*, New York: M.E. Sharpe (East Gate; revised edition).

Guo, F.C. and Wei, P.F. (1995) *Sheng Shi Zizhiqu Shaoshu Minzu Jiaoyu Gongzuo Wenjian Xuanpian, 1977–1990 (Province, City, Autonomous Region Ethnic Minority Education Work Documents, 1977–1990)*, Chengdu: Sichuan Minzu Chubanshe.

Ha, J.X. and Teng, X. (2001) *Minzu Jiaoyu Xue Tonglun (A General Survey of Ethnic Minority Education)*, Beijing: Jiaoyu Kexue Chubanshe.

Hansen, M.H. (1999) *Lessons in Being Chinese: Minority Education and Ethnic Identity in Southwest China*, Seattle: University of Washington Press.

Harrell, S. (1996) *Cultural Encounters on China's Ethnic Frontiers*, Hong Kong: Hong Kong University Press.

Harrell, S. and Ma, E. (1999) "Folk Theories of Success: Why Han Aren't Always Best," in G. Postiglione (ed.) *China's National Minority Education: Culture, Schooling and Development*, New York: The Falmer Press.

Heberer, T. (1989) *China and its National Minorities: Autonomy or Assimilation*, New York: M.E. Sharpe.

Iredale, R., Bilik, N., Wang, S., Fei, G., and Hoy, C. (2001) *Contemporary Minority Migration, Education and Ethnicity*, Northampton, MA: Edward Elgar.

Jiacuo, S. (1995) "Education is the Wing of the Economy: An Investigation into the Rural Education," unpublished manuscript, Tibet University of Agriculture and Animal Husbandry, Lhasa.

Liu, T.T. and Faure, D. (eds.) (1996) *Unity and Diversity: Local Cultures and Identities in China*, Hong Kong: Hong Kong University Press.

Mackerras, C. (1994) *China's Minorities: Integration and Modernization in the Twentieth Century*, Hong Kong: Oxford University Press.

Mackerras, C. (1995) *China's Minority Cultures: Integration and Identity Since 1912*, New York: Longman.

Mackerras, C. (1999) "Religion and the Education of China's Minorities," in G. Postiglione (ed.) *China's National Minority Education: Culture, Schooling and Development*, New York: The Falmer Press.

McDermott, R. (1987) "The Explanation of Minority School Failure, Again." *Anthropology and Education Quarterly*, 18: 361–364.

N.A. (1986) *Zhongguo Jiaoyu Chengjiu Tongji Ziliao 1980–1985 (Achievements of Education in China 1980–85)*, Beijing: People's Education Press.

N.A. (1995) *Zhongguo Jiaoyu Dituji (Education Atlas of China)*, Shanghai: Shanghai Kexue Jishu Chubanshe.

N.A. (1997) *Essential Statistics in Education in China (Zhongguo Jiaoyu Shiye Fazhan Tongji Jiankuang)*, Beijing: Department of Planning and Construction, State Education Commission (January).

N.A. (1999) *"Xizang Zizhiqu Minzu Jiaoyu 50 Nian"* (50 Years of Ethnic Education in the Tibetan Autonomous Region), in *Zhongguo Minzu Jiaoyu 50 Nian (50 Years of Ethnic Education in China)*, Beijing: Hongqi chubanshe.

N.A. (2000a) *Zhongguo Jiaoyu Tongji Nianjian 1999 (Educational Statistics Yearbook of China 1999)*, Beijing: People's Education Press.

N.A. (2000b) *Guanyu Shishi Kejiao Xingguo Zhanlue Gongzuo Qingkuang de Baogao, Guowuyuan Fuzongli Li Lanqing (Situation Report Concerning the Strategic Work to Enliven the Country Through Education and Science)*, Zhonghua renmin gongheguo quanguo renmin daibiao dahui changwu weiyuanhui (Gazette of the Standing Committee of the National People's Congress of the People's Republic of China), August 24, Beijing, No. 5.

N.A. (2000c) *Shaoshu Minzu Jiaoyu Yanjiu Lunwen (Ethnic Minority Educational Research Selections)*, Lanzhou: Xibei Shifan Daxue, Xibei Shaoshu Minzu Jiaoyu Fazhan Yanjiu Zhongxin (Lanzhou: Northwest Normal University, Northwest Ethnic Minority Educational Research Center), March.

N.A. (2001a) *China Education Daily*, May 30, 2001. Document available on-line, http://www.jyb.com.cn/gb/2001/05/30/zhxw/jyzx/3.htm (accessed May 20, 2006).

N.A. (2001b) "Xibu Dakaifa De Jiben Guoqing Yu Jiaoyu Fazhan" (Basic Situation of Educational Development in Western China), in *2001 Zhongguo Jiaoyu Lupishu (2001 Green Paper on Education in China)*, Beijing: Jiaoyu Kexue Chubanshe, July.

N.A. (2003) "Spending More in Rural Classrooms," *China Daily*, October 8, http://www.chinadaily.com.cn/en/doc/2003–10/08/content_269822.htm.

Ogbu, J. (1991) "Immigrant and Voluntary Minorities in Comparative Perspective," in J. Ogbu and M. Gibson (eds.) *Minority Status and Schooling: A Comparative Study of Immigration and Involuntary Minorities*, New York: Garland.

Postiglione, G. (2000) "National Minority Regions: Studying School Discontinuation," in J. Liu, H. Ross, and D. Kelly (eds.) *The Ethnographic Eye: An Interpretive Study of Education in China*, New York: The Falmer Press.

Postiglione, G., Teng, X., and Ai, Y.P. (1995) "Basic Education and School Discontinuation in National Minority Border Regions of China," in G. Postiglione and W.O. Lee (eds.) *Social Change and Educational Development: Mainland China, Taiwan and Hong Kong*, Hong Kong: Centre of Asian Studies.

Sautman, B. (1999) "Expanding Access to Higher Education for China's National Minorities: Policies of Preferential Admission," in G. Postiglione (ed.) *China's National Minority Education: Culture, Schooling and Development*, New York: The Falmer Press.

Sino-Tibetan Agreement on Measures for the Peaceful Liberation of Tibet (17-Point Agreement of May 23, 1951), available in P.P. Karan, (1976) *The Changing Face of Tibet*, Lexington, KY: The University Press of Kentucky, pp. 89–91.

Smith, A.D. (1997) "Toward a Global Culture," in M. Featherstone (ed.) *Global Culture: Nationalism, Globalization and Modernity*, London: Sage Publications.

Smith, W.W. (1996) *Tibetan Nation: A History of Tibetan Nationalism and Sino-Tibetan Relations*, Boulder, CO: Westview Press.

Stites, R. (1999) "Writing Cultural Boundaries: National Minority Language Policy, Literacy Planning and Bilingual Education," in G. Postiglione (ed.) *China's National Minority Education: Culture, Schooling and Development*, New York: The Falmer Press.

Trueba, H., Spindler, G., and Spindler, L. (eds.) (1989) *What Do Anthropologists Have to Say About Dropouts?* New York: The Falmer Press.

UNESCO (2000) "Dakar Framework for Action Education for All: Meeting our Collective Commitments," Electronic document posted to http://www2.unesco.org/wef/en-conf/dakfram.shtm.

Upton, J. (1999) "The Development of Modern School Based Tibetan Language Education in the PRC," in G. Postiglione (ed.) *China's National Minority Education: Culture, Schooling and Development*, New York: The Falmer Press.

World Bank (2004) World Bank Group data, http://devdata.worldbank.org/edstats/SummaryEducationProfiles/CountryData/GetShowData.asp?sCtry=CHN, China (accessed May 20, 2006).

Xia, Z. (2001) "Fazhan Shaoshu Minzu Jiaoyu Xuyao Zhengce Qingxie" (The Needed Policy Inclinations for Developing Ethnic Minority Education), paper delivered at the Conference on the Development of Ethnic Minority Education in Western China, Baptist University, Hong Kong, October 8.

Xia, Z., Ha, J.X., and Abadu, W. (1999) "Xizang Zizhiqu Minzu Jiaoyu 50 Nian (50

Years of Ethnic Education in the Tibetan Autonomous Region)," in *Zhongguo Minzu Jiaoyu 50 Nian* (*50 Years of Ethnic Education in China*), Beijing: Hongqi chubanshe.

Zhang, T. (1995) *Population Development in Tibet and Related Issues*, Beijing: Foreign Language Press.

7 Educational attainment of migrant children

The forgotten story of China's urbanization

Yiu Por Chen and Zai Liang

Introduction

A major challenge facing China's education system today is that of how to educate migrant children—the children of rural labor migrants, sometimes referred to as the "floating population," who are entering China's cities in ever-greater numbers. Under China's household registration system, or *hukou* system, these individuals remain official residents of rural areas, and do not have full citizenship rights in the cities where they now reside (see Cheng and Selden 1994, for the historical development of the *hukou* system). The scope of the challenge to China's urban education systems, while hard to gauge in precise terms, is vast. One report estimates that there are over 20 million migrant children in China overall, with about 10 percent being dropouts, and nearly half suffering from a delay in schooling (*Shi Jie Ri Bao* 2003). Another report estimates that there were 150,000 migrant children in Beijing alone in 2001. Of these, 30 percent had migrated while of "school age" (defined as between the ages of 5 and 16), and another 10 percent had been born locally, to temporary migrant parents (Lu and Zhang 2001). These numbers suggest a heavy burden for educational systems in the urban receiving communities.

This chapter addresses three questions: (1) how extensive is the migrant children's school enrollment problem? (2) what factors affect enrollment? and (3) what strategies might alleviate some of the problems of migrant children's education?

We review earlier studies, and present findings from our own analysis of the Survey on the State of Migrant Children's Education (hereafter MCE 2000), conducted in Beijing in the year 2000 by the Research Team on Migrant Children's Education at the Development Research Center, in the State Council Agricultural Department (Research Team on Migrant Children's Education 2000). The MCE 2000 was the first official, in-depth survey in China to focus primarily on migrant children's educational problems. It sampled 619 migrant workers' households with school-age children in three districts of Beijing: Fengtai, Haidian, and Chaoyang. The MCE 2000 focused on three topics: (1) migrant children's educational circumstances; (2) migrant parents' educational choices; and (3) the situation of migrant-sponsored schools.

The chapter is organized as follows: first, we discuss the size of the temporary migrant population and discuss trends in migration patterns. We then outline education policies that pertain to migrant children, as well as obstacles to their implementation. We offer an overview of current knowledge of migrant children's enrollment patterns. Next, we analyze MCE 2000 data to illustrate three factors that affect the education of migrant children in urban settings: (1) the cost of education; (2) low parental income; and (3) parental duration of stay. Finally, we discuss recent developments, including recent changes in educational policy and in the scope of non-formal migrant-sponsored schools, and recent dilemmas in migrant children's education. The chapter concludes with a discussion of the social implications of educating or not educating migrant children.

Context: children and migration in China

Migrant children in China's provinces today are part of a massive relocation of rural surplus labor to the urban sectors. While some of these children are migrating on their own, most are migrating with migrant worker parents. Migration, overall, has increased rapidly in recent decades. For example, inter-county migration increased from 30.5 million to 79 million between 1987 and 2000, according to those years' China One Percent Population Sample Surveys (Liang 2001: Table 2; Liang and Ma 2004: Table 1). Temporary migration has experienced especially rapid growth. The inter-county floating population rose from around 7 million in 1982 to 79 million in 2000—more than ten times increase in less than two decades (Liang and Ma 2004: 407).

The greatest increases have occurred in China's major cities. In Shanghai, for example, the number of temporary migrants increased from 1.7 million in 1986 to 4.4 million in 2000 (Liang 2001: Table 2; Liang and Ma 2004: Table 1). The 1997 Shanghai Census recorded 340,000 pre-school and school-age migrant children, comprising nearly 12 percent of the total migrant population. There was a 20 percent increase in the number of migrant children, when compared to 1993 data, while the total number of immigrants dropped by 5.6 percent during this period (Zhang 1998). Similarly, the number of temporary migrants in Beijing hovered around 70,000 in 1985, and increased dramatically to 2.9 million by 1996. According to 2000 Census estimates, economically active areas such as Shanghai, Zhejiang, Guangdong, and Beijing continue to be among the most popular migration destinations (ibid.: 13).

An important development has been a noticeable increase in family migration in recent years. For example, fully half of the 619 respondents in the MCE 2000 reported that they had migrated with their spouses, and 72 percent of them reported living with their spouses during the survey period. Over 36 percent of those who lived with a spouse in Beijing had children studying locally.

Another important development is that, while "floating" migrants are thought of as temporary, they are likely to remain for long durations in their host destinations. For example, over half of the respondents in a 1995 report by the Ministry of Agriculture stated that they had stayed for more than a year (Ministry of Agriculture Migrant Labor Survey Project 1995). Similarly, 28.9 percent of migrants interviewed in the 1997 Migrant Population Census in Beijing had stayed for at least three years, while 15.8 percent had stayed over five years (cited in Duan and Zhou 2001). Moreover, 20 percent of migrants 5 years old and under were locally born, even though they are referred to as "migrant children" (*liudong ertong*) (cited in Duan and Zhou 2001).

Educational policies for migrant children

In 1996, in an effort to deal with the increasing numbers of school-age migrant children, the first national legislation regarding the education of migrant children was drafted by the Ministry of Education (*The Economist* 2000: 54). This legislation was entitled the Provisional Acts regarding the Education of School-Age Children of the Floating Population and stated that state-run (public) schools need only enroll children who held local residence permits, which were nearly impossible for migrants to obtain (ibid.).

Six major locations were chosen as the testing grounds for this policy: Beijing, Tianjin, Shanghai, Hebei, Zhejiang, and Shenzhen (Zhang 1998). After the initial testing period, the Temporary Act on Migrant Children's Education was jointly drafted by the Ministry of Education and the Ministry of Public Security in 1998 to replace the Provisional Acts in 1996 (Duan 2001b). This legislation states that the governments at both the migrant origin and destination have the responsibility of providing education to migrant children. In particular, according to clauses 4 and 7, the migrant destination government is obliged to afford migrant children access to education, and to provide the necessary infrastructure to facilitate the education of migrant children. Moreover, according to the ninth clause, the host government can rally "social forces" (private organizations) to participate in the business of educating migrant children (Duan 2001b; Lu and Zhang 2001).

Notwithstanding the obvious merit of these above-mentioned efforts, little attention has been paid to this legislation at the local level (Duan 2001a: 55; Lu and Zhang 2001). For example, in Shanghai, formal enforcement of this legislation is virtually absent, as is any financial assistance to facilitate implementation, under the fiscally decentralized school finance system. The Shanghai government does not take the initiative to self-fund implementation (Zhang 1998: 424). In general, neither the sending nor the host areas have strong incentives to incur costs associated with migrant children's education, and a result has been rent-seeking behaviors on the part of individual schools. Public schools charge exorbitant fees to migrant parents for enrolling their children, making it impossible for these children to receive an education in the majority of urban public schools (Ling Dian Diao Cha 1997; Lu and Zhang 2001: 9; *The Economist* 2000: 54).

Finally, it is important to note that some of the education of migrant children is taking place outside of the state system. For example, education is occurring in low-cost, unlicensed worker-run kindergartens in the urban sector (Ling Dian Diao Cha 1997). Similarly, education is occurring in migrant-sponsored schools, which emerged as self-organized educational institutions, outside of the public system, in the early 1990s (Duan 2001a; Liu 2003).

These schools provide an affordable alternative to the basic education of migrant children. The motto of the central government in the 1990s was *bu qudi, bu chengren, zisheng zimie* ("do not ban, do not recognize, let it run its course") (Kwong 2004: 1079).

However, hopes on the part of the central government that migrant-sponsored schools would die out naturally were not to be realized (Kwong 2004). Numbers have flourished: at the end of the twentieth century, there were over 200 migrant-sponsored children's schools in Beijing, with over 40,000 students enrolled (Han 2001). An estimated 100 migrant-sponsored schools were found in Shanghai, while another 200 were found in Shenzhen (ibid.).

School enrollment of migrant children: what do we know?

Although the reported enrollment rates of migrant children are generally low, estimates vary widely from city to city, and from survey to survey. Among school-aged migrant children in Beijing surveyed in 1994, only 40.5 percent were reported as "enrolled" (Ling Dian Diao Cha 1997). A similar census in Shanghai revealed that about 64 percent of school-aged migrant children were enrolled in local schools (Zhu 2001). A more recent report published by Lu and Zhang (2001: 11) suggests a much more dire situation: according to a 2001 sample survey conducted in Beijing, there was only a 12.5 percent enrollment rate for over 3 million migrants between the ages of 6 and 14.

Using the 1995 China One Percent Population Sample Survey, Liang and Chen (2007) provide a more detailed and systematic analysis of the issues facing school-age migrant children in Guangdong Province, one of the major migration destinations in China. After categorizing the migrants by different lengths of duration of residence at the host destinations and *hukou* status, three major findings emerged. First, temporary migrant children, with around an 80 percent enrollment rate, were much less likely to be enrolled in school than local children, who were almost fully enrolled. Temporary migrants with less than one year of residence in the cities appeared to suffer the most serious consequences, with a mere 60 percent enrollment rate. Inter-estingly, permanent migrant children—meaning children of parents who had officially changed their residence status and thus enjoyed full citizenship rights—were more likely to be enrolled in school than local, urban children

(95 percent enrolled for permanent migrant children, versus 90 percent for local children) (Liang and Chen 2007: Figure 1). Second, and perhaps more importantly, when compared to non-migrant children at the place of origin, rural temporary migrant children from Guangdong also encountered a major disadvantage in terms of school enrollment. Overall, earlier work suggests that school enrollment rates for temporary migrant children tend to be low, but vary with the duration of residence in the host destination. In the next section, we use a case study in Beijing to investigate these issues further, along with the issue of affordability.

Analysis of migrant children's schooling in Beijing in 2000

Educational costs and affordability

The cost structure of basic education in urban public schools can be divided into several categories of "fees" (*fei*), including the "school" fee (*xue fei*), "placement" fee (*jie du fei*), "sponsor" fee (*zan zhu fei*), and "miscellaneous" fees (*za fei*). The school fee is the basic charge upon which all other fees are added. The reason for collecting the placement fee is to offset the financial burden to the local educational system caused by the attendance of migrant children. However, the sponsor fee is a rather new charge, arising in the early 1990s as a kind of "self-financing" fee. The miscellaneous fees cover all kinds of expenses incurred in school, including but not limited to books, uniforms, lunch and food, and so forth. Fees are set and collected by the individual public schools, usually with no formal bill issued. These fees are recorded in a school's "alternative" accounting journal that is rarely disclosed or subject to account auditing (Cao 1997: 4). While the State Council has implemented rules designed to regulate the pricing behavior of public schools, they are difficult to enforce at the local level. In large part, this is because under fiscal decentralization, educational tariffs are managed locally.

There are reports of skyrocketing fees that strain even local residents. A survey conducted by the China Economic Monitoring Center of 4,716 residents in the ten biggest cities in China showed that educational expenses account for approximately 15 percent of the daily budget, second only to food expenditure at 38 percent. Moreover, more than half of the respondents (54 percent) complained about the escalating tuition fees (*People's Daily* 2001).

One report on the attendance fees for a first-grade migrant student in Beijing showed that the school fee was 1,700 *yuan*, the placement fee was 480 *yuan*, and the sponsor fee ranged from between 500 and 2000 *yuan* for primary school, and between 10,000 and 30,000 *yuan* for high school (Cao 1997). Another report revealed that the sponsor fee was between 20,000 and 30,000 *yuan* for non-resident children for public school, while the yearly school fee was between 400 and 500 *yuan* for the migrant children's primary school (Zhu 2001).

We used the MCE 2000 to tabulate the different types of primary schools

Table 7.1 Educational indicators for temporary migrant children: average yearly school expenses by school type (in *yuan*)

School and fee type	Grade level					
	1	*2*	*3*	*4*	*5*	*6*
Urban public school[a]						
school fee (*Xue Fei*)	759	490	728	510	454	443
Placement fee (*Jie Du Fei*)	926	1581	1798	1842	1420	1503
Sponsor fee (*Zan Zhu Fei*)	3635	2583	4062	2412	2000	825
Miscellaneous fee (*Za Fei*)	467	423	917	809	433	650
Total[b c]	4422	3764	3563	5252	3774	6156
N = Number of respondents[d]	15	13	12	17	7	5
Migrant-sponsored school[a]						
school fee (*Xue Fei*)	930	1040	771.2	830	1400	1400
N = Number of respondents[e]	20	5	9	4	2	2

Source: MCE 2000.

Notes:
[a] Figures are based on expenditures/fees for the first child in the families. Migrant-sponsored schools only charged school fees.
[b] The total amount of urban public school fees may not match the sum of all fees because of missing responses for some fees. The total expenditure and the breakdown of expenditures are from different questions.
[c] The total yearly amount for the migrant-sponsored school fee is based on twice the semester school fee.
[d] N = Number of respondents who responded to the question for total school expenditures.
[e] N = Number of respondents who responded to the question of migrant-sponsored school fees.

and school fees by various grade levels. In Table 7.1, the total expenditure for studying in an urban public school was between 4,000 and 6,000 *yuan* per year, while the expenditure in a migrant-sponsored school was around 1,000 *yuan* for up to grade 4, and 1,400 *yuan* for higher grades per year. The low cost for migrant-sponsored schools is partly due to the fact that they charge school fees only. The additional charges by urban public schools for migrant families, such as sponsor fees (or endorsement fees) and placement fees are very costly expenses. It is difficult to imagine that a migrant parent with an average yearly income of 10,000 *yuan* could afford to send his or her children to an urban public school, considering that the yearly school fee is approximately 40 to 60 percent of the family's yearly earnings.

In this regard, the migrant-sponsored schools may represent the only feasible alternative, at present, for many migrant families. It is unfortunate that the elements of basic infrastructure—such as sound concrete building construction, qualified and trained teachers, adequate classroom facilities, playgrounds, and sometimes even a safe and hygienic environment—are often lacking in migrant-sponsored schools.

Undoubtedly, the ability to finance their children's education has always been a concern for migrant parents. According to a study by Duan and Zhou (1999), migrant parents in Beijing have an average yearly income of around 7,200 *yuan* and cannot afford to send their children to public school, given the aforementioned fees. The MCE 2000 also revealed that merely 10 percent of the 316 parents with a yearly income below 10,000 *yuan* could actually afford to send their children to a state-run public school, whereas the percentage jumped to 24 percent when the parents' yearly income is 10,000 *yuan* or above.

In fact, according to a 1994 Beijing survey, "family financial problems" was the top reason that precluded migrant parents from allowing their children to attend school in Beijing—accounting for half of those responses. Another 30 percent claimed that the "high local school fees" prohibited them from sending their children to school (Ling Dian Diao Cha 1997). The 1997 Beijing Census of Migrants showed that 42.9 percent of parents answered "high school fees" and 7.4 percent answered "no school acceptance" as the reason for not being able to pursue an urban education (Duan 2001a). More-over, in the MCE 2000 Survey, 47 percent answered that the reason for not letting their children come to Beijing was because of "parent income problems."

The MCE 2000 Survey also revealed that, given high costs, some parents may even prefer to send their children back home for education, such that 62.6 percent of respondents were "preparing to send their children back home" and only 21.8 percent of parents were planning to let their children attend school in Beijing. In fact, the problem is not new: among the top reasons migrant respondents cited in 1994 for not attending school in Beijing was "cannot afford, too expensive," which accounted for nearly 80 percent of respondents (Ling Dian Diao Cha 1997).

Effects of parents' duration of stay

Another important factor affecting migrant parents' choices for their children's education is their duration of stay in the host city. As shown in Table 7.2, the MCE 2000 survey revealed a relationship between parents' duration of stay and schooling choices. Schooling back home was the most popular parental choice for schooling overall (68 percent), but the longer parents stayed at the destination, the more likely migrant children would study in the destination. The MCE 2000 survey revealed that when parents' stay increased from less than a year to over nine years, the proportion of hometown schooling dropped by nearly one-third, from 83 percent to 53 percent; while the choice of public schooling increased from 3.4 percent to 34.5 percent. However, a striking finding is that the proportion of children attending migrant-sponsored schools maintained a steady 10 percent over the spectrum, but dropped slightly to 8.5 percent in the "less than one year" category, peaking around 14 percent for the 6–8 year group.

Table 7.2 Educational indicators for temporary migrant children: choice of children's schooling by parental duration of stay

School type (%)	Parents' duration of stay					
	1 year	*1–3 years*	*4–5 years*	*6–8 years*	*≥ 9* years	*Total*
Hometown school	83.1	77.0	62.8	69.2	52.9	67.7
Urban public school	3.4	6.6	14.9	19.6	34.5	17.2
Migrant-sponsored school	8.5	11.5	18.1	10.3	10.0	11.8
Pre-school	0.0	2.5	1.1	0.0	0.9	1.0
Dropped out	3.4	2.5	2.1	0.0	1.7	1.8
Other	1.7	0.0	1.1	0.9	0.0	0.6
N = Number of respondents[a]	59	122	94	107	119	501

Source: MCE 2000.

Note:
[a] N = Number of respondents who have children in school under 16 and have responded to the question of their children's schooling type.

In sum, as evidenced in Table 7.2, despite the decrease in migrant children's dropout rate as parents' duration of stay increased, only one-third of all migrant children whose parents stayed nine years or longer were able to receive an urban public school education. In this regard, the migrant-sponsored school, notwithstanding its "illegal status" and generally substandard quality of teaching, has become an important component of migrant children's basic education in urban China.

New developments

Policy changes pertaining to urban public schools

Although new measures, such as reducing school surcharges for migrant children, have been put in place recently in some large cities like Beijing, the scale of educational policies designed to help migrant children is very limited, to date (Zhang and Zhao 2003: 188). Only a few large cities have local regulations to address the problem of exorbitant school fees (Zhang and Zhao 2003). How these regulations can be extended to smaller cities, where local governments have limited local resources to finance the education of migrant children, is a serious problem (Park *et al.* 1996; see Li, Park, and Wang in this volume for a discussion of implications of fiscal decentralization for rural education). The "normal" or customary school fees for urban residents have reached very high levels, in historical terms, in recent years (*People's Daily* 2001). Of note, during the authors' May 2004 field visit to Beijing (two years after the Interim Measure of Beijing City of Implementing Compulsory

Education for Statutory Age Children and Young Persons in the Temporary Migrant Population 2002 was implemented for migrant children's education), it was evident that migrant parents are still paying much more than the normal tuition to local public schools, and school fees are still much higher than for migrant-sponsored schools. Thus, affordability is still one of the biggest issues for migrant families, in terms of planning for their children's education.

Growth in migrant-sponsored schools

Despite serious quality issues, migrant-sponsored schools are playing a key role in the education of migrant children. As noted earlier, the migrant-sponsored school as a self-organized educational institution emerged outside the conventional school system in China in the early 1990s, and by the year 2000, evidence suggests that numbers had flourished (Duan 2001a: 56, 2001b; Han 2001; Lu and Zhang 2001; Liu 2003). Migrant-sponsored schools address both psychological and economic barriers to education in the state system.

The psychological disincentives to attending state schools come from parental fears that migrant children will be looked down upon or ridiculed by local children. Consistent with this concern, "teased by other people (outsiders)" was the top issue that migrant children aged 7–17 ranked among problems they were worried about (Zhang and Zhao 2003: 78). An article from UNESCO detailing an interview of students attending a migrant-sponsored school in Shanghai also concluded, "One of the greatest challenges is to help [migrant children] pupils overcome a sense of inferiority wrought by their second-class status" (Irwin 2000). Migrant-sponsored schools can address this problem, as all students share similar origins. Migrant-sponsored schools can provide a bridge for migrant children to assimilate to their new environments.

The economic barriers to attending state schools are also somewhat-mitigated in migrant sponsored schools, which offer lower overall costs and more flexible payment terms. According to the MCE 2000, 72.5 percent of public school payments were made per semester, with 16.3 percent being made on a yearly basis. In contrast, at migrant-sponsored schools, 62.5 percent of school payments were made per semester, and 25 percent, monthly. The survey also showed that monthly payments—one of the more popular payment methods at migrant-sponsored schools—were not available in the public school system. In an interview conducted for the MCE 2000 in Beijing, a migrant parent indicated that although he had the money to pay a public school a lump sum for several years' worth of school fees, he preferred to use a flexible payment plan at the migrant-sponsored school (Liu and Zhang 2001). Migrant parents usually preferred this plan, due to uncertainty about where they and their family would be settling in the long term (ibid.: 26). Migrant schools sometimes also allowed delays in payment (ibid.).

Beyond affordability and flexibility in terms of payment plans, other aspects of migrant-sponsored schools may also be better suited to the circumstances of migrant families. These schools usually provide some form of extended program, enabling students to remain in school after the normal day has ended. In this regard, these schools also help care for migrant children while their parents are working (Zhang and Zhao 2003: 20).

While these "illegal" migrant-sponsored schools have been mushrooming in urban sectors as a result of the obvious advantages, not all of them will be able to remain operational because of current government regulations. While the Temporary Act on Migrant Children's Education, clause 9, states that the local governments at the migrants' host destinations can rally social forces (private organizations) to participate in the business of migrant-sponsored school, there are complaints that local officials have not yet given the schools formal approval. In other words, migrant-sponsored schools are not included in the category of "social forces," in practice. In other cases, schools have been demolished by local officials for alleged health and safety issues (Lin, this volume; Lu and Zhang 2001; Zhu 2001: 567). Thus, central regulations that encourage private investment in schooling are failing to assist in the task of offering private schooling to migrant children.

While new measures encouraging the participation of non-government organizations (NGOs) in migrant-sponsored schools are still in their early stages, for the time being, migrant-sponsored schools serve as functional alternatives to meet the needs of migrant children in different urban areas. Given poor resources and lack of official recognition, migrant-sponsored schools must be considered a problematic, though affordable and feasible, educational alternative.

Dilemmas

A problem has been that the legalization of migrant-sponsored schools has been a slow process since the Temporary Act on Migrant Children's Education in 1998. According to a report from the New China News Agency in 2002, a number of migrant schools have been granted legal status (*China Daily* 2002). Despite the increasing number of rural–urban migrants, there are only 519 legal migrant schools in Shanghai and 200 legal migrant schools in Beijing, among other cities (*Zhongguo Jiaoyu* 2002). These legalized migrant schools are now charging much higher fees than before. For instance, in Dongguan City in Guangdong Province, one of the most concentrated migrant worker cities in China, migrant-sponsored school fees have increased from 800 *yuan* to 1,300 *yuan* per semester for primary schools and from 1,300 *yuan* to 2,000 *yuan* per semester for junior high schools, due to legalization and expansion. Considering that a single wage earner family makes about 700 *yuan* monthly, it is undoubtedly a high burden to support a child studying at migrant children high school costing 2,000 *yuan* per semester (*Nanfang Ribao* 2005).

Another dilemma has appeared since the "legalization" of some "good quality" migrant-sponsored schools. While a handful of migrant-sponsored schools have been granted legal status and received supports from various government branches, the greater number of "low quality" migrant-sponsored schools have been closed down by force.

A third dilemma is that increasing use of the public school system to absorb school-aged migrant children may cause problems in local public finance. This problem has partially been addressed. When the national policy of the "unified school fee" (*yifeizhi*) in primary schools was implemented by the State Council in September 2004, the local public finance budget for schooling increased drastically, because of the rapid increase in student numbers and reduction in income from other fees. For example, in Beijing, the special subsidy for migrant children in public schools increased from 68 million *yuan* in the 2004 budget to 100 million *yuan* in the 2005 budget, according to a report from New China News Agency (Liu *et al.* 2005). The estimated number of school-aged migrant children in Beijing at the end of 2004 was 245,000, and around 217,000 of these have received public schooling in Beijing. Thus, if all migrant schools were demolished, even given the huge budget increment, a portion (about 10 percent) of those migrant children still would not receive urban schooling.

Relatedly, the implementation of the *yifeizhi* legislation in fact created public finance tensions between the public school systems, local education bureaus, and individual public schools. Under *yifeizhi*, although other fees may be waived, in most other places, endorsement fees are still required. Under fiscal decentralization, while local education bureaus are reluctant to provide public funding to public schools for migrant children, these local education bureau collect placement fees. However, headmasters of individual public schools would not welcome migrant children unless they receive educational endorsement fees for their own schools. During our field visits in 2005 and 2006, we were told that local education bureaus do not want to see migrant-sponsored schools licensed, because they want migrant children to be enrolled in local public schools, in order to make money. Since the placement fees go to the local education bureaus, not local public schools, local public schools have no interest in accepting migrant children (unless they receive educational endorsement fees). In this regard, in most other places, endorsement fees are still required and migrant parents may still not be able to afford the high fees.

A fourth dilemma is continuity of learning for migrant children. Given the unstable nature of migrant children's parents' jobs, migrant children may move from time to time with parents, or return to their hometowns. A lack of compatible curricular material across regions for these children is a particular problem. For example, municipalities such as Beijing and Shanghai have prepared their own reading material and examinations for the public high school system. However, migrant-sponsored schools use textbooks prepared by the People's Publishing Company, which have been used widely in other parts of the nation and for general entrance examinations for most of the country. In this regard, the migrant-sponsored schools' reading materials suit the living circumstances of migrant children, since those children may migrate to other places in the future (Kwong 2004: 1085).

A final dilemma is that of the so-called "left-behind children" (*liushou er tong*). Poor access to educational opportunities in urban settings often means that children are not brought with migrant parents into cities. As discussed here, if opportunities in the cities are not sufficient, these children are sent back home for education, where they are likely to live apart from their migrant parents. Current migration trends suggest that the number of left-behind children is drastically increasing, and the problems of living apart from parents are potentially significant (see, for example, Tolnay 2003).

It is only recently that the issue of children left behind has been brought to the attention of mainstream media and researchers (*China Daily* 2004; Duan and Zhou 2005; *Shi Jie Ri Bao* 2005). Using the 2000 Chinese census data, Duan and Zhou (2005) suggest that there are 14 million migrant children in destination areas and 23 million migrant children left behind in migrant-sending communities. In addition, nearly 87 percent of left-behind children are from rural areas. Duan and Zhou's detailed study also shows that left-behind children suffer from a serious dropout problem starting in their junior high school years, when compared to those children living with both parents.

As discussed in the Introduction to this volume and in Connelly and Zheng's Chapters 4 and 5, achieving compulsory education in rural areas is already a challenge, even without considering the additional problems faced by left-behind children. At present, policy-makers seem to be at a loss regarding policy options. When asked by a reporter, an official in charge of women's affairs at the State Council stated vaguely that "the government is not certain of what to do; perhaps the community can provide training for parents and better service for these children" (*Shi Jie Ri Bao* 2005). Clearly, more needs to be done, and sooner rather than later. As the tide of rural–urban migration continues to flow, the problem of educating migrant children remains staggering.

Policies that would allow migrant children to be enrolled in local public schools without paying prohibitively high fees are ultimately linked to the reform of China's *hukou* system. The well-publicized recent relaxation of the *hukou* system means that some rural areas near the urban coastal areas are allowed to change their rural *hukou* to urban *hukou*. However, the policy is very limited and is not allowing inter-provincial rural–urban migrants to apply for a change of *hukou* status. This limited *hukou* relaxation will likely have limited effects on migrant children's educational status, especially for those who are inter-provincial migrant children or those who come from remote rural areas.

Another option may be to support migrant-sponsored schools—rather than demolishing them—to help them to improve their physical infra-structure, ensure or facilitate the hiring of qualified teachers, and guarantee access to teaching materials and classroom supplies. Yet, as shown by the experience of migrant-sponsored schools that have been legalized, these steps may lead to substantial cost increases for families, in the absence of sufficient government support.

Conclusion

Migrant parents have high expectations for their children's education: among 494 MCE 2000 respondents, 62 percent would like their children to receive a college education or above. Yet, migrant workers have limited means to support their children's education. When they bring children with them into the cities, these children face problems accessing compulsory education because of residency policies (*Quan Guo Ren Da Chang Wei Fa Zhi Gong Zuo Wei Yuan Hui Sheng Ding* 2000). When they leave children in the countryside, children face the same infrastructure problems as other rural children, and also the stresses of life without parents.

Education has become critical for economic security in China—a point underscored repeatedly in Chapters 12 to 15 in this volume. Given this circumstance, the educational disadvantages faced by temporary migrant children today will undoubtedly bring negative personal and societal consequences down the road. Rising numbers of migrant children facing limited opportunities for upward mobility may well turn out to be significant future burdens on host cities.

The short-term implication of lack of schooling is the undermining of capacity for assimilation into the host society. In the longer term, blocked opportunities for migrant children may contribute to developments such as increases in crime and the creation of slums and ghettoes (Zhang 1998: 423–424). Child labor may also emerge as an issue. For example, a report from Shanghai revealed that there 2,300 child laborers in the city during the 1997 census of migrants; instances of child labor were also reported in Shenzhen (Shanghai Police Department Yearbook Editorial Board 1998; Zhang 1998; Liu 2003). Children living on the streets is another potential by-product of failure to educate migrant children. The Ministry of Civil Affairs estimates that there are over 152,000 street children in China, most of whom can be found in urban areas (*China Daily* 2000). It is important to address these problems. Many migrants plan to stay indefinitely in their host communities. Policy-makers need to take positive measures to provide for the human capital development of their children. Adequate schooling for migrant children may not avert the kinds of social problems described here, but inadequate schooling will certainly invite them.

Acknowledgments

This project is supported by a FIRST Award from the National Institute of Child Health and Human Development (1R29HD34878). We gratefully acknowledge their support. The authors would also like to thank Lu Shao Qing and Zhang Shou Li for permitting the use of their database, and Donna Espenberg for helpful comments on earlier versions of this chapter.

References

Cao, H. (1997) "Where to Put their School Desks?" *China News Digest*, 315: 4.

Cheng, T.J. and Selden, M. (1994) "The Origins and Social Consequences of China's Hukou System," *The China Quarterly*, 138: 644–669.

China Daily (2000) "Helping the Street Children," 23 October. Online. Available at <http://service.china.org.cn/link/wcm/Show_Text?info_id=3096&p_qry=Helping%20and%20the%20and%20Street%20and%20Children> (accessed April 2, 2002).

China Daily (2002) "Migrant Schools to Receive Legal Status," 15 August. Online. Available at <www.chinadaily.com.cn/en/doc/2002–08/15/content_132275.htm> (accessed August 13, 2003).

China Daily (2004) "Children Left Behind Face Tough Road," 2 June. Online. Available at <http://www.chinadaily.com.cn/english/doc/2004–06/02/content_335775.ht> (accessed April 11, 2005).

Duan, C.R. (2001a) "Education of Temporary Migrant Children in Beijing," paper presented at the Population Association of America, Washington, DC, March 29–31, 2001.

Duan, C.R. (2001b) "Yao Zhong Shi Liu Dong Ren Kou Er Tong Shao Nan De Jiao Yu Wen Ti (Concern is Needed for Temporary Migrant Children's Educational Problems)," *Ren Kou Xue Kan (Population Journal)*, 125: 54–57.

Duan, L.H. and Zhou M. (1999) "Liudong Renkou Zinu Yiwu Jiaoyu (Compulsory Education for Children of the Floating Population)," *Wenti Yanjiu (Problem Research)*, 2: 6–8.

Duan, C.R. and Zhou H. (2001) "Beijing Shi Liu Dong Er Tong Shao Nian Zhuang Kuang Feng Xi (An Analysis of Migrant Children in Beijing)," *Ren Kou Yu Jin Jie (Population and Economics)*, 124: 5–11.

Duan, C.R. and Zhou, F.L. (2005) "A Study on Children Left Behind," *Ren Kou Yan Jiao (Population Research)*, 29(1): 29–36.

The Economist (2000) "Schools for Children of Internal Migrants," 357 (November 18, 2000): 54.

Han, J.L. (2001) "Beijing Shi Liudong Ertong Yiwu Jiaoyu Zhuangkuang Diaocha Baogao (Education at the Margins: Survey on Compulsory Education of Beijing's Migrant Children)," paper presented at 2001 International Forum of Rural Labor Mobility in China, Beijing, July.

Irwin, J. (2000) "China's Migrant Children Fall through the Cracks," *The Courier*, September 2000. Online. Available at <www.unesco.org/courier/2000_09/uk/apprend.htm> (accessed August 13, 2003).

Kwong, J. (2004) "Educating Migrant Children: Negotiations between the State and Civil Society," *The China Quarterly*, 180: 1073–1088.

Liang, Z. (2001) "The Age of Migration in China," *Population and Development Review*, 27 (3): 499–524.

Liang, Zai and Chen, Y.P. (2007) "The Educational Consequences of Migration for Children in China," *Social Science Research*, 36(1): 28–47.

Liang, Z. and Ma, Z.D. (2004) "China's Floating Population: New Evidence from the 2000 Census," *Population and Development Review*, 30(3): 467–488.

Ling Dian Diao Cha (Horizon Marketing Company) (1997) "Liu Dong Er Tong Ji Chu Jiao Yu (Basic Education for Migrant Children)," in Ling Dian Diao Cha (Horizon Marketing Company), *Guan Cha Zhong Guo (Observing China)*, Beijing: Gong Shang Chu Ban She.

Liu, K.M. (2003) *Bian Yuan Ren (Migrant Labor in South China)*, Beijing: Xinhua Publishing.

Liu, J., Li J.T., and Zhan, Y. (2005) "The Entry of Children of Peasant Labors: A Drain on Educational Resources in Big Cities," Online. Available at <http://news.xinhuanet.com/focus/2005- 06/30/content_3152609.htm> (accessed November 10, 2005).

Lu, S.Q. and Zhang, S.L. (2001) "Bian *Yuan* Hua De Ji Chu Jiao Yu (A Marginalized Basic Education)," Ford Foundation Research Report, June 2001, Beijing.

Ministry of Agriculture Migrant Labor Survey Project (1995) "Rural Labor Mobility in Economic Development," *Zonggguo Nongcun Jingji (Chinese Rural Economy)*, 3: 3–13.

Nanfang Ribao (Nanfang Daily) (2005) "Zhuan Jia Re Yi Wai Lai Gong Zi Nu Jiu Xue," January 6, 2005. Online. Available at <www.nanfangdaily.com.cn/southnews/tszk/nfrb/jyzk/200501060365.asp> (accessed November 10, 2005).

Park, A., Rozelle, S., Wong, C., and Ren, C.G. (1996) "Distributional Consequences of Reforming Local Public Finance in China," *The China Quarterly*, 147: 751–778.

People's Daily (2001) "Surveys Find Education Investment Rising," 6 Oct. 2001. Online. Available at http://<www.english.people.com.cn/english/200110/06/eng20011006_81665.html> (accessed April 2, 2002).

Quan Guo Ren Da Chang Wei Fa Zhi Gong Zuo Wei Yuan Hui Sheng Ding (National People's Congress Law Making Working Committee) (eds.) (2000) *Zhong Hua Ren Ming Gong He Guo Jiao Yu Fa Lu Fa Gui Zhong Hui (1949–1999) (Education Laws and Regulations of the People's Republic of China (1949–1999)*, vol. 2, Beijing: Fa Lu Chu Ban She 2000.

Research Team on Migrant Children's Education, Development Research Center, Agricultural Department, State Council, the PRC (2000) "State of Migrant Children's Education Survey in Beijing," unpublished data set.

Shanghai Police Department Yearbook Editorial Board (eds.) (1998) *Shanghai Gong An Nian Jian 1998 (Shanghai Police Department Yearbook 1998)*, Beijing: Zhongguo Renmin Gong An Chu Ban She.

Shi Jie Ri Bao (World Journal) (2003) "Almost 20 Million Migrant Children, Only Half in School," November 7. Online. Available at <www.worldjournal.com> (accessed August 13, 2003).

Shi Jie Ri Bao (World Journal) (2005) "Problem with Left Behind Children Emerges," C7. August 31.

Tolnay, S.E. (2003) "The African American 'Great Migration' and Beyond," *Annual Review of Sociology*, 29: 209–32.

Zhang, S.H. (eds.) (1998) *Shanghai Liu Dong Ren Kou De Xian Zhuang Yu Zhan Wang (Shanghai Floating Population's Current Situation and Future Perspective: Shanghai's Sixth Floating Population Sample Survey)*, Shanghai: Hua Dong Shi Fan Da Xue Chu Ban She.

Zhang, L.M and Zhao, S.Y. (eds.) (2003) *Survey Report on the Temporary Migrant Children in 9 Cities of China*, Beijing: Office of Women and Children Affairs of the State Council, China Children Center, and United Nations Children's Fund.

Zhongguo Jiaoyu (Chinese Education) (2002a) "Beijing Liu Dong Shao Nian Jiu Yue Yi Re Qi Ke Jiu Jin Ru Xue Jie Du Fei Yong Biao Shun Jiang Di (From September 1st (2002), Migrant Children are Allowed to Enroll in Urban Public Schools Nearby Their Living Places; Their Placement Fee Will be Reduced By Then)," 22 April 2002. Online. Available at <www.edu.cn/20020422/ 3025257.shtml> (accessed August 13, 2003).

Zhu, M.H. (2001) "The Education Problem of Migrant Children in Shanghai," *Child Welfare*, 80(5): 563–569.

Part II
Educational quality

8 The growth and determinants of literacy in China

Donald Treiman

Introduction

A major factor in the transformation of China from one of the world's poorest nations to a rapidly industrializing nation with an unprecedented rate of per capita economic growth over the past 25 years has been the increasing literacy of the population. In a simple literacy test administered to a national sample of the Chinese population in 1996 (details are given below), the average number of characters correctly identified out of 10 ranged from just over two for those born in 1927 (and hence age 69 in 1996) to just over five for those born in 1976 (and hence age 20 in 1996). In China, gains in literacy are strongly linked to gains in years of schooling (see Figure 8.1). Thus, the

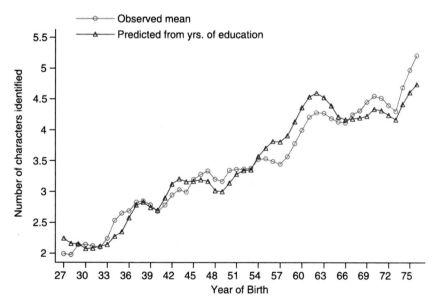

Figure 8.1 Number of characters identified by year of birth and number of characters identified predicted from the mean years of schooling of each cohort, Chinese adults, age 20–69 in 1996.

systematic expansion of education in China over the course of the twentieth century appears to be what mainly drove the expansion in literacy (Deng and Treiman 1997).

Nonetheless, education is not the sole determinant of literacy in China. We can see this from Figure 8.2, which shows substantial variation in literacy levels at each level of school completed. In the figure, the middle line shows the median level of literacy for a given level of schooling, the top line shows the 95th percentile, and the bottom line shows the 5th percentile. This figure thus shows the range of literacy at each level of schooling, excluding extreme outliers. For example, among those with three years of schooling, some people are effectively illiterate while others can identify as many as six characters, the median level achieved by university graduates. Determining the sources of the variability in literacy within levels of education is the task of this paper.

There are several possibilities. First, in China, as in other nations, the quality of schooling varies widely from place to place, and differentials are particularly sharp between urban and rural places (Unger 1982). Although in the data set analyzed here, there is no direct information on the quality of schooling, evidence that literacy is greater among those educated in towns and cities than among those with the same level of education who attended school in rural areas provides indirect support for a claim of differential schooling quality. Of course, urbanites also may be more likely to retain or

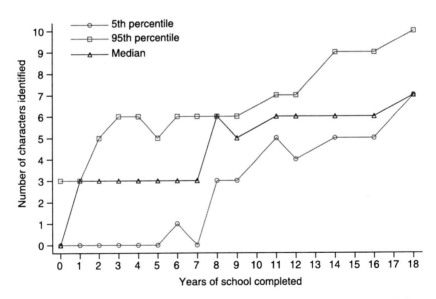

Figure 8.2 Number of characters identified by years of school completed, Chinese adults, age 20–69 in 1996.

Note: The circles and squares show the 5th and 95th percentiles at each year of schooling and the triangles show the median.

enhance their literacy as adults because they are much more likely to have to handle written materials in their work and daily lives than are rural people. For both reasons, we would expect urban residents to be more literate than rural residents with the same amount of schooling.

For much the same reason, it is likely that the literacy of nonmanual workers, whose work demands the manipulation of written materials—reading and writing—will increase over their working lives while that of manual workers will, if anything, decline.

In addition, reading skills are likely to depend not only on schooling but also upon the cultural capital of the family of origin—parental education, of course, and perhaps parental occupational status, but also such measures of cultural capital as the number of books in the household and the reading habits of parents.

Finally, given the dominant role of males in Chinese society, manifest in preference for male children (Banister 1987; Zeng *et al.* 1993; Lee and Wang 1999), higher survival levels of male infants in contemporary China (Lavely and Mason 2002), higher levels of education for sons than for daughters (see Table 8.4), and the greater propensity of men than of women to read, we would expect men to be more literate than equally educated women.

Apart from the factors affecting the literacy of individuals at any point in time, we might well expect variations over time in the level of literacy in China. In particular, it is possible that literacy declined during the 1966–1977 Cultural Revolution, relative to the amount of schooling obtained by individuals. Although the average level of education actually systematically increased during the Cultural Revolution (see Figure 8.1), mainly through the establishment of many new rural schools (Hannum 1999), many of these schools had very low standards and were closed after the end of the Cultural Revolution. Moreover, secondary schools were closed from 1966–1968 and when they re-opened were largely devoted to ideological indoctrination (Unger 1982); and universities were closed from 1966–1972 and also had a large political component to the curriculum when they re-opened. The re-establishment of academically oriented schooling did not occur until 1977, the year after Mao died (Unger 1982). Given the disruption of both the standard curriculum and school attendance, it would be surprising if the Cultural Revolution was without cost. A simple way to assess one possible cost is to analyze the effect of the Cultural Revolution on literacy, controlling for the other factors hypothesized to affect literacy. Some suggestion that there was, indeed, a cost can be seen in Figure 8.1, which shows that for cohorts born between 1955 and 1966 (and therefore age 11 between 1966 and 1977) the average level of literacy was lower than that expected from the overall relationship between years of schooling and literacy. The remainder of the chapter assesses the hypotheses sketched in the above discussion.

Data, variables, and methods

The analysis is based on data from a stratified national probability sample of Chinese adults age 20–69 carried out in 1996 (N = 6,090) (for details, see Treiman 1998; Walder *et al.* 2000; Wu and Treiman 2004). This is a very high quality survey, with little missing data. Except where noted, all the analysis is based on the 5,962 cases with complete data for the variables considered here. The basic strategy of the analysis is to estimate a series of OLS regression models predicting literacy from the factors discussed above. However, since the data are weighted and clustered, survey estimation procedures are used to obtain correct standard errors (StataCorp 2001, vol. 4: 15–101). I then show a series of graphs highlighting specific results by holding the other independent variables constant (usually at their mean).

The *dependent variable* for each of the analytic models is a transformation of a 10-item character recognition test in which respondents were shown each character and asked to identify it by name. The items, listed in the order they were presented to respondents, along with the percentage answering correctly,[1] are shown in Table 8.1. The items were chosen from three Chinese dictionaries, representing common words, words of medium difficulty, and difficult words. This proved to be a sub-optimal procedure for choosing words since it resulted in a very uneven distribution of difficulty, clustering into what are effectively four categories (see Table 8.2). To determine whether the sub-optimal distribution had any important substantive consequences, several transformations of the dependent variable I explored (scores derived from a Rasch model [Weesie 1999], the midpoints of the percentile range for each level of correct responses, and the normal transformation of the percentile scores [Powers and Xie 2000: 202–205]), and also estimated an ordered logit model parallel to that reported in Table 8.5. All of these alternatives to a simple count of the number of correct responses suggested that the simple

Table 8.1 Characters used in the literacy scale, with the percentage responding correctly to each item

Character	Pinyin (description)	Percentage responding correctly
一万	*yiwan* (ten thousand)	80.9
姓名	*xingming* (full name)	77.7
粮食	*liangshi* (grain)	76.4
函数	*hanshu* (function)	49.1
肆虐	*sinue* (wreak havoc or wanton massacre)	34.2
雕琢	*diaozhuo* (carve)	38.0
彳亍	*chichu* (walk slowly)	1.4
舛谬	*chuanmiu* (erroneous)	1.7
耆耄	*qimao* (octogenerian)	1.7
饕餮	*taotie* (glutton)	0.6

Note: Items listed in order of their inclusion in the questionnaire.

Table 8.2 Percentage distribution of number of correct responses to the 10-character vocabulary scale, and percentile midpoints, Chinese adults, age 20–69 in 1996

Number of correct responses	(%)	Cumulative percentage	Percentile midpoint
0	19.0	19.0	9.5
1	3.0	22.0	20.5
2	2.0	24.0	23.0
3	23.2	47.2	35.6
4	12.6	59.8	53.5
5	11.7	71.5	65.6
6	25.1	96.6	84.1
7	2.2	98.8	97.7
8	0.7	99.5	99.1
9	0.4	99.9	99.7
10	0.1	100.0	99.9

count underestimates the importance of place of residence at age 14 for literacy. I thus chose the simplest of the transformations, the midpoints of the percentile ranges corresponding to each number of correct responses (see Table 8.2), as the dependent variable and estimated OLS regression models. The regression coefficients can be interpreted as indicating the difference in the predicted percentile (the percentage of respondents with the same or a lower level of literacy) for two respondents who differ by one unit with respect to the corresponding independent variable but are identical with respect to each of the other independent variables. For example, in Model 2 of Table 8.5, each year of additional schooling would be expected to increase the level of literacy by 4.9 percentile points, among people who are identical with respect to father's years of schooling, gender, and place of residence at age 14.

Among the *independent variables*, gender (male = 1, female = 0), years of schooling, and father's years of schooling are all coded in a straightforward way. In preliminary analysis, I also considered mother's education and father's occupational status,[2] but neither variable had any net impact. Thus, in the interest of simplicity, they were dropped from the analysis reported here.

Residence at age 14 is a six-category classification formed by cross-tabulating whether the respondent had rural or urban residential status (*hukou*) at age 14 by the type of place of residence at age 14: village, town, or city.[3] Residential status is a crucial determinant of life chances in China, with urban registrants enjoying many privileges, including access to superior schooling; mobility from rural to urban residential status is very difficult to achieve.[4] Although the children of holders of urban *hukou* residing in rural areas (engineers working in rural facilities, teachers, health workers, etc.) can be sent to the cities for schooling, it is not clear how many actually are sent nor whether other aspects of the rural environment affect their level of literacy. It thus seems prudent to consider all combinations of registration and residential status at age 14. Technically, this is done by representing each category except the first (rural *hukou* and village residence) by a dichotomous variable, scored one for people in the category and scored zero otherwise; the omission of one category is necessary to estimate the equation. Regression coefficients for each dichotomous (or "dummy") variable are then interpreted as deviations from the coefficient for the omitted category, which is implicitly zero.

Also included are two measures of family cultural capital when the respondent was age 14: the number of books in the household, and whether the respondent's father ever read a newspaper. Since the number of books in the household is an ordinal variable with no clear metric, this variable is converted to a set of dichotomies, scored 1 for people in the category and scored 0 otherwise, with no books in the household as the omitted, or reference, category. Although the number of books in the household dominated a factor analysis in which several indicators of parental reading behavior were included, it has been suggested[5] that the measure is vulnerable to the possibility that in households with relatively few books a large fraction may be school books, or books brought into the household by a child who liked to read, thus rendering the number of books dependent upon the respondent's education or literacy rather than vice versa. Thus a second measure is included, whether the father ever read a newspaper when the respondent was about age 14, which is unambiguously causally prior to educational attainment or literacy.

To consider whether the level of literacy changes over the life course because of the demands of work, respondent's current occupation is divided into two categories: nonmanual (ISCO codes 0001–4999) and manual (ISCO codes 5000–9999) and those not currently employed are excluded from the analysis. Although the rate of intragenerational occupational mobility is quite low in China, especially between manual and nonmanual occupations (in these data 84 percent have never changed categories over the course of their work lives), in a second analysis the 16 percent who have been mobile are excluded. As we will see, the basic result holds up.

Finally, to analyze the effect of the Cultural Revolution on literacy, three cohorts are defined, based on the year of birth corresponding to the year the respondent turned age 11: (1) the pre-Cultural Revolution cohort includes people born in 1955 or earlier (and hence turning age 11 in 1966, the start of the Cultural Revolution, or earlier); (2) the Cultural Revolution cohort includes people born between 1956 and 1966, inclusive (and hence turning 11 between 1967 and 1977); and (3) the post-Cultural Revolution cohort includes people born in 1967 or later (and hence turning 11 in 1978 or later). While it is difficult to decide at what age(s) particular cohorts are most influenced by events occurring in a specific period, age 11 seems an appropriate point to assess literacy since it corresponds to about four years of schooling,[6] by which time children are expected to know more than 2,000 characters (Ren 1998).

Analysis

The analysis begins with descriptive statistics showing the distributions of the variables included in the analysis (Table 8.3) and the simple relationships (without controls) between selected independent variables and, respectively, years of schooling attained and the level of literacy achieved (Table 8.4). With one possible exception, these relationships are just what we would expect: men achieve more schooling and higher literacy levels than do women; and education and literacy increase with increasing father's education, for those whose fathers read newspapers when they were growing up, and who had more books in their households when they were growing up. The exception is that it turns out that even among those with urban registration at age 14, village

Table 8.3 Descriptive statistics for an analysis of the determinants of literacy, Chinese adults, age 20–69 in 1996

	Mean	*S.D.*
Continuous variables		
Number of characters recognized (out of 10)	3.6	2.2
Percentile transformation of characters recognized	50.0	28.3
Years of schooling	6.4	4.1
Father's years of schooling	3.1	3.7
Age (reduced sample [see text]: N=4,768)	39.6	12.1
	Percentage	
Male	51.9	
Father ever read newspaper when respondent age 14	23.3	
Number of books in household when respondent 14		
None	21.1	
1–10	21.3	
11–20	19.6	
21–50	20.3	
51–100	10.8	
101–500	6.0	
501 or more	0.9	
Total	100.0	
Residential status and size of place of residence at 14		
Rural *hukou*, village residence	77.6	
Rural *hukou*, town residence	3.0	
Rural *hukou*, city residence	1.3	
Urban *hukou*, village residence	1.4	
Urban *hukou*, town residence	5.7	
Urban *hukou*, city residence	11.0	
Total	100.0	
Current occupation is nonmanual (N=4,768)	17.7	

Table 8.4 Mean years of school completed, mean number of characters identified, and mean level of literacy (percentile transformation of number of characters identified), by selected variables, Chinese adults, age 20–69 in 1996

	Years of schooling	*Number of characters identified*	*Literacy percentile*
Male	7.3	4.1	56.0
Female	5.5	3.1	43.5
Father ever read newspaper when respondent age 14?			
Yes	9.2	5.1	69.2
No	5.6	3.2	44.2
Number of books in household when respondent 14			
None	2.2	1.4	23.2
1–10	5.5	3.2	43.5
11–20	7.2	4.0	54.3
21–50	8.2	4.6	61.5
51–100	9.2	5.1	69.5
101–500	10.2	5.5	74.6
501 or more	11.2	6.3	84.7
Residential status and size of place of residence at 14			
Rural *hukou*, village residence	5.7	3.2	44.6
Rural *hukou*, town residence	7.6	4.2	57.5
Rural *hukou*, city residence	8.8	4.9	66.4
Urban *hukou*, village residence	7.9	4.5	61.6
Urban *hukou*, town residence	8.7	4.9	67.5
Urban *hukou*, city residence	9.6	5.4	73.6

residence is costly, precisely about 1.7 years of school and 12 percentile points on the literacy scale relative to those with urban registration who grew up in cities. Thus, urban registration does not completely protect individuals from the disadvantage of growing up in a village. On the other hand, the advantage of city residence is substantially stronger for those with a rural *hukou* than for those with an urban *hukou*—3.1 additional years of schooling and nearly 22 percentile points on the literacy scale.

Determinants of literacy

The next step is to see whether the relationships between these factors and literacy continue to hold when the other factors are controlled. Table 8.5 shows the coefficients for five models predicting the level of literacy (the percentile-transformed scale of the number of characters identified). Consistent with Figure 8.1, it is evident that the level of literacy is largely a result

Table 8.5 Coefficients for models of the determinants of literacy (percentile transformation of number of characters recognized), Chinese adults, age 20–69 in 1996

	Model 1		Model 2		Model 3		Model 4		Model 5	
	b	s.e.	b	s.e.	b	s.e.	b	s.e.	b	s.e.
Years of schooling	5.46	0.06	4.93	0.09	4.42	0.11	4.88	0.09	4.40	0.11
Father's yrs. of schooling			0.82	0.15	0.50	0.16	0.45	0.16	0.25[f]	0.16
Male			3.85	0.56	4.28	0.52	4.00	0.56	4.37	0.52
Residence at age 14 (reference category is rural registration (*hukou*), residence in village)[a]										
R. *hukou*, town residence			3.34	1.15	2.86[d]	1.23	2.80[e]	1.18	2.50[f]	1.27
R. *hukou*, city residence			5.84	1.36	5.19	1.41	5.65	1.32	5.10	1.37
U. *hukou*, village residence			5.62[c]	2.31	5.72[d]	2.31	5.34[e]	2.32	5.52[f]	2.32
U. *hukou*, town residence			6.84	1.24	6.42	1.25	6.21	1.22	6.00	1.23
U. *hukou*, city residence			7.99	0.79	7.70	0.80	7.23	0.78	7.20	0.78
Number of books in household at age 14 (reference category is none)[b]										
1–10					4.56	0.94			4.57	0.94
11–20					7.02	1.00			6.90	1.00
21–50					9.31	1.13			8.98	1.12
51–100					11.44	1.11			11.00	1.12
101–500					10.91	1.91			10.15	1.97
501 or more					13.45	2.70			12.65	2.70
Fr. newspaper reader: R 14							4.16	0.65	3.08	0.66
Constant	15.02	0.48	12.42	0.60	10.29	0.54	12.96	0.61	10.66	0.53
R^2	0.639		0.656		0.668		0.659		0.669	

Notes:
[a] Wald tests on the set of coefficients for residence are significant for all models at beyond the .0005 level.
[b] Wald tests on the set of coefficients for number of books are significant for all models at beyond the .0005 level.
[c] All coefficients are significant at .01 or beyond except that marked (p=.018).
[d] P-values for marked coefficients, going down the column, are .024 and .017.
[e] P-values for marked coefficients are .022 and .026.
[f] P-values for marked coefficients are .136, .054, and .021.

of education. About 64 percent of the variance in literacy scores is due to variation in the number of years of school completed, and each additional year of schooling results in an expected increase of 5.5 percentile points on the literacy scale. Thus, for example, while the average person without any schooling would be expected to be at the 15th percentile of literacy (the intercept), the average high school graduate would be expected to be at the 81st percentile of literacy (since 15.02 + 5.46*12 = 80.54).

Model 2 takes account also of father's years of schooling, gender, and size and type of residence at age 14. All these factors contribute significantly to literacy and the effects of all but the father's years of schooling are substantial in magnitude. For example, among equally educated people with equally educated fathers and living in the same type of place with the same residential status, men would be expected, on average, to score nearly four percentile points higher on the literacy scale than would women. Also, education continues to strongly affect literacy, although, since the size of the education coefficient drops from 5.46 to 4.93, a modest portion of the total effect of education shown for Model 1 is due to the correlation of education with father's education, gender, and residence. However, the real story in Model 2 is the strength of the effect of residence. Relative to those who at age 14 had rural *hukou* status and resided in a village, those with urban *hukou* status residing in cities would be expected, on average, to be eight percentile points higher on the literacy scale. That is, the difference between the two extreme residential circumstances for otherwise similar people is the equivalent of about 1.6 years of schooling (since 1.62 = 7.99/4.93).

Models 3 and 4, respectively, add a measure of cultural capital when the respondent was age 14, the number of books in the household and whether the father read a newspaper, and Model 5 includes both measures of cultural capital. For our purposes, it is sufficient to discuss Model 5. The first point to note is that years of schooling continue to be the most important determinant of level of literacy, although the coefficient drops moderately relative to that for Model 2, suggesting that part of the effect of education is due to family cultural capital. Still, the coefficient of 4.4 tells us that people of the same gender whose fathers are equally educated, who live in the same type of place with the same residential status, and who come from families with the same amount of cultural capital, but who differ by a year of schooling, would be expected to differ, on average, by 4.4 percentile points on the literacy scale. Thus, the difference in percentile points between a person with no more than primary schooling and a high school graduate would be 26.4 percentile points (= 4.4*(12–6)). Second, when family cultural capital is controlled, father's years of schooling has no significant impact. Thus, the reason that the children of more educated fathers are more literate, net of their own level of schooling, is that homes with educated fathers are more literary—there are more books and fathers read more. Third, the impact of interest in the written word is very strong. The difference between the expected literacy levels of otherwise similar people coming from households with many books (501 or more) and from households with no books is nearly 13 percentile points, the equivalent of the effect of nearly three years of schooling. Whether the father read a newspaper also has an impact on literacy, controlling for all other factors, but it is much more modest, about three percentile points. Finally, once other factors are taken into account, it turns out that there is a clear advantage in having an urban *hukou*. Even urban *hukou* holders living in villages have higher expected percentile scores than do any rural *hukou* holders, even those living in cities. Further, urban residence at age 14 turns out to be much more important for rural *hukou* holders than for those with urban *hukou*. For rural *hukou* holders, those living in cities at age 14 had percentile scores more than five points higher than those living in villages, holding constant all other factors. However, for urban *hukou* holders, this gap was only 1.7 percentile points (= 7.2 − 5.5). This result suggests that urban registration status immunizes individuals from the disadvantages of village life when it comes to their level of literacy. Moreover, the cost of rural *hukou* status is substantially reduced among those who were raised in cities: 2.1 percentile points (= 7.2 − 5.1) compared to 5.5 percentile points among those raised in villages. Exactly what mechanisms (other than schooling, father's education, family cultural capital, and gender) differentiate urban and rural *hukou* holders living in villages but not those living in cities is unclear and requires further study.

Changes in literacy over the life course

We now turn to consideration of the suggestion made earlier that literacy is differentially reinforced over the life course because of the kind of work people do. Some work requires the manipulation of symbols—reading and writing (and also computing)—much more than does other work. A large fraction of the work that professionals, managers, and clerical workers do involves handling written materials, but this is much less true of manual workers and farmers. Thus, we might expect that the level of literacy at school-leaving age would be reinforced and enhanced over the life course for nonmanual workers but would, if anything, decline for manual workers.[7] As a simple test of this hypothesis, I consider those currently employed (as of the survey date); this reduces the sample size from 5,962 to 4,768 since some people are in school, waiting for work, keeping house, retired, or not in the labor force for other reasons. For those with a job, I extend Model 5 of Table 8.5 by adding a distinction between nonmanual and manual workers at the time of the survey, age at the time of the survey, and the interaction between the two variables. The interaction term allows both the slope and the intercept of the relationship between literacy and type of work (nonmanual vs. manual) to vary with age. The coefficients of the model are not reported since they differ little from those in Table 8.5, Model 5. However, in Figure 8.3, the relationship between age and literacy for nonmanual and manual workers is shown when all the remaining variables in Model 5 of Table 8.5

are set at their means. Inspecting Figure 8.3, it is evident that among equally well educated people with equally well educated fathers, equal family cultural capital, the same gender, the same residential status, and the same type of place of residence at age 14, there is no difference in the level of literacy of nonmanual and manual workers among those age 20. However, among nonmanual workers the level of literacy increases substantially as age increases, while among manual workers the level of literacy decreases as age increases.

This result makes it tempting to attribute the change in literacy with age as confirming the hypothesis that nonmanual work reinforces literacy over the life course while manual work suppresses it. Before accepting this conclusion, however, we need to rule out an alternative explanation—that the observed differences between those of different ages in 1996 simply reflect historical changes in China that result in differences among birth cohorts that remain constant over the life course. There are two reasonable possibilities: that schools have systematically improved or declined since the mid-1930s when our oldest cohorts first entered school until the date of the survey in 1996; or that a shift in the composition of the labor force—an increase in the percentage of workers who hold nonmanual jobs—causes the observed effects. However, neither possibility is consistent with the pattern of results. If there were a decline in the quality of education,[8] we would expect the level of

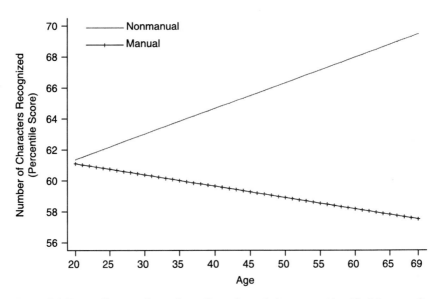

Figure 8.3 Percentile transformation of number of characters identified by age, for nonmanual and manual workers, controlling for education (evaluated at nine years of schooling), Chinese adults, age 20–69 in 1996.

Note: All remaining variables shown in Table 8.5, Model 5, are set at their means.

literacy for each level of education to decline for successive cohorts (that is, increase with age) for *both* nonmanual and manual workers. Similarly, if there were an increase in the quality of education, as might be expected in the long term given the sustained economic development of China since 1978, we would expect the level of literacy for each level of education to increase for successive cohorts (that is, decline with age) for both nonmanual and non-manual workers. However, since the level of literacy diverges with increasing age for the two groups, overall changes in the quality of education in China over time cannot explain the pattern and there is no basis for positing a complex scenario in which the quality of education declined for nonmanual workers but improved for manual workers.

The second alternative explanation fares no better. On the assumption that, in China, as elsewhere, the proportion of the population engaged in nonmanual work has been increasing over time, a genetic determinist might argue that the average "quality" of both nonmanual and manual workers has declined, as the best and the brightest of those who formerly would have become manual workers increasingly achieve nonmanual occupations. But this scenario is inconsistent with the facts. Somewhat surprisingly, the non-manual sector has not been growing in a linear fashion; rather, it follows a U-shaped distribution, declining during the Cultural Revolution and only by the 1990s regaining the relative size of the pre-Cultural Revolution period.[9] Moreover, a claim that the Chinese labor force is increasingly sorted by talent[10] is inconsistent with the diverging age trends for nonmanual and manual workers; under such a claim we would expect exactly the opposite pattern, a *converging* trend with age or, putting it in cohort terms, a *diverging* trend across cohorts. It thus appears that the pattern of increased literacy with age for nomanual workers and decreasing literacy with age for manual workers, net of education and the other factors in Model 5, is best understood as a life course effect—over the life course, nonmanual workers utilize their literacy and thus reinforce and enhance it, while nonmanual workers by and large do not, and hence suffer some decline in literacy.

There is, however, another possibility that needs to be taken seriously—that over the life course the more literate are upwardly mobile, from manual to nonmanual jobs, and the less literate are downwardly mobile. Although the overall rate of intragenerational mobility is quite low in China (only 16 percent of those with jobs at the time of the survey had ever worked at both manual and nonmanual jobs), there is a great deal of mobility into nonmanual jobs, with fully 65 percent of current nonmanual workers having had experience at manual jobs and having, on average, spent about half (51.4 percent) of their total working lives in such jobs. Thus, it could be the case that the diverging literacy of nonmanual and manual workers with age simply reflects the sorting of the more literate into nonmanual jobs as workers age. To test this possibility, I restricted the analysis to those who had never been mobile across the manual–nonmanual divide in the course of their careers; this reduced the sample size to 3,121 (results not shown). With this restriction, the slope for the gain in literacy with age for nonmanual workers is somewhat reduced relative to the corresponding line in Figure 8.3, and the intercept shifts downward, both indicating that part of the effect observed in Figure 8.3 is, in fact, due to the infusion into the nonmanual sector of especially literate workers over the life course. However, the basic pattern is unchanged: there is a divergence of literacy with age between "permanent" manual and nonmanual workers, strongly suggesting that literacy is reinforced or undercut by the demands of work.

A similar pattern holds for urban and non-urban residents. Changes in literacy with age for two groups—those living in villages both at age 14 and at the time of the survey and those living in cities both at age 14 and at the time of the survey—were compared. Here the argument is that city life demands literacy while rural life does not, so that a similar pattern of divergence in the level of literacy with age for rural and urban residents would be expected as just observed for nonmanual and manual workers. Again, the results are consistent with the claim. Village residents start (at age 20) with a slight disadvantage, about four percentile points on the literacy scale, but this disadvantage grows to 16 percentile points among the oldest respondents (those age 69). And again there is no basis for assuming variation across cohorts, specifically variation of a kind that leads to greater literacy among rural residents net of all other factors in the model and declining literacy among urban residents. Thus, the appropriate conclusion is that urban life does, indeed, promote literacy over the life course while rural life undercuts it.

The effect of the Cultural Revolution

The 1966–1977 Cultural Revolution in China was a cataclysmic event in which the entire society was thrown into chaos.[11] Unleashed initially by Mao Zedong and his agents as a device for purging Mao's (perceived) political enemies, it soon acquired its own escalating dynamic as an uncontrolled mass movement. Universities were shut down entirely from 1966 to 1972, and secondary schools from 1966 to 1968 and, when they re-opened, schools at both levels were concerned primarily with political indoctrination until the restoration of academic standards in 1977.

At the same time, many new primary schools were opened in villages, but typically with a very low academic standard (Unger 1982). Students and other urban workers, especially the "intelligentsia" (those with upper secondary or tertiary education working in professional or technical jobs), were "sent down" to the countryside to work as peasants, and political loyalty rather than competence became the main criterion for both educational and occupational advancement. Under these circumstances, especially the school closures and abandonment of the academic curriculum for several years after schools re-opened, it would be surprising if the quality of education did not suffer. In particular, since an important aspect of schooling is the expansion of literacy—the ability to identify increasing numbers of characters—we should expect that, relative to their level of schooling, students educated during the Cultural Revolution would be able to identify fewer characters than those educated before or since. Of course, differences in the number of characters identified at the time of the survey, when respondents ranged from age 20 to 69, is hardly an ideal measure of the number of characters learned in school since, as we have seen, literacy appears to vary over the life course, increasing for nonmanual workers and those living in urban areas and decreasing for manual workers and those living in rural areas. Still, the number of characters identified is the only measure available, and its use is warranted given how little is yet systematically known about how the Cultural Revolution affected the development of adult intellectual skills.

To estimate the effect of the Cultural Revolution on literacy, I explored a number of different spline models, each including all the variables in Model 5 of Table 8.5 and in addition allowing the net trend in literacy (that is, the trend controlling for all the other independent variables) to vary across three cohorts: (1) the pre-Cultural Revolution cohort, which consists of those born in 1955 or earlier; (2) the Cultural Revolution cohort, which consists of those born between 1956 and 1966, inclusive; and (3) the post-Cultural Revolution cohort, which consists of those born in 1967 or later. The models all have knots at 1955 and 1966 but differ with respect to the presence or absence of discontinuities at those years and also with respect to whether or not the Cultural Revolution period was represented by a straight line or a curved line. The best fitting and most parsimonious model (shown in Figure 8.4) was that which posited a discontinuity at birth year 1955 (people who turned 11 at the start of the Cultural Revolution in 1966), a curvilinear trend during the Cultural Revolution, and a knot but no discontinuity at 1966, which allows the trend to change for those who turned 11 in 1977, the end of the Cultural Revolution. Although the table is not presented here, all features of this model are statistically significant. Moreover, the cost of the Cultural Revolution was mainly felt by those who turned 11 between 1966 and 1968, when the disruption of schooling was greatest. The literacy scores of such students dropped about four percentile points relative to those who were age 11 in the year before the beginning of the Cultural Revolution, a decline the equivalent of about one year of schooling. In the same sense that reading scores in US schools are calibrated to "grade level," with reports phrased as "the students at such and such a school read two years below grade level," we can say that the cost of the Cultural Revolution, at least at the outset, was to reduce literacy scores by about one grade level—a strong effect.

Conclusion

Literacy in China is strongly socially structured. Of course, as elsewhere, literacy is a skill mainly acquired in school. Thus, as education has expanded over the twentieth century in China, literacy has increased as well. But the level of schooling is not the sole determinant of literacy. There are also

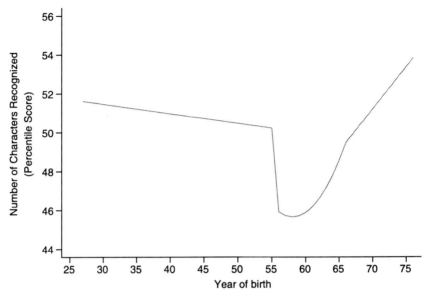

Figure 8.4 Percentile transformation of number of characters identified, before, during, and after the Cultural Revolution, Chinese adults, age 20–69 in 1996.

Notes: All remaining variables shown in Table 8.5, Model 5, are set at their means.
Spline function, with a discontinuity at 1955, a knot at 1966, and a curve between 1955 and 1966.

dramatic differences in the quality of schooling, particularly between urban and rural areas. Although we have no direct measures of school quality, such differences are well established and account, at least in part, for differences in the level of literacy between those with the same amount of education who attended school in villages, towns, and cities. In addition to school effects, however, there are individual, family, environmental, life course, and historical effects. First, in still another manifestation of male dominance in China, males tend to be more literate than females with the same amount of schooling, whether through greater engagement with written materials after leaving school or for some other reason. Second, those from families invested in reading (as indicated by many books in the household and newspaper reading on the part of the father) are more literate than their equally well educated classmates whose families were less prone to read—who had less "cultural capital." Third, the advantage of urban residence clearly reflects more than differences in the quality of schooling, since even controlling for the level of schooling and the other factors in the model, permanent residents of cities start out (at age 20) with an advantage in literacy over permanent village residents equivalent to that of an extra year of schooling, and this advantage increases over time to the equivalent of about three years of extra schooling, because over the life course the literacy of city dwellers increases and that of village dwellers decreases. Similarly, while equally well educated manual and nonmanual workers start out (at age 20) equally literate, the literacy of non-manual workers increases over the life course while that of manual workers declines. In both cases, the most plausible interpretation is that it is differential engagement with the written word—reading and writing—that creates the increasing gap over the life course. The old adage, "Use it or lose it," clearly applies here. Finally, literacy is responsive to historical events, specifically the Cultural Revolution, which created a massive disruption of the educational system. Among otherwise similar people, particularly people with identical levels of schooling, the cohort that was, or should have been, in school during the Cultural Revolution ended up, as adults, with a level of literacy a full year lower than similarly educated people who were in school prior to or after the Cultural Revolution.

Acknowledgments

Revised version of a paper presented at the Oxford Meeting of the Research Committee on Social Stratification and Mobility, 11–13 April 2002. Thanks for helpful comments are due to Richard Arum and Eric Grodsky, and for bibliographic assistance to Shige Song.

Notes

1 All other responses—answering incorrectly, the respondent saying s/he does not know the meaning of the character, or refusing to answer altogether, are coded as "not correct." Since fewer than 1 percent refused to answer each item, the responses can be taken as an accurate indication of the ability of the Chinese adult population to identify each character.
2 The ISEI; see Ganzeboom *et al.* (1992).
3 The seven-category urban hierarchy coded in the 1996 data (villages, townships or towns, county seats, county-level cities, prefecture-level cities, provincial capitals, and provincial-level cities (Beijing, Shanghai, and Tianjin)) is collapsed into three categories. Villages remain distinct; townships or towns and county seats are coded as towns; and the remainder are coded as cities.
4 See Wu and Treiman (2004).
5 I thank Eric Grodsky (personal communication) for suggesting this possibility.
6 In the data set used here, both the median and the mode of school entry age (among those who ever attended school) was seven, which is consistent with the claim of Hannum and Xie (1994: 76) that, in China, children typically begin school when they are seven years old.
7 The theoretical literature on the effect of age on verbal skills, summarized in Wilson and Gove (1999: 257–258), suggests that such skills should either increase or remain stable from young adulthood until old age (that is, over the entire age span included here). However, there has been little consideration of age trends differentiated by type of work performed or other attributes that might affect verbal skills.
8 Some claim that this is true of the USA, for example, Glenn (1994) and Alwin (1999), but see also the critique of this position by Wilson and Gove (1999) and the critiques and rejoinders that follow.

9 The same pattern holds when cohort variations in the proportion nonmanual are considered for the first job after leaving school, for the job held at age 20, and for the job held at age 25.
10 As claimed for the USA by Herrnstein and Murray (1994).
11 For good general accounts, see Bernstein (1977) and Lee (1978). For analyses of its effect on education, see Unger (1982) and Deng and Treiman (1997).

References

Alwin, D.F. (1999) "Family of Origin and Cohort Differences in Verbal Ability," *American Sociological Review*, 56: 625–638.

Banister, J. (1987) *China's Changing Population*, Stanford, CA: Stanford University Press.

Bernstein, T.P. (1977) *Up to the Mountains and Down to the Villages: The Transfer of Youth from Urban to Rural China*, New Haven, CT: Yale University Press.

Deng, Z., and Treiman, D.J. (1997) "The Impact of the Cultural Revolution on Trends in Educational Attainment in the People's Republic of China," *American Journal of Sociology*, 103: 391–428.

Ganzeboom, H.B.G., De Graaf, P.M., and Treiman, D.J. (1992) "A Standard International Socio-Economic Index of Occupational Status," *Social Science Research*, 21: 1–56.

Glenn, N.D. (1994) "Television Watching, Newspaper Reading, and Cohort Differences in Verbal Ability," *Sociology of Education*, 67: 216–230.

Hannum, E. (1999) "Political Change and the Urban–Rural Gap in Basic Education in China, 1949–1990," *Comparative Education Review*, 43: 193–211.

Hannum, E. and Xie, Y. (1994) "Trends in Educational Gender Inequality in China: 1949–1985," *Research in Social Stratification and Mobility*, 13: 73–98.

Herrnstein, R.J. and Murray, C. (1994). *The Bell Curve: Intelligence and Class Structure in American Life*, New York: Simon and Schuster.

Lavely, W. and Mason, W.M. (2002) "The Effect of Village-level Birth Planning Policy Variation on Infant Mortality in China," paper presented at the annual meeting of the Population Association of America, May, Atlanta.

Lee, H.Y. (1978) *The Politics of the Chinese Cultural Revolution: A Case Study*, Berkeley, CA: University of California Press.

Lee, J.Z. and Feng, W. (1999) *One Quarter of Humanity*, Cambridge, MA: Harvard University Press.

Powers, D.A. and Xie, Y. (2000) *Statistical Methods for Categorical Data Analysis*, San Diego, CA: Academic Press.

Ren, C. (1998) "Xue Xi Xin Li Yu Ke Mu De Zu Zhi" ("Psychology of Learning and the Organization of Subjects."), in Xianglu Cui (ed.) *Su Zhi Jiao Yu Shi Shi Fang Fa* (*The Implementation of Quality Education*), Jinan: Shangdong Education Publishing House.

StataCorp (2001) *Stata Reference Manual: Release 7* (4 vols), College Station, TX: Stata Corporation.

Treiman, D.J. (ed.) (1998) *Life Histories and Social Change in Contemporary China: Provisional Codebook*, Donald J. Treiman and Andrew G. Walder [principal investigators]; People's University, Beijing [producer]; Los Angeles: UCLA, Institute for Social Science Research, Social Science Data Archive [distributor].

Unger, J. (1982) *Education under Mao: Class and Competition in Canton Schools, 1960–1980*, New York: Columbia University Press.

Walder, A.G., Li, B. and Treiman, D.J. (2000) "Politics and Life Chances in a State Socialist Regime: Dual Career Paths into the Urban Chinese Elite, 1949–1996," *American Sociological Review*, 65: 191–209.

Weesie, J. (1999) "The Rasch Model in Stata," electronic document posted to http://www.stata.com/support/faqs/stat/rasch.html.

Wilson, J.A. and Gove, W.R. (1999) "The Intercohort Decline in Verbal Ability: Does It Exist?" *American Sociological Review*, 64: 253–266.

Wu, X. and Treiman, D.J. (2002) "The Household Registration System and Social Stratification in China: 1955–1996," *Demography*, 41: 363–384.

Zeng, Y., Ping, T., Baochang, G., Yi, X., Bohua, L. and Yongping, L. (1993) "Causes and Implications of the Recent Increase in the Reported Sex Ratio at Birth in China," *Population and Development Review*, 19: 283–302.

9 Academic achievement and engagement in rural China

Emily Hannum and Albert Park

Introduction

An important aspect of social stratification in post-reform China is that educational opportunities available to children are increasingly diverse. Heightened economic inequalities associated with market reforms, coupled with school finance policies that have strengthened the link between local resources and the provision of education, have led to great variability in investments in education by local governments, and by families. As the studies in this volume by Connelly and Zheng and Postiglione indicate, access to education is closely linked to characteristics such as location of residence, socio-economic status, gender, and ethnicity.

These and other studies have long attested to disparities in access to education, particularly at the secondary level. However, little research has examined the precursors to these outcomes that occur among children at lower levels of education, while they are still enrolled in school. As ever-larger proportions of China's children enter school, and as the school and home circumstances in which children function increasingly diverge, understanding educational achievement, attitudes, and practices among China's most vulnerable children becomes increasingly important.

This chapter investigates children's school performance and academic engagement—favorable educational attitudes and practices—in rural Gansu Province, a poor setting in interior China. The chapter begins with a discussion of recent changes in China's provision of education to rural children. Then, after providing a brief description of data and methods, we analyze educational achievement and engagement. We consider disparities by gender and socio-economic status, and analyze whether these disparities can be linked to differences in the home environments in which children develop or the characteristics of classroom teachers with whom children study. We close with a discussion of factors that support favorable schooling outcomes among students in poor rural areas of China.

Educational access and inequality in China

Education in China has undergone dramatic changes in the wake of market reforms dating from the late 1970s and early 1980s. On the positive side, market reforms have stimulated unprecedented economic growth and poverty reduction, enabling increased family investments in education. In addition, government policies encouraging educational expansion have emerged. Most notably, the Law on Compulsory Education of 1986 designated nine years of education, six years of primary school and three years of lower secondary school, as compulsory for all children (Ministry of Education 1986). New laws in the 1990s and into the twenty-first century have reaffirmed the government's commitment to achieving compulsory education in impoverished regions and expanding educational access (Hannum and Adams 2006).

On the other hand, rising regional economic inequality and fiscal decentralization set the stage for new educational inequalities. Inter-provincial income inequality increased markedly from the late 1980s to at least the mid-1990s, and the urban–rural gap in income and living standards remained great (Carter 1997; Khan and Riskin 1998). Coinciding with new economic inequalities was the decentralization of the administration and finance of primary, secondary and tertiary education. As of the early 2000s, the central government ran and financed certain institutions of higher education, and provincial, county, township and village governments respectively took responsibility for schools at the tertiary, upper secondary, lower secondary, and primary levels (Tsang 2002: 13). In general, the government budget finances only teachers' wages, while other costs must be covered from local resources, either through specially raised earmarked funds collected from households, collective contributions, school-generated revenues, or fees charged directly to students (Hannum and Park 2002). Student fees can be a major component of school finance, especially in poor rural communities where other options for generating school revenues are limited. New fees have coincided with new opportunity costs associated with educating children: in the years since market reforms allowed rural households greater freedom to engage in different income-generating activities, children have been able to contribute directly to the family economy.

Studies of educational inequality in China have emphasized these policy shifts and their implications for social disparities in enrollment and attainment. These studies have generally shown a trend of improving enrollment rates in the later 1980s and through the 1990s and the year 2000 (Hannum and Liu 2005; Connelly and Zheng, Chapter 5 in this volume). However, studies also attest to the continuing enrollment disadvantages associated with rural residence and household poverty (Brown and Park 2002; Connelly and Zheng, Chapters 4 and 5 in this volume; Hannum and Liu 2005). Rural children in low socio-economic status households and households that are credit-constrained are disproportionately likely to drop out of school (Brown and Park 2002; Hannum 2003). Still other studies have traced the disproportionate enrollment and attainment disadvantages associated with residence in remote and poor communities (Michelson and Parish 2000; Hannum 2003; Adams and Hannum 2005; Connelly and Zheng in Chapter 4 in this volume). Finally, analyses of survey data through the early 1990s have suggested that poor rural girls were at heightened risk of dropping out of school or not making the transition to junior high school (Brown and Park 2002; Hannum 2002). These studies also indicate that the enrollment disadvantages of poor children emerge at the stage of junior high school, when costs associated with schooling increase.

Prior research has convincingly established family economic constraints as a major contributor to school-leaving in rural China. Yet, presumably, when parents come to the decision that school is too expensive, other factors enter into this decision, such as how well the child is doing in school and how the child feels about school. Brown and Park's (2002) study in officially designated poor counties found evidence that girls' performance in primary school significantly affected whether or not they advanced to middle school. However, with the exception of Brown and Park's work, children's performance and attitudes remain largely unexplored as contributors to educational stratification.

Further, little is known about the role of classroom factors that might reinforce, or mitigate, inequalities. Because decentralization led to dramatic variation in school resources and teacher qualifications, it is likely that the quality of schooling varies greatly from place to place. In particular, the prevalence of less-qualified teachers in the poorest rural areas is significant, and teacher qualifications can be systematically linked to student learning (Park and Hannum 2001). However, whether qualifications of teachers may contribute to gender and socio-economic inequalities in school performance and engagement remains unknown.

In summary, the majority of studies of children's schooling inequalities have focused on the issue of access disparities: enrollment versus non-enrollment, or successful transitions to higher levels of education. However, little research has investigated children's experiences inside the school system that may contribute to these outcomes. We begin to address this gap by investigating factors associated with academic achievement and engagement among primary students in a poor setting in interior China. Specifically, we analyze achievement and engagement differences by gender and socio-economic status, considering both the scope of these disparities and how they are linked to differences in home environments and the classroom teachers with whom children study.

Data and methods

This chapter focuses on Gansu Province, which is located in northwest China and is one of the nation's poorest provinces. Gansu encompasses 390,000 square kilometers of flat Loess Plateau, Gobi desert, mountainous and hilly areas, and vast grasslands. In 2000, the year of our survey, Gansu Province had a population of 25.62 million, 76 percent of whom resided in rural areas (United Nations Economic and Social Commission for Asia and the Pacific (UNESCAP) 2005). Gansu's socio-economic and educational profiles resemble those of other interior provinces. Relative to the nation as a whole, Gansu exhibits low per capita income, high rates of illiteracy, and low per-child educational expenditures. Rural residents are predominantly employed in subsistence farming or animal husbandry.

This study uses data from the Gansu Survey of Children and Families (GSCF). The GSCF, conducted by the authors in the summer of 2000, is a survey of 2000 children aged 9 to 12 and their families in rural areas of 20 counties in Gansu Province. The survey consisted of extensive, linkable questionnaires administered to children, their parents, teachers, school principals, and community leaders. The multi-stage sampling scheme drew children from lists of all school-aged children in selected villages, enabling us to avoid concerns about selection bias that afflict school-based samples. The analysis presented below excludes children in junior high school (N = 50) and children not currently in school (N = 23), leaving a maximum sample size of 1,927 for analyses. We focus on a subset of items that cover achievement and engagement with schooling, children's and their teachers' demographic and socio-economic characteristics, and social and cultural resources in the family. Here, we describe our measurement strategies.

Child achievement and engagement

We measure both student achievement and engagement. Academic achievement is measured as the math and Chinese end-of-semester average test scores, which were scored out of 100. These scores are the key determinant of students' progress through school.

Considering children's engagement, we consider four types of measures. First, to tap into children's hopes for their educational future, we asked about aspirations with the following question: What is the highest level of education you want to achieve? (primary, junior high school, senior high school, college or higher). Second, to tap diligence, the target child was asked about the amount of time spent on homework on a daily basis: "Last semester, or when you were in school, how much time did you spend doing homework every day?" (less than 1 hour, 1–2 hours, 3 hours or more). Third, to understand children's academic confidence, we asked, "Are you a good student?" (no, somewhat, yes). Finally, to understand the child's feelings of alienation from school, we asked children to strongly disagree, disagree somewhat, agree somewhat, or strongly agree with the statement, "A lot of the time, I don't want to attend school."

Child gender and socio-economic status

We focus on two historically important lines of social inequality: gender and socio-economic status. We measure gender using an indicator variable for whether the child is female. We consider two dimensions of family socio-economic status. Wealth, specified in quintiles for descriptive purposes and in log form in estimation models, is a direct measure of family material resources. The family wealth variable was constructed from detailed measures of household assets, including the value of housing, fixed capital, and household durable goods. We also consider mother's years of education. Mother's education may reflect the long-term economic position of the family, the mother's bargaining power within the household, or be an indicator of family human capital. Mother's human capital, more than father's, is likely to matter for children's schooling outcomes, as mothers are likely to take more responsibility for socialization and childrearing activities.

Home environment for learning

To consider the role of the home environment for learning, we use three measures. First, to capture the cultural environment in the home, we use mothers' reports of whether there are children's books in the home (no, yes). Second, as a measure of social capital in the home, we consider mothers' reports of the frequency with which parents help children with homework (never, sometimes, often). Finally, as a measure of family norms about schooling, we consider mothers' aspirations for their children's education (primary school, middle school, high school, college or above).

Teacher characteristics

The increasingly unequal economic circumstances of China's schools may be reflected in great diversity in the quality of teachers. Just as the home environment is important for learning, characteristics of teachers are thought to matter for children's school outcomes. We consider four measures of teacher quality.

First, we describe teacher's education with two indicator variables for whether the teacher has completed high school- or college-level education. High school-level education includes regular high schools and specialized teacher training schools attended after middle school (*zhongzhuan*). College-level education includes regular universities (very rare) and normal colleges (*dazhuan*) following the completion of high school. Second, we employ two measures of experience: total years of teaching experience and years taught in the current school. Total years of experience reflects accumulated human capital in the field of teaching. Years of experience in the current school may capture school-specific human capital, e.g. familiarity with procedures and networks in the local school. Third, we measure teacher income as the log of total monthly income received by teachers. Fourth, we measure whether the teacher is a formal teacher—a government employee. In China, most teachers are government employees whose wages are paid out of county government budgets and who are assigned to schools by county education bureaus. In addition, some schools also hire "unofficial" teachers using locally raised funds, especially when there is a shortage of available qualified teachers. Additionally, we measure two characteristics of teachers that cannot be considered as part of standard conceptualizations of teacher quality. First, we measure teacher gender using an indicator variable for whether the teacher is female. It is possible that female teachers may relate to children differently than male teachers. Second, we consider whether or not a teacher is from the local village. Local teachers may connect to children or motivate them in ways that teachers from the outside cannot. We use an indicator variable coded as one if the teacher is born and raised in the village in which the school is located.

Other control variables

Because siblings are commonly perceived to "dilute" family resources— economic, social, or cultural—we also control for sibship size. Finally, because there may be developmental changes in children's attitude reporting, we include age in our analysis.

Results

This section presents gender and socio-economic differences in educational achievement and engagement. We then discuss differences by gender and socio-economic status in home environments and teacher characteristics. Finally, we present a multivariate analysis of student outcomes that considers the collective impact of gender, socio-economic status, home environment, and teacher quality on student outcomes.

Differences in achievement and engagement

One essential question for this chapter is whether historical enrollment disadvantages for girls and low socio-economic status children are mirrored in patterns of achievement and engagement. We begin to address this question in Table 9.1, which shows mean math and language scores as well as selected categories of the four engagement measures, tabulated by gender, family wealth quintile, and mother's educational attainment. For math score and language score, we also show *p*-values from F-tests of the null hypothesis of no difference in means by gender, wealth quintile, or mother's education. For other variables listed in column 1, we list *p*-values for chi-square tests of independence between each variable[1] and gender, wealth quintile, or mother's education.

Table 9.1 Achievement and engagement measures by gender and socio-economic status

1	2	3			4						5				
Variables	Gender				Wealth quintile						Mother's education				
	Total	Male	Fenn.	P*	Lowest	2	3	4	Highest	P*	None	Prim.	JHS	SHS+	P*
Grades															
Mathematics (average)	74	74	74	0.42	73	72	74	75	76	0.00	72	75	76	79	0.00
Language (average)	73	71	74	0.00	71	71	73	74	75	0.00	71	73	75	77	0.00
Engagement															
Highest level of schooling you want to complete (% college)	48	51	45	0.04	42	44	50	53	52	0.03	45	48	55	71	0.01
Usually finish homework (% usually finish all)	77	72	83	0.00	81	79	76	77	72	0.03	78	74	78	80	0.52
Are you a good student? (% yes)	42	40	46	0.01	44	42	47	41	37	0.04	45	43	35	44	0.05
Usually don't want to attend school (% yes)	11	10	11	0.86	13	12	10	11	7	0.00	12	10	9	7	0.00

Note:
* For the continuous variables math grade and language grade, p-values represent F-tests of the null hypothesis of no differences in means by gender, wealth quintile, or mother's education. For all other variables listed in column 1, p-values represent chi-square tests of independence between that variable and gender, wealth quintile, or mother's education.

The gender gap is mixed, but surprisingly, in many ways favors girls. Girls and boys perform similarly in math; girls are significantly, if slightly, advantaged in language (the difference in average language scores is about 0.2 standard deviations). There is a significant difference in aspirations that favors boys, but both girls and boys have aspirations that far exceed likely outcomes: 51 percent of boys and 45 percent of girls aspire to a college education ($p = 0.04$). Girls are more likely to report usually finishing homework than boys (83 percent versus 72 percent, $p = 0.00$) and are more likely to classify themselves as being good students than boys (46 percent versus 40 percent, $p = 0.01$). There is no significant gender difference in children's desire to attend school.

Socio-economic differences in educational outcomes generally favor wealthier children and children of better-educated mothers. Considering achievement, the mean math score for the wealthiest fifth of children is 76, compared to 73 for the poorest fifth ($p = 0.00$, a difference of about 0.2 standard deviations); for language scores, the corresponding figures were 75 and 71 ($p = 0.00$, a difference of about 0.3 standard deviations). Differences by mother's education were more striking: children of mothers with no education have a mean math score of about 72, compared to 79 for mothers with a senior high school or better education ($p = 0.00$, a difference of about half of a standard deviation). For language, comparable figures were 71 and 77, ($p = 0.00$, a difference of 0.45 standard deviations).

Children from wealthier families and with better-educated mothers were also significantly advantaged in aspirations. For example, 45 percent of children of mothers with no education aspire to a college education, compared to 71 percent of children of mothers with a high school or better education ($p = 0.01$). Further, children from poorer families and with less educated mothers are more likely to feel alienated from school. For example, about 13 percent of the poorest fifth of children completely agreed with the sentiment of not wanting to attend school most of the time, compared to only 7 percent of the wealthiest fifth of children ($p = 0.00$).

However, certain exceptions to the pattern emerge. There is no difference by mother's education in the degree to which children report finishing homework, and poorer children were actually more likely to report regularly finishing homework than wealthier children. There are significant differences by both socio-economic status measures in the degree to which students report themselves as being good students, but patterns are not consistent. These exceptions illustrate dimensions of engagement that do not behave as direct functions of socio-economic status.

Differences in the home environment and teacher characteristics

A second important question is how the resources at home and in the classroom differ for male and female children, and for higher and lower socio-economic status children. Table 9.2 shows measures of the home environment

Table 9.2 Home environment for learning and teacher characteristics by gender and socio-economic status

	Gender				Wealth quintile						Mother's education				
Variables	Total	Male	Fem.	P*	Lowest	2	3	4	Highest	P*	None	Prim.	JHS	SHS+	P*
Home Environment for Learning															
Children's books (% yes)	55	56	53	0.28	39	43	52	64	75	0.00	46	64	62	74	0.00
Parental help with homework (% often)	36	37	34	0.36	33	31	34	41	42	0.00	29	44	44	41	0.00
Mothers' aspirations (% college)	27	29	25	0.00	25	22	27	29	32	0.00	24	25	37	33	0.00
Teacher Characteristics															
Gender (% female)	35	35	36	0.59	32	33	34	36	42	0.02	32	38	42	42	0.00
Total years of experience (mean)	15	15	14	0.04	15	15	16	14	14	0.18	15	15	15	14	0.84
Years experience at this school (mean)	7	7	7	0.85	8	7	7	7	6	0.02	7	7	7	6	0.24
Education (% tertiary)	13	12	13	0.73	7	9	14	15	18	0.00	10	14	18	17	0.00
Formal teacher (% yes)	78	80	75	0.03	72	79	77	81	79	0.03	75	80	80	83	0.04
Location of birth (% village)	40	38	43	0.03	50	43	41	34	32	0.00	46	35	32	36	0.00
Income (mean wages)	497	508	484	0.03	449	481	486	523	548	0.00	467	517	540	541	0.00

Note:
* For the continuous variables children's books, both measures of years of teacher experience, and income, *p*-values represent F-tests of the null hypothesis of no differences in means by gender, wealth quintile, or mother's education. For all other variables listed in column 1, *p*-values represent chi-square tests of independence between that variable and gender, wealth quintile, or mother's education.

and teacher characteristics by gender and socio-economic status. For both years of teacher experience and teacher's income, *p*-values are for F-tests of the null hypothesis of no differences in means by gender, wealth quintile, or mother's education. For all other variables listed in column 1, *p*-values refer to results from chi-square tests of independence between each variable and gender, wealth quintile, or mother's education.

Table 9.2 shows no significant gender differences in the degree to which children have access to books or parental help with homework. Mothers' aspirations for children do show significant gender differences. However, the difference in mother's aspirations for girls and boys is modest: 29 percent of boys' mothers aspire to a college education for them, compared to 25 percent of girls' mothers. There are several significant gender differences in the kinds of teachers children have. Boys are more likely to be placed with slightly more experienced teachers, with formal teachers, with teachers from outside of the village, and with better-paid teachers. For reasons that will become clear in the multivariate analysis below, these differences carry mixed implications for gender disparities in student outcomes.

Considering socio-economic status, the home environment differences are much more striking. For example, only 39 percent of children in the poorest wealth quintile have access to children's books at home, compared to 75 percent of children in the wealthiest fifth wealth quintile. About one-third of children in the poorest wealth quintile had parents who regularly help them with homework, compared to about 42 percent of children in the top wealth quintile. About one-fourth of uneducated mothers aspire to a college education for their children, compared to about one-third of mothers with a senior high school or better education. All of the differences in home environment by wealth quintile and mother's education are statistically significant.

Lower socio-economic status children also have teachers with different characteristics than teachers of wealthier children. For example, about 7 percent of the poorest children have teachers with a tertiary education, compared to 18 percent of children in the wealthiest households ($p = 0.00$). Poorer children, and children of less-educated mothers, are significantly more likely to be taught by male teachers, non-formal teachers and teachers from the local village. Striking differences emerge in teacher wages experienced by poorer and wealthier children, and children of more and less educated mothers. For example, average wages of teachers of the poorest fifth of children, at 449 RMB, are nearly 100 RMB less than the average wages of teachers of the wealthiest fifth of children, at 548 RMB ($p = 0.00$).[2]

Multivariate analysis of achievement and engagement

Table 9.3 considers the implications of gender, socio-economic status, the home environment for learning, and teacher qualifications for student achievement and engagement in a multivariate context. We model each of the outcome variables listed in Table 9.1, using OLS regressions for test scores

Table 9.3 Regressions of achievement and engagement outcomes

	(1) Math score	(2) Language score	(3) Highest education you want	(4) Finish homework	(5) Good student	(6) Not want to attend school
Panel 1: Baseline Models						
Logged wealth	1.073*	1.229**	0.156**	-0.134*	0.003	-0.181**
Mother's years of education	0.499**	0.502**	0.052**	0.010	-0.017	-0.046**
Sex (female)	0.831	2.770**	-0.211*	0.631**	0.259**	-0.058
Age (years)	-0.705*	-0.632*	-0.034	0.076	-0.085*	-0.177**
Number of siblings	-0.302	0.178	-0.040	0.148+	0.003	0.154*
Constant	69.919**	64.653**				
Observations	1902	1896	1918	1923	1922	1923
Panel 2: Baseline + Home Environment Variables						
Logged wealth	0.478	0.689+	0.092	-0.171**	-0.039	-0.137**
Mother's years of education	0.389**	0.409**	0.040**	0.010	-0.022	-0.036*
Sex (female)	0.997	2.956**	-0.150	0.680**	0.255**	-0.092
Age (years)	-0.801*	-0.618+	-0.028	0.083	-0.079+	-0.195**
Number of siblings	0.326	0.603	-0.006	0.173*	0.038	0.136+
Mother's aspirations (years)	1.031**	0.789**	0.113**	0.035	0.028+	-0.040*
Parental help with homework (sometimes)	-0.478	0.021	0.023	-0.109	-0.197	0.079
Parental help with homework (often)	-0.126	0.524	0.000	0.221	-0.066	-0.105
Children's books (yes)	1.901*	1.671*	0.126	0.097	0.260**	-0.171+
Constant	62.918**	58.574**				
Observations	1852	1846	1868	1873	1872	1873
Panel 3: Baseline + Home Environment Variables + Teacher Variables						
Logged wealth	0.308	0.649	0.080	-0.193**	-0.039	-0.137**
Mother's years of education	0.326**	0.387**	0.037*	0.015	-0.027+	-0.034*
Sex (female)	0.676	2.655**	-0.190+	0.631**	0.237*	-0.092

Age (years)	-0.737*		-0.024	0.104+	-0.060	-0.196**
Number of siblings	0.568	0.772+	-0.008	0.194*	0.013	0.129*
Mother's aspirations (years)	1.003**	0.769**	0.104**	0.043*	0.027	-0.035*
Parental help with homework (sometimes)	-0.497	0.064	-0.029	-0.087	-0.185	0.086
Parental help with homework (often)	-0.206	0.498	-0.004	0.265	-0.034	-0.089
Children's books (yes)	1.758*	1.645*	0.164+	0.155	0.281**	-0.195+
Teacher sex (female)	1.205	0.935	0.278*	0.100	0.186	-0.111
Teacher total years experience	-0.035	-0.042	-0.010	0.002	0.000	-0.005
Teacher years experience at this school	0.045	0.069	-0.011	0.001	-0.004	0.018*
Teacher status (formal)	5.521**	1.797	-0.186	-0.117	-0.202	0.034
Teacher education (secondary)	1.608	1.780+	0.037	0.337+	0.187	-0.122
Teacher education (tertiary)	1.833	1.713	0.377+	0.224	0.111	0.001
Teacher birthplace (this village)	1.812+	2.000*	0.365**	0.447**	0.178	-0.165
Logged teacher income	3.505**	1.501	-0.077	-0.127	-0.042	-0.039
Constant	39.957**	46.805**				
Observations	1804	1798	1818	1823	1822	1823

Notes:

[a] Achievement models are estimated ordinary least squares regressions. Other outcomes are modeled using ordered logit models.

[b] Robust standard errors in parentheses; cut points not shown for ordered logit models.

[c] + Significant at 10%; * significant at 5%; ** significant at 1%

and ordered logit models for the other student outcome variables. In panel 1, we first predict outcomes using demographic and socio-economic variables alone. In panel 2, we add home environment for learning variables, and in panel 3, teacher characteristics.

Panel 1 confirms many of the gender associations discussed in the preceding paragraphs. Specifically, girls are significantly advantaged in language scores and finishing homework, and are more likely to describe themselves as being good students, but they have significantly lower aspirations. There is no gender difference in math scores or in the alienation measure. Panel 1 also underscores the benefits of socio-economic status for school achievement and engagement, net of demographic controls. Wealth and mother's education positively predict math scores, language scores, and aspirations, and negatively predict alienation from schooling. Consistent with inferences drawn from the descriptive tables, wealth negatively predicts diligence. Wealth does not exert a consistent effect on confidence; mother's education predicts neither of these outcomes.

Panel 2 adds the home environment variables, and thus allows both an assessment of their role in explaining socio-economic and gender differences, and an assessment of their independent effects on student outcomes. Adding the home environment variables weakens the implications of wealth for many of the educational outcomes. With environmental factors incorporated, logged wealth continues to predict alienation, but it is no longer a significant predictor of math scores and it becomes just marginally significant in the case of language scores. The negative relationship between diligence and wealth persists. Maternal education effects are relatively stable. Gender effects are also stable, with the exception of children's aspirations, where the gender effect disappears.

A home environment variable that consistently predicts children's outcomes is mother's aspirations. Mother's aspirations significantly positively predict math scores, language scores, and children's aspirations, marginally significantly predict confidence, and are significantly protective against alienation.[3] The presence of children's books also exerts significant positive effects on math scores, language scores, and whether a student perceives himself or herself to be a good student, and exerts a marginally significant protective effect against alienation. Net of other variables in the models, parental help with homework fails to show any significant effects.

Panel 3 adds teacher characteristics, and thus allows us to consider both the degree to which differences in the human resources in the classroom explain socio-economic differences in child outcomes, and the degree to which these factors matter as independent influences on child outcomes. With the incorporation of teacher characteristics, for wealth, only the negative effect on diligence and the protective effect against alienation remain. Mother's education effects remain stable, as does the general pattern of gender differences.

Focusing on teacher variables, just a few teacher qualification measures appear to matter. Children with formal teachers and higher paid teachers have significantly higher math scores. Effects of better-educated teachers are not very striking, with only a few marginally significant positive effects showing for language (secondary), aspirations (tertiary), and finishing homework (secondary). Teacher experience does not show significant effects, with the exception of one counter-intuitive effect: children with teachers who have been in the current school longer are more likely to be alienated. We speculate that this finding may be linked to teacher burnout among teachers working in the same village school for long periods of time.

Most interesting, however, are two results that are not included in typical measures of teacher qualifications: teacher gender and teacher birthplace. Children with female teachers have, on average, significantly higher aspirations, net of other characteristics in the model. More striking is the effect of local teachers. Children with local teachers show significantly better language scores, higher aspirations, and are more likely to report regularly completing their homework. They also show marginally significantly better math scores. These findings suggest that female and local teachers provide some form of motivation to students that male and outside teachers do not.

Discussion

These analyses yield several interesting insights about the nature of educational inequality in rural China. Notably, gender disparities at this age are not in line with expectations that one might derive from a simple reading of the literature on son preference in rural China. At the primary ages, girls perform equally to or better than boys in terms of high-stakes tests; they report a more diligent attitude toward schoolwork, and they report a somewhat higher level of confidence in their abilities as students. Girls and boys fare similarly in terms of the presence of children's books in the home and whether they receive parental help with homework.

However, some evidence of a male advantage does emerge. One area is the significant gender differences in the aspirations of children. Yet, despite this gap, the level of aspirations among both girls and boys is strikingly high: just under half of girls and just over half of boys aspire to college educations. There is also a statistically significant gender gap in mother's aspirations. However, while statistically significant, this gap is also modest in scope. A second area where gaps emerge is that boys are slightly more likely to study with teachers with more experience, formal teachers, teachers from outside of the village, and better-paid teachers. The placement of boys with teachers with better formal credentials and better pay offers them an advantage. However, the placement of more girls with local teachers confers an advantage on them. Overall, these results suggest that gender differences in the schooling experience are subtle, and not exclusively favorable to boys.

In contrast, the educational advantages of high socio-economic status children are less ambiguous. Results attest to significant advantages of wealthier children and children of better-educated mothers, in terms of achievement, aspirations and alienation.[4] Results also highlight the advantages of higher socio-economic status children in terms of the home and school environments in which they learn. Higher socio-economic status children had significantly greater access to children's books in the home and parental help with homework, and their mothers had higher aspirations for them. They were much more likely to have a teacher with tertiary education, and somewhat more likely to have a formal teacher. Teachers of the highest socio-economic status children were much better paid than teachers of the lowest socio-economic status children.

Further, multivariate analyses indicate that some home environment differences were important mechanisms of the observed socio-economic differences in outcomes. In particular, mother's aspirations and books appear consequential for a variety of children's educational outcomes. On the other hand, while children of higher socio-economic status parents enjoy more help with homework, the link from homework help to performance failed to emerge in multivariate analysis.

Similarly, certain of the teacher differences were important mechanisms of the disparate educational performance of high and low socio-economic status children. Family wealth effects were mitigated once teacher quality measures were controlled, and certain teacher quality measures were important predictors of achievement. Teacher wages and formal teacher status exerted strong effects on math achievement; marginally significant results suggest that teacher education is important for children's language achievement, aspirations, and diligence in completing homework. Results suggest that different environments at school often served to reinforce patterns of socio-economic disparity in rural China.

However, teacher-related factors were also important independent dimensions of advantage and disadvantage. Having a female teacher, for example, is associated with increased aspirations. Further, certain teacher effects appear to militate against, rather than reinforce, both socio-economic and gender inequalities. For example, while girls and low socio-economic status children are more likely to be in classrooms with non-formal and lower paid teachers, they are also more likely to be in the classroom of local teachers, whose students show a marginally significant advantage in math achievement, and significant, sizable advantages in language achievement, aspirations, and diligence in homework completion. These advantages suggest that local teachers are better able to connect with local children, to communicate with them, or to model successful outcomes of education for them. The beneficiaries of these advantages are precisely those children thought to be at greatest risk of early school-leaving: girls and socio-economically disadvantaged children.

Finally, we acknowledge potential limitations to the generalizeability of these results. First, as we have emphasized, our focus is on young children, at a stage of schooling where the economic burdens on families for educating children are relatively light. While the patterns observed here carry implications for subsequent achievement and attainment, they may work differently at higher levels of education, where stronger socio-economic and gender selection forces may be at work. Second, while Gansu shares many social and economic characteristics with other poor interior provinces, there may be significant cultural variations across western China, particularly with regard to gender, that may contribute to different patterns elsewhere. Third, the mechanisms by which gender differences in placement with teachers emerge remains unclear. This result may be an artifact of gender differences in distributions across grades, and the variation in these differences with community level of economic development, or it may be more directly linked to family agency; further research is needed to explore this result. Fourth, while family provision of a strong home environment for learning clearly influences children's behaviors, to some degree the behavior of children *vis-à-vis* their education or other unobserved child factors may influence parental likelihood of providing such an environment. Longitudinal data may help to tease apart these mutually reinforcing relationships. Despite these caveats, we believe that these results point to potentially important mechanisms of stratification in rural China that merit greater attention.

Conclusion

At the beginning of this chapter, we emphasized the importance of understanding educational achievement, practices, and attitudes among those children who are most vulnerable to dropping out in China. One significant implication of this work is that it suggests new mechanisms behind well-established patterns of disparity in dropping out that emerge as children transition into higher levels of schooling. Even in the relatively poor setting of rural Gansu, our results attest to significant advantages of wealthier children and children of better-educated mothers, in terms of achievement, aspirations and alienation. Our results also show that higher socio-economic status families are able to provide more academically supportive home environments, and in many ways the children of these families benefited from studying with teachers who had better qualifications. Boys enjoy advantages in mothers' and own aspirations, and there is a slight tendency for boys to be placed with better-qualified, higher-paid teachers.

These results represent mechanisms of educational advantage for wealthier children, and to a lesser degree, for boys, that go beyond the economic factors that have dominated research on enrollment at later stages in the schooling process, namely the ability to pay tuition and the opportunity costs of enrolling children in school. These findings are significant in suggesting that educational advantages emerge not only through family economic considerations about the costs and benefits of schooling, but also through effects of home environment and teacher characteristics on children's own performance in and attachment to schooling. These findings highlight the need for further research focused not only on family decisions about schooling, but also on children themselves, to better understand the multiple factors that contribute to early school-leaving in poor rural areas.

A second insight to emerge from this analysis is that the expected advantages for higher socio-economic status children and boys do not emerge across all measures. Advantages for higher socio-economic status children did not emerge in terms of whether they think of themselves as being good students or in terms of diligence. Further, we do not find evidence of across-the-board disadvantages for girls. Instead, results show advantages for girls in many dimensions of achievement and engagement. These findings are surprising in light of earlier studies that have underscored the disadvantages of poor rural girls, but are perhaps less surprising in the context of more recent evidence suggesting a national trend of declining gender inequality (Hannum and Liu 2005). These more encouraging findings highlight areas where historically disadvantaged groups of children are narrowing the gaps with the more privileged.

Finally, results suggest factors that may offer protection to vulnerable children. For example, while the home environment for learning and some teacher qualifications are distributed in ways that tend to favor higher socio-economic status children, the independent effects of these factors, after accounting for socio-economic status differences, suggest an encouraging interpretation that these factors can contribute to favorable educational outcomes, net of the economic resources available to households.[5]

More strikingly, the disproportionate placement of low socio-economic status children, and to a lesser degree, girls, with local teachers appears to confer a protective effect on these children. There are at least two plausible explanations for this finding. First, there may be less social distance between teachers and students, and the potential for better communication may improve students' performance. A second possibility is that local teachers may serve as role models for students. In isolated rural settings where the majority of children's contacts are involved in agricultural pursuits, students may see teachers as successful models of the value of schooling for personal life trajectories. In either case, this finding suggests the value of considering attributes of teachers other than formal credentials that may signal ability to connect with and motivate children.

We believe that these results suggest potentially significant new lines of thinking about how to support the schooling of children in poor areas. Most importantly, socio-economic status and gender remain salient concepts in rural Chinese settings, but their implications for educational outcomes may be less deterministic and more complex than they are sometimes portrayed. Socio-economic advantages are conferred not only through parental ability to pay fees, but also through a myriad of other resources that support children's schooling. Advantages to boys early in the educational process are subtle. At the same time, girls are favored in several dimensions of achievement and engagement, suggesting that any disadvantages that emerge for girls at subsequent stages in schooling cannot be linked to an average, lower level of school performance. Of course, poor performance may affect girls' and boys' subsequent educational trajectories in different ways, as has been suggested in earlier research and can be tested only with longitudinal data. Further, other resources may influence children's education, net of gender and economic status. Additional research on these other resources—in particular, further work to understand the nature of benefits associated with having local teachers and the salient characteristics of home environments for learning—may yield policy-relevant insights into how non-economic resources can support vulnerable children's schooling outcomes, and further illuminate important processes of educational stratification in poor rural areas.

Acknowledgments

Data collection for the Gansu Survey of Children and Families was supported by The Spencer Foundation Small and Major Grants Programs, by NIH Grants 1R01TW005930–01 and 5R01TW005930–02, and by a grant from the World Bank. The first author was supported while conducting this research by a fellowship from the National Academy of Education.

Notes

1 For brevity, we only display one category of each categorical variable. Chi-square tests used the full set of categories for the variables listed in column 1. Full tabulations of the variables are available from the authors upon request.
2 RMB stands for Renminbi (*yuan*). One US$ was about 8.3 Chinese Renminbi in the year 2000.
3 Some of the effects of maternal aspirations may reflect the fact that mothers of high-performing children are more likely to have high aspirations for them. Due to the cross-sectional nature of the data, we are unable to definitively infer a causal effect of maternal aspirations. However, the established significance of parental aspirations in the status attainment literature suggests the plausibility of a causal effect.
4 Advantages did not emerge in terms of academic self-concept or in terms of diligence. In fact, wealthier children were less likely to say that they were good students.
5 We acknowledge that these factors are not fully independent of economic circumstances. For example, mother's aspirations are probably linked at least in part to their perceptions of the family's ability to economically support the further schooling of children. The number of books in the home is also linked in part to family wealth. Wealthier communities are likely better able to attract and retain teachers with better formal qualifications.

References

Adams, J. and Hannum, E. (2005) "Trends in Children's Social Welfare in China: Access to Health Insurance and Education," *The China Quarterly*, 181 (March): 100–121.
Brown, P. and Park, A. (2002) "Education and Poverty in Rural China," *Economics of Education Review*, 21(6): 523–541.

Carter, C. A. (1997) "The Urban–Rural Income Gap in China: Implications for Global Food Markets," *American Journal of Agricultural Economics*, 79: 1410–1418.

Connelly, R. and Zheng, Z. (2003) "Determinants of School Enrollment and Completion of 10 to 18 Year Olds in China," *Economics of Education Review*, 22: 379–388.

Hannum, E. (1999) "Political Change and the Urban–Rural Gap in Education in China, 1949–1990," *Comparative Education Review*, 43(2): 193–211.

Hannum, E. (2002) "Educational Stratification by Ethnicity in China: Enrollment and Attainment in the Early Reform Years," *Demography*, 39(1): 95–117.

Hannum, E. (2003) "Poverty and Basic Education in Rural China: Communities, Households, and Girls' and Boys' Enrollment," *Comparative Education Review*, 47(2): 141–159.

Hannum, E. and Adams, J. (2006) "Structuring Inequality: Rural Poverty and Educational Opportunity in China," in D. Davis and W. Feng (eds.) *Creating Wealth and Poverty in China*.

Hannum, E. and Liu, J. (2005) "Adolescent Transitions to Adulthood in China," in J. Behrman, C. Lloyd, N. Stromquist, and B. Cohen (eds.) *Studies on the Transition to Adulthood in Developing Countries*, Washington, DC: National Academy of Science Press.

Hannum, E. and Park, A. (2002) "Educating China's Rural Children in the 21st Century," *Harvard China Review*, 3(2): 8–14.

Khan, A.R and Riskin, C. (1998) "Income and Inequality in China: Composition, Distribution and Growth of Household Income, 1988 to 1995," *The China Quarterly*, 154: 221–253.

Michelson, E. and Parish, W.L. (2000) "Gender Differentials in Economic Success: Rural China in 1991," in B. Entwisle and G. Henderson (eds.) *Redrawing Boundaries: Gender, Households, and Work in China*, Berkeley, CA: University of California Press.

Ministry of Education (1986) People's Republic of China Law on Compulsory Education. Beijing: Ministry of Education, electronic document: http://www.moe.edu.cn/

Park, A. and Hannum, E. (2001) "Teacher Influences on Child Learning in Developing Countries: Evidence from Rural China," paper presented at the Social Science Research Council Conference, Rethinking Social Science Research on the Developing World in the 21st Century, June, Utah.

Tsang, M. (2002) "Education and National Development in China since 1949: Oscillating Policies and Enduring Dilemmas," available at: http://www.tc.columbia.edu/centers/coce/pdf_files/d1.pdf

United Nations Economic and Social Commission for Asia and the Pacific (UNESCAP) (2005) *Population and Family Planning in China by Province: Gansu Province*, electronic document: http://www.unescap.org/esid/psis/population/database/chinadata/gansu.htm (accessed October 21, 2005).

World Bank (2003) "Country Brief: People's Republic of China," Washington, DC: World Bank. Electronic document: http://lnweb18.worldbank.org/eap/eap.nsf/Countries/China/42F2084B942D74C685256C7600687DBF?OpenDocument (accessed March 28, 2003).

10 Supporting China's teachers

Challenges in reforming professional development

Lynn Paine and Yanping Fang

Introduction

China's teachers have a long and complex history. Confucius, the intellectual architect of the traditional system of social relations, is also remembered as the country's preeminent teacher. With this tradition, China has long officially recognized the importance of teachers. Teaching in China, however, has often been a less distinguished profession than its proponents would hope or claim. A popular adage, paraphrased, recommends that "as long as there is rice in the house, don't be a teacher." Yet, in the political rhetoric of reform-era China, national development goals hinge on reforms to the educational system. Teachers, their training, and their professional development stand at the center of successful educational reform.

Given China's size, resources, and diversity, however, providing qualified teachers for its schools has posed significant challenges. In 2004, there were 9.1 million full-time teachers in the nine-year compulsory education system, with over 5.6 million working at the elementary level and over 3.5 million at junior secondary (Ministry of Education 2005a). Significant investments in training in the reform era produced impressive gains in the teaching force. Yet, by 2004, there were still over 313,000 teachers (95,128 at the elementary level and 218,781 at junior secondary) who lacked the required credentials (Ministry of Education 2005a). Moreover, teacher shortages persist in some communities and certain fields.

Those challenges have put pressure on systems of teacher education and professional development which, for a range of reasons, are already strained. For much of the late twentieth and early twenty-first centuries, teacher training, central to the development of an effective teaching force, faced key dilemmas about its location, character and systematic nature. Established in the late nineteenth century, teacher education was a foreign concept (Paine 1995). With the creation of the contemporary teacher training system in the early 1950s, teacher education developed into a set of specialized institutions at different levels (Paine 1986). In-service education, devoted to further training for teachers already on the job, has typically been offered through a variety of kinds of sites, ranging from local schools to special in-service teacher training colleges, correspondence programs, and television. As a result of global trends and market pressures, in recent years, specialized teacher training institutions have faced severe competition from comprehensive universities. The long-separate pre-service and in-service institutions have gradually merged into specialized teacher education institutions, charged with working with teachers across the career continuum. Web-based resources have been made increasingly accessible for teacher professional development purposes. The proliferation of routes into teaching and opportunities for further professional development creates problems of quality and control.

At the heart of these changes are dilemmas about the basic character of teacher education and professional development. In light of a long-standing view of the teacher as one who combines knowledge mastery and lofty morality, who transmits culture, knowledge, and social values, and who educates the future labor force, teacher education traditionally has focused not only on academic learning but also on the cultivation of political morality. In terms of academic study, however, the attention to subject matter knowledge dominates. The time spent in formal professional study—in courses on pedagogy, educational psychology, subject-specific teaching methods, and a practicum in schools (of two to eight weeks)—has remained small, despite reform efforts. This situation is regularly criticized by teacher educators and educational researchers (Paine *et al.* 2003). Many have wondered what the "special character" of pre-service teacher education is, and how it should best be expressed in institutional and curricular practices (Paine 1995).

The focus of in-service training has also shifted over time to reflect social and economic changes and changes in the needs of schools and backgrounds of their teachers. Training has changed, particularly, as a manifestation of the upgrading of teacher qualification at different levels. The systemic quality of teacher education—pre-service and in-service—is both a hallmark of and dilemma for China's teaching training. In the reform era, the Ministry of Education developed a comprehensive teacher education network that provided a variety of supports for teachers at different stages in their careers and in need of different kinds of learning. However, the uneven social and economic development discussed in this volume in chapters by Postiglione and Connelly and Zheng continues to cause imbalances in the original teacher development network across regions.

This chapter explores these challenges of reforming professional development in China in a period of broader educational reform. We begin by describing the shifting professional development task. We then juxtapose and discuss vignettes of two teachers to illustrate some of the range of professional development approaches and constraints facing Chinese teachers today. We conclude by considering three challenges that beset professional development and its reform: (1) creating professional development across and in spite of disparities; (2) building a professional development system; and (3) constructing professional development at a moment of significant educational reform—as the key to reform but as needing to respond to that reform.

Sources of evidence

This chapter draws on fieldwork conducted over several years. We use data collected during 1998–2000 in Shanghai as part of a study focused on new teacher induction and teacher learning. During that time, we interviewed and observed teachers and lessons in 27 schools; we conducted additional focus group interviews of teachers and professional developers from across Shanghai; we interviewed education researchers, teacher educators, and administrators at in-service institutes and two teacher education universities; and we also interviewed key municipal education policy people.

Over the course of 1999–2000, as a part of the Middle Grades Mathematics and Science Teacher Induction (MGM) study, a National Science Foundation-supported project, we interviewed 30 new and young teachers, as well as 45 other, experienced teachers who serve as mentors or play other roles pivotal to the life of new teachers and the school. We observed 29 classes in 21 schools. We also had the opportunity to interview 22 school-level administrators and 39 district-level administrators and professional development providers. We concentrated data collection on four districts and made at least two different trips to each of these districts and their colleges of education (centers of professional development), and in some cases repeated trips to schools in each of these districts. We observed induction-related and other in-service activities in three districts and interviewed about them in each. Each visit also included interviews, many repeatedly, with officials at the Shanghai Municipal Education Commission, the authority responsible for Shanghai's educational system.

While we concentrated on learning about induction practice, we also interviewed teachers and administrators not directly involved in induction work in order to understand the context in which new teachers are learning and the systems of provision in professional development. We made repeated visits to the two universities primarily involved in preparing secondary school teachers and providing in-service for experienced teachers, interviewed 20 math department faculty and university-based education researchers, and observed a few classes. We also benefited from the support of researchers at Shanghai's Academy of Educational Sciences, whom we met on each visit.

After earlier exploratory work, as part of the MGM project, three trips of two weeks each occurred in May 1999, October 1999 and May 2000, with analysis of data in between that helped us refine our data collection requests. Two researchers conducted work in each of the first two trips. A team of three researchers participated in the third. In addition, Yanping Fang remained on in Shanghai for additional data collection after both the May 1999 and May 2000 trips, conducting an additional month of fieldwork each time.

Our fieldwork was valuably supported by efforts of our Shanghai collaborators to gather documentary materials for us in advance and after individual trips. Our analysis is also informed by prior work that both Paine and Fang had conducted separately in earlier research in Shanghai and in other regions of the country, including, in particular, Fang's extensive involvement in the research work conducted by the Shanghai Institute of Human Resources Development (later a branch of the Shanghai Academy of Education Sciences) from 1990 to 1998.

Unevenness in the national teaching force: defining the professional development task

As described in the Introduction to this volume, beginning in the late 1970s, China's political and educational leaders began to forcefully and consistently argue for the importance of education to modernization. Central to their argument is the claim that improving education depends on improving teachers and teaching. It is thus not surprising that China has undertaken an energetic and wide-ranging approach to education reform focused on teachers.

For good reason. At the beginning of the twenty-first century, China's national teaching force was characterized by great unevenness, and serious problems with qualifications and quality still remain in some areas. The changing demographic composition of China's school and teacher population compounds the problem.

The situation of China's teaching force—both the needs for professional development and the difficulties related to it—is strongly affected by four dimensions. First, student and teacher demographic changes have raised the standards and foci for both pre-service and in-service education. Second, as Hannum, Park, and Cheng address in the Introduction, the widening urban–rural disparity in socio-economic development has shifted strategic planning for basic education and teacher development to the most needy, mainly China's West. Third, computer technology and the Internet have extended the access to qualification upgrading and professional development resources to teachers nationwide and reshaped what constitutes teacher development. Fourth, the continued institutional restructuring in the provision of both pre-service and in-service education has responded to the increasingly diverse training needs but created instability as well. Together, these new demands on and contexts of professional development have redefined the kinds of training and support teachers need and receive. We discuss each dimension below.

Issues of student and teacher demographic changes

As Table 10.1 shows, China has an enormous population of elementary and secondary students (over 177.8 million for nine-year compulsory education in 2004) and perhaps the largest teaching force (over 9 million in 2004) in the world. With the continuation of the one-child policy nationally there was a persistent drop in the school-age population and primary school enrollment from the end of the century, 135,480,000 in 1999 to 112,462,300 in 2004, a

Table 10.1 Enrollment changes in regular elementary and secondary schools, 1999 and 2004

Level of schooling	1999	2004	Change rate (%) from 1999 to 2004
Elementary	135,480,000	112, 462,300	−16.70
Junior secondary	58,117,000	65,275,100	+12.32
Senior secondary	10,497,100	22,203,700	+111.52
Total	215,500,000	199,941,100	−7.22

Sources: Ministry of Education (2000; 2004; 2005a), Shanghai Zhili Kaifa Yanjiusuo (1999).

Table 10.2 Teachers and percentage with required qualifications, 1999 and 2004

	1999		2004	
	No. of teachers	% with required qualifications	No. of teachers	% with required qualifications
Elementary	5,860,500	95.90	5,628,900	98.31
Junior secondary	3,187,500	85.50	3,500,500	93.75
Senior secondary	692,400	65.85	1,190,700	79.59

Sources: Ministry of Education (2000; 2004; 2005a), Shanghai Zhili Kaifa Yanjiusuo (1999).

decrease of 16.70 percentage points in less than five years. The baby boom generation led to an over-expansion of junior secondary education in the late 1990s. As this cohort completed their nine-year compulsory education, the enrollment of junior secondary schools started to fluctuate, with some decreases, for instance, from 66,906,300 in 2003 to 65,275,100 in 2004. Yet, this does not apply to places such as China's West, where the 12–14-year-olds will continue to peak from the 10th five-year planning period (2001–2005) onwards (Ministry of Education 2005b). Taken together, however, from 1999 to 2004, the junior secondary enrollment witnessed an increase of 12.32 percentage points. In addition, regular senior secondary education enrollment (not including specialized and vocational schools) continued to expand, from 10,497,100 in 1999 to 22,203,700, doubling in less than five years.

Such enrollment changes put strains on the number and distribution of teachers, and contribute to the problem of unqualified teachers. Table 10.2 shows that with a decreasing primary population, the number of elementary teachers has decreased, while those at the secondary level increased by large margins, particularly at the senior secondary level. In recent years, the proportion of teachers with required qualifications at all three levels (primary, junior secondary, senior secondary) has risen (*Xinhua* 2002). According to China's teacher qualification standards as of 1998, elementary teachers had to finish at least secondary teacher training (*zhongdeng shifan*) (the equivalent of a secondary school-level education); junior secondary teachers, at least a three-year college (*zhuanke*) program; and senior high school teachers, a four-year undergraduate education (*benke*). With a diminishing number of secondary teacher training institutions and a higher percentage of junior secondary teachers having received three-year college education, the required qualification for elementary teachers in most cities has been upgraded to completion of three years of college education. But given the rapid expansion of senior secondary education, there is still a long way to go to for all teachers to reach the required qualification standard (*Zhongguo Jiaoyubao Wangzhan* 2005). The combination of raised standards for teaching and shifts in student population produces a demand for professional development.

Yet, this new demand comes at a time when the nature of the current composition of the teaching force constrains teacher professional development. In recent years, there has been a rapid loss of senior experienced teachers as more teachers reached retirement age. The *China Education Daily* reported that in 2004, nearly half (46.8 percent) of all elementary teachers were below 35 years old and about 30 percent were between 36 and 49 (*Zhongguo Jiaoyubao Wangzhan* 2005). Only 17 percent were between 51 and 55 and 3.9 percent between 56 and 60. At both junior and senior secondary levels, the age distribution pattern was even more skewed towards younger teachers, with 78.90 and 80.70 percent respectively being younger than 40 and those 40 or older only accounting for 21.10 and 19.30 percent, respectively. This situation is most severe in the case of the rural teaching force. Traditionally, Chinese administrators view a balance between old, middle-aged and young teachers as most desirable. The current imbalance in the age structure of the teaching force adds to the professional development burden. For example, there are fewer senior teachers to lead and more young ones who need to grow in experience. Given the relative youthfulness of the teaching force, particularly in the rural areas, although teachers have time in their careers for professional development, this age distribution makes the scope of the task considerably greater.

Issues of urban and rural disparity

With two-thirds of China's 1.3 billion population in rural areas, 70 percent of the students and teachers for basic education are located there too (Zhu 1999). As Hannum, Park, and Cheng discuss in the Introduction to this volume, economic reforms associated with the market economy have widened the gap in economic development and income distribution between the rural and urban areas. Educational finance policies characterized by decentralization have also intensified the difficulty of provision in rural education (see Li, Park, and Wang, Chapter 2 this volume). For instance, market pressures have encouraged many experienced and qualified teachers in rural counties and townships to migrate to urban communities or leave teaching for good. The severe shortage of teachers has forced these areas to find substitute teachers, also called out-of-quota *minban*[1] teachers, to fill the void and meet the increasing demand for secondary education. Even though the government has tried since the late 1980s to discourage the growth of *minban* teachers by converting experienced and qualified *minban* teachers into *gongban*, government-paid teachers, the number of substitute teachers in the rural areas is on the increase again, especially in the poor areas in the West and Southwest. Chai (2005) reported that 50 percent of the substitute teachers were found in China's west. By the end of 2004, for primary education alone, there were about 600,000 substitute teachers (ibid.).

Given the high and increasing proportion of unqualified teachers in rural areas, rural schooling poses particular challenges for improving the teaching force. It is also in the rural areas that the problems of meeting the national standards for teacher qualifications, teacher salaries, and educational expenditures are the most acute. Yet, the quality of the rural teaching force is key to the effective implementation of compulsory education in the country as a whole.

To address these issues of disparity, the State Council's Action Plan for Rejuvenating Education 2003–2007 made educational reform and development in rural areas a top priority (*Renmin Ribao* 2003). With large numbers of students now completing nine-year compulsory education in poor rural areas, there is new, unmet demand for secondary and tertiary education. One of the chief strategies for improving the labor force and decreasing unemployment, particularly in rural areas, is expanding vocational and technical education (Ministry of Education 2005b). The Action Plan has made developing vocational education a significant focus for promoting secondary and post-secondary education. Such a shift in the orientation of secondary and post-secondary education has created a need to recruit and train qualified teachers who not only can support academic learning but also know and are able to teach vocational and technical education in a practical field.

The role of technology

Another contextual change affecting the provision of professional development involves the growing role of technology. One measure to combat growing disparity is called "informatization construction." For example, the China Education and Research Network (CERNET) (http://www.edu.cn/), established in 2004, makes information on educational research, classroom teaching resources, important official documents, statistical information and educational news accessible on the Internet. It is also linked to important educational newspapers and other national and local networks on the web.

Technology has become increasingly important in the actual delivery of professional training. In the case of the K-12 Teachers' Continuing Education Program, which was created to provide professional development to 10 million K-12 teachers from 1999 to 2002, for example, "about 70 percent of the training courses were delivered by satellite TV" (Zhu 2004: 1). According to the Chinese National Commission for UNESCO (2004: 17), school networks of different scales and remote satellite signals have been established in over 10,000 elementary and secondary schools in the rural areas. To build training and a life-long learning environment for teachers, a project called Union (or Alliance) of National Teachers' Network was also established in 2003 (Fu 2003). This Internet network has started to provide qualification-related courses, a credit system, and database resources such as information on outstanding teachers' classroom teaching and rural teachers' classroom research. Technology has begun to play a powerful role in reaching teachers in remote areas (Zhu 2004).

Issues of institutional arrangements: institutions for pre-service and in-service education

The establishment of new networks comes at a time of significant shifts in the institutional arrangements for teacher education and teacher professional development. We discuss both pre-service and in-service education below. Initially separated, their recent integration affects the delivery of professional development (Lu 2000; Paine *et al.* 2003).

In the early 1950s, a pre-service teacher training system comprised of specialized institutions at three different levels was established, each level of institution charged with the preparation of teachers for different levels of schooling. For a long time, senior secondary teachers have been trained at four-year teacher training universities (*shifan daxue*); junior secondary teachers, at three-year teacher training colleges (*shifan yuanxiao*); and elementary teachers, at secondary teacher training schools (*shifan xuexiao* or *shizhong*).[2] In 1998, there were 229 four- and three-year teacher training universities and colleges with an enrollment of 663,600 and 875 secondary teacher training schools with an enrollment of 921,100 (Zhu 1999). Low economies of scale and rather modest facilities and equipment limited the training capacities of these institutions. Policy-makers and some policy analysts argue that these institutions also had relatively weaker faculty and resources (Fang and Paine 2000; Paine *et al.* 2003). In addition, the pattern of teacher hiring often led to graduates of the different levels of institutions ending up teaching at the same level. In our fieldwork, we often heard criticism that specific missions of different types of institutions were therefore blurred and redundant (Zhu 1999; Lu 2000). By the 1990s, there was considerable debate among both teacher educators and policy-makers about improving the system in ways that recognized the need for efficiency, higher institutional quality, and the preparation of a different kind of teacher, one more suited for the demands of teaching in the twenty-first century (Paine *et al.* 2003; Cheng 2004).

A restructuring of pre-service institutions ensued, which expanded the size of institutions and upgraded the training levels. In 2001, the number of teacher education universities and colleges decreased from 229 to 221 with an enrollment of 1,350,383, almost doubling that of 1998. Standards for teacher qualification rose so that elementary teachers in urban areas are required to have college training, so the number of secondary teacher training schools quickly shrank. By 2001, secondary teacher training schools decreased to 570 with an enrollment of 662,353 (see Table 10.3). The latest available statistics show that two years later, in 2003, the number of specialized teacher education institutions at both tertiary and secondary levels still kept decreasing by large margins with increasing enrollment at the tertiary level and decreasing enrollment at the secondary level.

Such restructuring was engendered by the growth of the market economy, competition, and demand for a highly trained labor force. For teacher preparation, there is a market arising from a change in the supply and demand structure of teachers, as a surplus of teachers in some areas allowed the hiring institutions to select among teachers (Cheng 2004). In the meantime, the general public has had "a crisis of confidence in specialized teacher training institutions" (ibid.) and, in the late 1990s, started debating whether to let comprehensive universities join in the task of teacher preparation. Currently, in the wake of policy change, non-teacher-training tertiary institutions already account for 54 percent of all higher learning institutions that provide pre-service teacher education (Chinese National Commission for UNESCO 2004).[3]

Such restructuring has had both positive and negative impacts. By allowing other universities besides normal colleges and universities to enter the teacher education market, these traditionally specialized institutions have been forced to reform and compete against comprehensive universities in recruiting students for admission and in positioning their graduates in the job market. With this pressure and encouraged by educational, teaching, and technological reforms underway in Shanghai's schools, the two universities worked hard in recent years to revise their curriculum and training materials to respond to the various market demands, experiment with new practices for student teaching, and promote their unique features as specialized teacher training institutions.

Table 10.3 Pre-service institutions and enrollments, 1998, 2001, and 2003

	1998		2001		2003	
	No. of institutions	Enrollment	No. of institutions	Enrollment	No. of institutions	Enrollment
Four- and three-year universities and colleges	229	693,000,000	210	1,350,383	188	1,673,200
Secondary normal schools	875	921,100,600	579	662,353	317	317,300

Sources: Ministry of Education (2000; 2004; 2005a), Shanghai Zhili Kaifa Yanjiusuo (1999).

The negative impacts are also quite noticeable in two major aspects, as observed by Cheng (2004). In recent years, to face the competition, some teacher training institutions began to offer non-teacher-training programs and neglected to nurture their historic strength in teacher education, while comprehensive universities started to provide teacher education programs with only a weak background in teacher education. Because of this, Cheng argued, the teacher training quality in general might well be weakened. At the same time, reforms to upgrade teacher qualifications have led to the rapid demise of the secondary teacher training schools in many places. Responsibility for training elementary teachers has been shifted to higher education institutions that do not have the rich experience for preparing elementary school teachers that secondary normal schools did. Quite a few of those institutions had distinguished national and international reputations in the professional training of elementary teachers.

In-service education, likewise, has had a long history of a specialized system with a hierarchical arrangement of specialized institutions. Since 1976, aiming to improve the capacity of the general teaching force, China established an in-service training system made up of Colleges of Education (*jiaoyu xueyuan*) in urban areas (at both city and district levels) and Teacher Refresher Schools (*jiaoshi jinxiu xuexiao*) in counties (Paine 1997). In both cases, these were institutions devoted chiefly to providing professional development to practicing teachers in the nearby community. In 1998, there were 214 Colleges of Education (COEs) at the city and prefecture level engaged in both pre-service degree education[4] and in-service teacher training; and there were 2,087 teacher refresher schools (Shanghai Zhili Kaifa Yanjiusuo 1999). These institutions have made significant contributions to preparing qualified teachers for basic education. By the 1990s, however, the in-service system, like the pre-service system, became the subject of much policy debate and local reform. By 2003, the number of COEs and teacher refresher schools had decreased to 103 and 1,703, respectively, as a result of mergers (such as between the Shanghai College of Education and East China Normal University) (Ministry of Education 2004). In addition, by the late 1980s or early 1990s, most places had achieved their earlier goal of bringing teachers up to the nationally required qualification standards[5] (Fang and Paine 2000). In many communities, refresher schools and COEs, which had provided qualification upgrading programs as a focus of teacher in-service training, faced a redefined mission— raising teachers' educational levels and offering teachers continuing education.

In light of China's uneven educational development, the new standard for teacher qualifications is that all secondary teachers by 2010 will at least have a four-year university education and, where conditions permit, elementary teachers will have at least three years of college (Ministry of Education 2002). This policy acknowledges the challenge of achieving higher qualifications across diverse levels of socio-economic development. In fact, it would endanger the educational enterprise if it was uniformly taken as the major work of teacher professional development. This is especially true for rural areas, where a large number of unqualified teachers have the more pressing need for fundamental knowledge and skills required to teach adequately the basic curriculum. Analysts we interviewed thus predict that through 2010, the professional development tasks and pace will vary for the advanced, medium-level, and least developed regions and provinces.

Professional development, in the face of the kind of disparities outlined above, encounters a challenge it cannot ignore. That professional development is crucial seems clear from the attention policy-makers have given it of late. The promulgation of a series of legal documents, for instance, the Teacher Law (Ministry of Education 1994) and Teacher Certification Requirements (Ministry of Education 1995), has placed teacher education and professional development high on the agenda of national educational development. That its goals and approaches must be complex, varied, and dynamic also seems clear. Yet, determining those goals, and developing systems that can support them, is no simple task.

Vignettes as windows on broader issues in professional development

The unevenness of and shifts in the teaching force are so significant that they force continual redefinition of the goals of professional development. Even in educationally more advanced areas, there remain complex dilemmas related to professional development. Below, we explore three challenges central to the reform of professional development in China: (1) the problems of responding to growing inequalities to create professional development able to serve an increasingly diverse teaching force and increasingly unequal schools; (2) the challenge of making professional development widely accessible and systemic; and (3) the dilemmas of reforming professional development in the midst of reform. We begin with two brief vignettes as a way of illustrating the many factors at play in creating the needs and challenges associated with reforming teacher development in China. Our claim is that professional development is not only about structures and policies, but sets of experiences, constraints and knowledge of individual teachers. A full examination of professional development therefore needs to take into account the work of teaching, educational needs, and structural supports available to classroom teachers. These vignettes highlight two very different situations, both of which have significance for the challenges of teacher improvement in China today.

Professional development through the eyes of Ms Li Mei: starting with support

Li Mei[6] was in her second year of teaching middle school math in Shanghai when we first met her. She teaches 13 periods a week, six each to two different 6th grade classes and one to an elective "activity class" that is to deepen students' interest in math and develop creativity. In addition, Ms Li works as a *banzhuren* or "class head" (what is sometimes inadequately translated as a homeroom teacher). In that role, she manages the study and extracurricular lives of 48 students in one of the 6th grade classes she teaches. Her duties are to help nurture the "all-round development" of each student and the class as a collective. She was assigned two mentors: one experienced math teacher to work with her on her teaching, and one mentor supporting her in learning about what being a class head entails.

Ms Li's days start early. She comes to school by 7:00; a half hour before her students arrive for their morning review work. If she is not teaching a class, she spends most of her day in her office, which she shares with other teachers, correcting student assignments and meeting with individual students. In the office, she blends her math teaching work and her dealing with students' personal, social, and academic problems, as students pop into the office with questions, concerns, or little triumphs to share. She doesn't leave school till about 6:00. She likes to concentrate on class preparation on the weekends.

Ms Li's busy days of blending math-focused and class head work have their parallels in the routines of her week. On Mondays, during the school day, Ms Li takes part in weekly meetings of all the class heads. Tuesdays include weekly meetings of both the *jiaoyanzu* (teaching research group) and the *beikezu* (lesson preparation group). The *beikezu* meetings vary in length, depending on what the group needs to accomplish. The *beikezu* includes all three of the sixth grade math teachers (and occasionally a fourth, part-time instructor). Their meetings provide a time to "discuss where we've gotten in our teaching so far, plan lessons together, share our teaching experiences and how students have learned, discuss how to assess students, and analyze exam results." She finds this group especially important for giving her a chance to ask older teachers how to teach. Her *jiaoyanzu* involves all the math teachers in the school, regardless of the grade level they teach. Those meetings she sees as occasions to focus on "bigger issues of teaching." They have also provided chances to see teaching in other schools and participate in district professional development events.

For Ms Li, a graduate of a teacher education program at one of the local universities, pre-service education provided valuable preparation. As a math department graduate, she felt she had a solid preparation in the content she was to teach, but saw the knowledge as being chiefly theoretical. As she entered teaching, she felt that moving from "my student role to a teacher role" involved some areas that were "unfamiliar." She needed help in learning how to "teach a class" (*shangke*) and "prepare a lesson" (*beike*). Her student teaching practicum gave her some opportunity to learn about these, but once she began full-time as a teacher, she realized that she also needed to understand students and develop skills in managing and communicating with them. It was only once she was on the job that she "really understood" some of the things she had been asked previously to learn. "The university laid an important foundation for our subject matter knowledge, but to be a good teacher, you need to learn on the job." She wanted support on learning how to make her teaching connect for students in ways that "attracted" them to the lesson, focused their energies on learning (and thereby averting discipline problems) and encouraged active participation in the learning process.

In that initial year of teaching, Ms Li felt surrounded by help of many kinds, provided by different people. She and her math mentor worked together in the same *beikezu*, regularly jointly planning lessons and discussing their teaching and their students' learning in great detail. They also met often as a pair. After she taught each class, Ms Li would bring her lesson plan and tell her mentor about what had worked and what hadn't. They would analyze each week's work, exploring, in the words of her mentor, "all the areas in the past week that hadn't succeeded, where there were failures and why, and where there were successes."

As she plans a lesson, she is careful to start with looking at the teaching materials and reference guides, to focus on what commonly are seen as the "important" and "difficult" points in a lesson. She spends much time preparing on her own, sharing that lesson plan with others—her mentor as well as others who unofficially mentor her in her lesson preparation group (*beikezu*) and teaching research group (*jiaoyanzu*), and revising it before she teaches it. And she has multiple opportunities to get feedback on her actual teaching, thanks to frequent observation by her mentor, by others in the school, and as part of participation in "open" lessons and district teaching competitions.

Inside the school, she found others in the school who offered guidance—the principal (also a math teacher), the head of the teaching research group, and others; outside the school, she also took part, as all first year teachers are required, in district-organized induction programs. She found talks there given by "expert teachers" to be useful; they gave her ideas she could "apply" and offered encouragement and inspiration. Finally, she spent and continues to spend time observing others' teaching. There she studies how teachers teach a lesson, how they motivate students to learn and attract their attention. She sees teachers as having different styles and is working on developing her own.

Professional development under challenging conditions facing Ms Song: in-service education to meet high demands with few resources

Teacher Song persuaded herself to stay in her one-teacher village school in a remote village in Inner Mongolia Autonomous Region in Northwest China, despite the fact that she was not paid for several months.[7] Being a *minban* or community supported teacher (as opposed to state-supported, salaried), she depended on the village and township resources to get paid. Without her, the village would have a young generation growing up illiterate. With her two teenage children taught by her in this school and sent to the township central (*zhongxin*) school to continue their schooling and returning home only on the weekends, Ms Song still found herself busy after school—feeding the four pigs and the dozen chickens her family had raised, and helping her husband work in their courtyard vegetable plots and wheat fields.

Her school, a cottage of about 30 sqm, had clay walls and a thatched roof strengthened by a few wooden beams. Inside the cottage, there were two rooms: the inner, smaller room for pre-schoolers aged 4–5 and the front, more standard classroom for children aged 6–12, who should be first to fourth graders. After fourth grade, children had to go the township central elementary boarding school 15 miles away to continue their schooling. She was skillful in teaching the compound classes. For instance, when we observed, she was teaching older children mathematics while the younger ones were drawing. After she finished teaching and assigned seat work, she went to check on younger children's drawing in the other room.

Teacher Song had just finished her teacher qualification training and was taking continuing education courses at the township central school during the weekend. She was trained there to familiarize herself with the new textbooks, watch videotapes of experienced teachers teaching the new content, and make simple teaching tools. Because this was a rare opportunity, especially as a collaboration between UNICEF and the Chinese government that focused on rural teachers, her family supported her to purchase a bicycle that she pedaled on the sandy path every weekend to receive training. The video equipment for the professional development sessions had to be sent in a donkey-pulled wagon from another township school after those teachers had finished using them. An experienced teacher's teaching had been broadcast from the China Central Television Teacher Training Courses and recorded at the county training center or larger townships centers. About 30 teachers came from the township and village schools to participate in these weekly training sessions. They did not get paid for their training, and they used their free time to receive training. She especially enjoyed the time when she could discuss teaching problems with teachers from other places and share experiences about making and using teaching tools.

Making sense of the vignettes

Together, these two vignettes begin to capture some of the tremendous range of challenges facing professional development in China. The story of Ms Li, and of Shanghai more generally, may be seen as a best case scenario: a teacher with strong professional preparation, well supported by colleagues in her school, and working with a district that provides many and varied professional learning opportunities to her and her colleagues. As a new teacher, she is also supported by Shanghai's induction program, a larger professional development system, which represents what many in China see as the direction of the future. Ms Song, the teacher in Inner Mongolia, by contrast, is faced with rather limited resources, and has markedly different goals for her professional development. The challenges of distance, of low preparation, and financial constraints clearly influence both the content and processes of teacher support available to Ms Song.

Discussion

As diverse as the lives of Ms Song and Ms Li are, their stories echo key assumptions that drive the work of teacher development in China. There is an unquestioned assumption that professional development is in fact both worthwhile and urgent, and that improving teachers will improve learning for children. There is also a view that investing in models of new approaches, and providing key opportunities to learn these, will have a ripple effect in education more generally. For Ms Song and Ms Li, the efforts to develop systems and infrastructures for teacher development have had visible as well as less tangible effects on their teaching and their commitment to the profession.

Looking at both Ms Song and Ms Li's experiences of professional development helps us see the complex challenges facing those who hope to create powerful systems of professional development in China. Set against the backdrop of the national story of the teaching force and educational reform, it is clear that professional development is an urgent task. It is certainly one that requires resources and creative policy effort.

Shanghai's experience has been held up as a model by some within China, in the tradition of using models to support reform and learning. In fact, at the close of the Ministry of Education-led analysis of Shanghai's professional development reform experience, there is the suggestion that one could think of Shanghai in terms of "borrowing the hen to lay the eggs" (*jieji xiadan*) (or borrowing the idea generated in one place as a seed for reforms elsewhere) for the rest of China's teacher development reform. The report wisely cautioned that provinces and local communities need to consider their own situations. But taking that into account, Shanghai's experience must also be read critically in ways that recognize the inevitable dilemmas of making systems for such complex and inherently uncertain practices as teaching and teacher learning. We have nominated three, all of which, like dilemmas of any kind, require management rather than resolution. First, systems need to work in spite of and to remedy the inequalities that characterize China's educational system. The vision of video equipment being pulled by a donkey cart to Ms Song's in-service program captures some of the tensions of trying to develop new capabilities in teachers, and new approaches to teacher development, amidst structural and conceptual constraints. Second, making administrative systems that allow coherence in the provision of teacher development must be understood as requiring fundamental and contentious discussions about the knowledge base for teaching and teacher development. As hackneyed as the theory/practice debates may seem, they are nonetheless important. Finally, reforming professional development in a period of reform is a bit like changing the tires on a car while the car is in motion. It is an almost impossible task. Together, these three dilemmas point to the complexity that underlies the seemingly straightforward work of supporting China's teachers.

Acknowledgments

Support for Shanghai-related fieldwork came from the Division of Research, Evaluation and Communication of the U.S. National Science Foundation (NSF Award #9814083). We are grateful for that support and in particular to the NSF REC program officers Larry Suter and Elizabeth VanderPutten who encouraged and provided helpful feedback as the Middle Grades Mathematics and Science Teacher Induction (MGM) study progressed. The MGM study involved researchers from Michigan State University and WestEd; we greatly benefited from the collaboration with our colleagues Ted Britton, Dan Chazan, Violetta Lazarovici, David Pimm, Senta Raizen, Jian Wang, and Suzanne Wilson.

Our work in China was made possible by the generous help of many people. In particular, Zhang Minsheng, Zhang Yuhua and Zhang Fusheng at the Shanghai Municipal Education Commission offered crucial support. Professor Gu Lingyuan and colleagues at the Shanghai Academy of Educational Sciences facilitated arrangements, mobilized districts to gather statistical data, and were gracious in offering us many opportunities to interview them. We spent considerable time interviewing and observing Shanghai educational policy-makers, researchers, professional developers, teacher educators and teachers. They are too numerous to name here, but their generosity on our many visits was vital to our work. Finally, we thank Emily Hannum, Albert Park, and Maria Teresa Tatto for extensive and thoughtful feedback on drafts of this work.

Notes

1 *Minban* teachers are hired and paid by the local communities, and are not salaried teachers employed by the state.
2 *Shifan xuexiao* or *shifan zhongxue* have been senior secondary schools specially established with the mission of training elementary teachers. Their curriculum includes a combination of general secondary education and professional education.
3 It is important to note that this does not reflect proportionately the numbers of teachers trained.
4 Colleges of education often provided what could be seen as degree education to teachers who lacked appropriate academic credentials.
5 Established in the 1980s, this requirement expected elementary teachers to obtain a secondary school-level teacher training diploma, junior secondary teachers a three-year college diploma, and senior secondary teacher a four-year college degree training.
6 Here and in all references to teachers, we use pseudonyms. This vignette draws on data collected during fieldwork in 1998–2000 in Shanghai.

7 This vignette draws on Fang's fieldwork as a researcher with the Shanghai Institute of Human Resources Development and Distance Education Department of China's Ministry of Education in Inner Mongolia in 1996. As part of that work, she documented a village teacher's life and training in the UNICEF-China Teacher Training through Distance Education Program.

References

Chai, B.L. (2005) "Heri Gaobie Daike Jiaoshi? (When Do Teachers Bid Farewell to Substitute Teachers?)" *Zhongguo Jiaoyubao (China Education Daily)*, (March 20), electronic document available at: http://www.jyb.com.cn/ (accessed January 30, 2006).

Cheng, X.Z. (2004) "Dangqian Shifan Jiaoyu Gaige Xuyao Zhuyi de yixie Wenti (Some Issues Worthy of Attention around Current Reform on Teacher Education and Development)," electronic document posted to: http://www.edu.cn/20041201/3123057.shtml (accessed January 25, 2006).

Chinese National Commission for UNESCO (2004) *Educational Development in China 2004*, electronic document posted to http://www.ibe.unesco.org/International/ICE47/English/Natreps/Reports/China.ocr.pdf. (accessed January 30, 2006).

Fang, Y. and Paine. L. W. (2000) "Challenges and Dilemmas in a Period of Reform: Preservice Mathematics Teacher Education in Shanghai, China," *The Mathematics Educator*, 5(1/2): 32–67.

Fu, D.X. (2003) Jiaoshi Wanglian Jihua: Jiaoshi Jiaoyu De Chuangxin (Teacher Network Alliance or Union Plan: Teacher Education and Development Innovation), interview with Guan Peijun, Head of Teacher Education Department, Ministry of Education. (October 14), published in *Zhongguo Jiaoyubao (China Education Daily)*, electronic document posted to: http://www.jyb.com.cn/gb/jybzt/2002zt/jsjy/379.htm (accessed January 30, 2006).

Lu, B.Y. (ed.) (2000) *Yi Tihua: Shifan Jiaoyu Gaige De Sikao Yu Shijian (Putting into One System: Thoughts and Practice on Teacher Education Reform)*, Shanghai: Huadong Shifan Daxue Chubanshe.

Ministry of Education (1994) *Jiaoshi Fa* (Teacher Law), electronic document posted to: http://www.moe.edu.cn/edoas/website18/info1428.htm (accessed June 8, 2006).

Ministry of Education (1995) *Jiaoshi Zige Tiaolie* (Teacher Certification Requirements), electronic document posted to: http://www.moe.edu.cn/edoas/website18/info5919.htm (accessed June 8, 2006).

Ministry of Education (2000) *Quanguo Jichu Jiaoyu Fazhan Tongji Gongbao (National Statistical Report on Basic Educational Development, 1990–2000)*, electronic document posted to http://www.edu.cn/20020308/3022088.shtml (accessed January 25, 2006).

Ministry of Education (2002) "Woguo Jiaoshi Jiaoyu Qude Changzu Jinzhan (Our Country's Teacher Education has Achieved Remarkable Progress)," electronic document posted to: http://www.edu.cn/20020917/3068525.shtml (accessed January 30, 2006).

Ministry of Education (2004) "Woguo Jiaoshi Jiaoyu Qude Changzu Jinzhan" (Big Improvements in Teacher Education in Our Country), electronic document posted to: http://www.edu.cn/20051227/3167 (accessed January 20, 2006).

Ministry of Education (2005a) *2004 Nian Quan Guo Jiaoyu Shiye Fazhan Tongji Gongbao (2004 National Statistical Report on the Development of Education Work)*,

190 *Lynn Paine and Yanping Fang*

April 2005, electronic document posted to: http://www.edu.cn/20050728/
3144984.shtml (accessed 23 May 2006).

Ministry of Education (2005b) "Guowuyuan Guanyu Dali Fazhan Zhiye Jiaoyu de
Jueding" (State Council's Decision on Rigorously Developing Vocational and
Technical Education)," November 10, 2005, electronic document posted to: http://
www.moe.edu.cn/edoas/website18/info17182.htm (accessed February 10, 2006).

Paine, L. (1986) "Reform and Balance in Chinese Teacher Education," unpublished
doctoral dissertation, Stanford University.

Paine, L. (1995) "Teacher Education in Search of a Metaphor: Teachers, Teacher
Education, and the State in China," in M. Ginsburg and B. Lindsay (eds.) *The
Political Dimension of Teacher Education*, New York: Falmer Press.

Paine, L. (1997) "Chinese Teachers as Mirrors of Reform Possibilities," in W.K.
Cummings and P.G. Altbach (eds.) *The Challenge of Eastern Asian Education*,
Albany, NY: SUNY Press.

Paine, L.W., Fang, Y., and Wilson, S. (2003) "Entering a Culture of Teaching," in
E. Britton, L.W. Paine, D. Pimm, and S. Raizen (eds.) *Comprehensive Teacher
Induction: Systems for Early Career Learning*, Dordrecht: Kluwer Academic
Publishers.

Renmin Ribao (*People's Daily*) (2003) "Woguo Xinyilun Zhongxiaoxue Jiaoshi
Quanyuan Peixun Quanmian Qidong (Our Country's New Round of Elementary
and Secondary Teacher Training Has Been Launched in Full Scale)," September 8,
electronic document posted to http://www.people.com.cn/GB/jiaoyu/1053/
2770506.html (accessed February 2 2006).

Shanghai Zhili Kaifa Yanjiusuo (Shanghai Institute of Human Resource Develop-
ment) (1999) *Woguo Xiaoxue Yu Chuzhong Jiaoshi Xueli Tishen Wenti Zhuanti
Yanjiu* (*Research on Elementary and Secondary Teacher Qualification Upgrade in
Our Country*), report commissioned by the Teacher Education Department of the
Ministry of Education.

Xinhua News Agency (2002) "Woguo Jiaoshi Xueli Buduan Tigao, Xinxing Jiaoshi
Jiaoyu Tixi Zhubu Xingchen," (March 22), electronic version posted to:
http://news.xinhuanet.com/newscenter/2002–03/22/content_327535.htm (accessed
January 30, 2006).

Zhongguo Jiaoyubao Wangzhan (*China Education Daily* Online) (2005) "Quanguo
Putong Xuexiao Jiaoshi Duiwu Xianzhuang (Current Status of National Teaching
Force for Regular Schools)," (April 16), electronic document posted to: http://
www.southcn.com/news/community/shzt/sd/scxz/200504160276.htm> (accessed
February, 1 2006).

Zhu, Y.M. (1999) *Zhongxiaoxue Jiaoshi Zhuanye Fazhan Yanjiu* (*Research Report
on Professional Development of Elementary and Secondary School Teachers*),
Shanghai: Shanghai Zhili Kaifa Yanjiusuo (Shanghai Institute of Human Resource
Development), Shanghai Academy of Educational Sciences.

Zhu, Z.T. (2004) "Teachers' Professional Development in Technology-Pedagogy
Integration: Experiences and Suggestions from China," paper presented at the
Elearning Conference 2004, UNESCO, Bangkok, electronic document posted to:
http://www.unescobkk.org/index.php?id=1292 (accessed February 10, 2006).

11 Incentives and the quality of teachers and schools

Weili Ding and Steven Lehrer

Introduction

A growing body of research in social sciences substantiates the pronounced positive association between education and incomes in developing countries.[1] The perception that high quality education yields greater economic and social benefits for its recipients has promoted development policies focusing on the improvement of human capital and substantially increased parental demands for access to quality education for their children. In developing countries where quality education is in great shortage, one of the primary challenges for education policy-makers is to develop systems that could enhance and expand high quality education resources to meet such demands. The challenge deepens when programs aimed at increasing access to education such as universal primary education and expansions of college education spread existing resources across a rapidly enlarging student population. This chapter describes and assesses the current policies in an urban county in Jiangsu Province designed to provide a high quality education through developing proper incentives for teachers and ensuring equal access to high quality teachers and schools.

A key factor in teacher performance—and thus educational quality—is the evaluation and compensation system used to determine pay and promotion. In addition to eliciting greater teacher effort, incentives that reward outstanding teaching performance can help retain talented teachers, who may have attractive alternative job opportunities in a growing market economy.

Although it may seem obvious that appropriate incentives should improve job performance, there is considerable controversy over what characteristics an optimal teacher incentive system should have. Opponents of merit pay have argued that reward systems that link pay to easily observed performance outcomes such as test scores can lead teachers to neglect less easily observed but important aspects of teaching. For this reason, we have argued in other work that incentive contracts based on a combination of objective performance measures (e.g. students' test scores) and subjective performance evaluations (e.g. assessments by colleagues) are likely to be the most effective (Ding and Lehrer 2001).

We next examine China's teacher performance evaluation, promotion, and compensation system, consider its incentive effects on teachers, and describe differences in student access to high-quality teachers and schools. China has established nationwide a rigorous, multifaceted annual evaluation procedure that determines a significant component of teachers' compensation. To date, this system does not appear to be well understood outside of China. Our study uses a unique data set we collected from ten secondary schools in a large county in Jiangsu Province. It includes detailed information on each teacher's background and professional ranking, allowing us to gauge the relationship between these measures of secondary teacher quality and student academic achievement, as measured by scores on college admission examinations. We demonstrate that China's teacher evaluation and compensation system has many desirable features that may hold lessons for other systems.

In the following section, we describe the secondary school teacher ranking/compensation system employed in Jiangsu Province. We examine empirically the performance of this system, looking at determinants for ranking, salary, and promotion. In the next section we discuss how students gain access to high-quality schools and we describe differences between key schools and regular schools. A concluding section summarizes our findings and discusses policy implications for teacher compensation and improving teacher quality in China.

Teacher incentives in China

Our research focuses on secondary schools in one county in Jiangsu Province. The county is large, with approximately one million residents in 1996, and is relatively wealthy, with a per capita income for both urban and rural households that was more than three times the national average in 1997. The generous cooperation of local officials allowed us to collect data from administrative records at ten of the county's 16 secondary schools. Our data set includes information on the academic records of nearly 1,600 students from junior high school through university, as well as individual-level information on more than 1,500 secondary teachers. For the teachers we collected information on demographic characteristics, education, salary, and employment, as well as on teaching loads, subjects taught, and quality rankings in 1995 and 1998. In China, local governments at all levels (provincial, metropolitan municipalities, and county) have bureaus of education responsible for providing educational services and implementing national educational policies. In our county, the local education bureau regulates the textbooks and minimum standards for grade promotion but allows teachers to use their own teaching methods. The expected workload of teachers is determined at the provincial level. Senior secondary school teachers are generally in the classroom for 10–14 hours per week.

Each teacher has a quality ranking based on the county-level education bureau's assessment of his or her educational background, professional accomplishments, and teaching skills. These rankings—which in increasing order include intern (newly hired), third class, second class, first class, and superior—are used along with years of teaching experience to determine teachers' salaries. In Figure 11.1 we plot the salary scale for teachers of different ranks over years of teaching experience using 1998 data.

It is clear from Figure 11.1 that salaries follow a rule of thumb rather than a complicated formula, and that teachers have a strong incentive to improve their ranking to superior within the first 20 years of their teaching career. Also, irrespective of years of teaching experience, the rank-based salary gap increases with the rank, which provides a strong financial incentive for teachers to improve their ranking. Teachers also may enjoy the social prestige associated with a higher ranking, and may be able to charge higher fees in outside employment opportunities such as tutoring. In conducting assessments and determining whether an instructor will be promoted in rank, the county education bureau examines five factors. First, teaching skills are assessed. College entrance examination scores and other measures of the candidate's students' performance are examined in relation to those of other instructors. Administrators and superior instructors within the same school district in that subject area randomly attend the candidate's lectures to evaluate the quality of classroom instruction. Furthermore, credit is given to teachers who introduce new and effective teaching methods in the classroom. Second, the county education bureau looks at the quality of the college attended and years of education completed by the candidate. A national five-point ranking system of higher education institutions is used to assess the quality of colleges and universities. This information is combined with the number of articles on instructional methods the candidate has published in

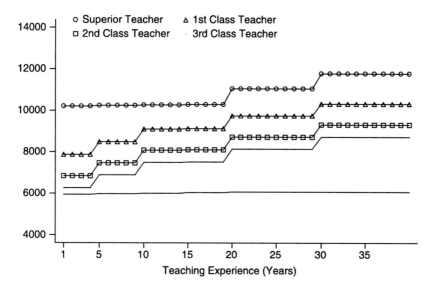

Figure 11.1 Salary schedule for teachers in 1998.

teaching journals to calculate a measure of professional knowledge. Third, the board evaluates the candidate's efficacy at evaluating and monitoring the performance of students, detecting problems that affect students intellectually or socially, and dealing with these problems. Fourth, the board assesses the candidate's enthusiasm and concern for students' performance (e.g. communicating with students' families). Finally, the board evaluates the candidate's work ethic.

County education bureau officials noted that the incentives to be ranked higher have increased recently as the salary differentials across ranks for a given level of teaching experience have widened. Increases in teachers' salaries are financed by local governments, reflecting the willingness and ability of local leaders, and indirectly the community, to reward its teachers. Local governments may want to attract highly qualified teachers for a variety of reasons, in particular because they may associate economic growth potential with the educational level of the local population. In fact, government reports advertise the number of superior teachers in the local school system in a bid to attract outside investment.

In Jiangsu, education officials pointed out that the nationwide introduction of the ranking system in the early 1980s noticeably altered teacher behavior. Instructors monitored student performance more closely and contacted family members either by phone or in person when a child encountered difficulties. As well, instructors increasingly provided tutoring—either directly or by establishing student peer groups—to students who were falling behind. These actions were taken by teachers in order to receive better subjective evaluations of their performance as well as to improve objective performance indicators such as student test scores.

The county education bureau also uses individuals outside the candidate's school to conduct subjective instructor evaluations. This helps the system avoid a common criticism of merit pay—that it creates an incentive for competition instead of collaboration among teachers.[2] At the same time, however, teacher incentives in China are targeted to individuals rather than to groups of teachers or schools,[3] which reduces the potential for unmotivated teachers to exploit the benefits earned by their harder-working colleagues.[4]

The determinants of teacher compensation

As mentioned in the preceding section, in recent years, rank-based salary differentials have widened among similarly experienced teachers. County education bureau officials believe that a successful ranking system must include financial incentives for attaining higher ranks, and that a promotion should entail not only a greater salary but also a higher growth rate in salary. To investigate the actual effect of rank on salary, we analyze information on teacher salaries in 1995 and 1998. Teacher salary is composed of a fixed component and a variable component based on rank and experience. Experience is measured in five-year intervals. We gauge the relative importance of rank and experience in determining salary increases by examining what percentage of the variation in teacher salary increases is accounted for by each variable. We find that rank is the major driving force in salary increases for teachers with less than 20 years of experience. Once a teacher has taught for more than 20 years, there appears to be a statistically significant return to experience, but this return is very small relative to that achieved by increasing rank.

We have already shown in Figure 11.1 that instructors have strong financial incentives to achieve promotion early in their career. In Figure 11.2, we illustrate the percentage of teachers at each rank for each year of experience attained in 1998. Note that at the ten-year mark, more than half of the teachers are ranked as first class and a small percentage of those with a superior ranking emerge. Another interesting phenomenon is the scarcity of second- and third-class teachers among those with more than 15 years of teaching experience.[5] As we do not have numerous repeated assessments of teachers in our data, we are unable to adequately address several dynamic questions related to teacher incentives or to calculate the ages at which teachers are promoted to first and superior class. However, we are able to predict which factors are associated with a teacher having a higher rank.

We use multivariate regression analysis to link these factors to teacher rank outcomes.[6] Explanatory variables for teacher rank in our regression model include individual characteristics thought to affect promotion (age, education, highest degree attained), factors that might influence teaching performance (course load, teaching the subject in which the degree was obtained, years of teaching experience),[7] a measure of objective performance (percentage of students accepted into college),[8] and a proxy for subjective performance measures (a value-added calculation).[9] Value added is assessed by statistically isolating the contribution of a teacher, as opposed to other factors, to the level of student achievement, controlling also for students' earlier performance.[10] The school administrator may consider this as an alternative objective performance measure if the value added can be assessed through objective measures.

The results are presented in Table 11.1.[11] In the first two columns we report the estimates for all of the ranked teachers in nine of our schools. In the last two columns, we report the results for all the ranked teachers in schools that provided information on teaching load and sections taught. We find a significant premium for education: the coefficient for a university degree is more than three times greater than that for a college degree. Instructors are also more likely to be ranked higher if they are teaching the subject in which they received their degree. Not surprisingly, teaching courses in more than one subject area is negatively related to the probability of promotion, which stresses the importance of specialization.

The inclusion of the number of different sections taught and the teaching load in the regression equation reduces the significance of specialization. This indicates that it is not so much the subject matter as it is the number of sections taught that has a negative effect on ranking. Instructors who teach

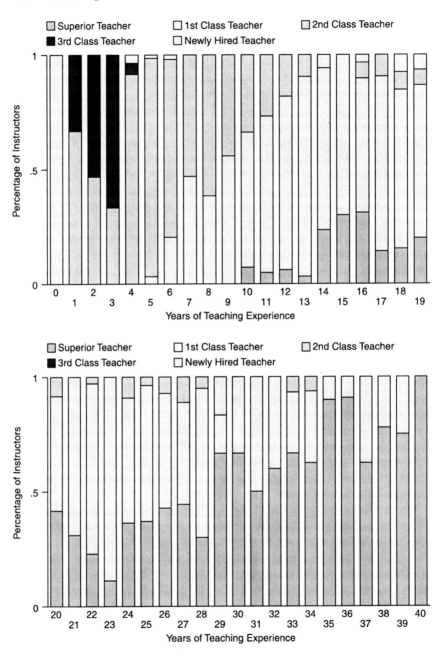

Figure 11.2 Percentage of teachers in different rank by years of experience.

Table 11.1 Factors affecting probability of promotion

Variable	(1)	(2)	(3)	(4)
Teaching experience	0.846**	0.609**	0.857**	0.608**
Teaching experience Squared	−0.030**	−0.025**	−0.029**	−0.025**
Teaching experience Cubed	3.22**10E-4*	2.20**10E-4*	3.49**10E-4*	2.56**10E-4*
Teaching subject	0.373**	0.420**	0.459**	0.451*
Degree is in teaching in more than one subject Area	−0.311	−0.342	0.143	−0.163
University degree	1.568**	1.457***	1.816**	1.624**
College degree	0.361*	0.409*	0.525*	0.526*
Trade school degree	−0.967**	−0.959**	−0.719	−0.747
Married	0.464**	0.429**	0.361	0.314
Female	−0.232*	−0.171	−0.220	−0.158
% of Students to tertiary school	1.737**	1.748**	1.845**	1.593**
Value added	0.008*	0.007*	0.004	0.004
Age		1.137**		1.324*
Age squared		−0.022*		−0.026
Age cubed		2.10*10E-4		2.56*10E-4
Teaching load			−0.066**	−0.066**
Sections taught			−0.070	−0.078*
Log likelihood	−544.863	−531.545	−290.138	−281.565
Number of observations	1051	1051	614	614

Note: This table reports coefficient estimates from ordered probit, * denotes significant at 5%; ** denotes significant at 1%.

more sections may have lower chances of promotion because they must prepare for more lectures and because they have less opportunity to become familiar with their students, which could reduce scores on their subjective assessments. Finally, being female has a negative effect on rank and being married has a positive effect, controlling for other factors.

In all columns the objective performance measure and proxy for the subjective performance measure are positively related to rank. The magnitude of the objective performance measure (percentage of students accepted to college) appears large and we investigated whether this was capturing school quality effects.[12] When we introduced school quality indicators into the equation and removed the objective performance measure, we found the school variables had an effect very similar to that of the objective performance measure. Yet, when we reintroduced the objective performance measure, we found it still had a statistically significant effect on the probability of promotion. Overall, these results indicate that in 1998, higher ranked teachers were associated with higher objective and subjective performance measures.

The effects of the explanatory variables on the probability of being higher ranked were generally small. However, for most variables they had larger impacts on the probability of being higher ranked for first-class and superior teachers. For instance (using the results in column 1), teaching the subject for which the degree was obtained raises the likelihood of having a higher rank by 0.091 on average. The average impact of holding a university degree is approximately four times larger than the effect of a college degree (0.275 vs 0.071), relative to no degree. The effect of a one-year increase in experience raises the probability of higher ranking by 0.032. Finally, it is difficult to compare the relative impacts of the two performance measures (1.318 and 0.006) since these variables are measured using different unit scales.

In additional specifications, we introduced an indicator variable for the subject that the instructor taught to see if higher ranked teachers were more likely to be in certain disciplines (other variables held constant). These estimates did not yield statistically significant results.[13] Similarly, we introduced a school indicator variable to see if promotions were more likely in certain high schools. Hypothesis tests rejected these conjectures.

Overall, we find that the teacher ranking/promotion system used in a county in China's Jiangsu Province has many desirable effects. Individuals with more experience, higher education, and stronger objective and subjective performance evaluations are more likely to receive promotion to higher ranks. Promotions occur frequently and fairly quickly in one's tenure at a school and subjective performance evaluations do not appear to favor any subject area or any one school.

Student access to high-quality teachers and schools

As teachers have formal rankings that indicate their experience and skill, schools themselves have characteristics that indicate their quality and teaching focus. Among the local population, it is well known whether a school is considered to be either a national or provincial model (or key) school, or one that focuses on teaching students trade skills.[14] The number of key schools is limited and these schools have the privilege of recruiting the best students. The philosophy behind these schools is that they are necessary to effectively train top-level manpower needed for China's development. In certain parts of China, such as Shenzhen, Xiamen, Shanghai, and Changchun, key schools have drawn criticism for being elitist and have been abolished in concept, although not in fact.[15]

Students compete for positions in the higher quality schools by taking a municipal-level high school entrance examination at the completion of junior high school. This exam tests knowledge in six subject areas and is held over a period of three days.[16] Scores on this exam are almost the sole determinant of high school admission.

Schools admit students who score above a cutoff level in their regular classes. Schools additionally admit one or two expansion classes of students who did not score above the cutoff level, but whose families pay a supplemental tuition fee, called a donation. The size of this donation varies both across and within schools, but is often greater than the household's annual earnings. A 2000 survey conducted by the Wuxi City Statistics Bureau found the average donation was 10,093 *yuan*.[17]

According to the local education bureau, no more than three families of students in each of the 11 schools elected not to make this donation when given the choice. Education has become an important part of family expenditure. An affiliated center of the State Statistics Bureau conducted a survey of 502 urban residents in Beijing, Shanghai, and Guangzhou, which revealed the following: (1) most families (85 percent) paid little attention to the amount of tuition fees and expressed willingness to pay higher fees to have their children attend a better school; (2) only 10 percent of families considered the amount of tuition fees in choosing a school for their children; (3) almost half (45 percent) of all families reported that the money they paid for education was "value for money"; and (4) 43 percent of families reported that education expenditure is an important part of their budget.[18] The importance of attending a better high school results in many students moving from their homes to reside in dormitories when attending school. The funds collected from students living in dormitories help to increase investments in the most desirable schools, which widen the quality gap across schools even further.

At the completion of high school, students are required to list their preferences for the combination of a specific major and college or university where they wish to enroll. Following the completion of this list, students take a three-day college entrance examination encompassing material in six subject areas. These test scores, coupled with the preference list, determine the major and the university or college in which the student is enrolled.

Given that secondary schools are ranked at quality levels, we examined how the resources available to each student differ across schools. We found that national or provincial key schools have a higher percentage of instructors in the superior class (23.9 percent vs 12.0 percent). However, average teaching experience is lower in key schools than in regular schools (10.27 years vs 12.01 years) because ranked schools can attract younger teachers with higher degrees. Teachers in these schools also are more likely to teach the subjects in which they have their degree (80.5 percent vs 63.1 percent). Most strikingly, only 52 percent of first-class and superior teachers in unranked schools teach the subject that was their study major.[19]

Our teacher data is matched with the annual local government school investment data. We also have the 1995 high school entrance examination scores for the incoming class at nine of the schools. For each of these schools we know whether students were admitted on a regular or expansion basis or because they had outstanding talent in some area. For example, schools give special consideration to students with exceptional art, music, or athletic ability, and place less emphasis on their examination scores. Other students are admitted in ranked schools prior to taking the entrance exam because of their strong academic records in junior high. Finally, for more than 1,600 students, we have data on the scores they received on the 1998 National College Entrance Examination, as well as the subject major, college or university, and national rank of the college/university in which the student subsequently enrolled. Thus, we are able to follow these 1,600-plus students from the completion of junior high school through their admission to a tertiary education institute.

We find that secondary schools of different qualities are significantly different in terms of the performance of incoming students, the success of graduating students, and the level of investment from government and private sources. Exam scores for incoming key school students average 8 percent higher and have less than half of the variation of scores for incoming unranked school students. Further, the average exam score for the national model school is 4 percent higher than average scores for the two provincial key schools. As a group, students in the expansion class have scores that are 1.5 percent lower than their regular class counterparts.[20] About 95 percent of the students from the national key school enrolled in tertiary education. The majority of students from most unranked schools were accepted into college level II programs or national rank 2 (where rank 5 is the highest). A surprising finding is that some unranked schools placed nearly 10 percent more students in tertiary institutions than did one ranked school. This is because the ranked school encourages students to apply to highly ranked programs in universities, whereas the unranked schools encourage students to apply to lower ranked programs, such as three-year associate degree programs in colleges. Most students who went on to tertiary institutions from ranked secondary schools were admitted to Bachelor degree programs (89.3 percent) while most students from unranked schools were admitted to associate degree programs (88.4 percent).

The local government invested substantially more funds in national and provincial model schools than those that were not ranked.[21] When we visited these schools, we observed that key schools tend to have more modern facilities. They also tend to receive more external donations than unranked schools, which exacerbates inequities across schools.

Conclusion

In China, the county education bureau annually assesses each teacher by looking at educational background measures, objective performance measures (e.g. attendance, student test scores), and subjective performance measures (e.g. colleague and student evaluations of teaching performance, and ethics). These assessments are used to assign and upgrade teacher rankings, and rankings are used, along with years of teaching experience, to determine each teacher's salary. Our data allow us to measure the contribution of secondary school teachers to their students' subsequent achievement on college admissions examinations, and to relate that contribution to the teachers' ranking.

Our estimates indicate that teachers' salaries and ranks are indeed positively related to measures of student performance. Promotions occur frequently and fairly quickly in one's career. Subjective performance evaluations do not appear to give ranking advantage to any particular subject area or school. Instructors who are more educated, married, male, experienced, and teach fewer students weekly are more likely to be ranked higher.

These findings suggest that China's teacher evaluation and compensation system may hold lessons for other nation's systems. The system appears to reward teacher quality to a greater extent than in many countries, even in a budgetary environment in which resources are scarce. This should encourage teachers to improve their teaching effectiveness by investing in their teacher-specific human capital and exert greater effort on the job. This is important because growing demand for education in a reforming, more open economy, and commercialization of the educational sector itself, are likely to put increasing pressures on China's educational system. In the future, China may have a greater diversity of school types, including more private schools, greater mobility of students and teachers, and an emerging market for teachers that could draw high-quality teachers from the public schools. This will make it even more important for teacher compensation schemes to recognize and reward quality. The challenge facing education policy-makers in this context is to offer incentives that continue to bring high-quality individuals into teaching, induce teachers to remain in public education, and motivate teachers to improve the quality of their work. Perhaps the first step should be the collection of experimental data to assess the relative effectiveness of alternative policies.[22]

Another set of policy concerns emerges from the growing reality that high-quality education can be bought, even in the public educational system. The system, through its differential investment in key schools, rations access to the best schools on the basis of both student ability (entrance scores) and, increasingly, monetary inducements. That some students gain entrance to key schools through cash "donations" challenges the philosophical underpinnings of China's performance-based school admission system and raises questions of elitism.

Since the period of the data collection many reforms have been implemented at the K-9 level. Senior middle schools have been neglected in these reforms, although admissions remain merit-based, the importance of "donations" has increased substantially over time. One response to the increasingly marketization of access to higher quality schools is to eliminate the system of key schools by discontinuing discriminatory school investment policies, abandoning entrance examinations at the K-12 level, and enforcing local admission. However, these seemingly equalizing steps may in fact have undesirable consequences.

First, adopting local open admission in lieu of performance-based admission may result in many parents with financial resources and/or social connections responding strategically to secure their children places at the former key schools—the generally perceived elite schools.[23] Such practice would merely push elitist public education underground; it would not create equal access to quality education. Second, abandoning public key schools might increase the demand for private elite schools, as many parents have shown themselves willing to pay substantial amounts to get high-quality peers for their children. These private schools would skim high-ability students and their high-contributing parents from the public school system, depriving it of talented students, significant parental investment, and associated educational resources such as highly ranked teachers. Taken together, the allocation of quality education resources will shift from schools that contain merit-based school populations towards schools composed of students of higher socioeconomic background. This could have large impacts on the access to quality education for low socio-economic status children.

Third, our research on the effects of peers on student achievement has shown that high-achieving students realize greater academic benefit from being grouped with similar-ability peers, or streaming, than from being grouped with peers of diverse abilities, or mixing (Ding and Lehrer forthcoming). Low-achieving students, however, may benefit more from mixing than streaming. In an era of increasing competition from private schools, these peer effects suggest that if the public school system does not provide achievement-based educational settings, private schools will substitute with elite education based on wealth and ability. This not only undermines the attractiveness and competitiveness of the public school system by taking away its best resources, but also denies top-quality education to students from poor families.

Rather than eliminating public key schools through measures that equalize school admissions, we believe that public school reform must instead address two seemingly conflicting goals: fortifying equal access of educational opportunity, and improving school competitiveness and quality. New educational policies should maintain competitiveness by allowing key schools to continue ability-based admission, and retain the best resources in the public school system and strengthen their accessibility to poor students by regulating access based on financial considerations.

Acknowledgments

We thank Thomas Rawski and the University of Pittsburgh China Council for research support at various stages of this project.

Notes

1 See chapters by de Brauw and Rozelle (Chapter 12), Zhao and Zhou (Chapter 13), and Zhang and Zhao (Chapter 14) in this volume. In addition, Maurer-Fazio's Chapter 15 in this volume describes additional (non-salary) labor market benefits from higher education.

2 Limited evidence from the USA suggests that many teachers who are not selected for merit pay become demoralized, think they have been treated unfairly, and become unwilling to work with each other.

3 Group incentives are fairly widespread based on standard arguments that individuals who share a common goal are likely to help and monitor each other.

4 Teamwork requires substitution among inputs which is not perfect within schools (a math teacher cannot teach music at the same level). In addition, Gaynor and Pauly (1990) provide empirical evidence suggesting that group incentives are more efficient, the smaller the group. Schools are relatively large organizations and it is difficult for teachers to monitor each other when they do not regularly observe their colleague's performance in the classroom.

5 This result may not be surprising since promotion from intern to third class and then to second class is almost automatic and years of experience are the prime determinant. The major challenges in the system are being promoted to first class and then subsequently to superior teacher.

6 Specifically, we consider an ordered probit estimator. This is a generalization of the linear regression model to the case of an ordered discrete outcome variable. It can capture the impact of explanatory variables on different levels of outcomes while preserving the underlying order of outcomes.

7 In our estimation, we include the square and cube of both age and years of teaching experience.

8 Note our results are robust to other objective performance measures such as college entrance examination test scores.

9 A proxy for the subjective performance measure is required since our data do not contain direct information on subjective performance evaluations.

10 Murnane (1975) found that the subjective evaluation of principals and school administrators of the effectiveness of the teachers is highly correlated with gains in student knowledge (value added) and practically uncorrelated with test scores.

11 Interpretation of these estimates is not straightforward. The ordered probit estimator estimates a threshold value for each rank. Using this information one could calculate a marginal effect for each variable separately for each rank. The sample mean of the response (other points could be used) is used in these calculations.

12 After all, higher ranked schools generally send more students to college.

13 This was accomplished using a conditional maximum likelihood estimator and running a Hausman test on the fixed effects.

14 The concept of key schools is similar to that of a magnet or college preparatory school in the USA.

15 In reality, changes have gone little beyond renaming these schools and/or enforcing local admission. With parents' perception of the quality of these schools unaltered, local admission becomes admission based on means of wealth and social connections, which raises serious fairness concerns.

16 There are two versions of the college entrance exams. The first is for students wishing to major in the arts and is composed of questions in Chinese, English, geology, history, mathematics, and political science. The second is for students who wish to major in the sciences and covers material in biology, chemistry, Chinese, English, mathematics, and physics. Both exams were scored out of 750 in 1998.

17 Source: *Wuxi Daily*, June 13, 2000. Note that 10,093 *yuan* is approximately $1225 US. As a point of comparison, disposable personal income per capita in 1999 in urban areas reached renminbi 5,854 (US$707). Per-capita net income for farmers was Rmb 2,210 (US $266.90).
18 Source: *Life Times*, April 15, 2000.
19 For teachers ranked second class or lower, the difference is only 3 percent between ranked and unranked schools.
20 All the schools admit an expansion class with the exception of the nationally ranked school. This school sends all the students in its expansion class to its affiliated school. This results in a surprising finding that the entrance examination scores are slightly lower for the regular class than the expansion class in this school. The affiliated school is famous for fine arts and many regular class students have exceptional ability in art or drama.
21 Tsang and Ding (2005) present a more detailed discussion of the disparity of school investment across fairly homogenous regions. Our results are complementary in demonstrating that even within one region there is substantial heterogeneity.
22 See Todd and Wolpin (2003) or Ding and Lehrer (2001) for a discussion of the distinction between the interpretation of coefficient estimates from non-experimental and experimental data in the context of student achievement.
23 See Chapter 3 by Jing Lin in this volume for a detailed discussion of the impacts of increasing fees and the demand for private schools.

References

Ding, W. and Lehrer, S.F. (2001) "Using Performance Incentives to Reward the Value Added of Educators: Theory and Evidence from China", mimeo, University of Pittsburgh.

Ding, W. and Lehrer, S.F. (forthcoming) "Do Peers Affect Student Achievement in China's Secondary Schools?," *Review of Economics and Statistics*.

Gaynor, M. and Pauly, M.V. (1990) "Compensation and Productive Efficiency in Partnerships: Evidence from Medical Groups Practice," *Journal of Political Economy*, 98: 544–73.

Life Times, April 15, 2000. The original article was originally at http://www.china.org.cn/english/2001/Nov/22548.htm

Murnane, R.J. (1975) *Impact of School Resources on the Learning of Inner City Children*, Cambridge, MA: Ballinger.

Todd, P. and Wolpin, K.I. (2003) "On the Specification and Estimation of the Production Function for Cognitive Achievement," *Economic Journal*, 113: F3–F33.

Tsang, M.C. and Ding, Y.Q. (2005) "Resource utilization and Disparities in Compulsory Education in China," *China Review*, 5(1): 1–31.

Wuxi Daily, June 13, 2000. An English summary of the article can be found at http://www.hku.hk/chinaed/chinaed_news/chinaednews_index_ed_and_finance.htm

Part III

Marketization and the economic impact of education

12 Returns to education in rural China

Alan de Brauw and Scott Rozelle

Through its roles in increasing production and promoting health status, education is considered to be of primary importance to sustained income growth (Schultz 1988; Barro 1991). People who are more educated are not only more efficient producers, they are also better able to communicate effectively and to make more informed choices (Sen 1999). In developing countries, access to education helps the rural poor build their human capital, increasing the value of the most abundant asset of most households, labor.

Within this context, it can be argued that rural education is of particular importance to development in China. In 2004, over 58 percent of China's population still lived in rural areas, and 46 percent of its economically active population worked in agriculture (NBS 2005). In a land-scarce country such as China, the nation will only truly modernize when its most abundant resource, labor, is made more productive. The importance of education in raising productivity is manifested in two ways: (1) by facilitating the shift of labor from agriculture to industry; and (2) by increasing the returns to labor when individuals find employment.

Despite the imperative of increasing the value of China's human capital stock in rural areas, the government has not given top priority to rural education in its development plan (Nyberg and Rozelle 1999). Rural education rates are low, only six years on average, compared to more than nine years in the rest of Asia (Psacharopoulos 1994). Moreover, unlike most other developing countries, China spends relatively little on rural education, and that amount is decreasing. China's government allocated 2.5 percent of GDP to all urban and rural education in 1980, but only 2.2 percent of GDP in 2000 (China National Statistics Bureau 2001). In comparison, other developing countries allocated an average of 3.3 percent of GDP to primary and secondary education in 2000 (World Bank 2001).

One reason for the adverse trend may be that, in China, investments in rural education are widely believed to generate relatively low rates of return. While measured rates of return in the world average in excess of 10 percent and exceed 9 percent in other Asian countries (Psacharopoulos 1994), most studies of education in China have found much lower returns. In the urban economy, until the recent estimates presented in the chapter by Zhang and Zhao, average returns to education have rarely been found to exceed 5 percent.[1] If anything, studies of education in the rural economy have found even lower returns (Parish *et al.* 1995; Meng 1996; Zhao 1999). If these studies are accurate, when combined with low average educational attainment levels, China stands out as an anomaly when compared to other countries. For China's level of average educational attainment, the typical return to a year of education found in the literature is less than half of the rate found in other countries.

Given the importance of education in the development process, such low estimated returns require an explanation. One possibility is simply that the private returns to education in rural China are lower than in other countries. It is possible that, given both its socialist legacy and the current transitional nature of its economy, China's reformers may have insulated managers from the pressures of markets (Weitzman and Xu 1994). Instead of forcing firms to look for the most qualified and educated workers to fill employment roles, managers may primarily use non-market factors (e.g. *guanxi*) to assign jobs to workers. When non-market assignment of jobs dominates, then investment in schooling does not lead to higher incomes, and it can be argued that the government should allocate less fiscal resources to school investments in favor of other investments that would lead to higher private and social returns. However, according to this explanation, if markets begin to function well in China, we should expect to see the rates of returns rise.

Alternatively, methodological shortcomings of previous studies could have systematically underestimated educational returns in China. Most studies that have calculated returns to education in rural China either chose a specification or selected a sample that may have contributed to lower estimated rates of return. If, in fact, low estimates of the rates of return to schooling can be attributed to methodology, previous research may have actually contributed to the problem of low educational investment, instead of helping policy-makers make more effective rural policy. In response to these shortcomings, use of a more sound methodological approach could produce higher estimates.

In this chapter, our primary goal is to further our understanding of the rates of return to education in China. To accomplish this goal, the chapter has two specific objectives. First, we review previous studies and examine the context in which they were generated. Second, we produce a new set of estimates. The new estimates will have two aims: to examine whether the returns to education are rising over time as China's markets have developed, and to explore the role that methodological and data shortcomings may have played in producing the lower estimates currently found in the literature. We show that among younger workers, by the late 1990s, the returns to education had reached levels found in other countries. Our finding is consistent with a message to policy-makers that budgetary allocations to education should be increased.

This set of objectives is extremely broad, and given our data limitations, we narrow our focus to studying rural education. While we review a wider set of studies on China's education, our examination of methodological problems mainly targets studies that have previously used the Mincer (1974) method of analysis.

To meet our objectives, the chapter will proceed as follows. The first two sections examine employment in rural China and review evidence on the relationship between wages and education. The next sections lay out our empirical framework and describe the data set that we use to generate our own estimates of the returns to education. In the results section, we report several new sets of estimates and examine how the estimates change when alternative specifications and samples are used. In the conclusion, we argue that previous low estimates of the returns to education in rural China are due both to weak labor markets, which have strengthened in recent years, and methodology.

Education and employment in rural China

The massive flow of labor into the off-farm sector brought new prosperity to millions of rural households during China's economic reform era. The proportion of the rural labor force that has found work off-farm rose from around 22 percent in 1988 to 34 percent in 1995 (Rozelle *et al.* 1999). By 2000, nearly 200 million people, or 43 percent of laborers, held off-farm jobs (de Brauw *et al.* 2002). The rise in wage earnings and income from self-employed activities can account for most of the increase in rural incomes in the late 1980s and 1990s (Parish *et al.* 1995).

Rural labor markets, however, do more for the development process than just providing a means for raising rural incomes (Todaro 1976). For China to develop successfully, labor markets must function well enough to facilitate the shift from a largely rural population to an urban one. As the rates of return to education are an indicator of the health and extent of labor markets, estimates of the rates of return can help evaluate their development. In determining their priorities with regards to economic development policy, China's leaders should be interested in knowing whether labor markets are developing in a way that rewards households and individuals for going to school, and may gauge their level of investment based on the returns being realized.

Although the focus of a considerable amount of research, scholars do not agree on the role that labor markets have played in contributing to China's economic growth during the first two decades of reform. Some researchers believe that significant barriers still exist in China's economy, and that the absence of well-functioning rural labor markets has hindered growth. For example, Benjamin and Brandt (1997) and Liu *et al.* (1998) provide evidence that on-farm labor markets did not function well during the 1990s. Others have focused on the *hukou* system and other institutional barriers and the constraints they place on the movement of labor, despite large wage gaps and positive expected gains from migration. Mallee (2000) and Yang and Zhou

(1996) argue that a number of barriers, such as land tenure arrangements and mandatory marketing delivery quotas, continue to increase the cost of out-migration and dampen off-farm labor market participation. Johnson (1995) worries that several prominent urban institutions, like the *hukou* system and the lack of social and educational services for rural residents in cities, restrict entrance into urban labor markets.

In contrast, others believe that rural labor markets have emerged in a healthy manner and are continuing to evolve positively. For example, Cook (1999) demonstrates the equalization of off-farm labor returns between wage earning and self-employed workers in her rural Shandong sample. Lohmar's (1999) analysis of the effect of land tenure and quota policies finds that, although more restrictive policies have some impact on household labor response to the off-farm sector, the magnitude is small. Knight and Song (2001) find that some urban firms have become less discriminatory in their hiring practices of those without an urban *hukou*. Finally, Zhang *et al.* (1995), Rozelle *et al.* (1999), the National Bureau of Statistics, and de Brauw *et al.* (2002), among others, have documented the explosion of migration and off-farm participation.

Wages, education, and previous estimates of the returns to education

If the relationship between education, access to employment and wages reflects the nature of labor markets, the record in the literature on China is somewhat mixed. Although the estimates of returns to education that appear in the literature indicate that they are lower than elsewhere in the world, several authors have found that education increases the probability of finding an off-farm job (e.g. Zhang *et al.* 1995, Zhao 1999). Furthermore, several more recent estimates indicate that returns may be increasing (Benjamin and Brandt 1997; Zhang *et al.* 2002).

Studies of the rural economy have found low returns compared with urban China and the rest of the world (de Brauw *et al.* 2002). Previous studies using the traditional Mincer method of estimating returns to education summarily find low returns.[2] Parish *et al.* (1995) and Johnson and Chow (1997) use nationally representative samples of individuals and find that the returns to education range between 1.8 to 4.3 percent. Examining individual workers in Sichuan province, Yang (1997) estimates that the return to education is only 2.3 percent. Meng (1996), Gregory and Meng (1995), and Ho *et al.* (2002) only examine workers in local enterprises in rural areas (i.e. those working in township and village enterprises) and find average returns of less than 5 percent. A number of other studies use other methods to examine the returns to education in rural samples and find average returns far below 5 percent (e.g. Zhao 1997, Hare 1999, Li and Zhang 1998, Zhao 1999, Yang and An 2002). In fact, with the exception the estimates of Ho *et al.* (2002: 5.1 percent); Benjamin *et al.* (2002: 6.6 percent); and Zhang *et al.*

(2002), who find a return of 9 percent between 1996 and 2002, there are no findings of returns to education above 5 percent.

In contrast, other studies have found compelling evidence of the importance of education to the rural workforce. A number of studies have documented the effectiveness of education in facilitating access to off-farm work. Zhao (1997), Zhang *et al.* (2002), and de Brauw *et al.* (2002) find that education has a positive and statistically significant influence on the probability that rural individuals can find a job. In fact, the survey data of Zhang *et al.* (2002) clearly show a positive and increasing relationship between education and off-farm employment. In all three years of the survey in seven northern Jiangsu villages—1988, 1992, and 1996—individuals with a middle school education and above had higher off-farm participation rates (Table 12.1). Perhaps more importantly, the difference between those with less and those with more education grew sharply over time. In 1988 and 1992 the off-farm participation rates of those with middle school or above exceeded the rates of those with less education by around 50 percent, and this gap rose to more than 100 percent by 1996.

In our northern Jiangsu sample, the relationship between education and wages strengthened between 1988 and 1996 (Table 12.2). In the late 1980s, wages for middle school graduates and above were actually lower than wages for those who had only graduated from elementary school, at least among older workers. By the mid-1990s, however, a sharp reversal had occurred. For all age groups, workers with a middle school education and above earned more on a per day basis than those with only an elementary education. Across all age categories, the real wage rose more than 10 percent faster annually between 1988 and 1996 for those with higher education levels compared to those with only elementary schooling.

In summary, then, it is not difficult to understand why researchers disagree regarding the nature of China's off-farm labor markets. Most econometric studies have recorded low measures of the returns to education. However, there are two reasons to believe that labor markets have begun to function better. Education has, or has begun to have, a positive effect on off-farm

Table 12.1 Labor market participation and education in Jiangsu Province, 1988, 1992, and 1996

Labor market participation	*1988*	*1992*	*1996*
Off-farm work (percentage in workforce)			
Primary school	41	33	33
Middle school and above	62	49	69
On-farm work (days worked per year)			
Primary school	67	113	80
Middle school and above	28	45	29

Source: Authors' survey.

Table 12.2 Wages by education and age in Jiangsu Province, 1988, 1992, and 1996

Age group	Level of education	1988	1992	1996
Young	Primary school	3.4	3.2	7.8
	Middle school and above	4.3	4.3	11.7
Middle aged	Primary school	10.2	5.5	14.7
	Middle school and above	4.0	4.5	20.9
Old	Primary school	11.0	5.7	4.5
	Middle school and above	4.9	7.7	6.3

Source: Authors' survey.

Note: The young are those between 16 and 30; the middle aged are those between 31 and 50; the old are those between 51 and 65. Wages in *yuan*.

participation. And furthermore, based on our descriptive statistics, more educated workers seem to earn a premium for their education, at least in recent years.

Some of the disagreement between previous measures of the returns to education and our descriptive analysis may be due to the timing of different studies. In this way, it is plausible that both sides of the debate are correct. Different sets of researchers may be describing two different economies—one in the early reforms, in which markets played only a marginal role, and another economy in the later reforms, when the private sector and markets began to dominate the economy. China's rural economy, in particular, has evolved remarkably over the past two decades. In the 1980s and early 1990s, decision-making in rural enterprises was heavily influenced by officials who were likely considering a number of non-market factors (Naughton 1995; Nyberg and Rozelle 1999).

In an economy with such rapidly emerging markets, it may not be surprising that returns to education were low during the early reform period, but have risen since. During the past ten years, several authors have shown that rural enterprises now operate in an increasingly competitive environment in which most managers have had fairly good incentives to respond to market signals (Jin and Qian 1998; Chen and Rozelle 1999; Li 2003). These changes may be showing up in more recent estimates of the returns to education. Not surprisingly, studies that found the highest returns use the most recently collected data (Benjamin *et al.* 2002; Ho *et al.* 2002).

However, when one takes a closer look at the studies that have estimated low returns, one questions whether the estimates also are low in part due to the methods or the nature of the sample being analyzed. In several studies, the method of measuring wages may have a negative effect on the estimated returns to education. In countries with underdeveloped financial markets, such as China, poorer people may drop out of school because they cannot finance the earnings they forego to attend school, while richer people can continue as they wish (Schultz 1988). Hence, richer people may systematically have more education. Moreover, once the rich and poor complete their education, differences in wealth endowments, which are associated with differences in preferences for leisure and tolerances for risk, may mean that the poor have to work more. The poor may have to work both more hours per day and/or more days per month or year. As a result, estimates of the returns to education based on daily, monthly or annual earnings could underestimate the true returns to schooling. Since hourly income is not affected by choices regarding the number of hours per day or days per month to work, it is the preferred measure (Schultz 1988; Card 1999). None of the previous Mincerian studies of rates of return in rural China use hourly wages.

The selection of the sample for some of these studies may also affect the measured relationship between wages and completed education. Several papers only consider workers in one industry or sector of the economy (Gregory and Meng 1995; Meng 1996; Ho *et al.* 2002). If that sector of the economy had lower rates of return to education than other sectors, perhaps for institutional reasons, national estimates drawn from such studies would not be representative. In addition, Becker (1964) warns that estimates of educational returns will be low if particular groups of workers are singled out for estimation, because the effect of selection into that portion of the off-farm labor force is ignored. Only one paper in the rural China literature corrects for sample selectivity bias (Zhang *et al.* 2002).

Empirical framework

To analyze the determinants of off-farm wages, we use the two-step model developed by Heckman (1974). The Heckman model avoids a possible bias that may result from excluding individuals from the sample who choose not to work for wages. Individuals choose whether or not to work for wages, and as a result ordinary least squares (OLS) estimation of the determinants of wages drops people who do not work for wages from estimation. However, individuals who choose not to enter the off-farm labor market believe the wage rate they would receive is lower than their reservation wage, or the wage they implicitly earn farming, in self-employment, or in doing tasks around the household. By dropping these people, the sample is not random, and so OLS estimates are not representative of the population as a whole. The Heckman two-step model allows us to include all individuals of working age in the analysis, avoiding sample selection bias and allowing us to interpret our results as applying to the entire sample.

In the first estimation step, we estimate a probit equation to determine whether or not an individual enters the off-farm labor market. We use two sets of variables to determine whether an individual enters the wage-earning labor force. The first set of explanatory variables are human capital characteristics, which include the years of education attained, work experience, and work experience squared, and an indicator variable that is 1 if the individual participated in a training or apprenticeship program, and 0 otherwise. The second set of explanatory variables are measures that may affect whether or not an individual decides to work off-farm, but should not affect the wage rate. These variables include an indicator variable for the marital status of each individual, the household size, and the household land endowment, which is the amount of land allocated to the household by the village. The results are used to calculate a sample selection correction term, an inverse Mills ratio, which then enters the second stage of estimation.

In the second step, we investigate the determinants of wages. We use the logarithm of the hourly wage as the dependent variable, and the explanatory variables are the same as the first set of explanatory variables used in the first step of estimation. As a result, our estimates exactly follow the Mincer (1974) method of estimating the returns to education, which has literally been used hundreds of times to measure the returns to education (Psacharopoulos 1994).[3] By using the hourly wage as our dependent variable rather than the daily or monthly wage and controlling for potential sample selection bias, we generate an estimate for the coefficient on the education variable that controls for both of the methodological factors we identified as possible shortcomings of the previous studies. We also address the representativeness of the previous samples by using our estimating framework on a sample that includes all rural workers, rather than a sample from a single sector of the rural off-farm labor force.

In addition to estimating the basic model defined by these equations, we perform a number of exercises to examine the returns to education within certain groups in the population. Specifically, because of the increasing importance of the migrant sector of the off-farm labor force, we examine the returns within this sector separately. This exercise may help to reconcile China's results with the returns to education in other countries, given that an overwhelmingly large fraction of the off-farm employment in other countries is in the *migrant* sector. In China, rural industry employs an unusually large portion of the population, whereas in other countries, workers who move off-farm must typically leave rural areas. To make our estimates even more comparable with other countries, and to control for possible differences in returns to education that might occur because of differences in the quality of education for those schooled during and after the Cultural Revolution, we also examine the effects of education on the wage rates of individuals under the age of 35 (henceforth, *young wage earners*).

Finally, we conduct two robustness checks on our results, to make sure that other biases that have been discussed in the broader literature do not affect our results (Schultz 1988; Card 1999). These robustness checks involve controls for individual ability and for school quality. To control for potential individual ability bias, we add variables that measure the grades that each person received in their final year of schooling, and their father's educational level. To control for a potential bias that results from differences in school quality, we sequentially add seven variables to a modified model that may measure school quality: the student–teacher ratio, average class size, the average education, experience, and wages of teachers, average expenditures per student, and an indicator variable for whether or not the school had a library.[4] To match up school quality variables with times that individuals were in school, the quality variables are measured in 1990 and these regressions are only estimated for individuals aged 35 and under who were raised in the village.

Data

The data set used in this chapter is from a national sample of 1,199 households in six provinces and 60 villages in rural China conducted by the authors in late 2000. In addition to collecting basic information on the farm household land and labor endowments, and other production-oriented activities, the survey included sections to collect detailed information about labor force participation and schooling. Enumerators questioned all household members about their employment and education, including children of the head who are still part of the household, but did not include children, individuals in school, and the elderly who no longer work. In total, the sample includes 3,363 individuals. Of those, 1,022 individuals worked for a wage off the farm, and 2,341 did not.

Several aspects of both the household and village level surveys are designed specifically to help answer the questions raised in our chapter. Hourly wages were computed by taking all monetary earnings over the course of the year (in multiple jobs, if the person held more than one wage earning job) and dividing by the *number of hours* worked during the year. The survey asked about school participation, eliciting information both about the number of years of schooling each individual attended and the final level of schooling attainment. Our questionnaire also asks respondents to identify if they lived at home while they were working or if they lived away from home, so we could categorize each worker as either a migrant or a local wage earner. To get proxies of individual ability, enumerators asked the respondent about the grades that each person received in the last year of their schooling (good, average, or poor), as well as the years of schooling attained by each person's father. A companion school survey was asked of each village primary school to construct variables measuring school quality.

Results

We estimated the system defined by the two equations to generate estimates of the rate of return to education (Table 12.3). Most of the coefficients are of the expected sign, strongly statistically significant, and robust across specifications. In particular, as described by other authors who examined the determinants of participation in the off-farm labor market (Zhao 1997), education has a strong effect on selection into the off-farm labor force. At

Table 12.3 Effects of education and experience on off-farm wages

Explanatory variables	All individuals		Individuals 35 and under		Individuals over 35	
	Selection equation	Wage equation	Selection equation	Wage equation	Selection equation	Wage equation
Years of	0.018	0.064	0.022	0.093	0.018	0.034
education	(5.90)**	(7.06)**	(3.48)**	(8.27)**	(5.32)**	(0.95)
Years of	0.002	0.032	0.023	0.068	−0.002	0.022
experience	(0.61)	(5.63)**	(2.66)**	(4.92)**	(0.47)	(1.15)
Experience,	−0.012	−0.047	−0.080	−0.134	−0.001	−0.033
squared (/100)	(2.82)**	(4.96)**	(2.49)**	(2.16)**	(0.23)	(1.22)
Skill training?	0.114	0.117	0.109	0.030	0.106	0.229
	(5.22)**	(2.17)**	(3.44)**	(0.53)	(3.67)**	(1.15)
Instruments						
Married?	−0.238		−0.350		−0.012	
(1 = yes)	(7.51)**		(8.84)**		(0.24)	
Household size	0.001		0.000		0.001	
	(0.13)		(0.03)		(0.11)	
Land	−0.004		−0.004		−0.003	
endowment	(2.39)**		(1.63)		(1.78)*	
Inverse Mills		−0.000		−0.180		−0.090
ratio		(0.00)		(1.34)		(0.14)

Notes: t-statistics are in parentheses. * indicates significance at the 90 percent level; ** indicates significance at the 95 percent level. Provincial fixed effects are included in all equations. Experience is measured as years since the person left school if they went to school, and age 6 if they did not. All regressions are done using the two-step method proposed by Heckman (1974) and standard error calculations take the method into account. 3,363 observations are included in columns 1–2; 1,513 observations are included in columns 3–4; and 1,850 observations are included in columns 5–6.

the mean level of education in the sample, given another year of education, a person becomes 1.8 percent more likely to find an off-farm job (row 1, column 1).

In addition to facilitating the process of finding an off-farm job, education has a positive and highly significant effect on hourly wages. When we used the entire sample, we found that the average return to a year of education is 6.4 percent (row 1, column 2). This coefficient implies that averaged across all of China, all age cohorts and sectors of the off-farm labor market, individuals in the rural economy who work off-farm receive 6.4 percent higher wages for every additional year of schooling.

The average returns to education, however, mask differences between age cohorts. Among young wage earners, the estimated returns to education are higher. Individuals below 35 years old receive, on average, 9.3 percent higher wages for each additional year of schooling (row 1, column 4). In contrast, the returns for those over 35 are statistically insignificant (row 1, column 6). The difference between estimated returns for younger and older workers may indicate that younger workers are much more mobile than older workers and that education is becoming increasingly important for new jobs in the labor market. One explanation for the low returns found among workers aged over 35 may be the low or different quality of education during the Cultural Revolution and earlier.

However, even when averaging across the whole sample, our estimated returns, 6.4 percent, are higher than estimates found in other nationally representative samples of rural areas (those studies discussed above). It could be that the higher rates of return that we find are primarily a function of the fact that our data are more recent, and that returns have been increasing over time. However, our estimate may be higher in part because of our methodology. In another paper, we decompose the gap between our findings and the average estimate in the current literature into a timing effect and a measurement effect (de Brauw and Rozelle 2006). In that paper, we demonstrate that 1.5 percentage points of the difference between the average return found in the literature (2.3 percent) and our findings (6.4 percent) is due to a difference in the timing of studies.[5] In other words, when comparing the estimates of the previous authors with calculations that use their specifications but our more recent data, the average returns rise from 2.3 to 3.8 percent. One interpretation of this rise is that it is due to the increased competition that has emerged in the rural economy during the 1990s. As markets have developed, it is possible that firm managers have begun to reward human capital more as they search for greater efficiency.

When we make further corrections to other authors' specifications, by using hourly wages as the dependent variable and by correcting for potential sample selectivity bias, we account for most of the rest of the gap between the average of other estimates and our estimate. After these corrections are made, the average return across other authors' specifications is 6.2 percent, which is nearly identical to our estimate (6.4 percent). Accounting for the methodological concerns, therefore, increases returns even more (2.4 percentage points) than accounting for the difference in timing of studies (1.5 percentage points).

Using our data and specifications in equations (1) and (2), we also show that migrants receive an even higher return to their education than other sectors of the rural economy (Table 12.4). When we restrict wage earners to migrants, we find that the returns to education rise to 8.3 percent (column 2). In contrast, in the local wage-earning sector, the average rate of return for a year of education is only 5.2 percent (column 4). Most noteworthy (although not shown here), among young migrants, the estimated rates of return are even higher, at 11.1 percent. Hence, our findings imply that the rates of return for China's rural laborers are higher for younger workers and for those who migrate, and are particularly high for young migrants. Given that much of the off-farm labor force in the rest of Asia (and the world, for that matter) is typically young and that the main off-farm jobs outside of China are found in cities (unlike China that has developed a large rural industrial sector), our

Table 12.4 Heckman regressions to determine effect of migration or local wage-earning status on hourly wages

Explanatory variables	All migrants		All local wage earners	
	Selection equation	Wage equation	Selection equation	Wage equation
Years of education	0.002	0.083	0.010	0.052
	(1.13)	(7.75)**	(2.50)**	(1.95)*
Years of experience	−0.005	0.038	0.010	0.042
	(2.74)**	(3.48)**	(1.72)*	(2.49)**
Experience, squared	−0.001	−0.070	−0.023	−0.023
	(0.46)	(4.02)**	(1.08)	(1.08)
Skill training?	0.065	0.106	0.029	0.061
	(4.07)**	(1.62)	(1.40)	(0.48)
Instruments				
Married? (1 = yes)	−0.169		−0.020	
	(6.31)**		(0.80)	
Household size	0.004		0.005	
	(0.88)		(0.62)	
Land endowment	−0.001		−0.005	
	(1.32)		(1.03)	
Inverse Mills ratio		0.086		0.076
		(0.55)		(0.16)

Note: t-statistics are in parentheses.
* indicates statistical significance at the 90 percent level;
** indicates statistical significance at the 95 percent level. Provincial fixed effects are included in all equations. Experience is measured as years since the person left school if they went to school, and age 6 if they did not. All regressions are done using the two-step method proposed by Heckman (1974) and standard error calculations take the method into account. 3,363 observations are included in the regressions.

estimates for these subsets of China's workforce may be more comparable to those found in the rest of the developing world, in general, and for those found in the rest of Asia, in particular.

The results of our analysis are found to be robust to two further tests that are designed to control for other effects that might be expected to affect rates of return. First, we test whether individual ability might affect the estimated returns to education (Table 12.5). When we add the three measures of ability to the base equations, we find that although having had good grades facilitated entry into the off-farm labor market (row 4, column 1), none of the ability measures directly affect the wage level (column 2). Even more importantly, we find that the estimates of the rate of return are nearly the same with and without the measures of ability, for the sample of all workers as well as the sample of young wage earners. As a result, we conclude that individual ability bias does not affect our estimates.

Table 12.5 Heckman regressions to determine effect of individual ability on wage

| Variables | All individuals 35 and under | | | |
| | All workers | | Migrants only | |
	Selection equation	Wage equation	Selection equation	Wage equation
Years of education	0.021	0.097	0.010	0.117
	(3.25)**	(8.20)**	(1.70)*	(8.78)**
Years of experience	0.022	0.073	0.014	0.081
	(2.53)**	(5.14)**	(1.75)*	(4.96)**
Experience, squared (/100)	−0.074	−0.148	−0.068	−0.159
	(2.27)**	(2.35)**	(2.24)**	(2.17)**
Skill training?	0.117	0.024	0.091	0.060
	(3.63)**	(0.41)	(2.94)**	(0.92)
Good grades?	0.045	−0.042	0.067	−0.123
	(1.25)	(0.65)	(1.97)**	(1.74)*
Bad grades?	0.016	−0.008	0.016	−0.003
	(0.40)	(0.11)	(0.44)	(0.03)
Father's education	−0.002	0.007	−0.005	0.016
	(0.49)	(0.84)	(1.25)	(1.63)
Instruments				
Married? (1 = yes)	−0.367		−0.359	
	(9.03)**		(9.51)**	
Household size	0.002		0.004	
	(0.15)		(0.39)	
Land endowment	−0.004		−0.003	
	(1.80)*		(1.16)	
Inverse Mills ratio		−0.163		−0.047
		(1.22)		(0.38)

Note: t-statistics are in parentheses.
* indicates significance at the 90 percent level;
** indicates significance at the 95 percent level. Provincial fixed effects are included in all regressions. Experience is measured as years since the person left school if they went to school, and age 6 if they did not. All regressions are done using the two-step method proposed by Heckman (1974) and standard error calculations take the method into account.

Second, we test whether our estimates are influenced by the inclusion of a measure of school quality. Since school quality would directly affect the return, we follow Behrman and Birdsall (1983) and interact the quality measure with educational attainment. Since we have no *a priori* expectation about which measure of school quality is best, we estimated the model seven times, each time using a different measure of school quality. Estimates of the coefficients for the interaction terms were never statistically significant. Most importantly, though, neither the estimated return to primary education nor the estimated return to post-primary education was affected significantly in any of the specifications, implying that differences in school quality across villages also do not substantially affect our results.

Conclusion

In this chapter, we have used a nearly nationally representative sample of workers in rural China to estimate the returns to education in off-farm work in 2000. Making corrections for selectivity into off-farm work and using the hourly wage rate, we find that across all individuals with off-farm jobs in our sample, the mean return to a year of education is 6.4 percent. The estimates are shown to be robust to controls for individual ability and for village primary school quality.

More importantly, our results go far in reconciling the low rates of return found in earlier studies with the higher ones that are typically found for the rest of the developing world. Experiments reported in de Brauw and Rozelle (2006) and summarized here demonstrate that returns have risen over time. The notion of increasing returns is also consistent with Zhang *et al.* (2002), who use a panel to show that returns to education rise over the reform period and claim that the improvement is likely due to improving labor markets.

We further find evidence that methodology has played an important role in the low estimates of returns in previous studies. When we define wages on an hourly basis, control for sample selectivity, and use a representative sample, the rates of return rise further. Finally, when the sample is used that includes workers who have demographic and employment profiles more like those found in the rest of the world (i.e. young and working in urban areas), the returns rise even more. In fact, when we find that the returns to a year of schooling are close to 10 percent for young wage earners and over 10 percent for those who work as migrants. These findings put China on a level that makes the returns to rural education very consistent with those in other developing countries (Psacharopoulos 1994).

Finally, these results strongly indicate that increasing access to education in rural areas would be a good policy instrument to increase rural incomes. Given the high returns to education that we find for younger workers, China's government would do well do make rural education a top priority, especially since the majority of children in China today are being raised in rural areas.

Acknowledgments

We would like to thank Qiuqiong Huang, Albert Park, Ed Taylor, Jim Wilen, and Yigang Zhang for comments on earlier drafts of the manuscript. Scott Rozelle is a member of the Giannini Foundation of Agricultural Economics. We acknowledge the US National Science Foundation for support for the project.

Notes

1 See Zhang and Zhao's Chapter 14 in this volume for a review of this literature.
2 The Mincer (1974) method involves regressing the logarithm of the wage rate against education, years of work experience, and years of work experience squared,

as returns to experience have been found to be concave. Since experience is often not directly observable, it is typically defined as experience = age − education − 6. Typically, studies that use the Mincer specification add other explanatory variables as well.

3 We include provincial dummy variables in both equations as well.

4 Furthermore, as we are limited to data on primary school quality, we further hypothesize that school quality will only affect returns to primary school, and adjust our estimation framework accordingly.

5 The average is taken only over studies that also use the Mincer method.

References

Barro, R. (1991) "Economic Growth in a Cross-Section of Countries," *Quarterly Journal of Economics*, 106(2): 408–443.

Becker, G. (1964) *Human Capital*, New York: Columbia University Press.

Behrman, J. and Birdsall, N. (1983) "The Quality of Schooling: Quantity Alone Is Misleading," *American Economic Review*, 73: 928–946.

Benjamin, D. and Brandt, L. (1997) "Land, Factor Markets, and Inequality in Rural China: Historical Evidence," *Explorations in Economic History*, 34: 460–494.

Benjamin, D., Brandt, L., Glewwe, P., and Li, G. (2002) "Markets, Human Capital, and Inequality: Evidence from Rural China," in R. Freeman (ed.) *Inequality Around the World*, New York: Palgrave.

Card, D. (1999) "The Causal Effect of Education on Earnings," in O. Ashenfelter and D. Card (eds.) *Handbook of Labor Economics*, Vol. 3A, Amsterdam: Elsevier Science Publishers.

Chen, H. and Rozelle, S.D. (1999) "Leaders, Managers, and the Organization of Township and Village Enterprises in China," *Journal of Development Economics*, 60: 529–557.

China National Statistics Bureau (2001) *China Statistical Yearbook*, Beijing: China Statistical Press.

Cook, S. (1999) "Surplus Labor and Productivity in Chinese Agriculture: Evidence from Household Survey Data," *Journal of Development Studies*, 35: 16–44.

de Brauw, A., Huang, J., Rozelle, S., Zhang, L., and Zhang, Y. (2002) "The Evolution of China's Rural Labor Markets during the Reforms," *Journal of Comparative Economics*, 30: 329–353.

de Brauw, A. and Rozelle, S.D. (2006) "Reconciling the Returns to Education in Off-Farm Wage Employment in Rural China," *Review of Development Economics*, forthcoming.

Gregory, R.G. and Meng, X. (1995) "Wage Determination and Occupational Attainment in the Rural Industrial Sector of China," *Journal of Comparative Economics*, 21: 353–374.

Hare, D. (1999) " 'Push' versus 'Pull' Factors in Migration Outflows and Returns: Determinants of Migration Status and Spell Duration among China's Rural Population," *Journal of Development Studies*, 35: 45–72.

Heckman, J. (1974) "Shadow Prices, Market Wages, and Labor Supply," *Econometrica*, 42: 679–694.

Ho, S., Dong, X., Bowles, P., and MacPhail, F. (2002) "Privatization and Enterprise Wage Structures during Transition: Evidence from China's Rural Industries," *Economics of Transition*, 10: 659–688.

Jin, H. and Qian, Y. (1998) "Public Versus Private Ownership of Firms: Evidence from Rural China," *Quarterly Journal of Economics*, 113: 773–808.

Johnson, D.G. (1995) "Is Agriculture a Threat to China's Growth?," Working Paper No. 95:04, Office of Agricultural Economics Research, University of Chicago.

Johnson, E.N. and Chow, G.C. (1997) "Rates of Return to Schooling in China," *Pacific Economic Review*, 2: 101–113.

Knight, J. and Song, L. (2001) "New Urban Labor Market Study," paper presented at CERDI Conference on Emergence of Markets in China, Cleremont-Ferrand, France, May.

Li, H. (2003) "Government's Budget Constraint, Competition, and Privatization," *Journal of Comparative Economics*, 31: 380–398.

Li, T. and Zhang, J. (1998) "Returns to Education under Collective and Household Farming in China," *Journal of Development Economics*, 56: 307–335.

Liu, S., Carter, M., and Yao, Y. (1998) "Dimensions and Diversity of Property Rights in Rural China: Dilemmas on the Road to Further Reform," *World Development*, 26: 1789–1806.

Lohmar, B. (1999) "The Role of Institutions in Rural Labor Flow in China," unpublished PhD dissertation, Department of Agricultural and Resource Economics, University of California, Davis.

Mallee, H. (2000) "Agricultural Labor and Rural Population Mobility: Some Observations," in L.A. West and Y. Zhao (eds.) *Rural Labor Flows in China*, Berkeley, CA: University of California Press.

Meng, X. (1996) "An Examination of Wage Determination in China's Rural Industrial Sector," *Applied Economics*, 28: 715–724.

Mincer, J. (1974) *Schooling, Experience, and Earnings*, New York: Columbia University Press.

National Bureau of Statistics (NBS) (2005) *China Statistical Yearbook (Zhongguo Tongji Nianjian)*, Beijing: China Statistical Press.

Naughton, B. (1995) *Growing Out of the Plan: Chinese Economic Reform, 1978–1993*, Cambridge: Cambridge University Press.

Nyberg, A. and Rozelle, S.D. (1999) *Accelerating China's Rural Transformation*, Washington, DC: World Bank.

Parish, W., Zhe, X., and Li., F. (1995) "Non-farm Work and Marketization of the Chinese Countryside," *The China Quarterly*, 143: 697–730.

Psacharopoulos, G. (1994) "Returns to Investment in Education: A Global Update," *World Development*, 22: 1325–1343.

Rozelle, S., Li, G., Shen, M., Hughart, A., and Giles, J. (1999) "Leaving China's Farms: Survey Results of New Paths and Remaining Hurdles to Rural Migration," *The China Quarterly*, 158: 367–393.

Schultz, T.P. (1988) "Education Investments and Returns," in H. Chenery and T.N. Srinivisan (eds.) *Handbook of Development Economics*, vol. I, Amsterdam: Elsevier Science Publishers.

Sen, A. (1999) *Development as Freedom*, New York: Alfred A. Knopf.

Todaro, M. (1976) *Internal Migration in Developing Countries: A Review of Theory, Evidence, Methodology and Research Priorities*, Geneva: International Labor Office.

Weitzman, M. and Xu, C. (1994) "Chinese Township-Village Enterprises as Vaguely Defined Cooperatives," *Journal of Comparative Economics*, 18: 121–145.

World Bank (2001) *World Development Indicators*, Washington, DC: World Bank.

Yang, D.T. (1997) "Education and Off-Farm Work," *Economic Development and Cultural Change*, 45: 613–632.

Yang, D.T. (1999) "Urban-based Policies and Rising Income Inequality in China," *American Economic Review*, 89: 306–310.

Yang, D.T. and An, M. (2002) "Human Capital, Entrepreneurship, and Farm Household Earnings," *Journal of Development Economics*, 68: 65–88.

Yang, D.T. and Zhou, H. (1996) "Rural–Urban Disparity and Sectoral Labor Allocation in China," Research Papers in Asian-Pacific Studies, Duke University, North Carolina.

Zhang, L., Huang, J., and Rozelle, S.D. (2002) "Employment, Emerging Labor Markets, and the Role of Education in Rural China," *China Economic Review*, 13: 313–328.

Zhang, X., Zhao, C., and Chen, L. (1995) "1994: A Real Description of Rural Labor's Cross-regional Flows (1994: nongcun laodongli kua qutu liedong di shezheng miaoshu)," *Strategy and Management (Zhanlue yu guanli)*, 6: 30–35.

Zhao, Y. (1997) "Labor Migration and Returns to Rural Education in China," *American Journal of Agricultural Economics*, 79: 1278–1287.

Zhao, Y. (1999) "Labor Migration and Earnings Differences: The Case of Rural China," *Economic Development and Cultural Change*, 47: 767–782.

13 Returns to education in urban China's transitional economy

Reassessment and reconceptualization

Wei Zhao and Xueguang Zhou

Some of the earliest reforms associated with institutional changes in post-Mao China were manifested in the education system. One of the major policy changes in 1977, only one year after Mao Zedong's death, was the resumption of the national examination for college admission, historically a primary gatekeeper of social mobility in China's social stratification system. The stigma associated with education in the Cultural Revolution disappeared overnight, and long queuing lines appeared at the doors of bookstores, libraries, and schools. Since then, the role of education has become salient in all spheres of political, economic, and social life. Beginning in the 1980s, new state policies have made education one of the most important criteria in cadre recruitment and promotion (Xu and Zhang 1992). Educational credentials help individuals open doors to prestigious jobs and work organizations.

In this chapter, we examine to what extent and in what ways the relationship between education and individual life chances has changed in China's reform era, focusing on changing returns to education in the transformation of the state socialist economy in urban China. We have two goals. First, we assess changes in returns to education from a historical perspective by comparing patterns in three selected years associated with distinctive historical contexts: 1965, 1978, and 1993. 1965 was the year before the disruption of the Cultural Revolution; 1978 marked the beginning of the economic reform; and 1993 was the year for which we have the most recent data for our study. Recent studies in this area have primarily focused on comparisons between the beginning phase of the post-Mao era and a more recent year in the reform process. One drawback of such a comparative framework is that, at the beginning of the economic reform in the late 1970s, Chinese society was still experiencing the aftermath of the Cultural Revolution, when the role of education had been severely suppressed by the radical state policies. Accordingly, returns to education in the early phase of the reform era may have underestimated the role of education in China's state socialist redistribution. Therefore, the longer historical perspective adopted here provides a more comprehensive picture and allows us to assess changes in the role of education in the ongoing transitional economy in a more sensible way.

Second, we go beyond a focus on returns to education in wage rates and develop a broader conceptualization of returns to education, especially in light of the role of education in social mobility in labor markets and in work organizations. In China's command economy, one's observable income was a poor indicator of socio-economic status and broadly defined life chances. Often, latent economic benefits were associated with job types, work organization characteristics, and managerial positions in the workplace. We believe that this pattern persisted through the early 1990s, when this survey was conducted. Therefore, the role of education in attaining these jobs and positions provides valuable information about *indirect* returns to education.

To motivate our study, we begin by reviewing key literature on returns to education in the transformation of state socialist economies. We then present an empirical assessment of changes in returns to education over time. We base our study partly on analyses of life history data of a national sample of urban residents drawn from 20 cities in China; we also incorporate findings on returns to education from our previous studies.

Returns to education as a theoretical and analytical focus

Most studies of returns to education in China and other transitional economies in former state socialist societies begin with the working hypothesis that there was a low rate of return to education in the state socialist economy and that the rate increased significantly in the post-socialist economy. This hypothesis seems to be well founded. The state socialist economy is organized on principles qualitatively different from those of a market economy. Under state socialism, the state ultimately determines the allocation of resources in both production and consumption. All resources, including human resources, are subject to "redistribution" through central planning, which follows a political logic rather than a market logic.

Several distinctive characteristics emerge with regard to the principles of human resource allocation in state socialist China. First, the political logic of redistribution emphasizes the importance of political loyalty over competence. For example, previous studies have revealed the common practice of rewarding political capital such as party membership rather than competence as indicated by formal education levels in the Mao era (Harding 1981; Lee 1991; Walder 1986). Second, because a large proportion of resources are allocated through work organizations, economic rewards are often tied *not* to individual attributes (such as educational qualifications) but to work organizations (Walder 1986, 1992; Lin and Bian 1991; Bian 1994; Zhou *et al.* 1997).

As a result, it is well known that the role of education in individual life chances is significantly different from that in market economies. In particular, returns to education are markedly low in state socialist societies relative to other types of economies. According to Psacharopoulos (1994), the rate of return to education is between 6 to 11 percent for each additional year of education in market economies, but the rate is only between 3 and 5 percent in state socialist societies (for similar findings in the case of Vietnam, see Moock *et al.* 1998).

Recognition of these distinctive mechanisms of human resource allocation provides an important empirical basis to assess the transformation of state socialist economies. To many economists, the rising returns to education associated with market transition represent expected corrections to the compression of wages characteristic of planned economies (Maurer-Fazio 1999; Newell and Reilly 1999). In sociology, Nee's (1989, 1991, 1996) and Nee and Matthews' (1996) market transition theory makes a similar argument. As Nee (1989: 678) wrote:

> A fundamental change in the processes of socio-economic attainment occurs in the transition from redistribution to markets, involving not only a reduction in the relative transfers of surplus from producers to redistributors but changes in opportunity structures and incentives resulting from market reforms.

Recent evidence appears consistent with the above argument that market mechanisms increase returns to education in transitional economies. In Chapter 12 in this volume, de Brauw and Rozelle contend that the increased returns to rural education in China in 2000 were comparable to those in other developing countries as reported by Psacharopoulos (1994). Similarly, Chapter 14 by Zhang and Zhao shows that in urban China returns to education increased dramatically from 1988 to 2003. In a comprehensive study of the rate of return to education in Central and Eastern Europe, Russia, and other former Soviet countries, Newell and Reilly (1999) found that returns to education "exhibited an upward tendency as labor-market reforms took hold," and they concluded, "the general pattern, in the most recent years available to us, was one of broad comparability with the estimates usually obtained in the literature for the set of high-income countries" (ibid.: 80).

But there are two unsettling issues in this literature. The first is about the mechanisms underlying the increasing role of education in the reform era. Although the importance of market processes is well recognized, there has been an ongoing debate among sociologists on the relative role of markets versus the state in the economic transformation of state socialism (Rona-Tas 1994; Stark 1996; Xie and Hannum 1996; Gerber and Hout 1998; Raymo and Xie 2000). Despite differences in emphasis and logic of explanation, in our view, researchers largely agree with Nee on the increasing importance of market economies in the processes of transformation. Disagreements are centered on the relationships between market mechanisms and other mechanisms of resource allocation, especially with regard to the role of the state in the reform process. In Nee's early formulation, markets and redistribution are seen as antithetical to each other. The rise of the former implies the decline of the latter.

In contrast, other scholars have emphasized the coexistence and continuing importance of the state and redistributive institutions in resource allocation in China's economic transformation (Walder 1995, 1996; Bian and Logan 1996; Parish and Michelson 1996; Guthrie 1997). Zhou (2000) argued that markets and politics not only coexist in the transformation processes but also coevolve in response to each other. That is, both have been transformed to such an extent that it is no longer meaningful to treat them as discrete and antithetical categories in empirical studies. In this framework, the coexistence of markets and politics is no longer conceptualized as a transitional phenomenon or "partial reform." Rather, their coexistence and interaction shape new institutional forms and stratification orders. This line of argument predicts that both markets and politics exert influence on resource allocation and the emergence of the new institutional forms. As a result, a more complicated picture of institutional changes emerges that defies a single logic of explanation. Vivid examples can be found in Khan and Riskin's (2001) comprehensive study of inequality and poverty over time in the reform era, based on 1988 and 1995 surveys in China.[1]

Second, the debates concerning the returns to education in state socialist economies are far from settled. Konrad and Szelényi (1979) developed early arguments that the Communist states in East European societies successfully incorporated intellectuals into the ruling class and rewarded them accordingly. This line of argument pointed to the importance of education in upward mobility and in the allocation of economic rewards in state socialist societies. That is, education credentials were likely to be rewarded even under the traditional model of state socialism.

The role of education in China presents a more complicated picture. Walder and his associates (Walder 1995; Walder *et al.* 2000) proposed a "dual career path" model to explain two distinctive elite (cadre versus professional) trajectories. Walder argued that the selection processes under state socialism involve both political loyalty and educational qualification. A dual career path has been developed for different kinds of elite positions, with two underlying processes: the first is a political screening process, and the second is a process of political incorporation. In this model, education is most important for entry into professional positions, which has "high occupational prestige but little authority and fewer material privileges" (Walder 1995: 309). In contrast, although education increases the likelihood of becoming a cadre, political credentials are more important determinants of attaining the more desirable administrative positions. In other words, securing professional positions only requires human capital, while securing administrative positions requires both human capital and political capital.

To complicate the matter further, evidence is not always consistent over time or across societies. Katz (1999) found significant and high returns to education under state socialism in the former USSR, in a sample drawn from a Russian city in 1989. Zhou (2000) found noticeably higher returns to education before than during the Cultural Revolution in urban China. In a comparative study of the redistributive patterns in the USSR and China,

Zhou and Suhomlinova (2001) showed that the rate of return to education was much higher in the USSR than in China, on the eve of the great transformations in both countries. In fact, the rate of return to college education in the USSR was higher than the rate in urban China even when the economic reform was well advanced in China.

Overall, returns to education reflect principles of human resource allocation that are part of fundamental institutional processes. The research issues and empirical evidence reviewed above suggest that the role of human resource allocation under state socialism and in transitional economies warrants further scrutiny.

Returns to education in urban China: context and hypotheses

Based on the issues set out in the preceding discussion, we now lay out the empirical implications of institutional changes and their effects on returns to education in urban China. First, we examine changes in the returns to education over time. We consider two alternative baselines for comparing changes in the reform era: the period just preceding the Cultural Revolution and the beginning of the economic reform in the late 1970s. Second, we examine variations in returns to education across economic sectors that are affected by the state and market forces differently. Finally, we propose a broader view to assess the role of education under state socialism and in transitional economies by considering the effects of education on status attainment, such as access to occupational positions and promotion opportunities in workplaces.

Changes in the returns to education over time

The increasing role of market mechanisms in the allocation of human resources, as elaborated in Nee's market transition theory, affects the returns to education in two ways. First, relative to central planning processes, market mechanisms can better utilize human resources. As a result, there may be higher returns to education than in a redistributive economy. Thus, Nee (1989: 674) predicted: "The transition to a market-like economy should result in higher returns to human capital characteristics." Second, the rise of the market economy may compete with socialist redistributive institutions and undermine state intervention in economic sectors. As a result, market mechanisms may create new opportunities outside of the traditional state sector and attract more educated and more able employees into the nonstate sector, likely leading to a higher rate of return to education. Accordingly, the emergence of labor markets may affect the returns to education through career mobility across sectors.

At the same time, we also argue that the salience of human capital in the reform era cannot be solely attributed to the emergence of a market economy. Instead, state policies play an important role in increasing returns to education in recent years, often indirectly by promoting cadres with educational credentials. Since the early 1980s, the state has followed policies that explicitly set youthfulness, education, expertise, and political loyalty as four criteria to recruit and promote a new generation of bureaucrats. Since then (even before the market reform in the urban areas took place since 1985), educational credentials have become one of the most important factors in obtaining political and positional power. According to official statistics, the proportion of cadres with college education (including *dazhuan* degree) increased from 22 percent in 1985 to 32 percent in 1990 (Office of Organization Structure 1993). Among all new cadres recruited in 1986, 55 percent were graduates of colleges and technical schools; this proportion increased to 83 percent in 1990. Empirical studies have also shown that educational credentials greatly contribute to status attainment of cadres or professionals in the reform era (Lee 1991; Bian 1994; Walder 1995; Zhou 1995, 2001; Dickson and Rublee 2000; Walder *et al.* 2000). Therefore, both the advance of market mechanisms and shifts in state policies in the reform era lead us to predict that *there is a significant increase in returns to education over time in the transformation of state socialism.*

Returns to human capital versus political capital

A more direct contrast between political and market mechanisms is with respect to the relative importance of human capital versus political capital. If the market logic and the political logic of redistribution are fundamentally incompatible, as posited by market transition theory, we would expect to find opposite changes in returns to these two types of capital in the reform era. That is, the increasing role of human capital is associated with the prevalence of market mechanisms, which in turn should diminish returns to political capital.

On the other hand, there are alternative arguments that point to the coexistence of both political and human capital in the processes of institutional changes. One explanation is the power persistence argument (Bian and Logan 1996) that emphasizes the continuing role of the state and redistributive institutions in resource allocation and the sustained importance of political capital. We also mentioned before that political and market processes interact in complicated ways that do not necessarily undermine each other. For instance, the advance of markets may also have changed political selection processes in the socialist society, increasing the importance of education in the recruitment of party membership and promotion. Evidence shows that educational credentials improve the chances of becoming party members in the reform era (Walder 1995; Dickson and Rublee 2000; Walder *et al.* 2000; Zhou 2001). In this view, human capital may overlap with political capital, and returns to education may be mediated by the continuing importance of political capital even in the reform era. *If political capital and human capital are antithetical, there should be a decline in the role of political capital relative to human capital in the reform era. On the other hand, if markets and state policies coevolve with each other, we should observe that both human capital and political capital make significant contributions to economic rewards in the reform era.*

Returns to education across sectors

Perhaps the most direct contrast between the roles of the state and markets is between the state and nonstate sectors. As is well known, there has long been a coexistence of a state sector and a nonstate sector in the Chinese economy (Lin and Bian 1991; Bian 1994; Zhou, *et al.* 1997). The state sector consists of state firms, public organizations, and government agencies. These organizations are under much stronger influence of state policies than those in the nonstate sector. The nonstate sector consists of collective firms, private firms, joint venture firms, and hybrid firms, which are more market-oriented and less affected by state regulatory or redistributive policies. Therefore, these two sectors may have developed distinctive channels of resource allocation and reward structures. Evidence shows that there are noticeable income differences across types of work organizations in the reform era. For example, Zhou (2000) found that organizations in the state sector (government agencies, public organizations, and state firms) offered higher economic rewards than collective firms and this pattern has not changed in the reform era. At the same time, private/hybrid firms have shown significant increases in economic rewards during the reform process. Maurer-Fazio (1999) also found significant variations in returns to education across these sectors.

What are the implications of these sectoral differences in returns to education? Some clues can be found in the evidence of talent being attracted from the state sector to the nonstate sector in the early years of the economic reform. As China began its economic reform, most educated personnel were concentrated in the state sector. In the early 1980s, many nonstate firms began to offer high salaries to attract talent from the state sector to the private sector. These pulling forces led the central government to adopt a series of new policies in 1983 that allowed professionals in the state sector to resign from their jobs or to perform work in the nonstate sector in their leisure time. Obviously, this movement was propelled by the significant variation in returns to education between the state sector and the nonstate sector. On the other hand, since the 1980s, state personnel policies have also strongly advocated educational qualification in the distribution of economic rewards. Accordingly, educational upgrading such as off-the-job training (*jin xiu*) is very popular in the state sector and important for career success, especially for those without educational credentials. Thus we expect that the state sector also witnessed an increase in returns to education that parallels that in the nonstate sector. That is, economic reform may have forced organizations in the state sector to increase returns to education and to replicate practices adopted in the private sector. Therefore, *if market competition is the main mechanism, we expect to find that returns to education increase faster in the nonstate sector than in the state sector in the reform era. If state policies also play an active role, we expect to find a parallel increase in returns to education in the state sector.*

A broader conception of returns to education

In the social science literature, returns to education are typically operational-ized as the effect of years of education on the wage rate. We suspect that this conceptualization is derived from a view of market economies in which labor service is exchanged for monetary payments in an open marketplace. Thus, one's wage rate (or monetary income) provides the most transparent, meas-urable indicator of economic rewards. However, the wage rate is not the only, and at times not even the most appropriate, measure of one's socio-economic rewards. In contemporary societies, social recognition and author-ity relationships associated with one's political status and positions in work organizations are also important aspects of one's socio-economic status.

This issue becomes especially salient in state socialist economies, where most resources are not allocated through market transactions, but through state redistribution. Hence, monetary rewards such as wages may not always be the best measure of economic benefits (Szelényi 1978; see also Khan and Riskin 2001).[2] Often, economic rewards are closely linked to one's political status and authority positions in work organizations. For example, since the salary reform in China's administrative system in 1985, position-based salary has become a significant component of one's salary. For a mid-level cadre (a "*chu*"-rank), the position-based salary is about two to three times one's base income (Chen and Zhang 1992: 143). Moreover, compared with other types of organizations, state-owned firms have provided much better welfare and housing benefits, in addition to monetary income (Zhou *et al.* 1997: 340–341). This recognition leads us to propose a broader conceptualization of the returns to education in state socialist societies. That is, we need to consider the role of educational credentials in access to different types of jobs and in the acquisition of managerial and professional positions.

Given the economic transformation in urban China in the past two dec-ades, especially the dual sources of economic reform, we speculate that *the role of education has increased significantly in the reform era not only through higher wage returns to education, but also in access to more prestigious jobs (cadres/managers and professionals), work organizations, and promotion opportunities in organizations.*

Research design

Data

The data used in our study are based on a sample of urban residents drawn from 20 cities through a stratified sampling scheme in 1993 and 1994. First, six provinces were selected, each representing a conventional geographical region in China. Second, within each province, the capital city of the province was chosen to represent large cities (population above 1 million) in that province; and a medium-sized city (population between 200,000 and 1 million) and a small city (population below 200,000) were randomly selected based on the 1990 *Yearbook of Chinese Cities* (State Statistical Bureau 1990). In addition, the data also included Beijing, the political center, and Shanghai, the largest industrial city in China. Third, within each targeted city, a systematic sampling procedure was used to select every *n*th block and the *n*th household within each selected block. Finally, in each household, a respondent aged 25–65 was chosen based on a random-number table. The data set included a total of 4,600 individuals. Using a pre-tested questionnaire, we collected information on the life histories of the respondents with regard to their educational experience, experiences in the labor force, and their job characteristics. In addition, we also asked for information about respondents' income in specific years. Recall errors are likely to occur in the collection of retrospective data. In order to check the reliability of the data, we have compared the key characteristics of our sample with the official statistics of the urban labor force. We find that the quality of our retrospective data is reasonably good (see Appendices in Zhou and Suhomlinova 2001). In our analysis, we excluded the information of the respondents after they had retired, because their income after retirement no longer reflected mechanisms of human resource allocation.

Dependent variables

Our dependent variables are logarithms of both basic and total (monthly) income. "Basic income" refers to the fixed income based on the official salary/ wage system. Total income is the sum of the respondent's basic salary or wage, bonuses, and any additional income earned by the respondent.[3]

In assessing the returns to education in the broad perspective proposed before, we consider the role of education in access to high-status jobs (managers, professionals), high-status organizations (government agencies, public organizations), political capital (party membership), and promotion opportunities.

Independent variables

- *Education.* For comparative purpose, we use a standard formula to convert educational levels into "years of schooling." Specifically, we use the following conversion formula: elementary school = 6 years of schooling; junior high = 9 years of schooling; senior high school = 12 years of schooling; junior college = 14 years of schooling; college = 16 years of schooling; post-graduate degree = 18 years of schooling. Given the fluctuations in China's educational system in the past, this scheme is used only as an approximation.

- *Party membership.* We use a dummy variable (party membership = 1) to indicate one's political status as a Communist Party member.
- *Labor force duration.* We follow the convention and use the following formula to capture one's work experience: labor force duration = age − years of schooling − 6. We use both the first- and the second-order effects of "labor force duration" to capture the potential life cycle factors in returns to experience. Returns to labor force duration also provide information on the effect of seniority on resource allocation.
- *Occupational groups.* We distinguish the following occupational groups: (1) top managers of a workplace; (2) mid-level managers in a workplace; (3) low-level managers in a workplace; (4) high-rank professionals; (5) low-rank professionals; (6) workers (including clerks, service workers, skilled and unskilled workers); and (7) private entrepreneurs. "Workers" are used as the reference category in our analyses. Information on managerial positions comes from respondents' self-reports of whether they held top, mid-, or low-level managerial positions in their work organizations. The category of high-rank professionals includes those who are at the rank of "engineer" or above. Low-rank professionals include assistant engineers and technicians.
- *The state and nonstate sectors.* In some analyses, we estimate returns to education for the state and nonstate sectors separately. We include the following types of organization in the state sector: (1) government agencies; (2) public organizations; and (3) state firms. The nonstate sector is composed of collective firms, hybrid firms, joint ventures, and private firms.
- *Gender and city effect.* For control purposes, we include a dummy variable (female = 1) to capture the gender effect. We also include a set of indicator variables for the 20 cities from which the data were collected.

Table 13.1 reports the descriptive statistics of the covariates.

Methods of analyses

To examine wage returns to education, we begin with the standard human capital model in economics. That is, we first estimate a Mincerian model in which the logarithm of income is regressed on years of schooling and work experience. To further assess returns to education, we then extend the Mincerian model to incorporate information on occupation and workplace locations in the model. In addition, we also include interactions between the occupation variables and years of schooling to identify and assess the specific channels that affect the returns to education. For our research purposes, we compare statistical models across time (1965, 1978, and 1993), between sectors (state sector versus nonstate sector), and for different types of income (basic income and total income).

Table 13.1 Descriptive statistics for variables used in the analysis

| | 1965 | 1978 | 1993 | | |
	Total	Total	Total	State sector	Nonstate sector
Total income in *yuan*, inflation adjusted (monthly)	45.0	57.8	111.4	111.6	111.1
Basic income in *yuan*, inflation adjusted (monthly)	42.2	48.9	51.8	50.9	54.3
Female	45.8	46.5	41.4	38.8	47.3
Years of schooling	8.4	9.1	10.7	11.1	9.7
Labor force duration	13.3	17.9	22.4	22.4	22.5
Party membership	18.9	20.4	23.4	26.5	14.7
Occupations					
Top manager	2.5	3.4	4.8	4.3	6.0
Mid-level manager	6.8	6.2	8.8	10.6	4.7
Low-level manager	12.0	10.9	13.3	15.4	8.4
Professional (engineer or above)	3.6	3.5	7.6	9.6	3.1
Technician	19.3	15.5	14.1	15.8	10.2
Private entrepreneur	–	0.4	3.5	–	11.3
Worker (including clerk)	62.5	66.6	58.7	56.4	64.0
Type of work organization					
Government agency	10.9	8.6	10.1	14.6	–
Public organization	14.7	11.1	12.6	18.1	–
Central government firm	48.6	51.9	46.8	67.4	–
Collective firm	23.3	25.7	22.0	–	72.0
Hybrid firm	1.6	1.7	2.6	–	8.4
Joint venture	–	0.1	0.9	–	2.9
Private firm	0.7	1.0	5.1	–	16.7
N	1,067	2,705	3,683	2,559	1,124

Notes: Income, labor force duration, and years of schooling refer to the means of these variables. All other numbers in the table refer to percentages in the designated category. Percentages in the occupational categories do not add up to unity because there are overlaps between administrative positions and professional positions. That is, a respondent can be in a managerial position and also be a professional at the same time.

Results

We first focus on variations in returns to education in wage rate over time and across sectors, and then we turn to consider the role of education in status attainment in work organizations.

Changes in returns to education over time

Table 13.2 reports the OLS regression estimates of the determinants of the wage equation in three selected years: 1965, 1978, and 1993. We estimate three models for each year. Model 1 for each year is the conventional

Table 13.2 OLS regression estimates of returns to education in 1965, 1978, and 1993

	1965			1978			1993		
	Model 1	Model 2	Model 3	Model 1	Model 2	Model 3	Model 1	Model 2	Model 3
Intercept	2.900***	2.967***	2.961***	3.226***	3.289***	3.264***	3.979***	4.038***	3.995***
Years of schooling	0.043***	0.032***	0.031***	0.028***	0.022***	0.024***	0.035***	0.027***	0.032***
Female	-0.250***	-0.243***	-0.242***	-0.183***	-0.168***	-0.165***	-0.203***	-0.190***	-0.186***
Labor force duration	0.063***	0.059***	0.061***	0.042***	0.040***	0.041***	0.017***	0.016***	0.015***
LF duration-squared/100	-0.123***	-0.118***	-0.125***	-0.054***	-0.053***	-0.056***	-0.024***	-0.025***	-0.023***
Occupations									
Top manager		0.091	0.319		0.194***	0.341**		0.259***	0.361**
Mid-level manager		0.211***	0.390***		0.160***	0.427***		0.132***	0.443***
Low-level manager		0.089**	0.203*		0.084***	0.167*		0.041	0.256***
High-rank professional		0.142**	0.216		0.048	-0.207		0.029	0.540***
Low-rank professional		0.108***	-0.102		-0.006	-0.053		0.076***	0.266**
Private entrepreneur					—	—		0.499***	-0.283*
Top manager*schooling			-0.021			0.014			-0.009
Mid manager*schooling			-0.017			-0.025**			-0.025**
Low manager*schooling			-0.011			-0.008			-0.018**
High prof*schooling			-0.003			0.020			-0.036***
Low prof*schooling			0.019**			0.004			-0.016*
Entrepreneur*schooling						—			0.086***
Party membership	0.061*	0.044	0.045	0.095***	0.055*	0.047*	0.101***	0.066**	0.056**
Adj-R²	0.37	0.39	0.39	0.26	0.27	0.27	0.39	0.41	0.42
N	1,124	1,124	1,124	2,612	2,612	2,567	3,625	3,625	3,625

Notes: "Worker" is the reference category for occupation. In all the models, a set of 19 dummy variables are included to indicate the specific cities in which the data are drawn. The coefficients for these control variables are not reported in this table. * $p < 0.10$, ** $p < 0.05$, *** $p < 0.01$.

Mincerian human capital model. Model 2 incorporates occupational variables in the model. Model 3 adds the interaction terms between years of schooling and occupational status.[4]

First, consider direct returns to education as measured by the coefficient for years of schooling. Across the three years, we observed a nonmonotonic trend. In 1965, the year before the Cultural Revolution, the rate of return to each year of schooling was about 4.4 percent (exp[.043] = 1.044). In 1978, the rate of return dropped to about 2.8 percent. In 1993, the rate increased to about 3.7 percent. Thus, there is no conclusive evidence about the extent of change in the role of education. If we use the year 1965 as the reference point, the rate of return to education in 1993 did not increase at all. If we compare 1978 and 1993, clearly there was an increase in returns to education during the economic transformation in urban China.

One may wonder whether the findings for 1965 were partly a consequence of a sampling attrition problem. That is, those with lower returns to education might have left the labor force and did not enter our sample framework. To explore this issue, we conducted sensitivity analyses by examining the 1965 cohort only and the patterns are consistent with those reported here. Furthermore, this empirical pattern is also consistent with corroborative evidence on drastic reductions in income differences by the radical "destratification" policies of the Cultural Revolution period (Parish 1984).

Interestingly, more dramatic changes are observed for returns to work experience. There was a sharp decline in returns to work experience over time, especially between 1978 and 1993. The peak year for returns to work experience also changed from nearly 40 years in the labor force in 1978 to about 30 years in the labor force in 1993. This pattern shows that, based on the egalitarian policies in the Mao era, seniority was used as the main criterion in the distribution of economic rewards. This criterion has given way to educational qualification in the reform era.

We now examine and compare returns to education and to Communist Party membership.[5] Adding "party membership" in the model does not change the effects of other covariates in any significant way. The main finding is that the returns to party membership, in Model 1, were only marginally significant in 1965. The party membership effect increased noticeably in subsequent years. Being a party member increased one's income by about 10 percent in 1978 and by about 11 percent in 1993. The markedly lower rate of return to party membership in 1965, relative to the subsequent years, does not support the view that state socialist practice rewarded political loyalty more than competence, other things being equal.

What are the specific channels through which education affects income? Model 2 and Model 3 in Table 13.2 explore this issue by including occupational positions and interactions between occupational positions and years of schooling in the estimation. First, note that in all three years the inclusion of occupational position variables (in Model 2) leads to a reduction in the direct returns to education (coefficients for years of schooling in Model 2 for those three years). This means that returns to education have been confounded with, and partially captured by, one's occupational status. But as Model 3 indicates, in 1965 and 1978 there is no systematic evidence of variations in returns to education across occupational positions, as indicated by the coefficients on the interaction terms between occupational positions and years of schooling. The only exceptions are the higher returns for low-rank professionals in 1965 and lower returns for mid-level managers in 1978, compared with the returns for workers (the reference category).

These patterns have changed in the reform era. Compared with 1978, managerial and professional positions as well as entrepreneurial jobs all contribute significantly to increases in income in 1993. In Model 3 for 1993, the interactions between occupational status and years of schooling show somewhat surprising patterns. Except for top manager positions and entrepreneurs, all interaction effects with respect to managerial and professional status show significantly negative effects. That is, the returns to education in these positions are lower than those for workers, controlling for the main effects of education and occupational status. In contrast, after controlling for returns to education for different occupational groups in Model 3, private entrepreneurs, on average, have lower income than the reference category of workers. However, there are increasing returns to education for private entrepreneurs, which result in the overall higher income for entrepreneurs than that for workers (see Model 2). How do we explain these patterns? One plausible explanation is that, in the reform era, income allocation in formal organizations is mainly based on positional power or official titles associated with positions. Because of the demography of promotions in the past years, many positions are still occupied by those in earlier cohorts with less educational credentials, and younger and more educated employees are still waiting along the promotion ladders. As a result, we observe the negative interaction effects, after controlling for returns to these occupational positions. We call this a "mismatch" phenomenon. In contrast, private entrepreneurs are free from these organizational constraints and, as a result, they directly capture all the benefits in returns to education.

Compared with empirical findings on the returns to education in other societies, our findings reveal several unique features of the distribution of economic rewards in urban China. First, returns to education in urban China are markedly lower than in other parts of the world (cf. Table A2 in Psacharopoulos 1994: 1342). This is consistent with the view that human resource allocation in a redistributive economy differs significantly from that in a market economy. Second, there has been a noticeable increase in returns to education in general between 1978 and 1993. Moreover, returns to education are more salient for private entrepreneurs in 1993, who are most distant from the state but closest to markets. The overall pattern, however, cannot be construed as solely driven by market mechanisms, as we discussed before. Increasing returns to managerial and professional positions in 1993 are even more salient than the returns to education. Moreover, the interaction terms in Model 3 show that returns to occupational positions are not necessarily congruent with the effects of education.

Returns to education across state and nonstate sectors

A major area of contention in market transition debates is the role of education in the allocation of human capital. To address this issue in a more direct way, we now examine returns to education in the state and nonstate sector during the reform era. Specifically, we treat governmental agencies, public organizations, and state firms as belonging to the state sector, and collective firms, hybrid firms, joint ventures, and private firms as part of the nonstate sector. Work organizations in the state sector tend to be more sensitive to administrative fiats and changes in state policies, whereas organizations in the nonstate sector are more subject to market mechanisms in the allocation of human capital as well as other resources. However, we hasten to add that this dichotomous categorization is only an approximation. Even within the state sector, work organizations face various extents of market competition in the reform era. Similarly, firms in the nonstate sector also vary in their relations to the administrative authority. For this comparison, we focus on the patterns in the year 1993 only. This is because there were only a small number of private, joint venture or hybrid firms in the nonstate sector in 1965 and 1978, making it impractical to compare the state and nonstate sectors.

We estimate OLS models for returns to education in the two sectors separately. In this set of analyses, we estimate models similar to those reported in Table 13.2. The parameter estimates for total income are reported in the first two columns of Table 13.3.

In terms of total income, there is a noticeable and large discrepancy in the returns to education between the state and the nonstate sector. Controlling for other covariates in the models, one additional year of schooling increases total income for employees in the state sector by 1.9 percent, but the rate of return is 5.7 percent in the nonstate sector. This difference is very large, suggesting that returns to education are significantly higher in the nonstate sector where the principles of human resource allocation are more governed by market mechanisms. A closer look at the effects of other covariates shows that in the state sector, total income is affected by other factors as indicated by the significant effects of managerial positions as well as high-rank professional positions. In contrast, in the nonstate sector, only top managers and low-rank professionals receive higher income than the reference category of workers. In the state sector as well as in the nonstate sector to a lesser extent, the interaction terms between these positions and years of schooling show lower rates of return to education for managers and professionals than for workers, after controlling for the effects of their positions. This is further evidence in support of our previous speculation that there is a "mismatch" between education and positional power (managerial and professional ranks)

Table 13.3 OLS regression estimates of returns to education in 1993, by sector

	Total income		Basic income	
	State sector	*Nonstate sector*	*State sector*	*Nonstate sector*
Intercept	4.020***	3.808***	2.887***	3.188***
Years of schooling	0.020***	0.047***	0.025***	0.023**
Female	−0.120***	−0.243***	−0.101***	−0.122***
Labor force duration	0.018***	0.017**	0.029***	0.011*
LF duration-squared/100	−0.026***	−0.028**	−0.032***	−0.013
Occupations				
Top manager	0.343*	0.618**	0.476**	0.556**
Mid-level manager	0.377***	0.291	0.246	0.752**
Low-level manager	0.313***	−0.172	0.467***	0.040
High-rank professional	0.441**	0.261	0.470**	0.668
Low-rank professional	0.211	0.500**	0.065	0.059
Top-level manager*schooling	−0.006	−0.039*	−0.025	−0.024
Mid-level manager*schooling	−0.021*	−0.015	−0.009	−0.053*
Low-level manager*schooling	−0.022***	0.019	−0.034***	0.002
High prof*schooling	−0.031**	−0.010	−0.027*	−0.048
Low prof*schooling	−0.012	−0.038**	−0.004	−0.000
Adj-R²	0.39	0.50	0.30	0.30
N	2,536	1,088	2,394	904

Notes: "Worker" is the reference category for occupational positions for both sectors. In all the models, we control for types of work organizations and their interactions with years of schooling. A set of 19 dummy variables are also included to indicate the specific cities in which the data are drawn. The coefficients for all these control variables are not reported in this table. * $p < 0.10$, ** $p < 0.05$, *** $p < 0.01$.

in formal organizations. Such organizational factors are especially prevalent in the state sector in which large, formal organizations are concentrated. Even if education has played an important role in these organizations, demographic factors may considerably delay the timing of a favorable match between positions and educational credentials.

The finding that there is a low return to education in the state sector is striking and troublesome. Given the aggressive state policies in emphasizing educational credentials since the 1980s, does this finding imply that these policies are merely symbolic or ineffective at all? To further explore this issue, we conducted additional analyses and examined the determinants of *basic income*. In China, basic income is largely determined by the administrative system and reflects the principles of human resource allocation and rewards in the corresponding state policies. In contrast, bonuses, which constitute an increasingly large proportion of one's total income in the reform era (see Table 13.1), capture individual or work unit performance. Accordingly, they are more flexible and are less subject to state policies. Generally, compared with basic income, bonuses and total income (including bonuses and subsidies) are poorly explained by the conventional human capital models and are less closely associated with education (Walder 1990; Bian and Logan 1996; Xie and Hannum 1996; Dickson and Rublee 2000). Thus, to assess the role of the state policies in returns to education, it is more instructive to consider the determinants of basic income.

Indeed, the story in the determinants of basic income is quite different. The findings in columns 3 and 4 of Table 13.3 show that, in terms of basic income, returns to education are quite comparable between the state and the nonstate sector, after controlling for other covariates in the models. This finding provides indirect evidence that both markets and state policies promote the role of education in the reform era and both exert influences on the increasing returns to education.

To sum up, we find both similarities and differences in the returns to education between the state sector and nonstate sector. On the one hand, the comparable returns to basic income across these two sectors are consistent with our argument that the state and state policies also actively promote the role of education. On the other hand, there is strong evidence that returns to education are significantly higher in those organizations that are more governed by market mechanisms. The significant differences in returns to education in total income imply different mechanisms in these two sectors. In the nonstate sector, it is likely that bonuses are a major component in total income and are closely related to employee performance, giving rise to the salient role of education. In contrast, in the state sector, subsidies and bonuses tend to be treated as routine elements of welfare benefits, hence they are not sensitive to education.

Toward a broader conception of returns to education: further explorations

As we argued before, a focus on returns to education in wage rates is too narrow to capture the role of education in individual life chances, especially in state socialist economies and transitional economies, where a large part of resources are not allocated monetarily or in the marketplace. We advocate a broader conception of returns to education by considering how education credentials affect one's access to job types, work organizations, political capital, and promotion opportunities in organizations. We now examine these dimensions.

Table 13.4 reports the impact of educational levels (junior high school or less education as the reference category) on a series of status-determining events in political life and in the workplace. These findings are based on analyses of life history data from the same sample of urban residents used in this study. We can group events into three categories. First is access to high-status managerial and professional jobs and high-status organizations such as government agencies and public organizations. Second, we consider access to political capital as indicated by Communist Party membership. Finally, we examine access to promotion opportunities in the national administrative system and in work organizations. Consistent with our emphasis on a historical perspective, we report the patterns for three historical periods: 1949–65, 1966–79, and 1980–93.[6]

Table 13.4 Discrete event history model of entry into selected jobs, organizations, and the Communist Party, and of promotions, by period

Covariates	1949–65	1966–79	1980–93
Entry into managerial job			
Senior high school	1.22***	0.94***	2.49***
College	1.42***	1.76***	3.71***
Entry into professional job			
Senior high school	2.97***	1.72***	2.83***
College	3.49***	2.88***	4.44***
Entry into government agencies			
Senior high school	0.74***	0.66***	1.60***
College	0.68***	1.32***	2.43***
Entry into public organizations			
Senior high school	2.38***	1.67***	2.17***
College	2.59***	2.43***	3.85***
Entry into the Communist Party			
Senior high school	–0.13	0.20	0.59***
College	–0.20	–0.12	1.02***
Promotion along administrative rank			
Senior high school	0.30	0.08	0.05
College	1.18***	0.69***	0.69***
Promotion in work organization			
Senior high school	0.02	0.43***	0.63***
College	0.70***	0.91***	1.10***

Notes: "Junior high school or lower education" is the reference category for the educational level. The models also include other control variables such as gender, parental status, residential locations, etc. Results from the last three types of events are drawn from another study by Zhou (2001). *** $p < 0.01$.

The empirical patterns show several interesting features. First, throughout the PRC's 45-year history, education has played an important role in access to high-status jobs and organizations, as indicated by the significant effects of high school and college education on the rates of entering these jobs and organizations, compared with the reference category of those with junior high school or lower education. Clearly, there are considerable variations across historical periods: in general, the positive effects of education were smallest during the Cultural Revolution period and most pronounced in the reform era. Second, the rate of entry into the Communist Party is significantly affected by educational levels only in the reform era. Finally, education, especially a college degree, has played a significant role in promotion in both national administrative systems and in work organizations for all three periods. Zhang and Zhao (Chapter 14) also find that college graduates were particularly rewarded in the reform era.

These findings have two important implications. First, the significant role of education in these important life events related to labor markets indicates that the role of education is likely to be far more important in this broad conception of returns to education than the typical human capital model indicates. The indirect returns to education are important especially in state socialist economies and, to a lesser extent, transitional economies where not all transactions take place in the marketplace. Because many economic benefits (e.g. housing space, fringe benefits) are associated with types of work organizations and positions, a narrow focus on wage returns to education is likely to underestimate the role of education in urban China, both before and during the reform era. Second, because a large proportion of these jobs and organizations are in the state sector, the events considered here are heavily influenced by state policies (Zhou *et al.* 1997; Zhou 2001). These state policies have contributed in significant ways to the returns to education, especially in the reform era, as evidenced by the noticeable increase in the relationship between education and the likelihood of these events. The increasing importance of education in both economic and political arenas underscores a more general trend. That is, in the reform era both economic and political arenas have become increasingly rationalized, as reflected in the increasing role of education and professional training in both spheres. This is the outcome of the coevolution of shifting state policies and emerging markets over time.

Conclusion

On October 26, 2001, *Forbes Global* announced the list of 100 richest businessmen and businesswomen in mainland China, whose wealth ranged from RMB 50 million to 8.3 billion. One statistic deserves particular attention: 73 of them experienced the disruption of education during the Cultural Revolution, but 86 of them received higher education after 1977. This statistic portrays vividly the close association of education and economic well-being in China's transitional economy; at the same time, it also points to the importance of the political processes in state socialist China that affect individual life chances in dramatic, often unpredictable ways. This image fits the theme of this study well.

In this chapter, we took returns to education as an analytical focus and examined changes in returns to education over time in three selected years (1965, 1978, and 1993) to understand the underlying processes. We estimated returns to education in urban China in terms of both the direct path of wage determination and of specific channels through which the role of education matters, such as occupational status and sectoral differences. We also proposed a broader conceptualization of returns to education in state socialist economies and transitional economies and provided some preliminary evidence on the indirect channels of returns to education through education's effects on status attainment in the labor force and in work organizations.

The main findings show that the returns to education varied considerably over time. There is a substantial increase in the reform era, compared with the baseline of 1978, and the increase is especially large in the nonstate sector where market mechanisms prevail. Among occupational groups, the returns to education are particularly high for entrepreneurs. In a companion study using the same data source (Zhao and Zhou 2002), we reported detailed comparisons of the returns to education in income between 1978 and 1993, a span of 15 years of economic reform in urban China. As we noted in that study, despite the still markedly low returns to education in urban China as of 1993, recent institutional changes have caused and are reflected in increasing returns to education, especially in the nonstate sector. The emergence of markets leads to new principles of human resource allocation different than those in the redistributive economy, as many economists and Nee's market transition theory have hypothesized. In Chapter 14, Zhang and Zhao further demonstrate that this trend of increasing returns to education was striking and robust in urban China from 1988 through 1999.

The findings reported in this chapter also point to two somewhat dissonant conclusions about the returns to education in the previous state socialist economy and in transitional economies in urban China. First, there is evidence that the wage returns to education were significantly higher in 1965 than in 1978. In other words, the strikingly low returns to education in the aftermath of the Cultural Revolution did not necessarily reflect the principle of human resource allocation under state socialism. Low returns to education in Mao's China were noticeably different than the pattern of high returns to education in the USSR. Second, adopting a broader conceptualization of returns to education, we find that education plays a significant role in access to high-status jobs and work organizations and to promotion opportunities, before and after the reform in urban China. Given the well-documented facts that economic benefits have been highly associated with jobs, organizations, and positions in China's state socialist economy, it is likely that a narrow focus on wage returns to education considerably underestimates the role of education in the allocation and rewards of human resources in state socialist societies.

Moreover, the continuing significance of political capital and occupational status indicates that state policies also contribute positively to the allocation of human resources in the presence of market expansion. Those observations under the broader reconceptualization also caution us about the sources of institutional changes in China's transformation of the state socialist economy. Our findings show that the returns to education significantly increased in the reform era in the proposed broad sense. These increases are undoubtedly related to the emergence of markets and market competition for human resources, as we discussed before. However, we also want to point out that a large proportion of the high-status jobs and organizations are still in the state sector, which are heavily influenced by state policies and often are directly administered by government agencies. As Table 13.1 indicates, of the urban labor force in our sample, 74 percent were in the state sector in 1965, 71.6 percent in 1978, and 69.5 percent in 1993. Moreover, it is difficult to attribute to market forces the significant effects of education on rates of entering the Communist Party and of promotion up the national bureaucratic ladder.

Given these considerations, we find it more instructive to consider the interactions between markets and politics in a coevolutionary framework. These different mechanisms may compete with each other, but at a different level they may also mutually adapt to and reinforce each other. For example, it is not difficult to imagine that the competition for able employees by the nonstate sector leads to a flow of talent from the state sector to the nonstate sector after barriers to job mobility have disappeared. Accordingly, it is plausible that organizations in the state sector may adjust their own incentive structures to retain employees and to attract able employees from other organizations. This scenario suggests that the interactions between the two sectors may induce institutional changes in both rather than one undermining the other. In this sense, it is useful for us to move away from treating political and market processes as fundamentally incompatible and to appreciate more complicated interactions between the two and their consequences for the emergence of new institutional forms and new stratification orders in urban China.

Acknowledgments

An earlier version of this study was presented at the Harvard Conference on Education and Reform in China (Cambridge, Massachusetts, July 2001) and at the RC–28 Conference (Berkeley, California, August 2001). We thank Donald Treiman, Yu Xie, the editors, and participants at these meetings for their helpful comments. This research is supported by a grant from the National Science Foundation (SBR–9413540), an ASA/NSF fund for the advancement of the discipline, and a Spencer Fellowship. We are grateful to the Departments of Sociology at Fudan University and the People's University, the Institute of Sociology at Tianjin Academy of Social Sciences and, in particular, Weida Fan, Qiang Li, Yunkang Pan, and Xizhe Peng for their assistance in data collection.

Notes

1 For instance, Khan and Riskin (2001) found that with the advance of the market economy, all types of subsidies have dramatically shrunk, while cash income tends to take higher proportion of the total income in urban China. Nevertheless, housing subsidies, as a legacy of redistributive economy, are still important, and the distribution of housing subsidies has become sharply unequal. With the privatization of urban housing under the banner of housing reform, this unequal distribution of housing subsidies as well as the rental value of owned housing has "a quantitatively large effect on overall inequality" in urban China (ibid.: 35–36).

2 Khan and Riskin (2001) decomposed the total income in urban China into eight categories. They found the "cash income of working members" took 44.42 percent in 1998 and 61.3 percent in 1995 of the total income (ibid.: 35).

3 In labor economics, wage rate or weekly wage is often used because these wage rates measure more precisely productivity-related rewards. In the Chinese context, since most urban employees are full-time workers, monthly wage serves the same purpose well.

4 Parts of the results in this section and the next section are reported in Zhao and Zhou (2002). That study also provides additional analyses, technical details, and interpretations of the results.
5 Because party membership information is missing in six cities in our data (about 20 percent of the sample), we estimated separate statistical models for the analyses in which party membership variable was included. We include the parameter estimates of party membership in this table for the purpose of illustration.
6 Although Mao Zedong died in 1976, most policies in the Mao era continued till the end of the 1970s in urban China. For the analyses of these events, it is more meaningful to consider their occurrences over a period rather than a single year.

References

Bian, Y. (1994) *Work and Inequality in Urban China*, Albany, NY: State University of New York Press.
Bian, Y. and Logan, J.R. (1996) "Market Transition and the Persistence of Power: The Changing Stratification System in Urban China," *American Sociological Review*, 61: 739–758.
Chen, S. and Zhang, H. (1992) *The Reform of the Salary System in Government and Public Organizations (Guojia jiguan he shiye danwei gongzi zhidu biange)*, Beijing: China Personnel Press.
Dickson, B.J. and Rublee, M.R. (2000) "Membership Has Its Privileges: The Socioeconomic Characteristics of Communist Party Members in Urban China," *Comparative Political Studies*, 33: 87–112.
Gerber, T. and Hout, M. (1998) "More Shock than Therapy: Market Transition, Employment, and Income in Russia, 1991–1995," *American Journal of Sociology*, 104: 1–50.
Guthrie, D. (1997) "Between Markets and Politics: Organizational Responses to Reform in China," *American Journal of Sociology*, 102: 1258–1304.
Harding, H. (1981) *Organizing China: The Problem of Bureaucracy, 1949–1976*, Palo Alto, CA: Stanford University Press.
Khan, A.R. and Riskin, C. (2001) *Inequality and Poverty in China in the Age of Globalization*, New York: Oxford University Press.
Katz, K. (1999) "Were There No Returns to Education in the USSR?—Estimates from Soviet-period Household Data," *Labor Economics*, 6: 417–434.
Konrad, G. and Szelényi, I. (1979) *The Intellectuals on the Road to Class Power*, New York: Harcourt, Brace, Jovanovich.
Lee, H. (1991) *From Revolutionary Cadres to Party Technocrats in Socialist China*, Berkeley, CA: University of California Press.
Lin, N. and Bian, Y. (1991) "Getting Ahead in Urban China," *American Journal of Sociology*, 97: 657–688.
Maurer-Fazio, M. (1999) "Earnings and Education in China's Transition to a Market Economy: Survey Evidence from 1989 and 1992," *China Economic Review*, 10: 17–40.
Moock, P.R., Patrinos, H.A., and Venkataraman, M. (1998) "Education and Earnings in a Transition Economy: The Case of Vietnam," World Bank Working Paper No. 1920.
Nee, V. (1989) "A Theory of Market Transition: From Redistribution to Markets in State Socialism," *American Sociological Review*, 54: 663–681.

Nee, V. (1991) "Social Inequalities in Reforming State Socialism: Between Redistribution and Markets in State Socialism," *American Sociological Review*, 56: 267–282.

Nee, V. (1996) "The Emergence of a Market Society: Changing Mechanisms of Stratification in China," *American Journal of Sociology*, 101: 908–949.

Nee, V. and Matthews, R. (1996) "Market Transition and Societal Transformation in Reforming State Socialism," *Annual Review of Sociology*, 22: 401–435.

Newell, A. and Reilly, B. (1999) "Rates of Return to Educational Qualifications in the Transitional Economics," *Education Economics*, 7: 67–84.

Office of Organization Structure, CCP Central Committee (1993) *The Grand Trend of the Administrative Reform in China (Zhongguo xingzheng gaige daqushi)*, Beijing: Economic Science Press.

Parish, W. (1984) "Destratification in Chinese Society," in J. Watson (ed.), *Class and Stratification in China*, Cambridge: Cambridge University Press, pp. 84–120.

Parish, W.L. and Michelson, E. (1996) "Politics and Markets: Dual Transformations," *American Journal of Sociology*, 101: 1042–1059.

Psacharopoulos, G. (1994) "Returns to Investment in Education: A Global Update," *World Development*, 22: 1325–1343.

Raymo, J.M. and Xie, Y. (2000) "Income of the Urban Elderly in Postreform China: Political Capital, Human Capital, and the State," *Social Science Research*, 29: 1–24.

Rona-Tas, A. (1994) " 'The First Shall Be Last?' Entrepreneurship and Communist Cadres in the Transition from Socialism," *American Journal of Sociology*, 100: 40–69.

Stark, D. (1996) "Recombinant Property in East European Capitalism," *American Journal of Sociology*, 101: 993–1027.

State Statistical Bureau, PRC (SSB) (1990) *Yearbook of Chinese Cities*, Beijing: China Statistical Press.

Szelényi, I. (1978) "Social Inequalities in State Socialist Redistributive Economies," *International Journal of Comparative Sociology*, 19: 63–87.

Walder, A.G. (1986) *Communist Neo-Traditionalism: Work and Authority in Chinese Industry*, Berkeley and Los Angeles, CA: University of California Press.

Walder, A. (1990) "Economic Reform and Income Distribution in Tianjin, 1976–1986," in D. Davis and E.F. Vogel (eds.), *Chinese Society on the Eve of Tiananmen*, Cambridge, MA: Harvard University Press, pp. 135–156.

Walder, A. (1992) "Property Rights and Stratification in Socialist Redistributive Economies," *American Sociological Review*, 57: 524–539.

Walder, A. (1995) "Career Mobility and the Communist Political Order," *American Sociological Review*, 60: 309–328.

Walder, A. (1996) "Markets and Inequality in Transitional Economies: Toward Testable Theories," *American Journal of Sociology*, 101: 1060–1073.

Walder, A.G., Li, B., and Treiman, D.J. (2000) "Political and Life Chances in a State Socialist Regime: Career Paths into the Urban Chinese Elite, 1949 to 1996," *American Sociological Review*, 65: 191–209.

Xie, Y. and Hannum, E. (1996) "Regional Variation in Earnings Inequality in Reform-Era Urban China," *American Journal of Sociology*, 101: 950–992.

Xu, S. and Zhang, L. (1992) *Handbook of Personnel Management in China (Zhongguo renshi guanli gongzuo shiyong shouce)*, Beijing: China Financial Economics Press.

Zhao, W. and Zhou, X. (2002) "Institutional Transformation and Returns to Education in Urban China: An Empirical Assessment," *Research in Social Stratification and Mobility*, 19: 339–375.

Zhou, X. (1995) "Partial Reform and the Chinese Bureaucracy in the Post-Mao Era," *Comparative Politics Studies*, 28: 440–468.

Zhou, X. (2000) "Economic Transformation and Income Inequality in Urban China: Evidence from Panel Data," *American Journal of Sociology*, 105: 1135–1174.

Zhou, X. (2001) "Political Dynamics and Bureaucratic Career Patterns in the People's Republic of China, 1949–1994," *Comparative Political Studies*, 34: 1036–1062.

Zhou, X. and Suhomlinova, O. (2001) "Redistribution under State Socialism: A USSR and PRC Comparison," *Research in Social Stratification and Mobility*, 18: 163–204.

Zhou, X., Tuma, N.B., and Moen, P. (1997) "Institutional Change and Job-Shift Patterns in Urban China, 1949 to 1994," *American Sociological Review*, 62: 339–365.

14 Rising returns to schooling in urban China

Junsen Zhang and Yaohui Zhao

Introduction

For any society, the economic returns to schooling provide important information about the incentives for individuals to invest in education, the efficiency of labor allocation in the economy, and the distributional consequences of differences in educational attainment.[1] As such, the returns to schooling directly influence fundamental economic outcomes of growth and equity. In this chapter, we summarize results of an analysis of a unique repeated cross-sectional dataset spanning much of China's economic reform period to estimate changes over time in the returns to schooling in urban China. We first evaluate past studies of the returns to education in China to establish the fact that returns to education were low in the 1980s and early 1990s. Second, we empirically estimate wage equations using regression analysis and demonstrate a rapid increase in the returns to education in urban China from 1988 to 2003. We verify the robustness of this trend by examining the sensitivity of our results to various specifications of the regression models and the inclusion of different control variables. Finally, we discuss how changes in the returns to education vary across groups defined on the basis of gender, experience, ownership, and region.

It is not surprising that the returns to schooling in China would increase over time as the economic system moved away from planning and became increasingly market oriented. It may be more interesting to observe how long it took the returns to education to increase in China, which reflects China's gradualist approach to economic transition.

Under the planning system, all workers and employers were matched to jobs by government labor bureau. Lifetime employment was guaranteed, but little labor mobility was permitted, either geographically or across occupations. During the socialist period, the Bureau of Labor and Personnel centrally determined and controlled the wages of all workers in urban areas through a grade system consisting of eight distinct grade levels for factory workers and technicians and 24 levels for administrative and managerial workers. Wage increases were based on seniority rather than productivity and allowed only small differentials based on the level of completed schooling.

Urban wage reforms were implemented incrementally. In the mid-1980s, reforms made it possible for larger income differences to arise among workers by allowing profitable firms to pay higher salaries and letting employers pay bonuses to more productive workers. Employment reforms also sought to end the system of permanent employment. In 1986, the State Council issued "Temporary Regulations on the Use of Labor Contracts in State-Run Enterprises," and formally introduced labor contracts to the labor market (Meng 2000). By 1997, one hundred million employees had signed labor contracts with their employers. In practice, firms were free to select and hire suitable workers; however, until the late 1990s, the government restricted the no-fault dismissal of workers. Nonetheless, more freedom in hiring increased the competition for productive workers.

Major changes in the labor market occurred in the late 1990s. Faced with large and unsustainable financial losses of SOEs that threatened the solvency of the banking system, the Chinese government finally moved ahead with an aggressive state-owned enterprise restructuring program, marking the end of the "iron rice bowl" of guaranteed employment and benefits for China's urban workers. The restructuring led to the lay-offs of tens of millions of workers, which led to major changes in the functioning of the labor market. Ownership reforms and a greater tolerance for private ownership led to a rapid increase in the size of the private sector. The flow of migrants to urban labor markets also increased substantially during the 1990s.

Prior studies

The most conventional method of calculating the returns to schooling using micro data sets, first estimated by Jacob Mincer (1974), is to estimate a regression equation in which the log of wages is specified to be a linear function of years of schooling, years of experience, years of experience squared, and other control variables, such as gender and region. As soon as micro data sets from China became available, economists began estimating Mincer-type earnings equations. In this section, we briefly review the findings from previous studies of the returns to education in urban China. The literature on the returns to education in rural China is reviewed in Chapter 12 in this volume by de Brauw and Rozelle. Interestingly, they also find that the returns to schooling remained low until the mid-1990s; by 2000, they estimate the returns to a year of schooling in rural China had reached 6.4 percent. This is higher than many early estimates of the returns to schooling in urban China, but well below our estimate of 10.1 percent in the same year for urban China. This difference is not surprising given that wage labor markets are much denser and better developed in urban areas.

Nearly all studies of the returns to schooling in the 1980s and early 1990s using individual-level data report low rates of return. It is important to point out that these are estimates of the private return to schooling, which may underestimate the social returns to schooling if educated workers are more likely to be paid wages below their marginal productivity.[2] Nonetheless, the private returns to schooling have the greatest effect on incentives to invest in education, and low private returns also are associated with inefficient allocation of labor and poor incentives for labor effort.

Using retrospective data, Zhao and Zhou find in Chapter 13 in this volume that the returns to schooling in urban China remained at low levels from 1965 to 1993, and were only 3.5 percent in 1993. Byron and Manaloto (1990) estimate a low rate of return of 1.4 percent for each additional year of schooling in China using data from a 1986 survey of 800 state industrial workers in Nanjing. Using state-sector data in the 1980s, Meng and Kidd (1997) find slightly larger but still low returns to education of 2.5 percent in 1981 and 2.7 percent in 1987. Fleisher and Wang (2005) use retrospective data collected in 1994 and find that returns to schooling did not recover from the low level during the Cultural Revolution until the 1990s. Although the estimates are not directly comparable due to differences in specifications and contexts, the consistently low values are in stark contrast to the findings of Psacharopoulos (1992) that the returns to schooling estimated using Mincer-type models in developing countries averaged 8 percent and the rate of return in Asian countries, excluding China, averaged 11 percent. Fleisher *et al.* (2005) conclude that China is an outlier in that its rapid economic growth is associated with returns to schooling remaining below world average for comparable countries.

The most widely used household data are the two waves of the Chinese Household Income Project (CHIP) conducted in 1988 and 1995. Different authors use different earnings equation specifications; thus, a range of estimates is generated. Maurer-Fazio (1999) uses the urban sample of the 1988 CHIP data and estimates that the returns to schooling were 2.9 percent and 4.5 percent for male and female workers, respectively. She also finds that the returns were higher for employees in the non-state sector at around 9 percent. Using the same 1988 CHIP data, Johnson and Chow (1997) produce estimates of the returns to schooling ranging from 2.8 percent to 4.0 percent, and Liu (1998) finds a 3.6 percent rate of return to a year of schooling. Liu also estimates rates of return relative to no education of 37.5 percent for university education, 19.1 percent for secondary education, and 7.5 percent for primary education. He also finds that Guangdong had higher returns than other provinces. Other studies using the 1988 CHIP data include Knight and Song (1991, 1993, 1995) who examine income inequality and wage structure, and Gustafsson and Li (2000) who examine gender wage gaps. The returns to education in these studies are uniformly low.

Scholars have also searched for evidence of increasing returns to education over time following the progress of economic reforms. Comparing the 1988 CHIP sample and the 1992 Chinese Labor Market Research Project (CLMRP) sample, Maurer-Fazio (1999) finds that the returns to a year of schooling increased by 0.8 percent for male workers and 0.4 percent for female workers. The availability of a second wave of CHIP data for 1995 led to a new set of estimates of the returns to education. Gustafsson and Li (2000) find a substantial rise in the returns to four-year college education relative to high school education for male workers, from 8.9 percent in 1988 to 15.5 percent in 1995. Using a similar specification but combining the male and female samples, Knight and Song (2003) find that the returns to college education, relative to high school, rose from 4.9 percent in 1988 to 15.0 percent in 1995. Yang (2005) shows that, on average, the rates of return to education at the city level increased from 3.1 percent to 5.1 percent over this seven-year period and the dispersion widened significantly.

One advantage of the 1995 CHIP data over the 1988 CHIP data is that information on working hours was collected to make it possible to test whether the previous low returns to education were due to measurement error in earnings. S. Li (2003) finds that the returns to education were higher using hourly wage rates because highly educated people worked fewer hours on average. However, the underestimation is less than 10 percent. Using hourly wages, the returns to schooling were 5.5 percent whereas, using annual earnings, the returns to schooling were 5 percent.

Most urban studies use a single year of data, and, due to differences in specifications of earnings functions, comparing the results across studies is problematic. The existing studies that use comparable data and consistent specifications over time, e.g. Gustafsson and Li (2000) and Knight and Song (2003), do not focus primarily on the returns to education. Hence, no information is provided on the robustness of the results or on between-group comparisons. Furthermore, these studies use data from only two points in time so that inferences about the trend may be influenced by transitory disturbances. In this chapter, we utilize annual micro data covering the entire period from 1988 to 2003 to document the trends in schooling returns. This chapter summarizes the main results found in Zhang *et al.* (2005), but adds additional results and discussion. In particular, it extends the time coverage from 2001 to 2003.

Data

The data used in this chapter come from 14 consecutive annual surveys of urban households in six provinces conducted by China's National Bureau of Statistics (NBS) from 1988 through 2001, and the NBS national urban sample in 2003.[3] About six thousand individual workers participated in each sample year from 1988 to 2001, and the sample size increased to over 16,000 in 2003. One undesirable feature of China's urban household surveys during this period is that migrant households living in urban areas without an urban household registration (*hukou*) were not included in the surveys. However, the exclusion of migrants allows us to restrict our attention to a relatively fixed group of people, which may enable us to better document the effect of economic changes on wage determination.

To examine changes over time, we use data from six provinces that are broadly representative of China's rich regional variation, namely, Beijing, Liaoning, Zhejiang, Sichuan, Guangdong and Shaanxi. Beijing is a rapidly growing municipality in the north; Guangdong and Zhejiang are dynamic high-growth provinces in China's south coastal region; Liaoning is a heavy industrial province in the northeast; Sichuan and Shaanxi are relatively less developed provinces located in the southwest and northwest, respectively.

To focus on wage determination in the labor market, we restrict our sample to workers engaged in wage employment. Following standard practice, we exclude employers, self-employed individuals, retirees, students, and household workers (Coleman 1993; Mwabu and Schultz 1996).[4] Moreover, as China's Labor Law sets the minimum working age at 16, we exclude all those younger than 16. Because most workers retire by age 60 in accordance with China's mandatory retirement age, individuals older than 60 also are excluded. Wage income consists of four major components, namely, basic wage, bonus, subsidies and other labor-related income.

About three-quarters of all workers are employed in the state-owned sector. Although this ratio did not change much between 1988 and 2001, an upward trend is observed during the first half of the data period, reaching 78.5 percent in 1996, followed by a downward trend thereafter. The shrinkage of state-sector employment coincided with the restructuring of state-owned enterprises and the lay-offs of millions of state-sector workers. In comparison to the state sector, the decline in employment in collective enterprises has been more dramatic and consistent. Between 1988 and 2001, the share of workers in the collective sector declined by almost half, from 24.8 percent in 1988 to 10.9 percent in 2001. The other ownership category consists of private enterprises, self-employed individuals, foreign-funded enterprises, and share-holding corporations that may have been spun off from the state and collective sectors. This sector enjoyed rapid growth in employment; in 1988, its share was less than 1 percent but, by 2001, its share had risen to 19.0 percent. The fastest increase occurred after 1991, following Deng Xiaoping's tour to the South in which he promoted openness and reform.

As reported in Table 14.1, mean years of schooling increase from 10.4 years in 1988 to 11.8 years in 2001.[5] Despite this somewhat small increment, dramatic changes in the structure of education occurred. Most noticeable are the more than doubling of the proportion of workers with college education and the decline by two-thirds in the number of workers with primary school education or less. The share of junior high school graduates also shows a sizeable decrease during the period, from 42 percent in 1988 to 25.1 percent in 2001. The decline in the share of workers in the low education categories is due primarily to the retirement of older, less-educated cohorts and the entrance into the workforce of younger, better-educated workers.

Two caveats concerning data limitations are in order. First, except for 2003, our data do not have information on working hours. Evidence from the CHIP data and from the rural returns to schooling calculations in Chapter 12 in this volume by de Brauw and Rozelle suggests that using hourly

Table 14.1 The distribution of schooling by years and levels, 1988–2001

Year	Schooling (years)	College and above (%)	Technical school (%)	Senior high (%)	Junior high (%)	Primary and below (%)
1988	10.4	12.6	11.8	22.6	42.0	10.5
1989	10.5	13.2	12.0	24.5	40.1	9.7
1990	10.6	14.1	12.8	24.3	39.5	9.0
1991	10.7	15.6	12.4	24.7	37.4	9.6
1992	11.0	18.2	13.3	26.2	34.8	7.4
1993	11.1	18.3	13.2	26.7	35.3	6.4
1994	11.3	20.4	14.1	27.1	32.9	5.2
1995	11.3	21.6	13.3	28.8	30.7	5.4
1996	11.3	22.1	13.7	28.1	31.2	4.7
1997	11.4	22.8	13.0	28.9	31.1	4.1
1998	11.5	24.5	14.2	29.1	28.3	3.9
1999	11.7	26.3	14.5	29.3	26.4	3.5
2000	11.8	28.9	13.2	30.3	24.1	3.4
2001	11.8	28.1	13.1	30.7	25.1	2.9

wages rather than monthly or annual wages increases the estimated returns to education. We can get a rough estimate of the bias by comparing results for hourly and monthly wages using the 2003 data. Second, we are not able to account for labor earnings in non-wage benefits, such as housing, health care benefits, and pension. If non-wage benefits are positively or negatively related to wage earnings, this omission leads to either an under- or over-estimate of the returns to education. However, its effect on observed trends is not obvious.

Estimates of the returns to schooling in urban China

Following Mincer (1974), we estimate a semi-logarithmic specification for earnings using ordinary least squares regressions in which log of monthly wage is specified to be a linear function of years of schooling (or indicator variables for different levels of schooling attained), years of experience, years of experience squared, a dummy variable for sex, and provincial dummy variables. The coefficient for the years of schooling is the estimated returns to a year of schooling.

The first column in Table 14.2 presents coefficients for years of schooling. By this measure, the returns to a year of schooling in the six sample provinces nearly tripled over the 14-year period, from 4.0 percent in 1988 to 10.2 percent in 2001 and 11.4 percent in 2003.[6] For the national sample (not reported in Table 14.2), the returns to a year of schooling was 10.9 percent in 2003, which is 0.5 percent lower than in the six-province sample. In 2003, the urban household survey included a question on hours of work, enabling us to calculate an hourly wage in addition to a monthly wage. Using hourly wages for

Table 14.2 Estimates of rates of returns to education in urban China, 1988–2003

Year	N	Years of schooling	College or above versus high school	Technical school versus high school	High school versus junior high	Junior high versus primary school
1988	6,087	4.0	12.2	3.1	11.0	13.9
1989	5,615	4.6	14.4	5.8	11.6	17.3
1990	6,194	4.7	16.6	9.9	11.5	12.8
1991	6,225	4.3	15.9	8.0	9.7	13.4
1992	7,853	4.7	20.1	9.2	9.8	10.8
1993	7,017	5.2	20.4	7.0	11.5	13.6
1994	6,752	7.3	28.7	15.3	14.5	20.2
1995	6,830	6.7	24.4	12.0	15.3	18.9
1996	6,651	6.8	25.2	10.4	15.6	14.9
1997	6,641	6.7	22.3	12.0	17.3	10.9
1998	6,331	8.1	32.1	16.5	16.2	12.2
1999	6,094	9.9	38.1	17.0	21.0	14.8
2000	6,197	10.1	38.7	16.2	20.5	16.4
2001	5,404	10.2	37.3	17.8	21.4	13.8
2003	16,538	11.4	–	–	–	–

2003, the returns to a year of schooling is even higher, 11.9 percent in the six provinces and 11.6 percent for the nation. The returns at the end of the period are now comparable to those found in other developing countries for the early 1990s as summarized in Psacharopoulos (1994).

Taking advantage of the annual data series, we observe that the schooling coefficient did not rise in a linear fashion over the period. Rather, returns rose by 0.6 points between 1988 and 1989, stagnated between 1989 and 1992, and increased by 2.6 points from 1992 to 1994. For another three years returns fell before rising by 3.5 points from 1997 to 2001.

Using dummy variables for discrete levels of schooling, we capture non-linearities in the returns to schooling. Table 14.2 presents the marginal return to completing each additional level of education, e.g. junior high school compared to primary school or below and senior high school compared to junior high school. We compare technical schools with senior high school, but they could also be compared with junior high schools since some technical schools target junior high school graduates. The returns to each level of education beyond junior high school have risen substantially from 1988 to 2001.[7] For senior high school, the rate of return varied between 9.7 percent and 21.4 percent, increasing sharply in 1994 and 1999. The levels of education exhibiting the greatest rise in returns to schooling were technical school and college graduates. For senior high school graduates, the return to completing technical school increased from 3.1 percent in 1988 to 17.8 percent in 2001. College graduates earned 12.2 percent more than senior high school graduates in 1988, but 37.3 percent more in 2001.

In order to test the robustness of the estimated increasing trend in the returns to education and to investigate whether education wage premiums occur mainly within or between job categories, we add ownership, occupation, and industry variables to the Mincer equation using the data from 1988 to 2001 and observe whether these additions change the estimated schooling coefficients. Often the inclusion of occupation and industry variables in wage regressions reduces the magnitude of schooling coefficients because of positive selection into high-paying industries and occupations by better-educated workers. In China, Zhao (2002) finds a similar positive selection in ownership categories, i.e state and foreign ownership. We find that the returns to schooling are lower when additional job-related variables are added. Adding ownership dummy variables reduces the estimated returns to schooling by about one percentage point. Adding industry dummies has a negligible effect on schooling coefficients in the beginning of the period but, by the end of the period, the effect is larger, reducing the returns to schooling by 1.5 percentage points. Hence, better-educated workers are increasingly being sorted into higher-paying industries. The effect of occupation on the returns to schooling is the largest of all three control variables; it reduces the schooling coefficient by about one-third. Finally, when we include all three of the job-related variables in the regressions, the magnitude of the schooling coefficient falls by about 40 percent at both the beginning and the end of the period. However, the trend of increasing returns to education over time is robust to the inclusion of job-related control variables. Hence, we conclude that rising returns to education are occurring within highly specific work categories and reflect broad changes in the labor market.

Next, still using the data from 1988 to 2001, we use the Mincer equations to examine whether the changes in the returns to education differ systematically by gender, experience, ownership, and region.[8] This analysis provides evidence on heterogeneity in the returns to education and sheds light on possible causes of the rising returns to education. We find that the returns to schooling are higher for females throughout the period, exceeding the returns to male education by an average of about 60 percent, and that the increase in the returns to schooling is also greater for women. We also find that the longer one has been out of school, the lower are the returns to education. Possible explanations for this difference include a vintage effect, the rising quality of education, or greater mobility among younger workers because they have made fewer employer-specific investments. However, the rise in returns to education is not confined only to young cohorts. The returns to education have increased at similar rates for all experience groups, more than doubling for both the youngest and oldest experience cohort. We find that the returns to education have been consistently higher for non-public enterprises. In contrast, the state-sector lagged behind the nonstate sector but caught up to narrow the gap over time. This suggests that the wage-setting behavior in state-owned firms changed substantially over the course of China's economic reforms, perhaps in response to competition for skilled labor coming from foreign-funded firms and domestic private enterprises. Finally, with respect to provincial differences in the returns to schooling, we find that the returns to schooling were initially higher in less developed provinces but that there is convergence over time.

Conclusion

Like other transition economies, China had an extremely compressed wage structure in the pre-reform period but experienced dramatic increases in the returns to education and inequality. Such changes occurred in the early period of transition in central and eastern European economies, as Svejnar (1999) and Rutkowski (2001) report. However, in China, returns to education and the level of inequality remained low until the early 1990s, more than a full decade after economic reforms began (H. Li 2003). This experience is consistent with China's gradualist approach to reform, a strategy that was at least partly born out of necessity.

Our study provides estimates of schooling returns in urban China over an extended period of economic reforms. We show a dramatic and robust increase in the returns to education in urban China, from 4.0 percent in 1988 to 10.2 percent in 2001 and 11.4 percent in 2003. Most of the rise in returns to education occurred in two periods, i.e. 1992–1994 and 1997–1999. The most prominent increase in the wage premium occurs for college-educated workers. However, the rise in schooling returns is observed across all groups of workers defined by gender, experience, region, and ownership, and is robust to adding other control variables.

This increase in the returns to schooling in urban China presents challenges for China's labor markets. Specific patterns suggest that institutional reforms played a key role in increasing the returns to schooling in China. Hence, the Chinese labor market has made significant progress during the 1990s in improving the efficiency of labor allocation and furthering labor market integration. An important consequence of the rising returns to education is that incentives for human capital investments have improved, which augurs well for the future quality of the labor force. Using our estimates for the returns to education and making assumptions about the costs of educational investments, we estimate that the private internal rate of return for a college degree is about 15 percent in China today.[9] However, rising returns to schooling contribute to higher levels of income inequality associated with differences in human capital.

Notes

1 Heckman (2003) argues that China spends too little on human capital investment and too much on physical capital based on the differences in the returns to human and physical capital.

2 Using firm-level data, Fleisher and Wang (2004) find that the wages of educated

workers were well below their marginal product, due to the monopsony power of state employers. The argument that the social returns to education are high in China is also supported by studies using aggregate data, e.g. Fleisher and Chen (1997), Demurger (2001), and Chen and Feng (2000).

3 The urban household survey is carried out by the Urban Survey Organization (USO) of the National Bureau of Statistics; it covers 146 cities and 80 towns. The choice of cities and towns and also households is based on the principle of random and representative sampling. USO (2001) provides details on the data. To assess the representativeness of the data, we compare several variables that are both available in our data and in the *Statistical Yearbook of China*. For 1988, our sample averages for household size, the number of workers in a household, and per capita household income are 3.7, 2.2 and 1,352, and the corresponding national averages are 3.6, 2.0 and 1,192 (*Statistical Yearbook of China* 1989: 726). In 2001, our sample averages for the three variables are 3.2, 1.8 and 7,763, compared with national averages of 3.1, 1.7 and 6,907 (*Statistical Yearbook of China* 2002: 321). Thus, the sample averages are reasonably close to those reported in the statistical yearbooks.

4 Following common practice, we also exclude individuals who earn less than half of the minimum wage under the assumption that such individuals are not full-time workers. Using data on official minimum wages for each province from 1988 to 2001, we calculate the ratio of the minimum wage to mean income for each province-year. Then, we take the mean share to estimate minimum wages for all province-years and use these values to exclude individuals.

5 The survey data include only information on the level of schooling attained. To construct a measure of years of schooling, we assume the following years of schooling for different levels of education: primary school = 6 years, middle school = 9 years, high school = 12 years, technical school = 15 years, and college or above = 16 years.

6 The 2003 estimate differs from those for earlier years in several regards. First, the sample size is much larger; second, incomes that are below 20 percent of mean income are excluded rather than those below 50 percent of the median wage; and third, the sample does not exclude self-employed individuals. However, self-employed individuals comprise less than 1 percent of the national sample and their exclusion does not change the estimated returns to schooling.

7 The return to completing junior high school relative to primary school fluctuates around 14 percent.

8 For a more detailed presentation of these results, see Zhang *et al.* (2005).

9 According to Table 14.2, an individual with a college education or above earns 37.3 percent more than a senior high school graduate. Because people with a master's degree or higher represent a small share of the work force with advanced degrees, we assume that the return to a college education for high school graduates is 35 percent. Annual earnings are 15,228 *yuan* in 2001 prices for a college graduate, assuming an annual growth rate of wages of 8.2 percent, tuition of $5,000 *yuan* per year, and the working life after college to be 40 years. Based on these projections, the internal rate of return for college education is 15 percent. In this calculation, the earnings and growth rates are actual numbers derived from our sample. Tuition is the 2001 tuition for undergraduates at Beijing University.

Acknowledgments

The authors acknowledge financial support from Research Grants Council of Hong Kong (Project no. N-CUHK417/01) and National Natural Science Foundation of China (Project no. 70131160745).

References

Byron, R.P. and Manaloto, E.Q. (1990) "Returns to Education in China," *Economic Development and Cultural Change*, 38: 783–796.

Chen, B. and Feng, Y. (2000) "Determinants of Economic Growth in China: Private Enterprises, Education, and Openess," *China Economic Review*, 11: 1–15.

Coleman, M.T. (1993) "Movements in the Earnings–Schooling Relationship, 1940–88," *Journal of Human Resources*, 28: 660–680.

Demurger, S. (2001) "Infrastructure and Economic Growth: An Explanation for Regional Disparities in China," *Journal of Comparative Economics*, 29: 95–117.

Fleisher, B.M. and Chen, J. (1997) "The Coast–Noncoast Income Gap, Productivity, and Regional Economic Policy in China," *Journal of Comparative Economics*, 25: 220–236.

Fleisher, B.M., Sabirianova, K., and Wang, X. (2005) "Returns to Skills and the Speed of Reforms: Evidence from Central and Eastern Europe, China and Russia," *Journal of Comparative Economics*, 33: 351–370.

Fleisher, B.M. and Wang, X. (2004) "Skill Differentials, Return to Schooling, and Market Segmentation in a Transition Economy: The Case of Mainland China," *Journal of Development Economics*, 73: 315–328.

Fleisher, B.M. and Wang, X. (2005) "Returns to Schooling in China under Planning and Reform," *Journal of Comparative Economics*, 33: 265–277.

Gustafsson, B. and Li, S. (2000) "Economic Transformation and the Gender Earnings Gap in Urban China," *Journal of Population Economics*, 13: 305–329.

Heckman, J.J. (2003) "China's Investment in Human Capital," *Economic Development and Cultural Change*, 51: 795–804.

Johnson, E.N. and Chow, G.C. (1997) "Rates of Return to Schooling in China," *Pacific Economic Review*, 2: 101–113.

Knight, J. and Song, L. (1991) "The Determinants of Urban Income Inequality in China," *Oxford Bulletin of Economics and Statistics*, 53: 123–154.

Knight, J. and Song, L. (1993) "Why Urban Wages Differ in China," in K.B. Griffin and R. Zhao (eds.), *The Distribution of Income in China*, New York: St. Martin's Press.

Knight, J. and Song, L. (1995) "Toward a Labor Market in China," *Oxford Review of Economic Policy*, 11: 97–117.

Knight, J. and Song, L. (2003) "Increasing Wage Inequality in China: Extent, Elements and Evaluation," *Economics of Transition*, 4: 597–620.

Li, H. (2003) "Economic Transition and Returns to Education in China," *Economics of Education Review*, 22: 317–328.

Li, S. (2003) "A Retrospect and Prospect of Individual Income Distribution in China," *China Economic Quarterly*, 2: 379–404.

Liu, Z. (1998) "Earnings, Education and Economic Reforms in Urban China," *Economic Development and Cultural Change*, 46: 697–725.

Maurer-Fazio, M. (1999) "Earnings and Education in China's Transition to a Market Economy: Survey Evidence from 1989 and 1992," *China Economic Review*, 10: 17–40.

Meng, X. (2000) *Labour Market Reform in China*, Cambridge: Cambridge University Press.

Meng, X. and Kidd, M.P. (1997) "Labor Market Reform and the Changing Structure of Wage Determination in China's State Sector during the 1980s," *Journal of Comparative Economics*, 25: 403–421.

Mincer, J. (1974) *Schooling, Experience and Earnings*, New York: National Bureau of Economic Research.

Mwabu, G. and Schultz, T.P. (1996) "Education Returns across Quantiles of the Wage Function: Alternative Explanations for the Returns to Education in South Africa," *American Economic Review*, 86: 335–339.

Psacharopoulos, G. (1992) "Returns to Education: A Further International Update and Implications," *International Library of Critical Writings in Economics*, 17: 102–123.

Psacharopoulos, G. (1994) "Returns to Investment in Education: A Global Update," *World Development*, 22: 1325–1344.

Rutkowski, J.J. (2001) "Earnings Inequality in Transition Economies of Central Europe: Trends and Patterns during the 1990s," World Bank Social Protection Discussion Paper No. 0117.

Statistical Yearbook of China (various years) Beijing: China Statistical Press.

Svejnar, J. (1999) "Labor Markets in the Transitional Central and European Economies," in O. Ashenfelter and D. Card (eds.), *Handbook of Labor Economics*, vol. 3B, Amsterdam: North-Holland.

Urban Survey Organization (2001) *User Manual for the Urban Household Survey 2002*, Beijing: National Bureau of Statistics.

Yang, D.T. (2005) "Determinants of Schooling Returns during Transition: Evidence from Chinese Cities," *Journal of Comparative Economics*, 33: 244–264.

Zhang, J., Zhao, Y., Park, A., and Song, X. (2005) "Economic Returns to Schooling in Urban China, 1988 to 2001," *Journal of Comparative Economics*, 33: 730–752.

Zhao, Y. (2002) "Earnings Differentials between State and Non-state Enterprises in Urban China," *Pacific Economic Review*, 7: 181–197.

15 In books one finds a house of gold

Education and labor market outcomes in urban China

Margaret Maurer-Fazio

China's urban labor markets underwent dramatic changes in the late 1990s. This chapter focuses on education as a determinant of urban residents' labor market outcomes in this turbulent period. Data from a 1999–2000 survey of urban workers are analyzed to examine the role of education in preventing lay-offs, obtaining re-employment, and determining earnings. The analysis reveals that by the late 1990s education had become a key factor in successful labor market outcomes. More educated workers were less likely to be laid off, more likely to find new employment if laid off, and were better paid. The education of workers who experienced a lay-off and then found new employment was rewarded more highly in terms of earnings than that of workers who managed to avoid lay-off.

Background

China's pre-reform urban labor system was decidedly far from that of a free market. The state asserted its ownership of workers' labor services and assigned workers to enterprises, usually for life. Wage rates were set according to national wage scales that left pay nearly equal regardless of worker effort, productivity, or performance.

The Chinese leadership embarked on a transition to a market economy. The process was slow and evolutionary largely due to concerns about open unemployment and social instability. However, in the mid-1990s concerns about state-sector inefficiency began to override concerns about dismissals and lay-offs. A policy of putting workers on *xiagang*, a form of lay-off in which workers were placed on inactive status and sent home with living stipends was developed. After several years of experimentation, the program was implemented nationwide in 1997. Its timing coincided with the unexpected financial crisis and slowdown of growth in Asian economies.

The effects were profound. By the end of 1997, while the official unemployment (*shiye*) rate increased to 3.1 percent of the urban labor force, or 5.8 million people (*China Labor Statistical Yearbook* 1998), an additional 11.5 to 15 million workers were suspended from their jobs (Li 1997, 1998).[1] Official statistics suggest that by the end of 1999 a total of 25.2 million

workers had been laid off (put on *xiagang*) and that 9.4 million workers still remained in the ranks of the laid-off (*China Labor Statistical
Yearbook* 2000). Recent estimates suggest that the true unemployment rate
amongst permanent urban residents rose from 6.1 percent in January 1996
to 11.1 percent in September 2002 (Giles *et al.* 2005). The plight of these
displaced urban workers was compounded by competition from large numbers of rural migrants seeking work. The security once enjoyed by urban
workers rapidly eroded. If we describe the early reform policies as causing
rust on the iron rice bowl, then we have to describe the 1997 *xiagang* policies
as totally smashing it.

Chinese urban workers are no longer shielded from market forces. Laid-off
workers experience substantial periods of unemployment with minimal stipends (Appleton *et al.* 2002). In the early reform period, increases in income
inequality meant that those at the low end of the income distribution lost out
relative to those at the high end of the distribution despite experiencing rising
incomes. In the current period of massive lay-offs, those at the low end of the
distribution are experiencing substantial reductions in income in absolute
terms (Meng 2004).

Enterprise restructuring is forcing workers to bear much of the cost of a
painful adjustment process. In one sense, this chapter can be viewed as examining how these costs are distributed amongst workers who differ in terms
of their educational attainments and acquisition of job training. In another
sense, this chapter can be viewed as exploring the role of education and
job training in determining the labor market outcomes of China's urban
residents during 1999 and 2000, a period in which workers faced both a great
deal of uncertainty and a rapidly changing work environment.

The data and sample characteristics

The data were gathered in the fall of 1999 and spring of 2000 as part of the
Urban Labor Market Integration Project.[2] The data set is rather unique in
that it is enterprise-based and ties together firm information with that of
workers of three different categories: employed urban residents, laid-off
urban residents, and employed migrants.[3] Surveys were conducted at 118
enterprises, roughly 20 in each of six cities: Beijing, Nanjing, Wuhan, Xian,
Tianjin, and Changchun.

Industry type (*hangye*) was the primary selection criterion for inclusion of
an enterprise in the survey process. In each city, several textile, mechanical
processing, and construction firms were selected. The remaining enterprises
were chosen according to the industrial mix of each city. Secondary selection
criteria dictated that, within an industry, enterprises were selected to provide
firms differing in scale, economic prosperity, and ownership. Firms known to
have laid off workers or to have both laid-off workers and hired migrants
were deliberately over-sampled. At the time of the survey, 83 of the samples'
118 enterprises had a number of laid off workers on their rolls.[4]

Approximately 800 individuals in each of the six cities mentioned above, each associated with one of the selected enterprises, were surveyed—4,873 individuals in total. Once an enterprise was chosen for inclusion in the sample, then roughly 15 workers of each type (employed urban resident, laid-off urban resident, and migrant) were selected. The employed urban residents were randomly chosen from those present at the job site at the time of the survey. The laid-off workers were called back to the enterprise to participate in the survey. This callback method introduces a potential source of bias into the sample—laid-off workers subsequently employed in other locations are most unlikely to have responded to the enterprise callback. Migrant workers were surveyed either at the job site or in their employer-provided dormitories. In all cases, survey overseers were present in the room while respondents completed the surveys. They were thus available to observe the process and answer questions. The worker surveys included questions regarding background information, work history, income, expenditures, and attitudes.

It is important to note that the workers designated here as "laid-off" (i.e. labeled as *xiagang gong ren*) are so designated because the enterprises that anchor the surveys identified them as such. Almost one-third of these "laid-off" workers reported finding jobs subsequent to their lay-offs although only one quarter remained employed at the time of the survey.

Men make up 52 percent of the sample of employed urban residents and only 44 percent of laid-off urban workers. There is little difference in age between the laid-off workers and the employed—the laid off-workers, at a mean age of 39, are about a year younger than their employed urban counterparts. Employed urban residents have a little more schooling than laid-off workers with means of 11.7 and 10.6 years of schooling, respectively. Over 8 percent of the currently/continuously employed have university educations while only 2.8 percent of the laid-off workers have attained this level of education. Although the majority of workers received some job training, the proportion of employed urban residents receiving such training was almost 17 percentage points higher than the proportion of laid-off workers.

Data on monthly income includes wages, subsidies, and bonuses but do not include the value of employer-provided benefits such as medical insurance, pension accruals, and housing. The pecuniary income of the urban workers (553 *yuan*/month) considerably exceeds that from the last job before lay-off for the laid-off workers (417 *yuan*/month). However, it should be noted that this mean income is a simple average of these workers' last reported income regardless of the year in which it was earned. Over one-third of the laid-off workers (37.7 percent) managed to find some type of work after being laid off and 27.4 percent reported still having a job at the time of the survey. The stated average monthly income of these re-employed workers at 571 *yuan*/month exceeds that of their urban counterparts who have not yet experienced being laid off. However, they work more hours per day (8.46) and more days per week (5.68) than urban workers who have never experienced a lay-off. Consequently, their hourly wage at 3.10 *yuan* is lower than that received by their urban counterparts who have never been laid off (3.37 *yuan*/hour).

In this sample, approximately 80 percent of the urban residents work or used to work for state-owned enterprises. This proportion exceeds the national proportion of urban workers employed in state-owned enterprises by 9 percent (*China Labor Statistical Yearbook* 2000: 14) and is an artefact of the sampling procedure that was aimed in part towards surveying large numbers of laid-off urban workers.

There is some variation in the method by which workers are paid, with a higher proportion of the laid-off workers than the continuously employed reporting being on a fixed wage contract. At their last job before being laid off, 86 percent of laid-off workers received fixed wages, 8 percent were paid by piece rate and 5 percent were compensated on an hourly basis while 77 percent of the continuously employed urban workers received fixed wages, 9 percent were on piece rate and approximately 10 percent were paid on an hourly basis. Medical insurance was provided by employers to 49 percent of the never laid-off urban workers while 54 percent of the laid-off workers used to receive this benefit.

Far fewer of the laid-off workers than the continuously employed report their latest job to be one from the higher rungs of the occupational scale— cadres, office/clerical workers, and engineers and technicians. The opposite is true for jobs at the lower rungs—higher proportions of the laid-off workers than those never laid off used to be production line workers, service workers, and sales workers.

Empirical analysis

Returns to education

Given the extent of wage compression in pre-reform China, we would expect human capital accumulation to be increasingly recognized and rewarded as the Chinese economic reforms progress and market forces permeate the work place. Since industrial reform did not significantly influence urban enterprises until 1984, Meng and Kidd's (1997) estimate of the returns to education[5] of 2.5 percent per year of schooling in 1981 is used as a benchmark of the returns to education in the pre-reform era. It is expected that the returns to education will increase until reaching a level consistent with those in well-functioning Asian labor markets.

As early as 1988, even though the rates of return for the employees in the state-owned sector remained low (2.6 percent), the rates of return for new labor market entrants (6.4 percent) and for collective (4.1 percent) and private-sector workers (9.6 percent) were higher and in the range that we find in East Asian market economies with smoothly functioning labor markets (Maurer-Fazio 1994). Econometric analyses of data from the early and mid-1990s corroborate these findings of low but increasing returns to education (Knight and Song 1993; Li and Gustafsson 1999; Maurer-Fazio 1999).

Given the further incursion of market forces into the urban Chinese workplace in the late 1990s, it seems likely that we should observe further increases in the returns to investments in schooling and training.[6] To the extent that the workplace exhibits features of both the legacy of its pre-reform assignment and reward system and the post-reform market system, it is possible that returns to education will vary according to the degree of marketization. It is thus hypothesized that workers who find their jobs through a competitive market means (as opposed to those who obtained their jobs through a non-market, uncompetitive mechanism) will have greater rewards to their human capital in general, and to their schooling in particular.

The group of workers who have experienced a lay-off and then found new employment is of special interest here. Given that these re-employed workers have each found their new job in the post-reform period, examining how, and to what extent, their productive characteristics are rewarded should prove revealing about the extent of change in, and marketization of, the workplace in urban China.

In the analysis that follows, the rewards to schooling are calculated from Mincerian earnings functions (Mincer 1974). The dependent variable in the underlying regressions is the natural log of hourly earnings, which include wages, subsidies, and bonuses but do not take into account employer-provided benefits such as medical insurance, pension accruals, or housing. The independent variables include years of schooling, years of work experience, the number of times a worker has changed his/her work unit (*danwei*), party membership, marital status, city of residence, enterprise ownership sector, health status, and payment method. The return to education is calculated and expressed in percentage terms by taking the coefficient on years of schooling from the Mincerian earnings function and multiplying it by 100.

Factors affecting the probability of lay-off

Which worker characteristics are likely to raise the probability of lay-off and which will reduce it? Characteristics that make a worker more productive should reduce the probability of lay-off, *ceteris paribus*. Therefore, both years of formal schooling and a "received training" dummy variable are used as explanatory variables. Firm-specific human capital is likely to increase with tenure at an enterprise so a variable that measures enterprise tenure in the analysis is also included. A worker's health status will affect his or her productivity, therefore, indicators of good and poor health are also included in the analysis.[7]

Other factors that may influence the likelihood of lay-off include: age, party membership, gender, and marital status. In the years just prior to the implementation of *xiagang* policies women were forced into early retirement in higher proportions than men, and older women in higher proportions than younger women (Maurer-Fazio *et al.* 1999). It is possible that lay-offs have also disproportionately affected working women. It is not necessarily the case, however, that the characteristics of age and femaleness raise the probability of lay-off after controlling for human capital characteristics. Party membership may provide a network of relationships that insulate and protect workers from lay-off.[8] The effects of each of the above-mentioned factors on the probability of lay-off are estimated and reported below.

It is possible that enterprises are more willing to lay off workers who have employed family members who can provide financial support to the laid-off worker than those who do not. Consequently, we control for the number of family members with paid employment in the empirical analysis.

Incentive schemes that tie productivity and/or effort to wages may lower employer costs relative to fixed-wage contracts and afford enterprises more flexibility in economic downturns. Therefore, a set of variables is used in the following analysis to control for whether workers are paid by piece rate or by the hour (as opposed to receiving a fixed salary).

To explore the effects of the above-mentioned factors on the probability of an urban worker being laid-off, a "within enterprise" probit model using a combined sample of all the workers with urban household registration (whether employed or laid-off) from enterprises reporting at least some lay-offs is estimated. The dependent variable is binary and set equal to one for all workers identified by the enterprise as ever having been laid off. Since all the enterprises in our sample were in existence and involved in production at the time they were surveyed, this means each laid-off worker was chosen for lay-off while others were not. (In no cases in our sample were all the workers of a firm laid-off.)

A note of caution is in order here. The sample employed here is not representative of the population of all workers in urban China. In each city, enterprises were chosen in such a way to yield reasonably large and nearly equal numbers of employed urban residents, laid-off urban residents, and migrant workers. Given this sample design, it is necessary to weight the observations to reflect the probability that a given worker of a particular employment status (employed vs laid-off) within a particular enterprise was included in our sample. Even with this weighting scheme, the lay-off probits need to be interpreted with care. For example, the marginal effect of an extra year of schooling should be interpreted as yielding the marginal effect of formal schooling in reducing the probability of lay-off *within enterprises choosing workers for lay-off.*

Factors affecting the probability of re-employment

One of the most important factors influencing the probability of re-employment is the state of the economy in the worker's locality. The cities in our sample vary considerably in terms of economic well-being, with Xian, Wuhan, and Changchun trailing far behind Nanjing, Tianjin, and Beijing. In the analysis that follows, the health of the local economy is controlled for by a set of geographic (city) dummy variables with Beijing as the base case.

Personal productive characteristics should also be listed amongst the most important factors in predicting the likelihood of rehire. Therefore, human capital variables (schooling, job training, and years of work experience) and health status variables (good health and poor health) are used as explanators.

It is possible that party membership provides a set of connections useful in finding work and a party-membership dummy is thus used to test this proposition. Gender and marital status are also controlled for in the re-employment probit estimation for reasons parallel to those explained above in the section on lay-offs.

The effect of the duration of lay-off is tested by including in the probit equation a variable that represents the number of months that a worker has been laid off. Workers without the support of either unemployment insurance or the income of other family members may be more inclined to accept early but less-than-ideal job offers than those with such support.

Sector dummies representing the ownership sector of the last job before lay-off are used as independent variables in the probit to allow for the possibility that employers place differing values on the experience (and work habits and attitudes) gained in previous employment at an enterprise of a particular form of ownership. State ownership is the base case.

Empirical results

Returns to education for continuously-employed urban workers

Table 15.1 reports two sets of returns to education based on Mincerian earnings functions that regress an individual's natural log of hourly earnings on an array of explanatory variables that measure his or her schooling and work experience as well as controlling for location, payment method, ownership sector, and health status. The first set of estimates allows us to look at the returns to schooling across all the firms in the sample and the second allows us to look at the returns to schooling within firms.

The first set of results reports returns to education for all of the continuously employed urban residents in our sample (that is, those not laid off by the firms that anchor the surveys). This set of workers is then divided first by gender, then by education level (high vs low), and finally by whether the workers used a clearly competitive method to find their jobs, as opposed to being either assigned to their position or being introduced by family members.

The coefficients on years of schooling in the underlying regressions were statistically significant for each of the groups in this first set. As revealed in Table 15.1, the returns vary from a low of 2.6 percent for the never laid-off females to a high of 5.5 percent to those who found work competitively. The return for the group as a whole was very low at 3.7 percent. This decidedly low overall rate of return does not reflect the expected continuing trend of

Table 15.1 Rates of return to years of formal schooling for "never laid-off" urban residents, Chinese urban labor markets, 1999–2000

Sector	Returns*	Significance	No. of Obs
(Based on regressions without enterprise controls)			
All urban workers	3.7	0.000	1546
Urban males	4.5	0.000	795
Urban females	2.6	0.000	751
Urban workers > 12 years of schooling	3.8	0.013	529
Urban workers <= 12 years of schooling	3.6	0.000	1017
Urban workers—competitively found jobs	5.5	0.000	452
Urban workers—assigned jobs	3.2	0.000	1088
(Based on regressions that control for enterprise)			
All urban workers	2.6	0.000	1544
Urban males	2.9	0.000	798
Urban females	2.6	0.000	756
Urban workers > 12 years of schooling	1.8	0.174	532
Urban workers <= 12 years of schooling	3.1	0.000	1022
Urban workers—competitively found jobs	3.0	0.001	454
Urban workers—assigned jobs	2.3	0.000	1093

Source: China Labor Market Integration Project.

Notes:
* Returns to schooling here are expressed as percentages which are calculated as the coefficients on years of schooling in the Mincerian earnings functions multiplied by 100.
　The dependent variable in the underlying regressions is the natural log of hourly earnings which include wages, subsidies, and bonuses but do not take into account employer-provided benefits such as medical insurance, pension accruals, or housing. The independent variables include years of schooling, years of work experience, party membership, marital status, city of residence, enterprise ownership sector, health status, and payment method.

increasing recognition of human capital in remuneration determination.[9] It is possible that this low return is due in part to the nature of the sample with its relatively high proportion of state-sector employees and over-sampling of firms engaged in lay-offs.

The second set of results in Table 15.2 deals with the same group of workers—the employed urban residents not laid off by the firms in our sample. This set of results differs from the first in that the underlying regressions control for firm characteristics by entering firm dummies in the regressions. (The controls for ownership sector and location are therefore necessarily left out.) These within-firm estimates of returns to education are consistently lower than the across-firm estimates and the statistically significant results range from a low of 2.3 percent for workers assigned to their jobs to a high of 3.2 percent for workers with 12 years or less schooling. That the across-firm estimates of returns to schooling are higher than the within-firm estimates implies that workers are sorting themselves with more educated workers going to higher-paying firms. Education is working here as a signaling device—the higher paying firms are employing higher proportions of more

Table 15.2 Rates of return to years of formal schooling for re-employed urban residents, Chinese urban labor markets, 1999–2000

Sector	Returns*	Significance	No. of Obs.
All re-employed workers	4.5	0.002	338
Re-employed males	7.1	0.001	129
Re-employed females	3.4	0.082	209
Re-employed workers > 12 years of schooling	1.1	0.851	55
Re-employed workers <= 12 years of schooling	2.9	0.161	283
Re-employed workers—competitively found jobs	11.6	0.024	70
Re-employed workers—introduced to their jobs	4.4	0.004	258

Source: China Labor Market Integration Project.

Notes:
* Returns to schooling here are expressed as percentages which are calculated as the coefficients on years of schooling in the Mincerian earnings functions multiplied by 100.
   The dependent variable in the underlying regressions is the natural log of hourly earnings which include wages, subsidies, and bonuses but do not take into account employer-provided benefits such as medical insurance, pension accruals, or housing. The independent variables include years of schooling, years of work experience, party membership, marital status, city of residence, enterprise ownership sector, health status, and payment method.

educated workers. Investing in education is a means of signaling ability and potential productivity.

It is possible to compare Meng and Kidd's pre-reform benchmark return to a year of schooling of 2.5 percent to a similarly defined group of urban employees here. In our data, the across-firm rate of return to education for men employed in the state-owned sector is 4.5 percent. Although the return to education increased by 80 percent from Meng and Kidd's estimate to ours, the return for men in the state-sector during this period of widespread retrenchment is only 2 percentage points higher than in the pre-reform period. It is important to note, however, that at least in one sense, these estimates of the rates of return to education are now under-estimates of the value of education. In the pre-reform period, workers pretty much kept their jobs for life. At the time the data analyzed here were gathered (late 1999 and early 2000), the work environment had changed considerably and urban workers faced a great deal of uncertainty about keeping their jobs—official unemployment stood at approximately 6 million with an additional 9 million workers in the laid-off category (of the over 25 million who had experienced a lay-off since 1997). Education's role in determining labor market outcomes is no longer restricted to earnings determination. It now plays an additional role as a causal factor in job retention.

Probability of lay-off

Each of the productive and ascriptive characteristic (with the exceptions of marital status and poor heath) posited above to affect the likelihood of lay-off does so in a statistically significant fashion. As Table 15.3 reveals, the observed probability of lay-off is 18.8 percent.[10] How does education affect the probability of lay-off? A one unit change, that is an additional year of schooling, evaluated at the sample means, reduces the probability of lay-off by 2.6 percent. Bear in mind that each of the marginal effects here is based on a sample of firms that has chosen to lay off some of its workers while keeping others on the job.

Employees who have received on-the-job training are 6.2 percent less likely to be laid off than those who have not received training. It appears that attachment to one's employer provides a small measure of protection—each additional year spent at the current employer (*danwei*) reduces the chances of being chosen for lay-off by 0.39 percent. Being in good health as opposed to average health reduces the likelihood of lay-off by 4.2 percent. (Being in poor health appears to increase the probability of lay-off but is not significant at the 10 percent level.)

The role of party membership in protecting workers from lay-off is larger than that of training—party membership reduces the probability of lay-off, *ceteris paribus*, by 6.6 percent. There is an advantage to men in the lay-off

Table 15.3 Probit model of the probability of lay-off

Variable	Marginal effect (%)	p>z
Years of schooling	−2.598	0.000
Years at latest *danwei*	−0.392	0.002
Age	0.334	0.015
No. of household members employed	−0.103	0.020
Male	−2.495	0.067
Married	−2.920	0.130
Party member	−6.638	0.000
Good health	−4.217	0.007
Poor health	3.568	0.241
Received job training	−6.170	0.000
Piece rate	−6.638	0.000
Hourly pay	−4.436	0.081
(firm dummies suppressed)		
Log likelihood	−631.770	
Wald Chi^2(93)	1834.200	
Prob > Chi^2	0.000	
Number of observations	2246	
Observed probability	0.188	

Source: Urban Labor Market Integration Project.

Notes: The base case consists of single females who did not receive job training and who are of average health and paid a fixed salary.

Entries for years of schooling, years at latest *danwei*, age, and number of family members with jobs are the marginal changes in the probability that an individual is laid off resulting from a one unit change in each of these factors, evaluated at the sample mean.

Entries for the other variables are the changes in the probability that an individual is laid off when these binary variables toggle from zero to one, evaluated at sample means.

process. Being male reduces one's probability of lay-off, *ceteris paribus*, by 2.5 percent. Marital status does not have a significant effect on the likelihood of being laid-off. Older workers are somewhat disadvantaged—the marginal effect of an increase in age of one year is an increase in the likelihood of lay-off of 0.33 percent. Being on flexible payment schemes as opposed to being paid on a fixed salary reduces the likelihood of lay-off quite significantly—by 6.6 percent for those paid by piece rate and by 4.4 percent for those paid by the hour.

Finally, the number of family members with paid employment significantly affects the likelihood of lay-off but not in the manner expected. Table 15.4

Table 15.4 Probit model of the probability of finding work after lay-off

Variable	Marginal effect (%)	p>z
Years of schooling	3.71	0.000
Years of work experience	0.38	0.642
Experience squared	−0.02	0.383
Duration of unemployment (months)	0.42	0.000
Received training at last job	10.36	0.003
Male	5.73	0.109
Married	−2.29	0.648
Party member	−2.61	0.813
Good health	−4.77	0.182
Poor health	−3.24	0.633
Last job provided unemploy.ins.	−1.31	0.719
Tianjin	5.16	0.424
Nanjing	1.65	0.788
Xian	−7.23	0.299
Changchun	−13.39	0.051
Wuhan	−10.92	0.083
Last employer collective ownership	7.05	0.226
Last employer joint venture	9.80	0.167
Last employer private enterprise	32.17	0.238
No. of household members employed	−0.02	0.924
Log likelihood	−597.703	
LR Chi^2 (20)	75.540	
Prob > Chi^2	0.000	
Number of observations	939	
Observed probability	0.410	

Source: Urban Labor Market Integration Project.

Notes: The base case consists of single females who are not party members and did not receive job training, are of average health, were formerly employed by a state-owned enterprise, and are residents of Beijing.

Entries for years of schooling, years of experience, experience squared, and duration of unemployment are the marginal changes in the probability that an individual finds work (after being laid off) from a one unit change in each of these factors, evaluated at the sample mean.

Entries for the other variables are the changes in the probability that an individual finds work (after being laid off) when these binary variable toggles from zero to one, evaluated at the sample mean.

reveals a decrease in the probability of lay-off of 0.1 percent for each additional income-earning member in the family.

Probability of re-employment once laid off

Schooling and job training stand out amongst the posited human capital factors predicted to affect the probability of re-employment once laid off (see Table 15.4). The marginal effect of an additional year of schooling is an increase in the probability of re-hire of close to 4 percent. (The overall probability of re-hire is 41 percent.) The marginal effect of a worker receiving training at his or her last job before being laid off is large—it increases the probability of re-hire by over 10 percent.

The coefficient on "male" borders on statistical significance and is large. It appears that men are favored in the re-employment process by 5.7 percent. Surprisingly, the posited network effect of being a party member is absent in our results—party membership does not help laid-off workers obtain new jobs. Years of work experience, marital status, health status, the number of family members with paid employment, and whether the last job provided unemployment insurance all also proved to be statistically insignificant in the re-employment regressions.

In terms of location, as expected, workers in Changchun and Wuhan have significantly lower probabilities of being rehired than workers in Beijing, with marginal effects of −13 and −11 percent, respectively. Surprisingly, given the poor state of the local economy, the coefficient on Xian, while negative, is statistically insignificant.

The only other factor beside schooling, training, gender, and location that has a significant role in explaining the probability of being re-hired is the duration of lay-off. Each additional month since being laid off increases the likelihood of being re-hired by approximately 0.4 percent.

How do the new positions of laid-off workers compare to their previous types of employment? Cai (2004) reports that many laid-off but re-employed workers experience an informalization of their jobs. In an earlier analysis of the data employed in this chapter, Maurer-Fazio and Dinh (2004) compare the pre- and post-lay off jobs and benefits of these re-employed workers. They find that on average these re-employed workers earn more in their new positions than in their previous ones but that they work longer days and more days per week. The increase in work hours is more pronounced for men than for women. The percentage of workers paid fixed salaries, as opposed to hourly or piece rates, dropped quite dramatically from over 80 percent in their pre-lay-off positions to 47 percent in their new jobs. The fraction of workers paid on a piece-rate basis almost tripled. As might be expected, there is a pronounced drop in the provision of benefits. The percentage of workers receiving medical insurance and pensions from their firms is cut in half. The ownership structure of employers is decidedly different in the pre- and post-lay-off worlds. In the past, over 77 percent of these re-employed workers were employed by state-owned enterprises; that percentage fell to only 37 percent in the new positions. Many of these laid-off workers are now either working in private firms (16 percent) or are self-employed (*getihu*)(20 percent).

Returns to education for re-employed urban workers

The final set of results in Table 15.2 are the returns to education experienced by workers who have been laid off and subsequently re-employed. The rewards to human capital accumulation appear to be greater for this group of urban workers (in arguably the most competitive sphere of China's labor system) than for those who have never been laid off. The return to a year of schooling for the group is 4.5 percent with male rehired workers realizing a return of 7.1 percent and women 3.4 percent. Those who reported using a clearly competitive method of finding work have a return of 11.6 percent to an additional year of schooling.[11]

Conclusions

In urban China's pre-reform labor system the state guaranteed workers a job. Wages were paid according to state-determined scales. Education was so poorly rewarded that some claim the pay scale exhibited a brain/brawn inversion. As the reforms proceeded, wage dispersion increased and market forces began to influence remuneration decisions. Nevertheless, out of apprehension about unemployment and social instability the Chinese leadership resisted giving enterprise managers the right to determine the size of their labor forces. In 1997, the leadership's concerns about the inefficiency of state-owned enterprises began to outweigh its worries about dealing with large numbers of unemployed urban workers. The leadership began to actively encourage lay-offs. Enterprises shed redundant workers in record numbers and, as mentioned above, by year's end 1999, over 25 million workers had been placed on *xiagang* status. Workers faced very real prospects of lay-off and unemployment.

The results of the above empirical analysis clearly demonstrate that by the end of the 1990s education had become a key determinant of workers' labor market outcomes and success. The smashing of the iron rice bowl increased the importance of education in labor markets. Its role was no longer restricted to its function in wage determination. Educational attainment became an important factor in the lay-off decision—the more education a worker has, the better his/her protection from lay off. Similarly, the more education a worker has, the better his/her chances of finding new employment if laid off. The education of re-employed workers, arguably those in the most competitive sphere of China's urban labor system, is rewarded more, as measured in terms of incremental earnings for each additional year of schooling, than that of the continuously employed.

As discussed above in the background section, in one sense this chapter can be viewed as examining how the costs of China's very painful adjustment process are being distributed amongst workers who differ in terms of educational attainment, job training, and other factors. Education and job training protect workers from lay off—workers with little education and no job training are more likely to suffer lay off than others. All else equal, women are more likely to be laid off than men. Party membership affords considerable protection from lay off, as does being in good health. Individuals who are paid by the hour or by piece rate are much less likely to be laid off than those with fixed salaries. Age increases the likelihood of lay off. Clearly, the costs of the adjustment as measured by the experience of losing one's job are borne disproportionately by those with little education and training, by women, by the elderly, by those who failed to enter the party, and by those employed on fixed salaries.

In the re-employment process, men are favored over women. Interestingly, party membership fails to provide any benefit to its members in terms of finding new jobs. Location is a very important factor in determining whether a laid off worker will find new employment.

Laid-off workers with higher levels of educational attainment and those who received job training in their previous employment have higher probabilities of finding new jobs than others. In post-reform competitive labor markets, the education of re-employed workers is rewarded more than that of workers who managed to avoid lay off. The market is recognizing and rewarding investments in human capital. The adjustment process, however, imposes significant costs on workers, even those fortunate enough to find new employment. Many of these workers suffer reduced benefits, job informalization, and increased uncertainty.

Notes

1 Li (1997: 9–13) reports National Bureau of Statistics estimates of 15 million redundant employees. Li (1998: 9–13) also quotes the former Minister of Labor, Li Boyong, as reporting 11.51 million lay-offs in 1997, of which 7.87 million were from state-owned enterprises.
2 The Urban Labor Market Integration Project was funded by the Ford Foundation, Beijing Office and was carried out by principal investigators Fang Cai (Population Institute, Chinese Academy of Social Sciences), Margaret Maurer-Fazio (Department of Economics, Bates College), Xin Meng (Research School of Pacific and Asian Studies, Australian National University), and Hansheng Wang (Department of Sociology, Peking University).
3 This chapter focuses exclusively on urban residents, that is, workers who hold urban *hukou*s, entitling them to legal status as urban residents. Readers interested in the role of education on the labor market outcomes of rural residents and rural-to-urban migrants should see, for example, de Brauw and Rozelle (Chapter 12 in this volume) or Maurer-Fazio and Dinh (2004).
4 Approximately half the firms had both migrant and laid-off workers. About one-third of the firms had laid-off workers but no migrant employees. A smaller number of the enterprises (approximately 15 percent) had hired migrants and had

never laid off members of their urban resident workforce. The remainder of the firms hired only urban residents and had no laid-off workers on their rolls.
5 The term "returns to education" is used here in the economic sense of a return on an investment. That is, a return of 5 percent to an additional year of schooling implies that investing in an additional year of schooling will, on average, raise incomes by 5 percent.
6 See Zhang *et al.* (2005) and Chapter 14 by Zhang and Zhao in this volume for evidence of increasing rates of return to education in urban China in the mid- and late 1990s.
7 Health status in this data set is self-reported as poor, average, or good.
8 Zhao and Zhou (Chapter 13 in this volume) directly explore the implications of party membership on the earnings of urban residents. They also explore the implications of party membership for workers' indirect returns to education, in terms of obtaining particular types of jobs and workplace authority. They find that education has played an important role in providing access to high status jobs and organizations.
9 Zhang *et al.* (2005) report a dramatic and robust increase in the returns to education in urban China from 1988 to 2001 from 4.0 to 10.2 percent.
10 This likelihood of lay-off is observed after weighting observations for probability of inclusion in the sample.
11 Our finding of a return of 11.6 percent for an additional year of schooling for re-hired workers who found their jobs by means of a competitive process echoes the findings of both de Brauw and Rozelle (Chapter 12 in this volume) of a return of 11.1 percent amongst young migrant workers. Zhang *et al.* (2005), similarly, found a return of 10.2 percent for urban workers in 2001.

References

Appleton, S., Knight, J., Song, L., and Xia, Q. (2002) "Labour Retrenchment in China: Determinants and Consequences," *China Economic Review*, 13: 252–275.

Cai, F. (2004) "The Consistency of China Statistics on Employment: Stylized Facts and Implications for Public Policies," unpublished paper, Institute of Population and Labor Economics, Chinese Academy of Social Sciences.

China Labor Statistical Yearbook (1998) Beijing: China Statistical Press.

China Labor Statistical Yearbook (2000) Beijing: China Statistical Press.

Giles, J., Park, A., and Zhang, J. (2005) "What is China's True Unemployment Rate?" *China Economic Review*, 16: 149–170.

Knight, J. and Song, L. (1993) "Why Urban Wages Differ in China," in K. Griffin and R. Zhao (eds.), *The Distribution of Income in China*, New York: St. Martin's Press, pp. 216–284.

Li, N. (1997) "Promising Reemployment Project," *Beijing Review*, August 18–24: 9–13.

Li, N. (1998) "Re-employment: A Solemn Scheme in 1998," *Beijing Review*, May 18–24): 9–13.

Li, S. and Gustafsson, B. (1999) "Zhongguo chengzhen zhigong shouru de xinbie chayi fenxi" (An Analysis of Gender Differences in Urban Workers' Income) in R. Zhao *et al.* (eds.) *Zhongguo jumin shouru fenpei zai yanjiu: jingji gaige he fazhan zhong de shouru fenpei (Further Research on the Distribution of Chinese Household Income: the Distribution of Income During Economic Reform and Development)*, Beijing: China Finance and Economics Publishing House, pp. 556–593.

Maurer-Fazio, M. (1994) "An Analysis of the Emerging Labor Market in the People's

Republic of China and its Effect on Rates of Return to Investments in Education," PhD. dissertation, Department of Economics, University of Pittsburgh.

Maurer-Fazio, M. (1999) "Education and Earnings in China's Transition to a Market Economy: Survey Evidence from 1989 and 1992," *China Economic Review*, 10: 17–40.

Maurer-Fazio, M. and Dinh, H. (2004) "Differential Rewards to, and Contributions of, Education in Urban China's Segmented Labor Markets," *Pacific Economic Review*, 9: 173–189.

Maurer-Fazio, M., Rawski, T.G., and Zhang, W. (1999) "Inequality in the Rewards for Holding Up Half the Sky: Gender Wage Gaps in China's Urban Labour Market, 1988–1994," *The China Journal*, 41: 55–88.

Meng, X. (2004) "Economic Restructuring and Income Inequality in Urban China," *Review of Income and Wealth*, 50: 357–379.

Meng, X. and Kidd, M. (1997) "Labor Market Reform and the Changing Structure of Wage Determination in China's State Sector during the 1980s," *Journal of Comparative Economics*, 25: 403–421.

Mincer, J. (1974) *Schooling, Experience and Earnings*, New York: Columbia University Press.

Zhang, J., Zhao, Y., Park, A., Song, X. (2005) "Economic Returns to Education in Urban China, 1988 to 2001," *Journal of Comparative Economics*, 33: 730–752.

Index

Note: *italic* page numbers denote references to figures/tables.

Lightning Source UK Ltd.
Milton Keynes UK
21 May 2010

154468UK00003B/9/P